MODERN ART AND THE IDEA OF THE MEDITERRANEAN

The Mediterranean is an invented cultural space, on the frontier between North and South, West and East. *Modern Art and the Idea of the Mediterranean* examines the representation of this region in the visual arts since the late eighteenth century, placing the 'idea of the Mediterranean' – a cultural construct rather than a physical reality – at the centre of our understanding of modern visual culture.

This collection of essays features an international group of scholars who examine competing visions of the Mediterranean in terms of modernity and cultural identity, questioning and illuminating both European and non-European representations. An introductory essay frames the analysis in terms of a new spatial paradigm of the Mediterranean as a geographic, historical, and cultural region that emerged in the late eighteenth century, as France and Britain colonized the surrounding territories. Essays are grouped around three vital themes: visualization of the space of the new Mediterranean; varied uses of the classical paradigm; and issues of identity and resistance in an age of modernity and colonialism. Drawing on recent geographical, historical, cultural, and anthropological studies, contributors address the visual representation of identity in both the European and the 'Oriental,' and the colonial and post-colonial Mediterranean.

VOJTÊCH JIRAT-WASIUTYŃSKI was a professor in the Department of Art History at Queen's University.

# Modern Art and the Idea of the Mediterranean

*Edited by Vojtěch Jirat-Wasiutyński*
*with the assistance of Anne Dymond*

UNIVERSITY OF TORONTO PRESS
Toronto Buffalo London

Toronto Buffalo London
utorontopress.com

Reprinted in paperback 2024

ISBN 978-0-8020-9170-3 (cloth)
ISBN 978-1-4875-6480-3 (paper)

Publication cataloguing information is available from Library and Archives Canada

Cover illustration: Young women of Provence at the well, 1892, Signac, Paul (1863–1935)/Musee d'Orsay, Paris, France, Peter Willi/Bridgeman Art Library

We wish to acknowledge the land on which the University of Toronto Press operates. This land is the traditional territory of the Wendat, the Anishnaabeg, the Haudenosaunee, the Métis, and the Mississaugas of the Credit First Nation.

University of Toronto Press acknowledges the financial support of the Government of Canada, the Canada Council for the Arts, and the Ontario Arts Council, an agency of the Government of Ontario, for its publishing activities.

Canada Council for the Arts
Conseil des Arts du Canada

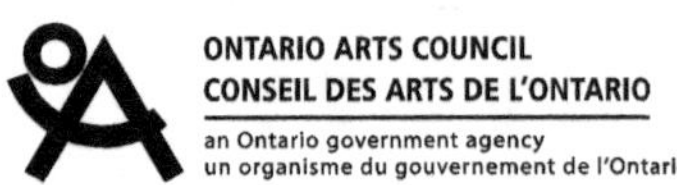


Funded by the Government of Canada
Financé par le gouvernement du Canada
Canada

*To the memory of Vojtěch Jirat-Wasiutyński, a probing scholar, a generous teacher, mentor, and colleague, and a caring friend*

# Contents

# Preface

In the fall of 2002, the Art Gallery of Ontario presented the exhibition Voyage into Myth: French Painting from Gauguin to Matisse from the Hermitage Museum, Russia. Co-organized with the Montreal Museum of Fine Arts, Voyage into Myth examined French Post-Impressionist and early modern responses to the concept of a mythological Golden Age (*L'Âge d'Or*) located in an ancient past. A central concern of the exhibition was to demonstrate how French artists at the turn of the century sought to 'update' history by marrying the idea of the Golden Age with their personal experience of a kind of Eden in the South of France. They created a myth of the Mediterranean as an earthly paradise, where calm replaced the fast pace of the modern industrialized world. Arcadian imagery and classical form in landscape painting defined one view of the Mediterranean, and this notion became a springboard for a symposium that occurred concurrently with the exhibition and examined a variety of topics and perspectives.

'Modern Art and the Mediterranean: Spaces, Bodies and Identities,' the brainchild of Professor Vojtěch Jirat-Wasiutyński of Queen's University's Department of Art and Alla Myzelev and John Potvin, then graduate students in the department's doctoral program in art history, investigated competing classicizing, Orientalizing, and resistant indigenous visions of the Mediterranean in the modern period. An outstanding roster of fourteen scholars – five from Canada, seven from the United States, and two from the United Kingdom – delivered papers over a two-day period (7–8 December 2002). The ten papers published here under the title *Modern Art and the Idea of the Mediterranean* are indicative of the conference's lively discourse and scholarly scope, encompassing European and non-European under standings of the Mediterranean in the modern period and investigating identity from geographical, historical, and cultural directions.

The conference 'Modern Art and the Mediterranean: Spaces, Bodies, and Identities' epitomizes the goal of the Doctoral Directed Studies Program, established with the support of Sandra Simpson, as a partnership of the Department of Art at Queen's University and the Art Gallery of Ontario to bring academic and curatorial practice together, thus leading to a valuable exchange of ideas and contributions to scholarship. We would like to thank Sandra Simpson for her patronage of the symposium and her support for continued collaborations between Queen's University and the Art Gallery of Ontario. This is the third such collaboration between the two institutions and the second publication to result from this very fruitful partnership.

'Modern Art and the Mediterranean: Spaces, Bodies, and Identities' was developed by the Queen's University and Art Gallery of Ontario Doctoral Directed Studies Program, and generously funded by Sandra Simpson and the Social Sciences and Humanities Research Council of Canada. The publication of this volume is supported by a grant from the general research funds of Queen's University. The encouragement of Professor Lynda Jessup in the Department of Art and the logistical support of the Office of Research Services at Queen's University have been invaluable.

MICHAEL PARKE-TAYLOR
Associate Curator, European Art
Art Gallery of Ontario

VOJTĚCH JIRAT-WASIUTYŃSKI
Professor, Department of Art
Queen's University

# MODERN ART AND THE IDEA OF THE MEDITERRANEAN

# 1 Modern Art and the New Mediterranean Space

VOJTĚCH JIRAT-WASIUTYŃSKI

The present volume examines the representation of the Mediterranean region in the visual arts since the late eighteenth century, placing the 'idea of the Mediterranean' – a cultural construct rather than a physical reality – at the centre of our understanding of modern visual culture. Although the region was not the birthplace or the principal production site of modern art, as it was for classical art in antiquity or much of Islamic art in the Middle Ages, the 'idea of the Mediterranean' informs much of modern art. Starting with the Romantics, artists from centres north of the Alps were drawn to the Mediterranean region by this idea. The essays in this volume analyse the visual representation of Mediterranean spaces and cultures in the nineteenth and twentieth centuries at a time when the area was transformed by modernization and the intervention of European powers, principally France and Britain, and by the responses of societies in the region to modernization and colonialism.[1] The authors consider competing visions of the Mediterranean, particularly classicizing and Orientalizing European approaches, and address the visual representation of identity in both the European and the 'Oriental,' the colonial and post-colonial Mediterranean.

Classicism and Orientalism have been studied extensively by historians of nineteenth-century European art and culture; more recently, post-colonial studies have addressed many aspects of visual culture in the Islamic world. These approaches have not, however, taken the Mediterranean as their primary focus. The present volume is framed by the argument that these issues and their visual representations are most fruitfully understood in relation to an 'idea of the Mediterranean' constituted by European knowledge. Use of the term Mediterranean to designate the sea located between Europe and North Africa, the Middle

East and the Atlantic Ocean, is modern; it does not crystallize in European languages until the eighteenth century.[2] No such term exists in Arabic or Turkish, in which it was known, from the time of its division in the seventh century CE between Islamic states and Christian ones, as the sea of the Christians (Roum), or sometimes as the Syrian or White Sea.[3] Repeated, standardized use of the term Mediterranean goes hand in hand with the recognition of this region as a distinct spatial arena of particular interest to European nations in their foreign policy for economic and cultural reasons.

In the words of Dr Johnson, recorded in 1776: 'The grand object of travelling is to see the shores of the Mediterranean. On these shores were the four great Empires of the world; the Assyrian, the Persian, the Grecian and the Roman. All our religion, almost all our law, almost all our arts, almost all that sets us above savages, has come to us from the shores of the Mediterranean.'[4] Significantly, the English writer puts the glory of these empires in the past tense, while the British Empire lay in the immediate future. The elaboration of the 'idea of the Mediterranean' was the work of modernity contemplating the past and the premodern in that arena. It was invented in visual image and text to represent, organize, and make comprehensible this ambiguous space, outside modern Europe yet intimately connected to it, through history, as a place of origin and exchange from antiquity to the early modern period. Paradoxically, the idea emerged when the old cultural and economic exchanges between Christian and Muslim states, based on rough parity and mutual need, increasingly gave way to conflict and warfare, inequality, and cultural dominance by the West.[5] The new Mediterranean (it is still with us) is not an actual geographical entity but a cultural construct that maps an imagined space;[6] there is no question here of subordinating history, or art history, to a geographical category. On the contrary, visual images – high art from Turner and Delacroix to Matisse and de Chirico, as well as the emerging mass media of print and photography – played a key role in the production and appropriation of the new Mediterranean space.

The Mediterranean thus conceived was a product of a Romantic myth that saw the region as remote in time and space, the site of great religions and cultures in ruins, now inhabited by exotic natives; though remote, it was paradoxically ever more readily available to Europeans – at first hand, in travel and tourism, and mediated, through scholarship and art. This remoteness in time and in space, the very basis of its allure or 'romance,' was the product of European modernity with its emphasis on history and progress, which remained the Mediterranean's absent comparator.[7] In this respect, the new Mediterranean was a construct like the Orient of Orientalism; Mediterraneanism, to use the term Michael Herzfeld has proposed, is a controlling and reductive Eurocentric viewpoint that, in a 'politics of knowledge,'[8] exoticizes, homogenizes, and restricts any account of the region.[9] Francesco Loriggio addresses these 'allegories of modernity' in his essay and develops the parallel between Mediterraneanism and Orientalism. Using Orientalism to inform his discussion of Mediterraneanism, he reveals the profound ambiguity of the West's relation to the Mediterranean, which is at once European, Asian, and African.

## A Mediterranean Space

Seen, since the earliest textual accounts, as the meeting place of three continents – Africa, Asia, and Europe – the Mediterranean has many of the qualities of a frontier where peoples and cultures meet and mix. Geologically, it is a zone of fracture and confrontation at which the African plate pushes against and plunges below the Eurasian; the unstable sea is shrinking at the rate of 1 cm a year, which will lead to its disappearance in the very distant future, about ten to fifteen million years from now. Yet, historically, the Mediterranean has also been at the centre of empires uniting disparate peoples and cultures: most convincingly, during the Roman Empire (figure 1.1) and, a second time, incompletely, under the rule of Ottoman Turkey (figure 1.2). In the nineteenth century, it would, once again, be seen as the centre of a region by Europeans strongly influenced by their Christian and classical heritage and motivated by their search for the origin of ancient civilizations in the Middle East. Bent on dominating this region as the Ottoman Turks weakened their hold, the European powers saw it as the gateway to the Orient, especially after the completion of the Suez Canal in 1869. Thus imagined and reconfigured, between North and South, West and East, the Mediterranean region was a modern invention, inseparable from the spread of European power and colonization, the retreat of Ottoman and Islamic empires, and the impact of technological and cultural modernity.

The new Mediterranean space was described, measured, and administered by European science, technology, and law, which thus helped to produce and legitimate the Romantic 'idea of the Mediterranean' as an objective fact. Natural science and geography established the Mediterranean as a bio-geographical region, united by climate and geology, flora and fauna. Used memorably by Braudel to define the Mediterranean theatre of history and still very much present in travel literature and government planning, such environmentalist ideas survive to this day as we identify the area with dry summers and mild, wet winters and with the cultivation of olive trees and vines (figure 1.3).[10] Any such privileging of geographical factors risks falling into environmental determinism and needs to be understood in its cultural context. Recent scholarship has questioned the validity of the idea of a Mediterranean environmental unity based on vegetation and climate, noting that the interpretation reflects a strong literary tradition reaching back through the classics to Homer, and has opted instead for a micro-ecological understanding of the region as defined by 'the unpredictable, the variable and, above all, the local.'[11] For historians of visual culture, however, such cultural determination of a scientifically validated concept of Mediterranean unity is revealing and of great interest. The stereotype, its uses, and our continuing involvement with it need to be studied.

Studying the flora of different sites around the sea ca. 1800, in Greece, Spain, North Africa, and the south of France, botanists found similarities and explained them by shared geology and climate, defining the region bio-geographically and, thus, also as a landscape.[12] In 1828, for example, a scientific expedition accompanied the French military force led by General Maison sent to expel Egyptian troops and consolidate Greek control of the Peloponnese. Clearly modelled on the Egyptian expedition of Napoleon that had just completed publication of its results,[13] it studied the flora, fauna, and geology of Morea, as it was then called, and published the results in two folio volumes and an atlas, Bory de Saint Vincent's *Expédition de Morée* of 1832. The studies that defined the new Mediterranean space scientifically were produced by government-funded expeditions, their campaigns made possible by British and French military power. Formulated at a most opportune moment to provide scientific support for the political and cultural imperatives of French and British colonialism, the bio-geographical space, or environment, of the Mediterranean cannot be understood apart from that context.[14]

Modern technologies facilitated the conquest and domination of the Mediterranean region; they also created and reshaped it as the space of Romantic vision and a product of the technological futurism central to capitalism. In 1869 the Suez Canal was inaugurated after ten years of construction. It is the most obvious symbol of this ambition and the resulting process of transformation. The idea of such a canal has a long history, even an antique precedent. In their technologistic and mystical vision of the Mediterranean as the centre of a world economy and culture, the French Saint-Simonians lobbied in the 1830s for the long-mooted project as the 'decisive act' in the 'marriage' of East and West.[15] When it was finally built, thirty years later, by the French engineer Ferdinand de Lesseps for the Khedive Ismail, the canal linked the Mediterranean to the Indian Ocean via the Red Sea, turning the inland sea, joined naturally only to the Atlantic Ocean at the straits of Gibraltar, into a passage between Europe and the Far East. Puvis de Chavannes's exactly contemporary mural *Marseille Porte de l'Orient* (figure 1.4), painted with its pendant *Massilia Colonie Grecque* to decorate the staircase of the Marseilles art museum in 1868–9, represents the modern port as the hub of the new Mediterranean and France's gateway to the Orient.

Christine Peltre has shown in her examination of French Orientalist painting that there was room for the celebration of modernity. In the case of the Suez Canal, some artists made explicit comparisons with the past: between, on the one hand, steam-powered dredges and the large, deep cut and, on the other, pharaonic pyramids and the biblical story of Moses crossing the Red Sea.[16] Whether this was explicitly acknowledged or not, the images of Suez were produced and perceived as documents of a dramatic meeting of modern Western technology and Egyptian ancientness. The historicist perception of place as a locus of time-space, as a chronotope[17] affected by a layering of past and present, is typical of the Romantic sensibility. In the case of the Suez Canal, such juxtapositions and historical symbolism both acknowledged Egyptian past achievements and, simultaneously, referenced the unexpressed contrast between past greatness and present decadence, which called for European intervention to supply the resources and technology to reform and modernize Oriental societies.

The Western desire to map and order Mediterranean lands, to bring them into relation with the modern world, made use of technology to accomplish the task. Images were produced in the languages of scientific description and empirical realism, employing the geometry of architectural projections and linear and aerial perspectives. Conquest and colonization were accomplished with the aid of the artist as well as the surveyor; paintings and prints, displayed in exhibitions, museums, and albums were another means of appropriating and remaking the world. W.J.T. Mitchell has underscored the central role of landscape imagery in the naturalization of power.[18] John Zarobell's essay on landscape painting in French-occupied Algeria shows that these images, particularly the limiting case of depictions of the desert – incommensurable and located at the edge of the French colony – can be aligned with the colonial regime's imposition of an alien concept of land ownership on the territory. Comparing legislative and geographical representations with artistic ones by Gustave Guillaumet and Eugène Fromentin, he argues that the representations share, across domains, an 'abstract space' that orders human activities and, ultimately, shifts perceptions and practices. *The Desert*, though exceptional in Guillaumet's oeuvre, is fully representative of colonial appropriation of the land.

## Classicism and Living Antiquity

Representation of the Mediterranean in the modern period was dominated by two tropes, classicism and Orientalism. Classicism was an old and well established vision of Mediterranean antiquity in the West; however, Orientalism, defined by Edward Said as a discourse 'by which European culture was able to manage – and even produce – the Orient,' was new, post-Enlightenment, Romantic and colonialist.[19] Initially focused on the Mediterranean region, the imaginary space of the Orient would come to encompass far more of the globe, including lands from North Africa through the Middle East and even to the Far East of India, China, and Japan. Deploying a Foucauldian understanding of the relation between power and knowledge, Said maps the imaginative geography of Europe's world order. The expansive energy, as well as excitement, of modernity made this vision across time and space possible. Below, I will argue that the classicizing vision of the Mediterranean, too, was radically affected by modernity and the division of the world into modern West and pre-modern Other, North and South, dominant and subaltern.

Well into the nineteenth century, the European idea of the Mediterranean was predominantly literary, anchored in classical texts and situated within the borders of the ancient Greek and Roman worlds. From the Renaissance, and earlier, the humanistic education of Western elites had focused on these texts, so that it was impossible to 'see' the physical elements of the region without a classical gloss – whether considering olive trees and vines or wind and sun.[20] In the eighteenth century, the princely collections and classical sites of Italy became goals of the Grand Tour. More adventurous travellers, especially archaeologists and architects, pushed on to Greece and the Ottoman Empire. Although Turkey and Egypt were visited and Islamic buildings and the ancient pyramids described as early as the sixteenth and seventeenth centuries, the Mediterranean of European scholars, artists, and architects on the Grand Tour remained a classical world for a long time. However, their approach to that classical Mediterranean changed fundamentally in the eighteenth century.

The case of Johann Wolfgang von Goethe is instructive. He travelled to Italy to experience the vestiges of antiquity at first hand, as shown in Wilhelm Tischbein's portrait of *Goethe in the Roman Campagna*, painted in 1787 (figure 1.5), and to complete his classical tragedy *Iphigenie auf Tauris* there. The journal of his 1786–7 trip reveals that this German writer steeped in the classics was a modern traveller with a Romantic imagination fleeing court duties at Weimar who immersed himself in what he saw as a spontaneous, pre-modern culture.[21] For Goethe, like many transalpine visitors, the contrast of a Catholic culture with that of the Protestant north also played an important role. Italy was full of classical sites and ruins. Equally important for the northern visitor, it was southern in climate and lifestyle. The stereotype of blue sky, blossoming and fruiting trees, and gentle breezes was quickly established. Living a great deal outdoors, simply and in harmony with their surroundings, Italians presented themselves to these northern visitors as happy and hospitable. They seemed unreflective and passionate, open and innocent, lighthearted and pious. Shaped by landscape and built environment and by the enduring Mediterranean climate, they seemed to be continuing the natural life of antiquity.[22]

From the German Enlightenment, Goethe accepted the new historical understanding of antiquity, established in Johann Joachim Winckelmann's revolutionary *History of the Art of Antiquity* (1764) and developed in the work of Johann Gottfried von Herder (1785). Winckelmann established a chronology and historical narrative of classical art and recognized four centres of antique culture around the Mediterranean, Greece, Rome, Etruria, and Egypt.[23] The high point of German Hellenism came in the writings of Friedrich von Hölderlin and Wilhelm von Humboldt, published after Goethe's Italian trip.[24] Classical culture as moral example was Goethe's primary focus, even though, in the spirit of the new historicism, he gave other cultures their due. A first draft of Tischbein's portrait showed Goethe against a background of obelisks.[25] The poet would go on to study the newly translated poetry of Persia, attempting to integrate the Orient into his vision in *West-Östlicher Divan* (1819).[26]

The contrast of North and South found in Goethe's *Journal*, so central to the modern image of the Mediterranean, has a long tradition, as the records of travellers coming from north of the Alps in the fifteenth and sixteenth centuries show.[27] In the eighteenth century, the *philosophes* put in place a new cultural geography of reason and progress centred on Western Europe. Travel away from the centre was read as a move back in time in terms of civilization and reason.[28] In their images of Italian ruins and pastoral life, local customs and costumes, writers and artists from the North assumed a contrast with modernity. Location in space implied a temporal dimension. Mediterranean Italy appeared not only as a survival from antiquity, in whose ruins these peoples dwelled, but increasingly seemed pre-modern and, so, exotic and 'primitive.' Southern European cultures, in Italy as well as Spain, Provence, and Greece, were seen as different and became the object of the emerging disciplines of anthropology and folk studies, as well as history. These pre-modern qualities, read positively as signs of Arcadia ca. 1800 by Goethe, were seen increasingly negatively by the mid-nineteenth century, in terms of Orientalism.[29]

Classicism persisted as a major trope in nineteenth-century images of the Mediterranean, although it had to compete with a proliferation of Orientalist representations by mid-century. Modernity not only identified the classical Mediterranean with a ruined past; it also made the classical vision of such canonical places as Italy problematic, as André Dombrowski argues in 'The Untimely Classicism of Hans von Marées.' Von Marées escaped to Italy after 1870, in the wake of the Franco-Prussian war and German unification, in search of a pre-modern culture, as had the medievalizing Nazarenes earlier. In the tradition of German Hellenism,[30] von Marées sought to develop a new classicism in response to French modernist painting and German nationalist art. However, his new classicism could not satisfactorily resolve the fundamental conflict between a timeless, Arcadian classicism – no longer available to him in the unproblematic way that it had been to Goethe less than a hundred years earlier – and a modern present, both erotic and geographical, as Dombrowski demonstrates.[31] Von Marées's male-centred imagery reminds us that the idea of the Mediterranean assigned gender roles (e.g., athletic, physically active males and solid, maternal females). The classical vision, as defined most recently by Winckelmann, was centred on the male body, athletic and sensual, in harmony with mind and environment.[32] The Orientalist Mediterranean was gendered female and so was, increasingly, the classical as the century advanced.

Mediterranean classicism remained a powerful language throughout the nineteenth and twentieth centuries. Such classicizing art has generally been understood as purveying a conservative vision of Western culture, contrasting with both Romanticism and modernism in its backward-looking visual language and imagery. Classicizing art has also been identified with the politics of the right because of its use by fascist regimes in Italy and Germany in the 1920s and 1930s and because of its exclusionary conception of Western culture. Although, in most cases, it was inseparable from a Eurocentric vision celebrating the Mediterranean as the Greek and Roman source of European civilization,[33] closer study reveals its changing and contested nature and its availability for use in both right and left political visions.[34] The cultural meanings of styles and imagery are malleable and entirely historically situated in time and space at any given moment. Classicism was the language of both left and right revolutions from the late eighteenth to the twentieth centuries; but then so was realism. Both Cézanne and Renoir painted Provence, and their works can be associated with the regionalist revival of the Félibres that celebrated the Greek and Roman roots of the French South.[35] Aristide Maillol's classicizing female nudes were given traditional gender roles and allegorical functions. The sculptor himself linked them with the nationalist Latinism of Charles Maurras.[36] An archaizing classicism could be seen as more authentically Mediterranean than a full-blown classicism associated with empire; in Italy, it was preferred by some artists and critics of the left who promoted the Etruscan revival of the 1920s.[37]

Classicism was reshaped as a modern visual language in Western art in the second half of the nineteenth century by science and naturalism and was used widely as the norm in a hierarchical view of the world.[38] Athena Leoussi characterized the change ideologically as one from a universalist, civic classicism based in the city to a naturalistic, particularist, and ethno-racial one privileging the countryside and nature.[39] The switch from an inclusive ideal to an exclusionary physical typology was the product of nationalist and colonialist politics, underwritten by racist biology and ethnography. In the aftermath of defeat in the Franco-Prussian War and the devastation of the Commune (1870–1), many French scholars and ideologues claimed a Mediterranean origin and Greek racial inheritance for the nation to distinguish it from the 'barbarian' Germans and encourage a healthy and fecund French population. The female nude played a central role in this gendered Mediterranean imagery.[40]

Mediterranean classicism did not necessarily signify a conservative ideology, however; it was a powerful imagery claimed by left as well as right. There was a long-standing tradition that saw the region as the cradle of democracy in France with an emphasis on individual and communal freedoms. Anarchist geographers associated the South with a tradition of freedom-loving citizenry and argued that the Mediterranean climate was conducive to anarcho-communism. As Anne Dymond shows in her chapter on Paul Signac, the anarchist painter used the pastoral to visualize an utopian communal future on the shores of the Mediterranean in a direct challenge to conservative classicizing visions of the South. In Signac's work, pastoral was a socially radical genre and classicizing compositions modelled on those of Puvis de Chavannes evoked, in their harmony and order, a hoped-for utopian future.

To Europeans, the modern Mediterranean appeared increasingly hybrid as the nineteenth century wore on, contaminated by the Orient even on its European shore. Among avant-garde artists, Henri Matisse devoted a major portion of his work to visualizing the Mediterranean; his paintings, gouaches, and cut-outs have become identified with southern light and colour. In 'Inventing Mediterranean Harmony in Matisse's Paper Cut-Outs,' John Klein argues that, in the 1950s – in the aftermath of French humiliation in the Second World War and in the face of growing colonial unrest – Matisse's cut-outs visualized such a hybrid Mediterranean as an idyllic refuge. Avant-garde artists discovered France's Mediterranean coast in the 1880s. Before their arrival, Provençal painters represented the South as a distinct geographical region by showing it as a bleached and dusty land dominated by sunlight to the exclusion of other climatic and meteorological phenomena.[41] Later in the nineteenth century, avant-garde artists formed by Impressionism translated the effects of intense sunlight into bright prismatic colour, for the most part using a division of colour based on complementary contrasts.[42] Southern sunlight, already exotic to the northerner, became colour in the works of Paul Signac and Vincent van Gogh; thus was built a link with the Romantic heritage of Eugène Delacroix and notions of Orientalist splendour that Henri Matisse would exploit.[43] The interaction of Matisse's line drawings and pared-down sculptures with the *fauve* colour of his paintings suggests a desire to marry Orientalism and classicism.

## Orientalism

We have seen that the Mediterranean region first became the object of intense European scientific and artistic study, underwritten by the new geopolitical realities of great-power rivalry and colonization, in the late eighteenth century. The region included religious and cultural monuments central to European cultural identity in the pilgrimage sites of the 'Holy Land,' as Palestine came to be known, and the archeological sites of Italy, Greece, the Middle East, and also North Africa. The Mediterranean as a whole bore the imprint of past civilizations and, most important for Europeans in the age of colonialism, of a variety of empires including the Roman. Delacroix saw in the inhabitants of North Africa antique figures rather than the decadent Turks he had expected to find;[44] later, French colonizers would claim to be recovering a Latin heritage from the invading Arabs.[45] Modern historicism and science transformed the educated traveller's relationship to the region's past and present. The Mediterranean region came to be seen in a new way, as a unit, a cultural and geographical area with shared characteristics that stood apart from contemporary enlightened Europe, as Francesco Loriggio argues in his essay. It appeared both ancestral and exotic: ancestral because it had been 'the cradle of European civilization' in a remote past and exotic because it now appeared distant culturally.[46] From this perspective, the Mediterranean needed to be modernized and its heritage recovered for Europe.

Napoleon's brief occupation of Egypt (1798–1801) was a 'decisive moment in the formation of a distinctively modern Orientalism,'[47] and the *Description de l'Égypte*, published 1809–28 by the scholarly commission that accompanied the French army, became the basis for future scientific and artistic appropriation of the Orient.[48] The modern Orientalist vision of the non-European Mediterranean is well represented by David Roberts's two lithographic albums; published between 1842 and 1849, the albums appeared at the very moment when tourist travel to the region emerged. Judging by the publication dates of the first British and French guidebooks, tourism in Egypt and the Middle East began in the 1840s. In the 1860s construction of the Suez Canal heightened interest; in 1865 Thomas Cook organized the first tour of Egypt. Roberts, his subscribers, and the broader public that visited his exhibitions shared a vision of the contemporary Mediterranean world as exotic and pre-modern, where the inhabitants lived in the splendid ruins of past civilizations. In *Temple of Dendereh* and *Gateway to the Great Temple at Baalbec* (figure 1.6), Roberts documents this vision of the historical sites and monuments. The lithographs, about 250 prints altogether, are based on his on-site drawings and inscribed with precise dates and locations. They were exhibited and sold widely to a wealthy, educated middle class avid for images of this newsworthy region, newly available to them as the Ottoman Empire lost control and Britain and France gained influence.[49]

Roberts travelled to the Middle East in 1838–9, at a moment when British forces asserted their presence in Syria and Palestine and biblical archaeology was beginning to transform Palestine into the 'Holy Land.'[50] Commentary in his diary and the inscriptions on some of the prints restore for us the cultural context of his representation of the sites in the album.[51] When he visited the Temple of Dendereh in 1838, it was without any human presence, which led Roberts to melancholy reflections, noted in his diary, on 'the instability of human greatness' and 'the perishable nature of even the most enduring works of human genius.'[52] Contemporary Muslim inhabitants were held responsible for the lack of repair and degradation of the monuments, as the caption on *Gateway to the Great Temple at Baalbec* makes clear. 'These beautiful structures, though replete with interest and delight, carry with them a mingled feeling of humiliation at the transitory greatness of all human conceptions, and regret that such proud relics should be in the hands of a people incapable of appreciating their merits and consequently heedless of their complete destruction.'[53] That these people needed Western colonial tutelage was the clear Orientalist conclusion; with modernization, the sites could be cleared and turned into monuments on exhibition in an uncanny realization of the plates in the *Description de l'Égypte*.[54]

The 1980s saw an upsurge of interest in Orientalist art, coinciding with the publication of Edward Said's ground-breaking *Orientalism* in 1978. Two exhibitions surveyed Orientalist painting of the Mediterranean: in 1982 Donald Rosenthal's *Orientalism, the Near East in French Painting, 1800–1880* and in 1984, MaryAnne Stevens's *The Orientalists: Delacroix to Matisse*.[55] The latter documents the primacy of French involvement, starting with the invasion and colonization of Algeria from 1830, and the Europe-wide scope of Orientalism in painting. It was Linda Nochlin's 'Imaginary Orient' that introduced Said's critical perspective to English-language art history, arguing that the descriptive images of the ethnographic painters were a value-laden, carefully constructed Orientalism set against the paradigm of European modernity and addressed to the fantasy of an implied Western viewer.[56] Writing at almost the same moment, Olivier Richon emphasized the imaginative aspect of Orientalism, the 'romantic dreams' and the 'fantasms' of the European centre, over the social and political factors noted by Nochlin.[57] In *Prayer in the Mosque of 'Amr*, ca. 1872 (figure 1.7), Jean-Léon Gérôme shows a cross-section of Egyptians, from a nearly nude *fellah* to a richly clad *arnavut*, praying together in the oldest Cairene mosque. This scene, presented in the deep space of a meticulously described, decaying structure infested by pigeons, is – to borrow Richon's terms – both a hyper-real slice of life and a posed tableau constructed, without any hint of the modern world and the Western viewer, as a metaphor of a timeless and static Orient. It is the Orientalist equivalent of Salon paintings of Christian piety set in the past of the Middle Ages or the rural provinces of contemporary Europe such as Bavaria and Brittany.

British artists too depicted an Orientalist Egypt; however, they had a particular religious motivation for focusing on Palestine.[58] Protestantism had rejected pilgrimage to Jerusalem as a Catholic ritual, but Jerusalem and the 'Holy Land' remained a powerful, ever-present image in its theology. Palestine was also of particular interest to Britain because of its strategic position alongside Egypt on the road to Mesopotamia and India. As they do today, strategic and religious interests reinforced each other; biblical archaeologists and military surveyors worked side-by-side in nineteenth-century Palestine. In an age of scientific investigation, Protestant religious cultures based in the direct authority of the Bible had a strong interest in recovering the true appearance of the landscapes and sites of the Christian sacred story set in the 'Holy Land.'[59] William Holman Hunt travelled to Egypt and Palestine in 1854 in order to paint biblical subjects accurately in the light, and with the models and settings, of the region. *Finding of the Saviour in the Temple*, 1854–60 (figure 1.8), shares Gérôme's modern documentary approach and creates a 'reality effect';[60] however, it does so using the luminous modern palette of the Pre-Raphaelites, rather than the sober, classically restrained one of the French artist.

At first glance, Holman Hunt's painting of the life of Christ might not seem to be an instance of Orientalism because of its subject. On a visit to Jerusalem with his parents, Jesus has slipped away to dispute scripture with Temple scholars. Hunt locates the scene in the Semitic East by using a variety of archaeological sources to construct a believable exotic setting.[61] However, in Marcia Pointon's words, 'Archaeological and biblical knowledge allied with the power of the brush ... permit Hunt to annexe the Middle East for the causes of Protestantism.'[62] Hunt's attitude to the contemporary Middle East, as opposed to the archaeological record, is clear from his letters: in his view, both the Jews and Arabs of Palestine were ignorant of the truth and degraded the sites. The painting depicts the rabbis as 'Oriental' in their garb and facial features; led by their blind elders, they are no match for the vigorous and youthful Jesus, founder of Western Christianity.[63] Marked by dress, language, religious practice, and occupation, Jews were seen as an alien and strange people in Christian Europe. In the post-Enlightenment sciences of anthropology, ethnology, and biology, their difference was explained by 'race' and they were located hierarchically, between the pinnacle of European whiteness and the nadir of African blackness, in the Semitic 'Orient.'[64] Hunt's depiction of the Temple scholars in *Finding of the Saviour in the Temple* coincides with the stereotype of the Jew as the Oriental Other.[65]

Orientalism could also, however, serve the Jews when they began to settle in Palestine and sought to establish their own culture and art production. Seeking to create a new art free of European models and to prove that they, like any genuine national culture, could produce an original style and imagery, the Zionist community launched the Bezalel School of Arts and Crafts in 1906 under the direction of Boris Schatz. The new Jewish art used biblical imagery and a repertory of natural motifs derived from Palestinian flora and fauna; it developed an appropriate visual language, filtered through a contemporary art nouveau sensibility, based on Orientalist stylization found in local crafts and on Hebrew calligraphy.[66] Bezalel closed in 1929 for financial reasons and, when it reopened in 1935, it had to compete with other visions of Jewish culture, most importantly the universalist aesthetic of modernism championed by the new Tel Aviv Museum of Art founded in 1932.[67] The Bezalel Museum, given a separate existence from 1935, was absorbed into the Israel Museum, an Israeli rather than a Jewish collection with a strong modernist and Western bias that rejected the earlier Orientalism of Bezalel's national art and, with it, the Palestinian context as Oriental and historically past.

Alla Myzelev's 'The Representation of Islamic Art in Israeli Museums: The Politics of Collecting' examines a particularly telling example of such Orientalism at work. According to Timothy Mitchell, Europe's Oriental Other was constructed as its opposite marked by three features, essentialism, otherness, and absence.

> Three features define this Orientalist reality: it is understood as the product of unchanging racial or cultural essences; these essential characteristics are in each case the polar opposite of the West (passive rather than active, static rather than mobile, emotional rather than rational, chaotic rather than ordered); and the Oriental opposite or Other is marked by a

> series of absences (of movement, reason, order, meaning and so on). In terms of these three features – essentialism, otherness, absence – the colonial world can be mastered, and colonial mastery will, in turn, reinscribe and reinforce these defining features.[68]

Mitchell linked Orientalism to a fundamental aspect of modernity that he called 'the exhibitionary order,' a system of representing the world applied not only to distant realities such as the Orient but, increasingly, to all experience, so that the world is understood as ordered and meaningful on the model of an exhibition.[69] Myzelev's prime example, the L.A. Mayer Museum of Islamic Art, collects and displays objects for the avowed purpose of fostering knowledge and understanding of Islamic culture in Israel. The museum's objective narrative, starting after the prophet Mohammed's death in the seventh century CE and ending with the demise of the Ottoman Empire in 1924, constitutes an abstract archive and carefully isolates Islamic art, placing it outside the Western narrative of artistic progress, but subordinate to it at key points. Myzelev draws a contrast with museum displays of the art and culture of Israel, which are linked directly to the Mediterranean of biblical and classical antiquity and thus Europe. The Mayer and other Israeli museums' treatments of Palestinian archaeology and Islamic art are recent examples of Orientalism, here motivated by Israeli nationalism.

While acknowledging an immense debt to Said's pioneering work, scholars have recently moved away from his monolithic concept of Orientalism with its binary opposition of Orient to Occident and foregrounding of Western mastery of a passive Eastern subject. Eschewing such binarism as early as 1983, Homi Bhabha characterized the space of colonial discourse as a 'process of subjectification' founded on ambivalence and excess and alerted us to the subaltern's powers of agency, limited though they may seem, to mimic, speak back, and thus negotiate a position and an identity.[70] To productively complicate the analysis of specific situations, Lisa Lowe has proposed a heterogeneous reading of Orientalism as a tradition 'crossed, intersected, and engaged by other representations' and 'an apparatus through which a variety of concerns with difference is figured,' differences of race, class, gender, and identity.[71] For her, Orientalism is no longer a one-way conduit of Western power applied to a colonial subject; the system and its institutions can be used by the Oriental subject for other purposes. Reina Lewis has analysed the gendering of the Orient as feminine and highlighted the agency of subaltern women within Orientalism.[72] Most recently, Frederick Bohrer has argued with particular cogency for use of the broader concept of exoticism in order to avoid binarism and because it is more inclusive than Orientalism. Not limited to geographical locales, it addresses time as well as space.[73]

By examining the Oriental Other's accounts of the West, scholars have enriched the Western view of Mediterranean history. Timothy Mitchell used accounts of the West by visitors from the Orient in arriving at his analysis of the 'exhibitionary order' of occidental modernity.[74] With a particular focus on the Mediterranean, historians of art and architecture have begun to chart the complex dialogues of such Orientalisms and Occidentalisms in the age of European colonialism. Zeynep Çelik's *Displaying the Orient* examined Ottoman self-representation in response to modernity at World's Fairs between 1867 and 1900 in the pavilions of Egypt, Algeria, and Tunisia.[75] Writing of the early twentieth century, Gwendolyn Wright has shown how colonial urbanism, used to order, pacify, and police indigenous societies while imposing European models of modernization, also engaged in a colonial contextualism of style and ornament to create a sense of continuity with local traditions for the indigenous populations and to revivify exoticism for the metropolitan culture. Colonial cities modelled a twentieth-century city that promised to combine 'the benefits of modernity with a strong sense of place and local history.'[76] Of particular relevance to the present volume is her discussion of modernization and architectural preservation in Morocco. Earlier, Prochaska analysed the colonial history of the Algerian city of Bône, now Adeba, with a specific focus on spatial politics.[77] In *L'atelier de voyage* and subsequent publications, Christine Peltre stressed the complex effect of the voyage on the perceptions and practices of Orientalist painters throughout the nineteenth century.[78]

Recently, Roger Benjamin has published a fascinating and revealing study of Orientalism in French painting. In *Orientalist Aesthetics: Art, Colonialism, and North Africa, 1880–1930*, he resituates the modernist art of the impressionist Auguste Renoir and the *fauve* Henri Matisse in the context of French Orientalism and its metropolitan and colonial institutions;[79] with equal attention, he analyses the art of their indigenous counterparts painting between the two world wars, Azouaou Mammeri and Mohammed Racim, as modernist 'emulator' and 'hybrid' neo-traditionalist respectively.[80] Racim's miniatures (figure 1.9) celebrate the sixteenth- and seventeenth-century corsairs of al-Djezira and the Barbary Coast, as well as the earlier Caliphate of Andalusia. These images, based on Islamic models, reconstruct a heroic age before the European invasion, when Islamic rulers and corsairs controlled much of the Mediterranean. Racim's revivalist art, successfully practised with French support, now appears to us, from our post-colonial vantage point, as a counter-discourse of political resistance.[81] Benjamin studies Orientalist institutions as well as individuals in an 'art-historical test of Said's thesis, his Foucauldian insight that the links between colonial governance and aesthetic production ... were constitutive in fundamental ways.'[82]

## Nationalism, Identity, and Post-Colonialism

National states and nationalism are modern European phenomena developed in the nineteenth century.[83] Their emergence in the Mediterranean regions of the Ottoman Empire coincided with European military intervention and colonization, which fostered the founding of certain states quite early in the nineteenth century, while others were created by indigenous nationalist groups that forced the abandonment of colonial rule after the Second World War. These post-colonial countries were modelled on the modern nation-state and mapped in relation to boundaries established by European empires and colonies. On the European side of the Mediterranean, Italy was finally united in 1870 with Rome as its capital. In the Ottoman Empire, Greece achieved separate statehood in 1830; Serbia and other Balkan nations emerged throughout the nineteenth century, with the Treaty of Berlin in 1878 recognizing many of these developments. Visual art played an important role in the invention of the cultures and traditions of all new nations, including those of the new Mediterranean space.[84] Each of these states worked to produce a national culture with both fine arts and handicrafts playing key roles.

Perceived since the Enlightenment as the source of Europe's democracy and culture, Greece was of particular interest to European cultural elites and a strong philhellenic movement supported the Greek national uprising. Byron's poetry and personal involvement and Delacroix's paintings are among the best-known artistic responses. Greek philhellenes, with the aid of foreign supporters, set out to recreate an imagined Greek nation using as their model Periclean Athens from two millennia earlier. However, this neo-classical culture administered by a monarch imported from Germany was perceived as a foreign imposition by most Greeks and clashed with popular sentiment, which identified the nation with the religious and folk culture safeguarded by the Orthodox church through centuries of Ottoman rule.[85] In opposition to its Islamic rulers, the Greek population defined itself as *romaiosyne,* Christian of the Roman Empire, which is precisely how Islamic cultures referred to the West and the Mediterranean. Nina Athanassoglou-Kallmyer examines this paradoxical confrontation between two competing national visions in 'Classicism and Resistance in Late-Nineteenth-Century European Art: The Case of Greece.' She interprets the classicism fostered by England, France, and Germany as an ideologically charged colonial language and analyses Greek images of religion and folklore as instances of a counter-discursive resistance.

Palestinian nationalism, also, has had to resist a Western vision of its lands. We have seen that, as the 'Holy Land' of the Bible, Palestine was as much of a Mediterranean lodestone for European power and scholarship as Greece. It was part of the European sphere of influence by the 1830s, protected in the Crimean War. The British took a particular interest in the area as a way of guarding the land route to India, for which purpose they carried out military surveys. Palestine was the focus of biblical archaeology that overlaid a sacred geography on the Arab landscape, a visual imperialism clearly represented in the works of Roberts and Holman Hunt, as well as numerous photographers.[86] Many of these images (e.g., figure 1.8) recorded the presence of Jews in the population of Palestine, marginalized as historical curiosities. During the 1920s and 1930s, under the British Mandate, growing Jewish settlement provoked by European anti-Semitism was a source of friction and there was a major uprising of Palestinians in 1927. Once the state of Israel was declared in 1948, biblical archaeology was used to document and visualize a historical narrative that connected the modern state of Israel to the early history of Jewish tribes and kingdoms in the area. In the process, Arab Palestinian archaeology and history were marginalized; ultimately, Islamic culture was to be safely located in the museum past, as Myzelev demonstrates.

Palestine and the Middle East were represented in the nineteenth-century work of European photographers (figure 1.10) as lands largely emptied of their people.[87] The inhabitants were largely invisible in these landscapes, even though traces of their agricultural activity and views of their settlements registered. In Palestine the focus was on sites and historical monuments associated with the Bible. The result was a landscape freighted with the past, existing in a curiously languorous, fated present – waiting for something to happen, that something being the arrival of Western modernity. Here we might recall Zarobell's analysis of the representation of Algerian landscape in French painting as empty and made available for the colonialist enterprise. Yet this was, in reality, a productive agricultural landscape worked by Arab villagers, albeit for absentee landlords, much of it overgrazed.[88] In 1862 Mary Rogers published an account of her 1850s visit to Palestine and described a flourishing Mediterranean landscape of fruit trees, vegetable gardens, and wheat fields that she observed on her way from Jaffa to Jerusalem. This is a precious document even though it, too, is framed by an Orientalist judgment of the Palestinians as 'decadent, destructive and passive,'[89] and the author, a member of the British ruling elite, seems to anticipate Palestine's transformation by (imperial) modernity.

In the twentieth century, Palestinian artists and writers have used an idealized memory of this Mediterranean landscape and the villages dotted through it to visualize their homeland in the face of European intervention, Zionist settlement, and recent Israeli colonization on the West Bank and in Gaza. Palestinian Arabs do not reside in one, continuous territorial setting; their communities are found in settlements within territory occupied by Israel since 1967, in refugee camps, and in exile in Europe and North America. The Mediterranean landscape of Palestine, increasingly besieged and fragmented, is the ground on which Arab artists imagine their national community and identity.[90] As in the nineteenth-century art of many European nations, pastoral and folkloric depictions visualize a longing for a lost past, driven by nostalgia, which may never have existed in the form depicted. Olive trees, peasant women, village houses, cacti, the earth, and stones are the recurring reference points as the mood shifts at the end of the twentieth century from utopian memory to melancholy fragments and absence, the technique from painting to installation art.

The identities of national communities of the southern and eastern Mediterranean were asserted and visualized against the colonial order. Insofar as the Mediterranean was a European idea, as I have argued, these new identities would seem to have had little room for it. In fact, that debate had been engaged in the 1920s and 1930s. In Italy, Mussolini's fascism asserted a classicizing vision based on a Roman Mediterranean, as did important segments of the French colonial administration; yet these cultural regimes were far from monolithic and left a place for other aesthetics including the avant-garde. In her essay, Emily Braun examines the complex case of Amedeo Modigliani, Italian and Jew, both insider and outsider in Paris and Europe. Locating himself in the foreign community in Montparnasse, Modigliani portrayed mostly Eastern European Jews and Slavs, in a collective Otherness marked by sightless eyes. His most desirable images were seductive female nudes that were Mediterranean in their Italian and Oriental references. Drawing on both European and non-Western sources, combining African and Cambodian models with classical and early Renaissance ones, Modigliani created a hybrid image and identity for himself and his sitters. His successful Italian reception and posthumous display of the 1920s and 1930s marked the recuperation of an avant-garde art, consecrated by its Parisian success, for the fascist nation.

The nationalist appeal of Latinity and classicism was just as strong in France as in Italy.[91] Yet Jean Ballard's *Cahiers du Sud* (founded 1925) defended an alternative, open, and inclusive view of the Mediterranean that welcomed Islam and all cultures. In poetry and prose, Paul Valéry, André Suarès, Albert Camus, and others celebrated the Mediterranean region as a source of creative inspiration;[92] however, as Said has cautioned in the case of Camus, despite his criticism of the colonial administration, this is a celebration of a European North Africa, for all its exotic hybridity.[93] *Cahiers du Sud* was widely read around the Mediterranean, in Algeria, Tunis, and Egypt, as well as in Europe. Egyptian writers such as Taha Hussein argued that the culture of the nation was Mediterranean, but many more reacted by asserting the Islamic, Arab, and Oriental character of Egypt and rejecting a Mediterranean alliance with Europe. During the political crisis of the 1930s, liberal intellectuals sought an alternative way of maintaining their links with Western culture as Arab nationalism established itself and the Moslem Brotherhood (founded 1928) asserted Islam against the Orientalists.[94]

In the lands bordering the Mediterranean, there was an important tension between the idea of a cosmopolitan, hybrid, and modernizing culture focused on the sea and major ports and the new national cultures that 'turn their back to the sea'[95] to ground themselves in the land and indigenous tradition. Economically and historically, ports such as Barcelona, Marseille, Genoa, Beirut, Alexandria, and Tangiers were open cities.[96] Rising nationalist sentiment reacted against their cosmopolitanism and modernity, seeking purity and tradition in the hinterland. The Félibres of the late nineteenth century rejected Marseille as cosmopolitan and foreign, seeking their national tradition in the old towns and rural culture of Provence. The new Turkish republic of Kemal Atatürk, founded in 1924, turned from cosmopolitan Istanbul and the Mediterranean, its link to the lost empire of the Ottoman past, to an inland capital at Ankara that re-emphasized Asia and the Seljuk heritage of Anatolia. Similarly, in 1948 Israel founded a modern Hebrew state that rejected the Mediterranean context of Palestine. Jewish writers and scholars were generally hostile to the Graeco-Roman tradition and the idea of a Mediterranean unity because the Hellenic and Roman worlds of antiquity had been enemies of the Jewish people. Here, the juxtaposition of Tel Aviv's modernist architectural development with the port of old Jaffa may be taken as emblematic.[97]

Images are vital to establishing and representing cultural identity; after 1840 photography was given a central role in that process and the national institutions fostering it. Modernity brought with it to the Mediterranean the documentary impulse; but the practice and purpose were not neutral, as we have seen in the case of both classicizing and Orientalist painting. Photography was one of the Western technologies that was used to order, manage, and put on display the world as knowledge. It had a particular claim to objectivity because it was presented as simply recording, in a physical process, what was in front of the lens. Photographers fanned out to document the physical world; in the Mediterranean region, they followed in the footsteps of artists, recording antique monuments, landscapes, and, increasingly, the inhabitants seen as types, often photographed posed in the studio with props.[98] In 1856–7 Félix-Jacques-Antoine Moulin produced six albums of *Algérie photographiée* containing three hundred photographs of the provinces of Algiers, Oran, and Constantine,[99] and in 1873 Osman Handy, the Turkish, Paris-trained pupil of Gérôme, hired Pascal Sébah to make a set of photographs for a catalogue of costumes of the Ottoman Empire.[100] Although these projects may have been unusual in their ambition to produce comprehensive surveys, even more modest documentary practices shared with them the idea of an archive. Images from such, often partial, archives were sold to tourists as souvenir photos and then, later, as postcards.

David Prochaska examines this colonial photographic regime and its subversion in the post-colonial present through the prism of contemporary Moroccan-French photographer and video artist Yasmina Bouziane. In a critique and reworking of colonial practices, Bouziane looks back from her contemporary vantage point and responds to the colonial past.[101] In her series *Untitled Self-Portraits*, Bouziane interrogates the Orientalism of earlier studio-photography practices. Gender is central to her practice: how the colonial photography studio was gendered, the gendered gaze of colonial postcards, and what it means to be a woman photographer and filmmaker of hybrid French and Moroccan background living in a post-colonial world today. Focusing on selected photographs from the *Untitled Self-Portraits* series, Prochaska links them to past Orientalist photography: Arab women veiled and unveiled, dressing in disguise and cross-dressing, and the 'timeless' biblical Holy Land / Palestine. What emerges is the historical 'situatedness' of the photograph, or any image for that matter; at any given moment, its meaning is entirely historically situated in time and space.

## Conclusion

Our account of the idea of the Mediterranean as a region has taken us from its beginnings in Romantic thought through its colonialist heyday to the present, a process that has involved an examination of its classical, Orientalist, and post-colonial representations. The idea of the Mediterranean continues to carry with it most of the Eurocentric premises that structured it ca. 1800. In the aftermath of the collapse of the Soviet Union and the East European communist bloc and of the hopes raised by peace negotiations between Israel and Palestine in the 1990s, there was a strong impetus to revive the idea of a shared Mediterranean economic and cultural space. It remains largely a Western concept today, as it was at its inception more than two hundred years ago, with nation-states vying for influence.[102] For that reason, the recent initiatives of the European Union and the United Nations to create such a space were problematic from the outset and have become even more so since September 11, 2001. Besides fundamental cultural divisions, which after all are the attraction as well as the challenge, there are huge economic and political divides between Europe and the rest of the Mediterranean region. Add to this the fact that the Mediterranean has not been a viable economic and political unit since the sixteenth century and the enormity of the task becomes apparent.

The economic, political, and ideological forces that play across the Mediterranean come from outside and dispose of the region; extremist visions and local responses roil the stage. Yet there is hope as well as tension as, for instance, Turkey negotiates entrance into the European Community. The challenge is to imagine a dialogue among cultural equals, based on meaningful agency, understanding, and respect, that would lead to the series of true partnerships that are needed to turn a Western and colonial idea of the Mediterranean into a shared cultural space, in which different traditions and lifeways can not only coexist, but also enrich each other. Reaching this imaginative horizon of expectations requires a genuine and deep comprehension of the past, based in real humility and openness, as well as a clear-eyed view of the present, leading to trust and action. Thierry Fabre's journal *La Pensée de Midi* has been an important contributor to this process since 2000. We see the present volume as another very modest contribution.

## NOTES

Preparing an introduction on the topic of modern art and the Mediterranean has taken me well beyond the scope of my normal art-historical expertise and has required the assistance of many generous colleagues. The authors of the nine papers, as well as others who spoke at the original conference, have commented on drafts of the text, making this a truly collaborative venture; in particular, I thank Emily Braun, Athena Leoussi, Alla Myzelev, and David Prochaska for their pertinent interventions. I have also benefited from conversations with Pat Berman, Anne Godlewska, Rudolf Harmsen, Lynda Jessup, and Joan Schwartz.

1 Fernand Braudel, *The Mediterranean and the Mediterranean World in the Age of Phillip II* (1949), English trans. Siân Reynolds (London: Collins, 1972–3); Peregrine Horden and Nicholas Purcell, *The Corrupting Sea: A Study of Mediterranean History* (Oxford: Blackwell, 2000).

2 Thierry Fabre, 'La France et la Méditerranée: Généalogies et représentations,' in Jean-Claude Izzo and Thierry Fabre, *La Méditerranée française* (Paris: Maisonneuve et Larose, 2000), 28–38; Gregor Meiering, 'Genèse et mutations d'une mémoire collective: La Méditerranée allemande,' in Wolfgang Storch and Gregor Meiering, *La Méditerranée allemand* (Paris: Maisonneuve et Larose, 2000), 41ff.

3 For earlier visualizations of the Mediterranean world see Sadok Boubaker, 'La perception de la Méditerranée en Tunisie,' in Emna Belhaj Yahia and Sadok Boubaker, *La Méditerranée tunisienne* (Paris: Maisonneuve et Larose, 2000), 17–42; and Fabre, 'France.'

4 [James Boswell,] *Boswell's Life of Johnson*, 6 vols. (Oxford: Clarendon Press, 1887), 3: 36.

5 See William Dalrymple, 'The Truth about Muslims,' *New York Review of Books*, 4 November 2004: 31–4.

6 Derek Gregory, 'Imaginative Geographies,' *Progress in Human Geography*

19, 4 (1995): 447–85; Joan Schwartz '*The Geography Lesson*: Photographs and the Construction of Imaginative Geographies,' *Journal of Historical Geography* 22, 1 (January 1996): 16–45.

7 See 'Romantic' in Raymond Williams, *Keywords: A Vocabulary of Culture and Society*, rev. ed. (London and New York: Oxford University Press, 1985); for the relation of Romanticism to history, see Jerome J. McGann, *The Romantic Ideology: A Critical Investigation* (Chicago and New York: University of Chicago Press, 1983) and Marjorie Levinson, Marilyn Butler, Jerome McGann, and Paul Hamilton, eds, *Rethinking Historicism: Critical Readings in Romantic History* (Oxford and New York: Blackwell, 1989).

8 Michael Herzfeld, *Anthropology through the Looking Glass: Critical Ethnography in the Margins of Europe* (Cambridge and New York: Cambridge University Press, 1987); Herzfeld, 'Practical Mediterraneanism: Excuses for Everything, from Epistemology to Eating,' in William V. Harris, ed., *Rethinking the Mediterranean* (Oxford: Oxford University Press, 2004), 45–63.

9 Horden and Purcell, *Corrupting Sea*, 486–7.

10 Braudel, *Mediterranean*, 1: 231–75.

11 Horden and Purcell, *Corrupting Sea*, 13.

12 W.J.T. Mitchell, ed., *Landscape and Power* (Chicago: University of Chicago Press, 1994); 2nd edition with new preface and essay by Edward Said (Chicago and London: University of Chicago Press, 2002); Alain Corbin, *The Lure of the Sea: The Discovery of the Seaside in the Western World, 1750–1840*, trans. Jocelyn Phelps (Cambridge: Polity, 1994).

13 The *Description d'Égypte*, based on research started during Napoleon's military campaign by a committee of scientists, engineers, historians, and some artists, was published between 1809 and 1828 in twenty-three oversized volumes. Edward Said, *Orientalism* (New York: Pantheon Books, 1978), 83, saw the *Description* as the end product of Napoleon's project 'to render [Egypt] completely open, to make it totally accessible to European scrutiny.' See David Prochaska, 'Art of Colonialism, Colonialism of Art: the *Description de l'Égypte* (1809–28),' *L'Esprit créateur* 34, 2 (Summer 1994): 69–91, for a comparative study.

14 Emma C. Spary, 'L'invention de l'expédition scientifique. L'histoire naturelle, Bonaparte et l'Egypte,' in Marie-Noëlle Bourget, Bernard Lepetit, Daniel Noordman, and Maroula Sinarellis, eds, *L'invention scientifique de la Méditerranée: Egypte, Morée, Algérie* (Paris: École des Hautes Études en Sciences Sociales, 1998), 119–38; also J. Browne, 'A Science of Empire: British Biogeography before Darwin,' *Revue d'histoire des sciences* 45 (1992): 453–75.

15 Michel Chevalier, *Politique industrielle*: *Système de la Méditerranée* (Paris: Aux bureaux du Globe, 1832), cited in Fabre, 'France,' 28–38; Philippe Regnier, 'Le mythe oriental des Saint-Simoniens,' in Magali Morsy, ed., *Les Saint-Simoniens et l'Orient*: *Vers la modernité* (Aix: Edisud, 1989), 39–40.
16 Christine Peltre, *Orientalisme* (Paris: Terrail, 2004), 183–7. See Darcy Grimaldo Grigsby, 'Geometry/Labor = Volume/Mass?' *October*, Fall 2003: 3–34, for a recent reading of nineteenth-century technology and the building of the Suez Canal.
17 Mikhail M. Bakhtin, *Speech Genres and Other Late Essays*, trans. Vern W. McGee, ed. Caryl Emerson and Michael Holquist (Austin: University of Texas Press, 1986), 42.
18 Mitchell, *Landscape and Power*.
19 Said, *Orientalism*, 3.
20 Horden and Purcell, *Corrupting Sea*, 26–7.
21 For an account of a parallel development in the perception of Greece see Suzanne Saïd, 'The Mirage of Greek Continuity,' in Harris, ed., *Rethinking the Mediterranean*, 267–93.
22 My interpretation of Goethe's account of his Italian journey draws on the study of time and space (the chronotope) in Goethe's work and thought by Mikhail Bakhtin, 'The Bildungsroman and Its Significance in the History of Realism' (1938–9), in *Speech Genres*, 25–50.
23 Alex Potts, *Flesh and the Ideal: Winckelmann and the Origins of Art History* (New Haven and London: Yale University Press, 1994).
24 Meiering, 'Genèse,' 44–9.
25 Ibid., 51.
26 An idyllic Italian culture continuous with the past could also be envisioned around the Christian faith. The German painters who called themselves the Nazarenes lived in an abandoned monastery and painted altarpieces and frescoes in a pre-Raphaelite, quattrocento manner.
27 Horden and Purcell, *Corrupting Sea*.
28 Edward Soja, 'History: Geography: Modernity,' in Simon During, ed., *The Cultural Studies Reader* (London and New York: Routledge, 1993), 135–50; Larry Wolff, *Inventing Eastern Europe: The Map of Civilization on the Mind of the Enlightenment* (Stanford: Stanford University Press, 1994).
29 Nelson Moe, *The View from Vesuvius: Italian Culture and the Southern Question* (Berkeley and Los Angeles: University of California Press, 2002), 13–36, discusses the case of Italy in a very illuminating way.
30 Eliza M. Butlin, *The Tyranny of Greece over Germany* (Cambridge: The University Press, 1935), and Suzanne L. Marchand, *Down from Olympus:*

*Archaeology and Philhellenism in Germany, 1750–1970* (Princeton: Princeton University Press, 1996).

31 For Alma-Tadema's contrasting, untroubled view of antiquity as modern see Elizabeth Prettejohn, 'Lawrence Alma-Tadema and the Modern City of Ancient Rome,' *Art Bulletin* 84 (2002): 114–29.

32 Robert Aldrich, *The Seduction of the Mediterranean: Writing, Art and Homosexual Fantasy* (London: Routledge, 1993), for a homosexual Mediterranean; and Kenneth Silver, 'The Body Politic,' *Art in America*, March 1991: 45–53, for a suggestive critique of Elizabeth Cowling and Jennifer Mundy, *On Classic Ground: Picasso, Léger, de Chirico and the New Classicism, 1910–30*, exh. cat., Tate Gallery (London 1990), in terms of gender and embodiment.

33 Silver, 'The Body Politic,' 47–8.

34 Christopher Green, 'Classicisms of Transcendence and of Transience: Maillol, Picasso and de Chirico,' in Cowling and Mundy, *On Classic Ground*, 269.

35 Nina Athanassoglou-Kallmyer, *Cézanne and Provence: The Painter in His Landscape* (Chicago: University of Chicago Press, 2004).

36 Green, 'Classicisms' in Cowling and Mundy, *On Classic Ground*, 267–8.

37 Emily Braun, 'Political Rhetoric and Poetic Irony: The Uses of Classicism in the Art of Fascist Italy,' in Cowling and Mundy, *On Classic Ground*, 345–6.

38 For a good discussion of the use of these typologies, albeit in England, see Mary Cowling, *The Artist as Anthropologist: The Representation of Type and Character in Victorian Art* (Cambridge and New York: Cambridge University Press, 1989).

39 Athena Leoussi, *Nationalism and Classicism: The Classical Body as National Symbol in Nineteenth-Century England and France* (Basingstoke: Macmillan; New York: St Martin's Press, 1998).

40 Tania Woloshyn, 'Health and Consolation in Renoir's Late Southern Works, c. 1895–1919,' MA thesis, Queen's University, Kingston, 2004, explored the related issues of a health-giving South; she is preparing a PhD thesis on a related topic at Nottingham University.

41 Vojtěch Jirat-Wasiutyński, 'École de Marseille? Région et histoire de l'art en France au 19e siècle,' in Christine Peltre, ed., *La notion d'école en histoire de l'art. Colloque de Strasbourg, 11–12 décembre 2003*, in press.

42 Georges Roque, 'La Méditerranée devient colorée,' in Françoise Cachin and Monique Nonnel, *La Méditerranée de Courbet à Matisse*, exh. cat., Galeries Nationales du Grand Palais (Paris, 2000), 109–36.

43 Vojtěch Jirat-Wasiutyński, 'Van Gogh in the South: Antimodernism and

Exoticism in the Arlesian Paintings,' in Lynda Jessup, ed., *Antimodernism and Artistic Experience: Policing the Boundaries of Modernity* (Toronto: University of Toronto Press, 2001), 177–91.

44 Eugène Delacroix, *Souvenirs d'un voyage dans le Maroc* (1832), ed. Laure Beaumont-Maillet, Barthélémy Jobert, and Sophie Join-Lambert (Paris: Gallimard, 1999), 98–9.

45 Fabre, 'La France,' 53–67.

46 Herzfeld, *Anthropology*, 7.

47 Derek Gregory, 'Emperors of the Gaze,' in Joan M. Schwartz and James R. Ryan, eds, *Picturing Place: Photography and the Geographical Imagination* (London and New York: I.B. Tauris, 2003), 196.

48 Prochaska, 'Art of Colonialism.'

49 [John Roland Abbey,] *Travel in Aquatint and Lithography, 1770–1860, from the Library of J.R. Abbey* (London: Curwen Press, 1955–6), vol. 1, no. 272 and vol. 2, no. 385, gives the details of the editions and publication of the albums between 1842 and 1849 as well as the prices. No edition size is noted, but the subscription lists suggest about 400. The graphic work preceded Roberts's paintings, which closely followed the drawings that were the basis for the lithographs by Charles Haghe.

50 Mehmet Ali, Pasha of Egypt, had seized these territories from the Ottoman Sultan in 1831, in retaliation for the loss of his fleet to the European powers at the Battle of Navarino; he was defeated again and the territories returned to the Ottomans in 1841. Roberts's visit coincided with the establishment of biblical archaeology and the overlay of a biblical geography on Arab Palestine by Protestant scholars. Neil Asher Silberman, *Digging for God and Country: Exploration, Archaeology, and the Secret Struggle for the Holy Land, 1799–1917* (New York: Knopf, 1982), 36–45.

51 Kenneth Bendiner, 'David Roberts in the Near East: Social and Religious Themes,' *Art History* 6 (1983): 67–81.

52 MaryAnne Stevens, *The Orientalists: Delacroix to Matisse*, exh. cat., Royal Academy of Arts (London 1984), 223.

53 Stevens, *Orientalists*, 224.

54 Gregory, 'Emperors,' 207. See also Anne Godlewska, *The Napoleonic Survey of Egypt: A Masterpiece of Cartographic Compilation and Early Nineteenth-Century Fieldwork.* Cartographica 25, 1–2 (Spring and Summer 1988), and Timothy Mitchell, 'Orientalism and the Exhibitionary Order,' in Nicholas B. Dirks, ed., *Colonialism and Culture* (Ann Arbor: University of Michigan Press, 1992), 289–317.

55 Rosenthal, *Orientalism, the Near East in French Painting, 1800–1880* (Rochester, NY: Memorial Art Gallery of the University of Rochester, 1982). See

also Lynne Thornton, *Les orientalistes peintres voyageurs, 1828–1908* (Paris: ACR, 1983), and Gerald Ackerman, *The Life and Work of Jean-Léon Gérôme with a Catalogue Raisonné* (New York: Harper and Row, 1986).

56 Linda Nochlin, 'The Imaginary Orient,' *Art in America* 71 (1983); repr. in Nochlin, *Politics of Vision: Essays on Nineteenth-Century Art and Society* (New York: Harper and Row, 1989), 33–59.

57 Olivier Richon, 'Representation, the Harem and the Despot,' *Block* 10 (1985); repr. in *The Block Reader in Visual Culture* (London and New York: Routledge, 1996), 242–57. See also François Pouillon, 'L'ombre de l'Islam: Les figurations de la pratique réligieuse dans la peinture orientaliste du 19e siècle,' *Actes de la recherche en sciences sociales* 75 (November 1988), 24–34.

58 Barbara W. Tuchman, *Bible and Sword: England and Palestine from the Bronze Age to Balfour* (New York: New York University Press, 1956).

59 Silberman, *Digging for God and Country*, 4–5.

60 Roland Barthes, cited in Nochlin, 'Imaginary Orient,' 38.

61 Frederick N. Bohrer, *Orientalism and Visual Culture: Imagining Mesopotamia in Nineteenth-Century Europe* (Cambridge and New York: Cambridge University Press, 2003), 191–4.

62 Marcia Pointon, 'The Artist as Ethnographer: Holman Hunt and the Holy Land,' in Marcia Pointon, ed., *Pre-Raphaelites Reviewed* (Manchester and New York: Manchester University Press, 1989), 27.

63 On racial types and the image of Christ see Cowling, *Artist as Anthropologist*, 109–11.

64 Tamar Garb, 'Modernity, Identity, Textuality,' in Linda Nochlin and Tamar Garb, eds, *The Jew in the Text: Modernity and the Construction of Identity* (London: Thames and Hudson, 1995), 20–30. On the 'blackness' of the Jew see Sander Gilman, *The Jew's Body* (New York and London: Routledge, 1991), 169–73.

65 Margaret Olin, *The Nation without Art: Examining Modern Discourses on Jewish Art* (Lincoln: University of Nebraska Press, 2001), 6–7.

66 Ibid., 40–4.

67 Ibid., 53–9.

68 Mitchell, 'Exhibitionary Order,' 289.

69 Ibid., 290.

70 Homi Bhabha, 'The Other Question: Stereotype, Discrimination and the Discourse of Colonialism' (1983), in Homi Bhabha, *The Location of Culture* (London and New York: Routledge, 1994), 66–7.

71 Lisa Lowe, *Critical Terrains: French and British Orientalisms* (Ithaca, NY: Cornell University Press, 1991), ix and 8.

72 Reina Lewis, *Gendering Orientalism: Race, Femininity and Representation* (London and New York: Routledge, 1996).
73 Bohrer, *Orientalism*, 17–41. Darcy Grimaldo Grigsby, 'Rumor, Contagion and Colonization in Gros's *Plague-Stricken of Jaffa* (1804),' *Representations* 51 (Summer 1995): 2, has proposed an Orientalism that 'represents its own incompleteness' and includes failure signalled by violence; see also her *Extremities: Painting Empire in Post-Revolutionary France* (New Haven, CT: Yale University Press, 2002), 4 and 65–6.
74 Mitchell, 'Exhibitionary Order.'
75 Zeynep Çelik, *Displaying the Orient: Architecture of Islam at Nineteenth-Century World's Fairs* (Berkeley: University of California Press, 1992).
76 Gwendolyn Wright, *The Politics of Design in French Colonial Urbanism* (Chicago: University of Chicago Press, 1991), 6.
77 David Prochaska, *Making Algeria French: Colonialism in Bône, 1870–1920* (Cambridge and New York: Cambridge University Press; and Paris: Éditions de la Maison des Sciences de l'Homme, 1990).
78 Christine Peltre, *L'atelier du voyage: Les peintres en Orient au XIXe siècle* (Paris: Le Promeneur, 1995) and *Orientalisme* (Paris: Terrail, 2004).
79 Roger Benjamin, *Orientalist Aesthetics: Art, Colonialism, and North Africa* (Berkeley and Los Angeles: University of California Press, 2003), 33–55, 159–90. See also Roger Benjamin, *Renoir and Algeria*, exh. cat., Clark Art Institute (Williamstown and New Haven: Yale University Press, 2003). In an important essay in this catalogue on the colonial context, 'The Other Algeria,' David Prochaska stresses the 'absence of the French colonial presence' and the dominance of the 'timeless Orientalist glow' (142) in Renoir's Algerian paintings.
80 Benjamin, *Orientalist Aesthetics*, 221–48. See also François Pouillon, 'Tableaux d'Occident et d'Orient: La synthèse Racim,' in *Mohammed Racim, miniaturiste algérien*, exh. cat., Institut du Monde Arabe (Paris 1992), 14–20, and *Les deux vies d'Étienne Dinet, peintre en Islam* (Paris: Balland, 1997).
81 Benjamin, *Orientalist Aesthetics*, 247.
82 Ibid., 5.
83 Eric Hobsbawm, *Nations and Nationalism since 1870: Programme, Myth and Reality*, 2nd ed. (Cambridge: Cambridge University Press, 1992), 9–12.
84 Eric Hobsbawm and Terry Ranger, eds, *The Invention of Tradition* (Cambridge: Cambridge University Press, 1983).
85 Hobsbawm, *Nations*, 76–7.
86 Kathleen Stewart Howe and Karen Sinsheimer, *Revealing the Holy Land: The Photographic Exploration of Palestine*, exh. cat., Santa Barbara Museum of Art (1997).

87 Abigail Solomon-Godeau, 'A Photographer in Jerusalem, 1855: Auguste Salzmann and His Times' (1981), in her *Photography at the Dock* (Minneapolis: University of Minnesota Press, 1991), 159; Yeshayahn Nir, 'Phillips, Good, Bonfils and the Human Image in Early Holy Land Photography,' *Studies in Visual Communication* 8, 4 (1982): 33–45; Howe and Sinsheimer, *Revealing the Holy Land;* Kathleen Stewart Howe, 'Mapping a Sacred Geography: Photographic Surveys by the Royal Engineers in the Holy Land, 1864–68,' in Joan M. Schwartz and James R. Ryan, eds, *Picturing Place: Photography and the Geographical Imagination* (London and New York: I.B. Tauris, 2003), 226–42.

88 Mark LeVine, *Overthrowing Geography: Jaffa, Tel Aviv and the Struggle for Palestine, 1880–1914* (Berkeley and Los Angeles: University of California Press, 2005), 28–59.

89 Roger Heacock, 'Al-Majd was-Sumood: Landscapes of Glory and Resignation,' in Ibrahim Abu-Lughod, Roger Heacock, and Khaled Nashef, eds, *The Landscape of Palestine: Equivocal Poetry* (Birzeit: Birzeit University Publications, 1999), 132–3.

90 Glenn Bowman, 'Tales of the Lost Land: Palestinian Identity and the Formation of Nationalist Consciousness,' in Erica Carter, James Donald, and Judith Squires, eds, *Space and Place: Theories of Identity and Location* (London: Lawrence and Wishart, 1993), 80–2.

91 See Cowling and Mundy, *On Classic Ground*, especially Marilyn McCully, 'Mediterranean Classicism and Sculpture in the Early Twentieth Century,' 324–32.

92 Fabre, 'La France,' 78–83, 90–105.

93 Edward Said, *Culture and Imperialism* (New York: Knopf, 1993), 169–85.

94 Mohamed Afifi, 'Les racines historiques de la notion de "méditerranéisme" en Egypte,' in Edouard Al-Kharrat and Mohamed Afifi, *La méditerranée égyptienne* (Paris: Maisonneuve et Larose, 2000), 29–48.

95 Yaacov Shavit, 'The Mediterranean World and "Mediterraneanism": The Origins, Meaning, and Application of a Geo-Cultural Notion in Israel,' *Mediterranean Historical Review* 3, 2 (1988): 96–117.

96 Christine Peltre, 'Tanger, un Euripe africain,' in *Le Maroc de Matisse*, exh. cat., Institut du Monde Arabe (Paris 2000), 237–45; Fabre, 'La France.'

97 Shavit, 'The Mediterranean World'; Olin, *The Nation without Art*, 53–66; LeVine, *Overthrowing Geography*.

98 For example, Gregory, 'Emperors of the Gaze,' 209–17.

99 Musée Galerie de la Seïta, *Photographes en Algérie au XIXe siècle* (Paris 1999), 39, and Nissan N. Perez, *Focus East: Early Photography in the Near East (1839–1885)* (New York: Abrams, 1988).

100 Sarah Graham-Brown, *Images of Women: The Portrayal of Women in Photography of the Middle East 1860–1950* (New York: Columbia University Press, 1988), 122–4.

101 For another instance, the installations of Houria Niati, see Salah Hassan, 'Nothing Romantic About It!' in Salah M. Hassan, ed., *Gendered Visions: The Art of Contemporary Africana Women Artists* (Trenton, NJ, and Asmara, Eritrea: Africa World Press, 1997), 205–26.

102 A prime example may be found in the French government's efforts to make Marseilles a leading Mediterranean centre with projects such as the Euroméditerranée zone and the Musée des civilisations de l'Europe et de la Méditerranée (www.musee-europemediterranee.org), a translation of the Musée des arts et traditions populaires from Paris to Marseille with a new vocation.

# 2 Allegories of Modernity: Space, Time, and the Mediterranean

FRANCESCO LORIGGIO

One of the defining historiographical gestures of the cultural criticism of the last thirty years or so has been to distinguish between early- and late-twentieth-century modernity in terms of their relations to space and time. During the first of the two phases, preoccupations with the temporal aspects of life and culture prevailed; during the second, preoccupations with space and spatial aspects. One was the age of Proust, Joyce, and stream of consciousness in literature, of Bergson and Heidegger, involuntary memory, and the ontology of temporality in philosophy; chronologically it coincided with the modernism of the first decades of the century and with the predominance of Eurocentric perspectives. The other is the age of such writers as Chinua Achebe, Salman Rushdie, and Derek Walcott, of ecology, geophilosophy (Gilles Deleuze), the culture of mass migration, exile, and displacement, of 'the empire writes back' and the politics of identity. Its macrohistorical referents are de-colonization, the rise of gender, race, and ethnicity as criteria of cultural analysis, and the emergence of new social groups and new social subjects.

So goes, plus or minus some names, the narrative. Needless to say, since we are still ensconced in one of the poles it conjures, the tale being spun is as much an exercise in self-fashioning and history-making, an attempt to let contemporary issues ripple in portrayals of modernity, as an exercise in history-telling as such. The overarching plot it furnishes offers the backdrop against which to gauge the individual geographies – 'real' or 'invented' – that the last century has deployed or has had sedimented on it. It constitutes the hypothetic preamble to begin with, the paragon to bounce data off or to amend and elaborate on, so that – circularly, as the tenets of the hermeneutic method would have it – a perhaps more accurate and more distanced history may accrue once we have adequately surveyed the specifics of modernity's dealings with space.

In other words, the dichotomy of time and space is not unproblematic. It is not just the binarism, the neatness and peremptoriness of it all. Doubts might legitimately arise about the direct analogies, implied in each of the antipodes of the dyad, between life and art, between the thematizing of space and time, or especially between the political and social events by which such thematizing was instigated and literary fiction or painting or any other artistic form. Are we getting one more illustration of how inescapably disciplines – and hence criticism – found their discourse on representationalist premises? Or is this instead an equally inevitable confirmation of the aporias of recent criticism, which has had to attest to the power of mimesis despite the suspicion mimesis has inspired? As well, explaining the predilection for space in literature or the arts through the parallels with social or historical phenomena may leave one at the mercy of opinion about those phenomena. In recent years, for instance, reservations about the usefulness of the concept of post-colonialism have been voiced. Some have maintained that, to the extent that it pertains to a general, abstract process, the word already, eerily 'describe[s] someone else's history,' the history of 'no-longer recognizable colonial power[s].'[1] For others, colonialism has, in any case, never ended, and the 'post' merely indicates that 'the culture of colonialism continues to resonate in what was supposed to be its negation.'[2] If this is true – and the evidence in support of it is compelling – then the imbrications of the watershed event that 'post-colonialism' stands for and the spatial turn of the arts would also have to be revised, and would become much more intricate than we have taken them to be. First, to posit the priority accorded to space in the manner in which it has been posited would entangle in inextricable difficulties the discussion of any single, specific space; second, the lingering reverberations of colonialism within post-colonialism would greatly attenuate the pluralizing of geography that is allegedly behind the pre-eminence of space in artistic and generally intellectual practice. As the term 'culture' in the above quotation reminds us, domination can occur on various levels and by various means, not only the ones tried in the classical, imperialist phase of colonization.

For anyone pondering that single particular space that is the Mediterranean, as I will be doing in some of the following paragraphs, the ambiguities being wrenched from the history of modernity are of fundamental relevance, however many-layered they may be (many gaps may have been overestimated, but our world also *is* different from the world of Proust and James Joyce or of Picasso and modernism, and the dichotomy *does* serve heuristic purposes). The region has received little attention in recent North American cultural debates partly due to the automatic associations with Europe it summons: it belongs with that which has to be intellectually decentred, about which we should be talking less than before. On the other hand, the Mediterranean has been politically, economically, and socially decentred within Europe and within the West for a number of centuries. It stopped being in the thick of things with the great seventeenth-century shift to the ocean and the rearrangement of roles and hierarchies that ensued. As European culture transmutes into North Atlantic culture and the seamlessness with history is broken, even the Renaissance can appear to be on the other side of the divide, a pre-modern accomplishment. It could thus be argued that Europe and the West have within themselves a geographical and cultural frontier zone to reintegrate – and reintegrate for its pastness, for its marginality, no more and no less than the non-Western margins have to be retrieved along with their 'pre-modernity,' their pre-colonial heritages. That this space has been both a political and economic backwater and an area whose culture the West could never disavow, has had to repeatedly measure itself by, again only shows how many other tensions have to be fitted in the equivocations inherent to our initial dichotomy once we move on to single individual locales.

But what the historical peculiarities of the Mediterranean force us to register most immediately and, perhaps, most emphatically is the very diverse consistency of the topographies privileged by late modernity, and thus perhaps some backtracking is in order before proceeding further.

When ecologists or, in literary studies, practitioners of ecocriticism speak of places, they mean actual, concrete locations, a nature that, constructed though it may be, exists partly on its own, and can deflect human intervention and even impinge on it. Natural catastrophes, some contemporary historians contend,[3] *have* altered human history, at a social as well as an individual level, not to mention the consequences for evolution. This recognition of the (limited) autonomy of the object vis-à-vis the subject and the subjective world, which has been hailed as the hallmark of a full-fledged, mature cosmopolitanism by sociologists such as Ulrich Beck,[4] underlies Carl Schmitt's conception of space.

History for Schmitt is the story of humanity's grapplings with earth, water, and air, of the subterfuges it has mustered to adapt to, defy, and conquer each of these elements. Thus, he attributes the political success of Britain from the seventeenth century on to its ability in exploiting technological know-how, such as the compass and the sail, to establish its primacy over the ocean. The British simply could criss-cross bigger chunks of the planet faster and more efficiently. Not to be overlooked, Schmitt's historiography links British naval supremacy to the socio-cultural peculiarities of British life and both of these to Britain's geographical positioning, its insularity. The ocean is a dimension that negates the existential security available on *terra firma*. You cannot settle permanently *in* water: you can stay *on* it only by building simulacra of *territorial* habitations, that is, as long as you have, as the etymology of the adjective instructs, some soil or soil-like steadiness under your feet. Beyond fixity, fluidity is beyond barriers, hence beyond treaties, jurisprudence, the rules of international governance – all accoutrements of land-based societies. The challenge of the high seas, unstable by definition, enhanced the ingenuity, the capacity for survival of the British and, according to the German philosopher, consolidated their penchant for freedom and individualism.[5]

By contrast, the other conspicuous spaces of modernity bear rather loose resemblance to historical geographies. The 'smooth space' trenchantly theorized by Deleuze and Guattari is modelled on the desert, the steppe, and the sea, surfaces that are presumed to permit unhampered movement and indeed to recapitulate the psycho-socio-anthro-politicological possibilities of movement as such. But we would not be doing it justice were we to try to measure its intellectual validity by comparing it to any 'real' deserts or steppes or seas, just as it would be wrong to fault the nomadism the two authors describe by invoking real Bedouins (whose life is not the perpetual 'intermezzo,' the perpetual motion between points, the becoming that never coalesces into stasis that Deleuze and Guattari lionize).[6] Even Edward Said's well-known analyses of Western Orientalism rest on tenuous, blurred geographical grounding. No historical Orient or, for that matter, self-representations by individuals who identify with any specific portion of the Orient are opposed to the complex process of invention that nurtures Orientalist attitudes, to the array of depictions, stereotypes, and stylistic devices ingrained into Western literature, social sciences, and arts by which the Orient is transformed into a staple of Western discourse formations, a rhetorical effect. Said is actually quite careful to avoid any suspicion that he may be highlighting the inauthenticity of Western versions of the Orient by pitting them against authentic versions. As he declared towards the end of his career, some twenty years after his path-breaking book was written, the Orient of *Orientalism* partakes of an 'imaginative geography.'[7]

There are other discrepancies in the late-twentieth-century reflection on space that merit some probing. Nomadic movement, as sponsored by Deleuze and Guattari, and the geography that post-colonialist critics championed are directed, in part, against the nation-state, whose authority they erode. Borders exclude no less than they include, and are perpetuated by the violence of bureaucratic power. Carl Schmitt seems, in contrast, bent on demonstrating that the same premises, the same mechanisms that hang over the nation – technological speed and the constructedness, the porousness of borders – can serve to aggrandize it, to widen its territory, to produce empires.

This approach to the politics of space ties in quite directly with the rationales that have justified, theoretically, the two-phase view of modernity. On this the touchstone is Said. Some of the essays he published during the 1990s, now collected in *Reflections on Exile*, zero in precisely on this duality. Said glosses perceptively early modernity's fascination with time by locating it within the legacy of Hegelian historicism. Especially emblematic for him were Gyorgy Lukacs's *Die Seele und die Formen* (The Soul and Its Forms) and *Theorie des Romans* (Theory of the Novel). The storyline these two works extract from Western fiction hinges around a protagonist who is in sync with the world in the classical and pre-modern epic and alienated from it in the novel, where the only overcoming open to him or her is in the intellectual sphere, through art and its forms. Said found this thesis-antithesis-synthesis pattern somewhat escapist: the compulsion to resolve the subject's rift with the object (society, the Other, the 'out there') inevitably led to a literature that either was happy to lose touch with history or was too indulgent towards history's solutions and hence towards the solutions of those in power. To the therapeutic idealism offered by the young Lukacs, whom he still much admired, he preferred Antonio Gramsci's '*geographical* sense,'[8] which espouses the 'outsider's perspective,'[9] never reroutes or reconciles the frictions that pervade reality, never loses sight of the fact that 'politics is a contest over territory ... to be won, fought over, controlled, held, lost, gained,'[10] that history is the history of 'ruler and ruled.'[11] Among the figures less close to the Marxist camp than Gramsci, Said's paradigms were the composer Arnold Schoenberg and the philosopher and music critic Theodor Adorno. Both were steadfast advocators of dissonance as a stance, adhering to twelve-tone music and undeterred by the loneliness to which the decision would consign any musician or music critic. Both theorized the artist's or the intellectual's refusal to abolish or to domesticate conflicts, to provide unity and synthesis in his or her own life and in his or her own practices '[T]he uncompromisingly critical thinker,' wrote Adorno in a passage Said quotes in 'On Lost Causes,' one of his most revealing essays, 'is in truth the one who does not give up ... [T]hinking is not the spiritual reproduction of that which exists. As long as thinking is not interrupted, it has a firm grip on possibility. Its insatiable quality, the resistance against petty satiety, rejects the foolish wisdom of resignation.'[12]

Said's updating of twentieth-century modernity has its own internal coherence. It pays due homage to *métier* and biography, the strains and constraints in his life that he, as he confessed, was 'required to negotiate.'[13] The 'contrapuntal' analysis that he propounded – to recall the locution he often used in lieu of 'dissonance' – overtly intertwines with the experience of exile he knew first hand. He put a premium on geographical awareness not simply because he felt it responded more faithfully to some of the pivotal swerves of history, but also – above all – because it forced literature, the arts, philosophy, and the social sciences to face up to the ethical issues that those events raised. Conversely, time and temporality had to be warded off, to be rebuffed because they are the 'sustaining element'[14] of identity, and identity, which is 'non-contradiction or, rather, contradiction resolved,'[15] was at odds with the plurality that is the bread and butter of ethics and the preamble to its allure for intellectual activity. It is why, while Said was sensitive to the plight and the pleadings of groups, movements, and emergent nations, he was always ill at ease with the controversies the notion of identity has fuelled.

The ethical thrust of Said's vision of modernity is, clearly, beyond dispute: we can only and should only acknowledge it and act upon it. But does ethics have to be proved? Is the intellectual and historical evidence Said is so keen on deploying really necessary for the ethical appeal to be persuasive? More importantly, is it entirely convincing or are we confronted with one tension that Said did not in the end satisfactorily negotiate? Surely in rehearsals of history some temporal sequence is warranted, along with spatial delimitation, the rootedness in the memory of the 'here and now' it entails, and the identity it buttresses, otherwise we would be culturally disenfranchising all individuals who do not travel or do not travel far enough. Surely, too, forging some prototype of the Lukacsian 'healing unity,'[16] which Said rejected, is among the tasks of literature and the arts, a task that is nothing more and nothing less than the flip side of the dissonance he would embrace: care for the spiritual well-being of the thinking subject (and thus of the reader) is also among the desiderata behind all utopias, and if the risk of the intellectual who embarks on such ventures is a heroism that may re-entrench the status quo, the risk of the heroism of aesthetic outsidership is professional pride, elitism, art for art's sake, a distance from the crowd that is complacent (and, after Romanticism, an equally traditional and equally commodified quality).

In a similar vein, when we associate a period with time or with space, we are talking of an emphasis, rather than neatly contoured, absolute prevalences. Literature, the arts, and criticism are topochronic or chronotopic, not purely topocentric or chronocentric, since time and space cannot be separated, as historically minded critics such as Mikhail Bakhtin have admonished.[17] We can at best say that after decolonization space and geography have acquired a new, socio-political salience, not that they had little or no salience before the late twentieth century or in historicist thought. The impact on human affairs that Montesquieu and Herder in the eighteenth century, and Hegel in the nineteenth century, attributed to climate and topography smacks too much of determinism for our taste, although current ecology has been conveying a message that is only a less strong variant of theirs. Furthermore, the works of these philosophers, such texts as Montesquieu's *De l'esprit des lois* (The Spirit of Laws), Herder's *Ideen zur Philosophie des Geschichte der Menschheit* (Ideas for the Philosophical History of Mankind), and Hegel's *Vorksungen über die Philosophie der Geschichte* (Lectures on the Philosophy of World History) endorse a history whose bias in favour of Europe is unacceptable for us. But in their pages space and geography do come into play up front. The early twentieth century itself was hardly the heyday of time and temporality it is made out to be. Until almost the 1920s, in literature, the benchmark of the modernism that counted was lyrical poetry, the genre in which the most advanced experimentations were being conducted, and the poetics that dominated the scene – vorticism, imagism – all exalted the fragment or the quick aphoristic stroke, the equivalent of the ideogram over narrative sequentiality. F.T. Marinetti, the author of the Futurist manifestos, enjoyed baiting his bourgeois audiences by declaring that Venice, a location for him pathologically redolent of the past, should be allowed to sink,[18] or that literary texts should eliminate declined verbs, which also exuded the temporal and the mnemonic.[19] One of the aims of Cubist and Futurist painters was to catch movement and time in the same image, to freeze them as it were, by juxtaposing on the space of the canvas each of their single stages. The great novelists who now embody the first portion of the century – Proust, Joyce, Woolf, Faulkner – had to reassert the value of narrative and time over strong competition.

This neglect of the internal dynamics of modernism aligns Said with other leftist thinkers who, like him, believed, to echo the title of one of his books,[20] that the world came before the text and the text before the critic and that '[c]ulture and the aesthetic forms it contains derive from historical experience,'[21] but who were first and foremost concerned with forestalling any charge of historicism. When we read Fredric Jameson on how 'the moderns were obsessed with the secrets of time, the postmoderns with that of space'[22] or on the 'end of temporality' and the 'reduction to the present'[23] brought about by the globalization of markets and by electronic media, we cannot help but conclude that, since both of these phrases would perfectly characterize the aspiration of practically all the vanguard, experimental art, literature, and music of the period between 1905 and 1915, his historiography corroborates, more than it interprets or contradicts, the *Zeitgeist*. The paintings of either Picasso or Boccioni or Mondrian, the poems of the Imagists, and twelve-tone music are to some degree forms that suitably anticipate today's societal conditions (rather than refract conditions of the early twentieth century, most of whose non-metropolitan regions were still un-modernized), or today's world – however it may have been attained, by whichever non-artistic devices – is the prosaic materialization of the assumptions about society that permeate the oracular visions of modernist art. With each of the options the split between modern and postmodern art and society or between modern and postmodern views of art and history becomes less wide and less straightforward. And we have not yet factored into our historiography the many demonstrations of the persistence of time and temporality, of the unabated vigour of their social or cultural prerogatives (the heightened institutional role of museums, the impact of the politics of memory, the popularity of autobiography, et cetera) that have been in the public domain during the age of the bias in favour of space.[24]

Put against this scanning of the 'details' of the dichotomy with which we began, the idea of the Mediterranean becomes one of the more obligatory litmus tests of the debate about the nature and the history of modernity and the issues that arise from it. The geography it covers is not just one of the exemplary spaces of modern Western literature and art, of the novels, the poetry, and the paintings that portray scenes of Mediterranean life or are set in some Mediterranean locality; it is, implicitly or explicitly, one of the chronotopes of the criticism, of the thought by which modernity has explained – or explains – itself to itself. When we reflect on the Mediterranean we are obliged to canvass not merely Joyce, E.M. Forster, Ezra Pound, Lawrence Durrell, Albert Camus, Amin Maalouf, Tahar Ben Jelloun, and their colleagues. We have to bring into the equation philosophers such as Martin Heidegger, Simone Weil, Hannah Arendt, Alisdair McIntyre, Marta Nussbaum, and the many others for whom the revisitation of pre-Socratic or post-Socratic Hellenism was a personal milestone. And just as we must query ourselves about the presence of expatriates from northern Europe and the Americas and the literary traffic internal to the Mediterranean, so must we ask ourselves about the circulation of intellectuals from other disciplines. Marinetti and his early-twentieth-century compatriot poet Giuseppe Ungaretti were born in Alexandria, as was the Greek Constantin Kafavy; Camus, a couple of generations younger than they, in Algeria. Our contemporaries Maalouf and Ben Jelloun, both winners of the Prix Goncourt, hail one from Lebanon and the other from Morocco, and have resided in Paris. The biographical data of these writers, their experiences away from the French or Italian metropoles in the early decades of the century or towards them in the last few decades are not insignificant. Neither are the biographical data or the experiences of such towering beacons of recent critical theory as Jacques Derrida and Hélène Cixous, who were also born in Algiers, Louis Althusser, who taught there, Michel Foucault and Roland Barthes, who taught in Tunis and Cairo, or Pierre Bourdieu, whose influential *Esquisse d'une théorie de la practique* (Outline of a Theory of Practice) was written after fieldwork in the Khabyle area of Algeria.

What I am suggesting is that the space and the time of the Mediterranean chronotope are as yet unachieved and that the paradoxical quality of this unfulfilled promise is what we must factor into modernity and its history. Consider space, the dimension where the incompleteness and the antinomies are more blatant. Like that of the Orient of *Orientalism*, the geography of the Mediterranean is invented, the product of acts of discourse and, in so far as its littoral is subdivided into nation-states, of the political imagination. Unlike the Orient of *Orientalism*, which has an abstract air to it, derived evidently from the type of essentializing representations foisted on it but also from the vectorality, the element of direction it carries with it (the Orient is, at its most general, just the lands to the East), the Mediterranean basin has more physically circumscribed lineaments: it is the territory around *that* sea. In spatial representations of the Mediterranean, the ambivalences are due first and foremost to the clashes and the overlappings between these cartographies – abstract and territorial – which are different in *kind* and thus foreshadow different ideological positions.

Very telling, in this regard, are the polemics triggered in the 1970s and the 1980s by the attempt to establish Mediterranean studies as a branch of anthropology. The efforts of the proponents of the new subunit reached their apex at that special juncture in recent intellectual history when structuralist-functionalist methods in anthropology had begun their downward curve. The fear of those who objected was that the theoretical past of the anthropologists promoting Mediterranean studies, most of whom had been groomed on fieldwork in smaller, simpler societies, would inevitably lead to essentialized notions of the Mediterranean, to the notion of a unified Mediterranean culture. The historical coincidences were just as worrisome: the sudden shift of focus on to the Mediterranean occurred in too visible conjunction with decolonization and the loss of anthropology's usual sphere of action.

The retreat to a terrain closer to home did not inspire any changes, any corresponding adjustments in the disciplines's intellectual tool kit: the risk, accentuated by the tendency of anthropologists to pitch their Mediterranean tents in small rural communities, was that one exoticism would be replaced by another, that, in order to retain the displacement, the observational distance they deemed to be obligatory for their discipline's proper functioning, they would transfer to the Mediterranean the attitudes and the logic typical of their research on the non-Western cultures of the colonies. Undertaken in such a manner, without any correctives, the anthropology of the Mediterranean could only be an apparently scientific appendix to the depictions already to be found in literature, the arts, popular culture, and travel guides, which describe the region as being perpetually peripheral, oscillating between Ariel and Caliban, the refined, genteel atmosphere of museums and raw emotions and sexuality, between Club Med comfort and the more perilous climes waiting around the corner, where Western post-industrialism joins Third World pre-industrialism; next to the reclining chairs and mineral water of the beaches, the unexpected is ready for an ambush. The rejection was often outright. For many of the anthropologists native to the Mediterranean, the ethnographies they read about parts of their countries '[were] basically written in English and addressed to an Anglo-Saxon audience' to satisfy tastes that had been instigated, cultivated, and promoted 'long ago (at least as far as the early nineteenth century)' by 'novelists, travellers, scholars, etc. both local and foreign'[25] and which 'preserve[d] for the English some of the charms of the old Empire.'[26] Not surprisingly, in the wake of Said's *Orientalism,* during the early 1980s, the term 'Mediterraneanism' was coined.[27]

The alternative these anthropologists opted for was an anthropology thoroughly modern, one that did not shut out the contemporary, near-to-home, undistanced context of the locale of fieldwork, that took into account written as well as oral traditions and therefore also the paraphernalia and apparatuses that hold together late-twentieth-century societies, from bureaucracy to political systems to systems of jurisprudence; in short, an anthropology for which the forms of governance, the machinery of social cohesion are segments of culture amenable to analysis, that interact with – affect and are affected by – other segments. As a result, the spotlight shifted from the village to the nation-state and to the inter-state cluster to which it belonged, specifically, in this case, the then burgeoning supranational European Union. Mediterranean topography became an object of anthropological study only as an appendix of Europe or of Western Europe.

It is hard now to judge whether, in substituting for the imaginative geography they labelled Mediterraneanist the imaginative geography of the state and of an incipient Europe, anthropologists were spurred on by the urge to latch on to the very process of invention while it was in the making or whether theirs was a defensive posture. Sometimes the impression they leave is that what they resented, what bothered them was not really the exoticism, its clichés, and its colonialist inheritances, but being grouped with the ex-colonies and the ex-colonized. Were you a Spaniard, a southern Italian, a Greek intellectual – a native of the favourite jaunts of the ethnographers scouting out Mediterranean culture – in the 1970s or the 1980s, in decades when Third Worldism was in crisis, you might not wish to hedge your bets. You went with Europe.

Going with Europe, however, does not annul the major conceptual difficulties that prevented anti-Mediterraneanist anthropologists from accepting the idea of a Mediterranean region with its own culture. Is Europe a solider notion on which to anchor research than that of the Mediterranean? Are its borders definable with more unimpeachable certainty? If not, methodological propriety does not guarantee logical adequacy, and the study of Europe is just as precarious as the study of the Mediterranean. What is more, jettisoning the Mediterranean prevented the discipline from exploring other theoretical avenues, including some that would have lent the repatriation of the discipline some much needed intellectual bite. Locating a site of fieldwork or a feature of some culture within the national and then the European context does afford that offshoot of the Western trunk that is anthropology a self-reflexivity, a depth it did not have before, but the return home cannot be fully accomplished without traversing the Mediterranean, regardless of the problems the operation poses. Facing those very problems is one of the names of the game.

This is the road taken by the most enticing recent work on the Mediterranean. Less attached than other anthropologists to the constructivist notion of culture, the authors I have in mind have been able to countenance inventions of space in which geography is not a passive effect of discourse, an inert domain to be handled at will, but can influence cultural representations. All of them deflect the issue of essentialism, of the unity of the Mediterranean by intimating in one guise or another that, as the Slovenian Predrag Matvejević has stated, the many Mediterranean cultures are simultaneously 'divergent and similar,' that the Mediterranean, although not homogeneous, is a 'unique' area.[28]

To properly survey the region's geography, Peregrine Horden and Nicholas Purcell remark in their *The Corrupting Sea,* both 'ecologising' and 'interactionist' approaches are required: there are micro-ecologies that extend no further than ten kilometres but also '"structures" which overcome the fragmentation'[29] and intense navigational patterns that put the diverse sub-units into contact with each other and make the Mediterranean littoral an entity 'as intelligible as "Europe" or the "Middle East."'[30] The Mediterranean is a corrupting sea because the 'relatively easy seabourne communications' always threaten the isolation of the 'coastlands and islands,'[31] as many Greek and Roman writers lamented. One of the epigraphs to Horden's and Purcell's book is a quotation from the Roman historian Strabo: 'Plato thinks that those who want a well-governed city ought to shun the sea as a teacher of vice.'

For the Italian philosopher Massimo Cacciari it is out of this predisposition for encounter inscribed into the environment that emanated the vocabulary of Greek and hence European philosophy. Without the multiplicity of other cultures around the next gulf or across the straight or at the end of the next journey, neither difference nor sameness could be conceived. Western history starts, as Herodotus narrates with strife,[32] when Greek city-states declare their mode of governance to be unlike that of their Asian neighbours, an act of division that also announces an adjacency, a co-existence: 'To distinguish,' Cacciari says in *Geo-filosofia dell'Europa* (Geophilosophy of Europe), 'is to-put-in-relation'; in so far as the distinction is 'absolute' and not 'casual, it renders necessary the element from which we are distinguishing ourselves,' so that we are 'necessarily connected' to the other we are separating ourselves from.[33] Geographically, geophilosophically, for Cacciari the Mediterranean is epitomized by the many islands that dot it, by the image of the archipelago.[34]

In another seminal work of this period, Franco Cassano's *Il pensiero meridiano* (Southern Thought), the inhabited geography of the Mediterranean, the awareness that in such a sea you are always near some land, always bound to meet other people, is opposed to the unfettered vastness of the ocean. The sense of freedom that being long away from land and from the laws that settled life instils can never be disjoined from the euphoric sense of mastery that the capacity to deal with the elements (and therefore with others) produces, and is thus synonymous with Western modernity, which has been, for Cassano, a North Atlantic modernity, the modernity of the glorification of speed, productivity, and technological prowess. The Mediterranean is, instead, the sea where you start your voyage knowing that someone else who may contradict you is always on the horizon. In an unblinkered and unblinking reading of the last section of Camus's *L'homme révolté* (The Rebel) devoted to *la pensée de midi*, or 'thought at noon,' Cassano revives the French writer's notion of *la mésure* (which can be translated as 'moderation' or 'measuredness'), identifying, as did his predecessor, the lesson that Mediterranean geography teaches with the rule of Greek tragedy, that there are limits to human endeavour by which it would be wise to learn to abide.[35]

Cassano's historicizing re-evaluation of the role of geography in representations of Mediterranean culture relativizes any too strict collating of geography with the dissonance Said speaks about. Having a spatial sense of life, rather than a temporal one, does not mean that you will dissent always in the same way or from the same things: you can disagree with positions and attitudes that are or have been themselves against the grain in other circumstances. Does this satisfactorily accommodate the full brunt of views of modernity such as Said's? That Camus and Cassano ultimately did not manage to interpret Mediterranean culture without resorting to a concept borrowed from classical Greek tragedy *could* seem another instance of covert Eurocentrism. And yes, the blind spot in Camus's and Cassano's argument is its failure to integrate into it any interrogation of North African or Middle Eastern sources: for us Mediterranean history has changed somewhat since Martin Bernal's *Black Athena* and its reconstruction of the exchanges between Greek and Egyptian and Phoenician cultures. But Cassano's reformulation of Camus's scathing post–Second World War critique of Northern thought, or thought 'at midnight,'[36] switches the axis of reference from the usual, horizontal, longitudinal East–West dichotomy to the vertical, latitudinal North–South one. For Cassano the forgotten cardinal point is the South, not the Orient, and, whatever the shortcomings of his actual mappings of Mediterranean culture, his intention is to obviate that forgetfulness. The Mediterranean that he describes is the place – the only place in the world – where three continents abut each other, where all cardinal points intermingle at once.

The analogies with Said here break down. Orientalism is a category of Western discourse: it is a phenomenon of discourse pertaining to how one culture has configured – has dominated – another culture, to how cultures configure – dominate – other cultures. As a phenomenon of discourse, its scope is larger than any debate on the Mediterranean. To the degree that it has to do with a specific geographical area, the Orient, on the contrary, the reverse has to be contemplated: Orientalism can be envisaged as a chapter in the debate on the Mediterranean. Banal quibbling though it may seem, some of the lands and peoples most frequently Orientalized by the West – Palestine, the Middle East, the Maghreb – *are* housed wholly or in part within the Mediterranean basin. And some of the Mediterranean cultures that Orientalized the Orient were also the object of some Orientalism, or its local variety, Mediterraneanism. Mediterranean geography and history bequeath us parallel structures of cultural dominance and cultural subalternity, with some countries – Spain, Italy, Greece – occupying two rungs. Last but not least, geography-wise Orientalism has been the major purveyor of the flow on which Europe has depended for the construction or the construal of its identity, much of the tracing of which involves the Mediterranean. From Homer to Herodotus to Virgil to the epic writers and the chroniclers of the Middle Ages and of the Renaissance, the history of Europe has unravelled with the course of the sun, along an East-to-West trajectory: the route travelled by Jupiter in kidnapping the young woman after whom Europe is named, by Ulysses, by Aeneas, by the Apostle Paul. At some period or another, most of the reigning houses, in Italy, Belgium, Germany, Holland, and elsewhere, large or small, furnished themselves with some pedigree rooted in the East, usually Troy.[37]

This third caveat should not be underestimated. In the *Aeneid*, the most explicit of the ancient epics, Aeneas lands in Africa, woos Dido, the queen of Carthage, but is commanded by the gods to depart and leave her behind so that he may fulfil his destiny as founder of Rome. That symbolical interdiction has cast a huge shadow over European history. It has legitimated an omission that has lasted centuries. Necessary, indispensable a notion as it is, Orientalism participates in the West's mutilation of geography and of history. Its obliviousness to the specifics of region and place has saddled it with the same exclusionary behaviour that we can detect in European culture and in Westernized versions of the Mediterranean. Today any analysis of Orientalized representations within the Mediterranean lands demands complementary gestures: the uncovering of the rhetorical armamentarium that imposes Western depictions on the Middle East or Maghreb societies *and* the uncovering of the occlusion of the African Moorish presence in North Africa, via, for example, such devices as the minimizing of figures or features that may foreground the relation between North Africa and sub-Saharan Africa. By the same token, the neglect of the South casts a different light on Europe's overeager inquisitiveness about the Orient, whose prestige – no match for the 'dark' continent, or perhaps any continent save, later, America – mobilized religious, iconographic components that bolstered colonial discourse but pre-dated it. Before the secular fog of mystery descended upon it, the East was where Jerusalem, the earthly paradise, the centre of the world were located; it was the seat of light and spirituality.

The paradoxes that the idea of a Mediterranean space spawns cannot by surmounted without momentous expenditure of cultural and socio-political capital. They are greater than decisions – already of some magnitude – about whether to admit or not to admit Turkey and Israel into the European Union, and the absence on the agenda of any provisions about the future entry of Palestine or Tunisia or Algeria or Libya. The nation-state is too firmly entrenched for a Mediterranean region to have any chance of materializing as an autonomous social reality. Even in a Mediterranean in which current political structures were fully safeguarded and the nation-state kept as the fundamental unit, any realignment of geography along the North-South axis would seem inconceivable without some miraculous intervention: Europe, for one, would have to graft its African and Arab and Islamic and Byzantine and Ottoman pasts onto its Graeco-Roman and Germanic core – improbable and, to repeat, implausible. For now the Mediterranean is destined to remain the invention of intellectuals, an unofficial space as unfeasible, as unachievable as it is partial and incomplete. This is its weakness but also – it should be quickly observed – the mainspring of its cultural attractiveness. The utopian tinges with which its representations are coloured do not diminish its cogency for us. Non-Lukacsian, non-Hegelian, the dilemmas out of which it is moulded have *some* reality. Bernal's insistence that Hellenic Greece was Mediterranean, and not Aryan, that it didn't come about out of invasions from the Caucasian North but through contact with the Egyptian or Phoenician South,[38] and Cassano's re-evaluation of the pre-Columbian, non-oceanic scale of the Mediterranean modify the coordinates of the mental maps upon which we act, as individuals.

Which brings us to time. In chronotopes – I have claimed – the spatial cannot be divorced from the temporal. How do the two collaborate? Time is less tangible, less concrete: there is no sea in Mediterranean time. And when it is private and interiorized, or in its manifestation as history, as collective memory, it is highly selective. Said's misgivings are comprehensible: time is the realm of the 'I–I' or the 'We–We' type of communication, in which preceding selves or preceding texts encroach upon their successors; space is where the 'I–You' communication between a subject and another subject takes place. The Mediterranean 'We' is extremely fragile; it is a 'We' that can be postulated only thanks to the extraordinarily frequent and extraordinarily large number of 'I–You' contacts the environment permits. How do you patch together a single temporal denominator out of that? You can only do so if time is as paradoxical as space, if it rests on similar assumptions, as it should in a chronotope – if it obeys the criterion of uniqueness, and not of unity.

The enclosedness, the smallness of the Mediterranean – the trait out of which the most tenable recent specifications have been gleaned – does not become conspicuous, historical until the ocean does, in the seventeenth century. The sudden predominance of the oceanic consciousness – unthinkable in classical cosmography, which relegated open water to the edges of the world, beyond the Pillars of Hercules – and the inability to properly answer its promptings was one of the epochal nails in the coffin of many Mediterranean countries, from Italy to Spain to Greece to Turkey to Egypt, each of which, in its own modality and modulations, has been overburdened by the lapsarian narratives, the declines they have had to cope with. Some of these countries (such as Italy) alleviated the distress with an official history emplotted according to a cyclical rhythm, an alternance of periods of dormancy and *rinascimenti* or *risorgimenti*, rebirths and resurgences. They underscored the double dissonances of Mediterranean temporality, in which irreversible temporality and manoeuvrable history have asymmetrical courses, and collective memory a dénouement definitively un-Lukacsian and un-Hegelian, neither pacified nor pacifying.

Let me conclude with an illustration, not from critical thought but from painting. One of Giorgio de Chirico's earliest canvases, the 1910 *L'énigme d'un après-midi d'automne* (The Enigma of an Autumn Afternoon, figure 2.1), portrays a scene with two males in brownish and bluish robes next to a gigantic statue on a large pedestal in an otherwise empty square. The statue, which has a truncated arm and no head, recalls the Venus de Milo. Disproportionately tall, it stands in front of a romanesque church-like structure with two doors, one rectangular, the other arched. In the right corner, enveloped in shadows, a portion of a high dark building can be discerned; to the left and to the right of the romanesque structure, a dilapidated wall with shut doors and shut windows encloses the square and joins the two buildings. Behind the wall, we have the mast and the white sail of a ship; a dark greenish sky hovers over the entire scene. The painting, rudimentary in form and content, is not vintage de Chirico and is rarely anthologized; nevertheless it anticipates egregiously – better than any other early piece – his more celebrated works, commonly allotted to the next fifteen years of his career.

Patently 'drawn' in its form, past- or tradition-laden in its imagery, *L'énigme d'un après-midi d'automne* clashes with the pre–First World War cult of the 'new' and with the output of the serious painters of the decade, the seemingly more adventurous cubists, futurists, constructivists, and expressionists (with whom de Chirico might have had some commerce, were it not for their anti-traditionalism or their iconoclastic imperative to distort). Its faithfulness to line and the residual anthropomorphism notwithstanding, *L'énigme* lets transpire a distinctly modern intellectual project. A cursory cross-check with the works of such late-nineteenth-century artists as Arnold Böcklin, who was equally antiquarian and whom the young de Chirico knew and was impressed by, is enough for us to ascertain how modern this early specimen was. Böcklin is somehow too beholden to typical Romantic concepts of the poetic, which he re-adapts to the canvas, rather than re-create them. In his paintings convincingly ancient men and women are put in a mythological situation surrounded by the appropriate atmosphere; the responsibility for the effect falls on the correspondence between the scene and the props, on the scene's ostentatiousness. The only assent *L'énigme* gives to Böcklinian coherence is through the two men, one of whom is shown with head hanging down and a hand screening his face, as if emotionally distraught or in deep meditation. Aside from this, inconsistency and disharmony preside over the canvas. The two men are dwarfed by the architecture and the environment, the real protagonists of the scene, as they will be in future paintings in which 'live' human beings will vanish from the picture almost altogether. The other components are discreetly but firmly out of kilter with each other. Of a size that overwhelms the church-like structure as well as the two men, the statue is presented with its back to us and is clad in a disconcertingly transparent veil tunic; it is of older manufacture than the church-like structure, which is older than the building, which is of a different era than the sail of the ship, which is superseded by the uncertain dating of the spigots of a fountain that protrude on the left and the right of the statue's base and by the curtains across the doors of the romanesque structure, the only inklings of modern civilization in the painting. The shadow of the building is inadequately short, unrealistically angled and, like the shadow of the statue and that of the two men, arbitrary, given that we have no indication of the time of the day. Most of all, the painting hides more than it displays. The small, slightly brighter spot on the upper right corner of the canvas may or may not be the sun (as in de Chirico's other works of the metaphysical period, light seems to be self-propagating). We do not know if the statue is really the Venus de Milo or how far the sea is, or if there is any sea. The wall, continued by the curtains across the open doors of the romanesque structure, prevents us from determining where or what is the landscape behind it. The objects, though not under erasure, are, like the statue, as if veiled.

Two principles, then, guide *L'énigme*: the juxtaposition of temporally incongruous fragments and the tension between the seen and the unseen. These are the principles that de Chirico refined in the following decade. In the works of *Pittura metafisica,* as he dubbed his project, forlorn statues appear in light-drenched piazzas with porticos, bits of ancient sculpture (busts, heads, hands, feet) sit next to draftsman's utensils or other modern, geometric bric-a-brac, mannequins have marble heads and, vice versa, statues sport mannequin faces. As in *L'énigme,* the canvas is subtly scrambled, with shadows more or less artificially tacked on, the architecture randomized, and the arrangement reducing, as much as fostering or assisting, sight. De Chirico's goal was to develop a style that transcended both realism and symbolism, both the perception of existing objects (however evoked: for de Chirico a still life by Cézanne or by Braque is a painting about something on a table)[39] and the perception of recondite, esoteric ciphers. The premium he put on juxtaposition would have smoothed any transition to avant-garde experimentation, as some of his works of a few years after *L'énigme* and later on, when he searched for variations to his basic formula, bear out: in *Composizione metafisica* (Metaphysical Composition), of 1916 (figure 2.2), the squares and triangles revert back to two-dimensional geometry, the plasticity of his modernist contemporaries, who attempted to transfer three-dimensional volumes to a flat surface by dissecting and reassembling the image into cubic or cylindric or spheric elements; yet the painting remains between the collage and cubist and constructivist reordering of space and form. What separates de Chirico's works from those of the avant-garde is the same difference that separates purely chromatic (as in Mondrian's work) or purely formal relations (in Cubism, some Futurism) from hieroglyphs: the push-and-pull he instals in his images is a friction between signifying items, hence one yielding a surplus of meaning. The geometry here is not entirely abstract: the triangles and squares have a palpable, recognizably wooden quality to them; they still contain dots that make us think of nails, appear to be more like the basic fragments, the building blocks of real, historical 'constructions' (frames of paintings, pieces of chairs, of tables, of draughtsmen's tools). The canvas banks on that which it withholds: it does not end with sight and perception.

Much of this applies to the more common fare of *Pittura metafisica*. Some of de Chirico's works pick up directly on one of the obsessions of avant-garde painting, the metropolis: they are cityscapes, compositions of urban materials (architecture, statues, squares, train stations, towers), which may seem ultra-figurative but are also painstakingly constructed. On this score, *Pittura metafisica* overlaps with Cubism and Futurism: Boccioni's celebrated *La città che sale* (The City Rises) also juxtaposes cut-offs of metropolitan urbanistics. The divergences have to do with the sign value of the representations. Boccioni convokes different moments of a portion of cityscape in order to stress the simultaneity, the 'reduction to the present,' as Jameson might have phrased it, that painting can produce. In de Chirico's works the ingredients of the assemblage – the buildings, the statues, the porticos, the train stations, the trains – are historically charged, and the different temporalities they carry introduce another semantic level into the image.

As I have stated, we do not have to enlist de Chirico among the progeny of symbolism. We best grasp his works if we think of them as representations of a mental theatre, another phrase for 'metaphysical.' His paintings stage the drama of time and history. They are highly self-reflexive works, art about art: not merely architecture or sculpture but also literature, often directly cited by the paintings (as in *Ettore e Andromaca* [Hector and Andromache]), and a major influence on his method and his imagery. All of the arts are machines against the devastations of time, and it is that struggle that the paintings testify to visually through their recourse to architecture and sculpture, the most concrete and durable among human fabrications. The stillness of the situations represented and the mythical aura of some of the items strive against sequence and time, but the non-contemporaneity of the items, together with their highly recognizable historical provenance, constantly reinsert sequence and time into the canvas. Juxtaposition ineluctably changes into narrative. Just as compromised, as undermined is the monumentality of the buildings or the statues, refuted by the layered historicity of the paintings and by the dismembered fragments of sculpture scattered, in some works, next to other objects or along the architecture: constructed, programmed endurance is not eternal. The statues of nineteenth-century notables that some paintings feature are ruins to be, as Graeco-Roman classicism now is.

The choreography of this theatre is there also to ensure that its spectators do not get off scot-free emotionally. The technique of concealment with which de Chirico booby-traps his juxtapositions, his collages that are not collages, heeds the tenets of a Romanticism less predictable, more rigorous and philosophical than the one Böcklin or enthusiasts of myth such as the Pre-Raphaelites revered. It sends us back to the Italian poet Giacomo Leopardi and his writings about the function of obstacles to visibility, which release the envisioning, visionary force of the imagination, or about the innate vagueness and therefore innate poetic properties of towers, which induce a sense of the infinite.[40] The same arches and porticos that have always been among the banners of Renaissance harmony can metamorphose into screens that filter light and shadow, into labyrinthine contraptions through which you see and do not see (figure 2.3, de Chirico's *Le voyage émouvant* [The Anxious Journey]). The conventional, the traditional, the expected can be strange, unexpected. Post-formalist, de Chirico's dramatizations defamiliarize by calling upon both the familiar and the unfamiliar. Of their many analogues, the most immediate and most à propos is Freud's essay on the uncanny, which also asks us to shudder in front of the dejà vu. Except that in de Chirico the *heimlich* and the *unheimlich* are of an ontological and historical – and not simply psychological – kind: the statues, the buildings, the hybrid mannequins both alert us to the passing of time and resist it, and do so as vestiges of a Western legacy that we know and, now, suddenly, in the context of modernity, do not know.[41] In addition, the process operates dialectically: the juxtposition with the time of tradition, of a tradition whose possible return (in the Nietzschean sense of the eternal return) is postulated, affects our perception of the modern items. In their surroundings, the mannequins, the modern monuments, the train stations may themselves suddenly become infused with strangeness. Unlike the Futurists and the majority of his contemporaries, de Chirico did not care for debunking as a strategy: his goal was to re-enchant both the past and the present of the world; whence the impeded visibility, the reduced perception of the object represented, the calling into play of the not there.

In all of this percolates quite a bit of de Chirico's own biography. He was an Italian born and raised in Greece, and his homecoming was that of the exile and the migrant: not simple.[42] But the many allusions to the Renaissance and to ancient classicism, to ships and the sea, invite observations of greater breadth. In the fifteenth or sixteenth century's yearning to relive Athens or Rome, to restore a continuity with an origin that it blamed the Middle Ages for interrupting, lurk anxieties similar to ours. For us, today, much of the gist of the humanist experience is encapsulated in Poggio Bracciolini's dismay at seeing shrubs and grass grow in the Roman forum. This is how the eminent fifteenth-century philologist narrates his re-enactment of the rendez-vous with the Mediterranean ruins:

> [W]ith wonder in our hearts ... we reflected on the former greatness of the broken buildings and the vast ruins of the ancient city, and again on the truly prodigious and astounding fall of its great empire ... How remote are these ruins from the capital that our Virgil celebrated: 'Golden now, once bristling with thorn bushes.' How justly one can transpose this verse and say: 'Golden once, now rough with thorns and overgrown with briars ... [F]ortune offers no more striking example of mutability than the city of Rome ... How much the more marvellous to relate and bitter to behold, how the cruelty of fortune has so transformed its form.[43]

'Prodigious,' 'astounding,' 'marvellous,' 'bitter': without stretching the semantics too much, for these adjectives we could substitute those that recur in the titles of de Chirico's paintings: 'enigmatic,' 'disquieting,' 'hermetic.' Renaissance texts such as Bracciolini's, which apparently rehash the well-trodden theme of Fortune's power over individuals and societies, are where the modern awareness of temporality insinuates itself into Western culture. Plaintive and ironic (could the 'cruelty' of 'mutability' be more flagrant and more punishing than in a period that had as its ideal the emulation, the preservation of the past?), the episode at the Roman forum pre-emptively broaches almost the whole inventory of issues that de Chirico wrestles with.

Here time finally brushes against space. The ruminations of Bracciolini the philologist, the retriever of the literary masterpieces of Greece and Rome, are about archaeology, the science of ruins, the science that recovers statues, monuments, buildings from the soil, from the substance of geography. After reading the excerpt, we appreciate de Chirico's debt to the Renaissance masters he venerated and the geniality of his self-reflexivity, his intuition that painting should adopt architecture and sculpture, and not painting itself, to comment on art. For us sculpture and architecture are 'metaphysical' arts that have been very efficient agents of power: they can be transported into the soil of another place, where they can become part of that place's buried memory.

Can the ontological hesitations that architecture and sculpture provoke and the symmetries in the history of those inhabitants of the Mediterranean who have had to meditate on the dissipation of some glorious past, on the grass growing in the ruins, override and redeem the archaeological disparities? Access to unofficial, personalized dissonance of the sort Said approved must pass, in the Mediterranean, through public pathos: intellectuals who have had their exposure to the monuments have had to take the uncanniness, the rupture between reversible memory and irreversible time, and live with the understanding that today is tomorrow's archaeological site and that excavations will unearth monuments that will seem familiar and foreign. The glitches in the European continuity of time, in that Greece-Rome genealogical line that Western civilization has privileged, have not translated into ecumenicity, into greater official recognition of the history of others, of the heterodox history in its soil (on the European shores, Arab or Byzantine buildings and other artefacts can be a stone's throw away from the Greek temples). More often than not, the ontological quivers have engendered defensive political postures: de Chirico did not refuse induction into the Royal Italian Academy when it was conferred on him by those Fascist authorities who dreamed of turning the Mediterranean into an Italian *mare nostrum*. And so the chronotope is still an imperfect one. For all this, if there are to be new starts, it is the trepidation of artists such as de Chirico or, especially, others like him in countries from the non-European shores that will signal them to us. In this respect, too, the Mediterranean is an allegory of modernity.

NOTES

I would like to thank the publisher's two anonymous readers for their very helpful comments on the article. Unless otherwise indicated, translations are mine. 

1 Vijay Mishra and Bob Hodge, 'What Was Postcolonialism?' *New Literary History* 36, 3 (2005): 381.
2 See Simon Gikandi, *Maps of Englishness* (New York: Columbia University Press, 1996), 14.
3 William H. McNeill, *The Global Condition: Conquerors, Catastrophes, and Community* (Princeton: Princeton University Press, 1993).
4 Ulrich Beck, 'The Cosmopolitan Society and Its Enemies,' *Theory, Culture and Society* 19, 1–2 (2002): 17–44.
5 Carl Schmitt, *Land and Sea*, trans. Simona Draghici (Washington: Plutarch Press, 1997), 49ff.
6 Gilles Deleuze and Felix Guattari outline the notion of 'smooth space' in *A Thousand Plateaus*, trans. Brian Massumi (Minneapolis: University of Minnesota Press, 1987), 474–500. On the 'intermezzo' see ibid., 380ff.
7 Edward Said comments on his earlier work on Orientalism in 'Orientalism Reconsidered,' now part of *Reflections on Exile and Other Essays* (Cambridge, Mass: Harvard University Press, 2000), 198–215. The book he reflects upon is, of course, *Orientalism* (New York: Random House, 1978).
8 Said, 'History, Literature and Geography,' in *Reflections on Exile*, 458.
9 Ibid., 472.
10 Ibid., 464.
11 Ibid., 465.
12 'On Lost Causes,' in *Reflections on Exile*, 553.
13 'Identity, Authority, and Freedom: The Potentate and the Traveler,' in *Reflexions on Exile*, 397.
14 'History, Literature and Geography,' 463.
15 Ibid.

16 'Traveling Theory Reconsidered,' in *Reflections on Exile*, 441.
17 Mikhail Bakhtin, 'Forms of Time and the Chronotope in the Novel,' in Michael Holquist, ed., *The Dialogic Imagination*, trans. Caryl Emerson and Michael Holquist (Austin: University of Texas Press, 1981), 84–5.
18 Filippo Tommaso Marinetti, *Selected Writings*, trans. R.W. Flint and Arthur Coppotelli (New York: Farrar, Straus & Giroux, 1971), 55ff.
19 Ibid., 40ff.
20 I am alluding to *The World, the Text, and the Critic* (Cambridge, MA: Harvard University Press, 1983).
21 Edward Said, *Culture and Imperialism* (New York: Knopf, 1993), xxii.
22 Fredric Jameson, 'The End of Temporality,' *Critical Inquiry* 29 (2003): 697.
23 Ibid., 711.
24 On this see Andreas Huyssen, *Twilight Memories: Marking Time in a Culture of Amnesia* (New York and London: Routledge, 1995).
25 J. Llobera, 'Fieldwork in Southwestern Europe: Anthropological Panacea or Epistemological Straitjacket?' *Critique of Anthropology* 6, 2 (1986): 25.
26 J. Cutiletro, quoted in Joao de Pina-Cabral, 'The Mediterranean as Category of Regional Comparison: A Critical View,' *Current Anthropology* 30, 3 (1989): 400.
27 See Michael Herzfeld, *Anthropology through the Looking Glass: Critical Ethnography in the Margins of Europe* (Cambridge: Cambridge University Press, 1987), 64.
28 Predrag Matvejević, *La Méditerranée et l'Europe* (Paris: Stock, 1998), 30.
29 Peregrine Horden and Nicholas Purcell, *The Corrupting Sea: A Study of Mediterranean History* (London: Blackwell, 2000), 79.
30 Ibid., 25.
31 Ibid., 5.
32 Herodotus, *The Histories*, trans. Aubrey de Sélincourt (Harmondsworth: Penguin Books, 1972), 3.
33 Massimo Cacciari, *Geo-filosofia dell'Europa* (Milan: Adelphi, 1994), 146.
34 The notion of the archipelago, as it pertains to the Mediterranean, is at the centre of another book by Cacciari, *L'arcipelago* (Milan: Adelphi, 1997).
35 Camus is a strong presence throughout Cassano's *Il pensiero meridiano* (Bari: Laterza, 1996), but one of the essays, 'Albert Camus: Necessità del pensiero meridiano,' 81–108, assesses his work directly. The edition of *L'homme révolté* I have used is the one in *Essais* (Paris: Gallimard, 1965), 423–709. On Cassano and Cacciari I have drawn from my 'Modernism, Memory and the Mediterranean: Italian Variations,' forthcoming in Domenico Pietropaolo and Luca Somigli, eds, *Modernity, Modernism and the Mediterranean* (Ottawa: Legas).
36 See *L'homme révolté:* 'Europe has not been anything but this struggle

between noon and night' (703). This sentence has to be read within the context of the paragraphs preceding it, some of whose lines are worth quoting: 'Perhaps the basic conflict of the century isn't so much the one between German ideologies of history and Christian politics, which in a certain way are accomplices, but the one between German dreams and Mediterranean tradition, the violence of eternal adolescence and virile force, a nostalgia exasperated by knowledge and books and a courage reinforced and enlightened by the experiences of life, between, ultimately, history and nature' (702).

37 On this, quite useful is Richard Waswo, 'The History Literature Makes,' *New Literary History* 19, 3 (1988): 541–64.

38 Martin Bernal's now classic *Black Athena: The Afroasiatic Roots of Classical Civilization*, 2 vols (London: Free Association Books, 1987–92) makes this point, but for a more specific statement by him see 'Greece: Aryan or Mediterranean? Two Contending Historiographical Models,' in Silvia Federici, ed., *Enduring Western Civilization* (Westport, CT: Praeger, 1995), 3–11.

39 See Giorgio de Chirico, *Il meccanismo del pensiero* (Torino: Einaudi, 1985), 54: 'The intimate intention of the cubist painter does not diverge intrinsically from that of any traditional painter, past, present or future. One need only note the titles of a catalogue of cubist exhibitions, perfectly identical to those of an exhibit of traditional painters: "Landscape," "Figure," "*Nature Morte*," "*Head of a Woman*," and yet again "Nature morte," "Landscape" ...'

40 This aspect of de Chirico's work has been explored in Paolo Baldacci, *De Chirico*, trans. Jeffrey Jennings (Boston: Little, Brown, 1997), 145. Here are some of the things Baldacci says: 'The theme of infinity brings us back to the poetics of Leopardi, which De Chirico knew well, and, as ever, to Nietzsche. For Leopardi infinity is not so much a matter of boundless immensity as vague indeterminacy, and is often associated with the image of an isolated tower.' Here are some of the passages from Leopardi's *Zibaldone* that Baldacci quotes in *De Chirico* (the pagination is that of his text): 'At times the soul desires a view which is restricted and confined in certain ways, just as in romantic situations. The motivation is the same – that is the desire for the infinite. The imagination takes the place of the view, and thus the fantastic takes the place of the real' (146). 'A building, a tower, etc. seen in such a way that it seems to rise above the horizon, which itself cannot be seen, produces a highly effective, even sublime contrast between the finite and the indefinite' (146). 'The height of an edifice or building, whether from within or from without, the height of a mountain, etc. is always pleasing to see, so much so that one forgives

disproportion. As in the case of an extremely tall and slender spire. Indeed, it is the disproportion itself that is pleasing, because it emphasizes the height and augments the appearance and impression and perception and sentiment and concept ... You already understand the natural and intrinsic and metaphysical causes of such effects' (146).

I would note that one of Leopardi's most famous poems is entitled 'L'infinito' ('The Infinite') and has to do with the stimulating effect on the imagination of a hedge that closes off the horizon to the viewer. The paragraphs by Leopardi on indeterminacy and vagueness that Baldacci does not quote are also of some interest. As, for example, the following, from Giacomo Leopardi, *Zibaldone di pensieri*, vol. 1 (Milan: Mondadori, 1973): 'Not only the cognitive faculty, or the erotic faculty, is capable of seizing the infinite or of thinking in terms of the infinite, but also the imagination, especially with regard to the indefinite or to thinking in terms of the indefinite. This delights us because the soul, not distinguishing borders, is left with the impression of a kind of infinity and confuses the infinite with the indefinite' (382); 'The human soul is so composed that it receives greater satisfaction from a small pleasure, from the idea of a minor sensation of which it cannot determine the limits than from a strong sensation, of which it can determine the limits ... Science destroys the main pleasures of the soul because it defines things, shows their borders' (971); 'Words such as "distant," "ancient" and others like them are very poetic and delightful because they give rise to ideas of vastness, to ideas that are indefinite, indeterminate and vague' (1147–8); 'Words such as "night," "nocturnal," etc., descriptions of night are very poetical because night renders objects more difficult to perceive, so that the soul can have of them only a vague, indistinct, incomplete image' (1150).

41 The two adjectives *heimlich* and *unheimlich* come, of course, from Freud's influential essay 'The Uncanny,' originally published in 1919 and now, among other locations, in *Collected Papers*, vol. 4, trans., Joan Riviere (New York: Basic Books, 1959), 368–407. I am aware that the thematic ambivalences of *Pittura metafisica*, the inevitable linkage with Freud's text that they inspire, and the equally inevitable enlisting of de Chirico's painting among the twentieth-century forerunners of Surrealism have encouraged psychoanalytical interpretations of his work. See, for instance, Hal Foster's *Compulsive Beauty* (Cambridge, MA: MIT Press, 1993), 57–98, which discusses *L'énigme d'un après midi d'automne* and the *heimlich* and *unheimlich* qualities of de Chirico's art in strictly Freudian terms, as an indirect manifestation of primal fantasies, of some unconscious and unresolved sexual tension. My focus is on the various degrees of historical

'uncanniness' that the paintings depict. Whatever else *Pittura metafisica* may be representing, in many of its images a sense of non-contemporaneity governs the relation among the various elements, as the buildings, the statues, and other items are chronologically marked. That feature has a dynamic of its own, certainly one that cannot be dismissed: to do so would be to exclude from interpretation a basic portion of de Chirico's work and practically all of his production after the 'metaphysical' stage of his career, which was much less 'disquieting' than the earlier work.

42 If, as de Chirico states in his account of the episode (see Baldacci, 76), *L'énigme d'un après midi d'autumne* was first conceived one autumn afternoon as he was sitting in Piazza Santa Croce, that epiphany can also be brought back to his biography through the fact that he is a returning migrant. To listen to Freud, uncanniness arises when sensations of familiarity and unfamiliarity intermingle, and it is connected to the encounter with the homely, with whatever reminds us of home. Valuable meaning can be derived from *Pittura metafisica*, I would submit, by just staying at that level. Suddenly in Piazza Santa Croce, in front of the church in which are buried many of Italy's cultural heroes, de Chirico, for the first time, recognized the puzzling historicity of the built environment around him, of the land that was his ancestral home and one of his cultural homes. Both the Greek and Italian pasts, his cultural inheritances, contain between them several historical strata whose continuity with modernity is not always obvious. This would explain why the images of *Pittura metafisica*, while definitely oneiric and perhaps anxiety-ridden, are not frightening, as they should be if they were representations of any of the primal fantasies of seduction, of castration, of the origin of sexuality and of intrauterine existence that Foster lingers on, as these should be according to Freud (the adjective 'frightening' recurs often in his description of uncanniness) and as are the images of other artists closer to Surrealism (for example, Max Ernst).

43 Giovanni Francesco Poggio Bracciolini, 'The Ruins of Rome,' in J.B. Ross and M. Martin McLaughlin, eds, *The Renaissance Reader* (Harmondsworth: Penguin, 1981), 379–84.

# 3 Abstracting Space: Remaking the Landscape of Colonial Algeria in Second-Empire France

JOHN ZAROBELL

This essay emerges from a recent dissertation on the representation of the colony of Algeria in French visual culture between 1830 and 1870.[1] The term visual culture here covers a broad range of modes of visual art and spectacle that recorded the colonial exploration and conquest of Algeria, including paintings, prints, photographs, illustrated books, and a panorama. The impulse to research such an array of media arose from an interest in the social character of colonial imagery, though this essay confines itself to a consideration of paintings in relation to geographical descriptions, both pictorial and textual. Following the groundbreaking, if often criticized, model of Edward Said,[2] I have sought to trace the relations between the political domination of Algeria and the images of Algeria that were generated in this period in France. In my view, such an inquiry follows the classic models of the social history of art, attempting to elucidate historical circumstances and the art produced in relation to them. But this analysis does redefine the terms of society, to consider not just art objects and the technical processes involved in creating them, but also the way visual images establish the means through which individuals interact with the world. While social historians of art have looked at paintings as images, analysing their symbolism and their inherent political and social messages, I propose to go further in an effort to reconsider the social character of works of art. Works of visual art educate our perceptual faculties, setting parameters for the apprehension of the world. It is crucial to examine the visual symbolism of art works, but it is even more central to investigate the relationship between world and image that a work of art proffers. This method allows new perspectives onto history and further illuminates our own means for understanding the history of art.

Considering the importance of the Algerian landscape to France in the nineteenth century, this view of the Mediterranean is one of political and semantic power, a story of outright domination and hegemony. Such trans-Mediterranean power plays date back as far as recorded history allows. Of course, conflict and domination also initiate exchange, but the terms of the exchange must be established in some language. What is the Arabic word for Mediterranean? Or the Kabyle word? The historical example of spatial representation and definition explored here can articulate a central problematic that continues to plague our best efforts today to find the terms in which to consider the hybrid and heterogeneous Mediterranean world. By attempting to consider and describe a series of spatial and cultural relations that go beyond the central dualities described by Said, Self/Other, Us/Them, Black/White, North/South, etc., we are all in some way begging the question: On what terms can such discussions take place? What kinds of relations between the self and the world are we proposing? and Is there any way that such conceptions could be not ours, or someone else's, but a hybrid of the two?

It would seem impudent to hazard answers to such questions, but the study offered here takes as its subject the negotiation of spatial and individual boundaries in the colonial context of Algeria under France's Second Empire. My subject involves the representation of the most distant and wild of Algeria's landscapes, the desert. Further, the paintings I consider are more experimental in their technique than other Orientalist paintings produced at this moment in France. Nevertheless, such a limit case illuminates one recurring theme in the history of artistic and colonial exploration: while works of art enhance a viewer's understanding of a world beyond view, they reflect and articulate a particular set of conceptions, an interpretation of the world. Such an interpretation exists in dialogue with other representations, but the terms of representation codify an existing set of values. In the case of landscape painting, it is space that is ordered into a pictorial language. Whereas landscape traditionally generates a world for viewers (creating land), the desert landscapes discussed here abstract space and actually deny the specific characteristics of the place that they purport to represent. This tendency leads to the erasing or obscuring of alternative interpretations of the spaces in which people lived and continue to live. In other words, the potential power of landscape paintings to enact a form of possession for the artist and viewer, when realized in representations of Algeria in the Second Empire, replaced the spaces of human activity with the space of pictorial representation. This analysis connects the development of new paradigms of landscape description in colonial geography to those that emerge in paintings of the desert. Territory, that raw material of colonialism, is nonetheless the result of colonial practices, the implementation of a certain view of the world upon the world and those who inhabit it.

The concern here is to trace a certain historical turn in spatial representations of the colony. This transformation had a visual character, as well as social and political dimensions in the French colonization of Algeria that occurred in the last years of the Second Empire, between 1863 and 1870. The space of France's colonial desert, the Algerian Sahara, was the very limit of its empire in the 1860s and, as such, it represented a liminal terrain both in material terms and as a symbol of French national landscape when depicted in works of art.

The French began their colonial occupation of Algeria in 1830, with the seizure of the city of Algiers. In 1834 the French government declared the region a colony and, in 1838, the name Algeria was formally adopted for it. Though indigenous resistance did occasionally flare up throughout the latter half of the nineteenth century, the French authority over the region was basically secured through the surrender of the native leader Abd-el-Kader in 1847. Thus, the period I am concerned with was part of a process of colonial development with a relatively short history. However, the French colonial experience in Algeria was significant because it was the prototype for French colonialism in the nineteenth century, the period in which this nation went from administering a few scattered colonial possessions to dominating an expansive empire abroad. This transformation could not have occurred without the success of Algeria, whose territory was transformed into an overseas homeland for the French and was officially incorporated into France in 1871. In order to analyse a metamorphosis of representations of colonial space in the last half of the Second Empire, it will be useful to compare legislative and geographical representations of Algeria with a handful of artistic ones created by Gustave Guillaumet and Eugène Fromentin.

In the 1860s a self-conscious colonial posture arose among many of the writers who addressed the issue of France's political problems in Algeria. The years between 1839 and 1844 were the most recent period when the future of colonialism in Algeria was a pressing political issue. Unlike in this earlier epoch, in the 1860s ethical concerns and practical problems that might complicate the unrestrained exploitation of the colony's resources were brushed aside. In the early 1840s the opposition criticized the colonial administration for its ineptitude and its unjust treatment of Algeria's indigenous population. In the 1860s the opposition criticized the colonial administration for its ineptitude and its overly generous treatment of Algeria's native population. Although the conquest was complete and the military administrators of Algeria were not entirely consistent, there is ample evidence that they continued to undermine native social and religious institutions during the Second Empire.[3] Therefore, it was the political rhetoric that shifted, partly as a result of the increased organization of the colonists that allowed them to voice their sense of entitlement.

While interesting in themselves, such political debates gloss over the deeper changes that constitute the foundation of the rhetorical arguments from this period of Algerian colonialism. Such a transformation of conceptions is difficult to pinpoint, but here it will be useful to turn to a recent French theorist of society and space, Henri Lefebvre. Central to my argument is his concept of abstract space:

> Homogeneous in appearance (and appearance is its strength), abstract space is by no means simple. In the first place, there are its constitutive dualities. For it is both result and container, both produced and productive ... For, while abstract space remains an arena of practical action, it is also an ensemble of images, signs, and symbols. It is at once lived and represented, at once the expression and foundation of a practice, at once stimulating and constraining, and so on.[4]

This quotation is not completely clear, but the basis of Lefebvre's notion is that lived space and the means of perceiving it through vision are intimately connected by representation. Abstract space is an order into which human activities are placed, but it is ultimately a conception of space that shifts practices. It constitutes a way of perceiving the world that changes what the world is and what happens there. For this analysis, the visual aspect of abstract space is crucial.[5]

## Social Dimensions of Desert Imagery

In the nineteenth century, particular landscape representations of Algeria coincided with emerging developments of colonial ideology in the political and cultural spheres of France. The Second Empire is particularly significant because, at this point, France initiated the legal and administrative process of fracturing Algerian terrain into units, thereby promulgating an abstraction of the colonial landscape. This process of rupturing the Algerian landscape in the service of French expropriation of it, corresponds to depictions of denuded, empty landscapes. It is not simply that the desert, described by Heffernan as 'the negation of Europe,'[6] represented the outer reaches of the colony that had been little explored and still retained an element of distant romanticism. Rather, the desert functioned as a powerful symbol. In his article 'The Desert in French Orientalist Painting during the Nineteenth Century,' the geographer Michael Heffernan argues for the desert's symbolic value, both as the land of 'desolation and infertility' and as simultaneously representing the power of (European) society and progress to restore the desert to a mythical former time of prosperity. Such an opposition of meanings, according to Heffernan, leads to an ambiguity that 'instead of breeding confusion and vacillation, became a source of imperial power. Europeans could, and did, profess admiration for a separate and distinctive Orient while at the same time promoting the necessity of a transforming and beneficial European imperial presence in the Orient.'[7] This ambiguity will play a role in an analysis of Guillaumet's desert landscape *The Desert* (1867) (figure 3.1), also known as *The Sahara*, but it is crucial to make the point at the outset that the desert existed as a symbolic construction of a land outside of time (history) and outside of civilization (society/progress). In the terms of nineteenth-century European conceptions of space, it was an empty landscape in the sense that it was by definition uninhabited (an oasis being within, though not part of, the desert) and therefore an open screen for the projection of whatever meaning a viewer might perceive in it.[8] In this case, the idea of a 'pure landscape'[9] has a meaning with historical relevance because a landscape image that features a denuded space is open, to both interpretation and potential settlement. A notion of the individual as the locus of legal and visual representations of space inheres in both pri-vate property and pure landscapes. Further, pure landscapes, like private property, are an accepted fiction, and just as deeds function to secure private territorial ownership, so a painting of the desert secures the notion that the colonial landscape is in fact empty, open to European settlement.

Guillaumet's *The Desert* could be described as a pure landscape because there are no traces of human presence here and the space is rendered in a direct, uncomposed manner. This work has received more attention in the last thirty years than in its own epoch, but the descriptions of it provided by contemporary historians are, for the most part, anachronistic. Donald Rosenthal has described *The Desert* as 'surreal' and has drawn a comparison between this work and the 'fantasy academicism' of Dali.[10] Philippe Jullian states that Guillaumet's landscapes 'might have achieved an abstract quality if he had not given too much emphasis to some of the details in order to convey the desolation.'[11] Perhaps the most compelling observation comes from Robert Rosenblum: 'Throwing aside any notion of perspective as useless in this context, he deploys a limitless space, half-way between documentary reportage and a nightmarish mirage.'[12] These comments all share a notion of abstraction common to twentieth-century viewers that would have been lacking in 1867. Only Rosenblum's remark details the way the artist ignored the conventions of perspective in order to achieve his effect. Rosenblum reminds us that the artist elected to deny perspective in order to achieve a sense of limitless space as well as the dreamlike quality of the work that makes it appear surreal. Théophile Gautier's 'Salon of 1868' provides a contemporary indication of the artist's ability to evoke a limitless expanse of space without contrivance: 'Never has the infinity of the desert been painted in a simpler, more grandiose or more moving way.'[13]

The effects Guillaumet achieved in this work are, in some ways, obvious to twenty-first-century viewers steeped in Impressionist and Post-Impressionist art. Through a denial of perspective and recognizable land masses, the artist has reduced the terms of this landscape depiction to the point that the viewer becomes aware of sensations of light and atmosphere. These effects are achieved through the artist's technique, the means employed to achieve effects such as the scumbling of paint in the sky and the use of light strokes of dry paint laid horizontally over darker, grey-green tones to give the illusion of light on a horizontal plane. Pastel tones inform the viewer that it must be either dawn or dusk. Traces of yellow pigment modelled on the blue surface of the sky suggest dust hovering above the ground and surrounding the viewer with light. A desiccated camel in the foreground provides a decisive form that contrasts with the evanescence produced by sand and sky. The image is also completely static. Despite the traces of the artist's hand that indicate the time it took to make the painting, the lack of movement only enhances the perception of a moment frozen in time.

In fact, the technical means, though they are visibly registered on the surface of the canvas, are subservient to the effect produced by them. When a viewer perceives a streak of dry pigment that depicts a slight rise in the terrain catching light, what registers is the effect of light on dry earth or perhaps a bit of dust catching the last or first rays of the sun. When one views this work, what the artist did in order to make the painting seems less important than how the viewer perceives the image depicted on the canvas. The transformation of landscape art initiated by this painting shifts the burden of representation from the artist to the viewer. Perception supplants creation as the central problematic of the work of landscape art.

This composition constitutes an interruption in Guillaumet's pictorial production. While he did, in other works, evoke this kind of vast space, it was always populated by exotic figures and trappings and therefore was more conventional as well as more appealing to the state. If one looks at an earlier work, *Evening Prayer in the Sahara* (Salon of 1863, figure 3.2), it is apparent that Guillaumet's career of official success began with a more standard Orientalist genre scene, albeit one that evokes a real place in southern Algeria that the artist had travelled to and seen for himself.[14] While this earlier work was rewarded with a Salon medal and a state purchase for the young artist, *The Desert* was mostly ignored by the press and the Salon judges in 1867 and entered the national collection only after the death of the artist in 1887. The question of what led the academically trained Guillaumet to produce such a radically simplified composition is compelling, perhaps because it is inherently impossible to answer with any certainty. However, the painting itself and its symbolic references continue to inform viewers about the depiction of the outer reaches of the French Empire in the 1860s. The emptiness of this landscape, its most profound pictorial legacy, is the aspect of the picture that demands interpretation. This emptiness is not only meaningful; it produces meaning as well. It is a representation of Algeria as a stretch of naked earth, a landscape with no inherent character, a placeless space full of light extending forever. The means through which *The Desert* makes this landscape available for the viewer's apprehension and interpretation are also worthy of exploration. Therein lie the mystery and power of this picture. After an investigation of colonial land policy in Algeria in this period, the significance of this emptiness will be easier to comprehend.

## Colonial Land Policy and the Political Economy of the Landscape

The *sénatus-consulte* of 22 April 1863[15] appears, on the surface, to be a piece of legislation enacted by the French government for the benefit of the Arab population of Algeria. It does, after all, begin by declaring the tribes of Algeria the rightful proprietors of all 'permanent and traditional' lands occupied by them. Considering the fact that this law put an end to the practice of *cantonnement*, or the direct expropriation of a portion of tribal territories by the French administration for the purposes of French settlement and colonization, it was indeed a step in the right direction for the indigenous inhabitants of Algeria. Further, in light of received ideas in France about Arabs in general and Algerians in particular,[16] the *sénatus-consulte* was an enormous improvement in the French conception of Arabs. This law formalized their status as individuals in the French Empire, granting them the right to hold property and, further, something French peasants had enjoyed since the Revolution, the ownership of the lands from which they generated their livelihood. This law was followed in 1865 by another *sénatus-consulte* granting the native inhabitants of Algeria full French citizenship under certain conditions. In other words, the law of 1863 was one in a string of legislative concessions to the natives of Algeria. It was the kind of metropolitan domination of colonial affairs that infuriated both the colonists and the military administration in Algeria. In the eyes of critics, such laws guaranteed the rights of the Arabs over and above those of the French settlers.[17]

In fact, the *sénatus-consulte* was not created in the interests of Algerian natives at all, but was designed to allow for the future expropriation of tribal lands for French settlement. As an added benefit to the French administration, it sought through legal means to fix the *douars* – the social groupings of Algeria's rural indigenous population – in place, replacing their nomadic existence with a sedentary one. This process had a history in the efforts of the *bureaux arabes* up to this point. As Patricia Lorcin explains:

> In the period up to 1858 a concerted attempt was made to sedentarize the nomadic population through the construction of houses and public utilities, such as fountains, wells, public baths and markets (but not mosques or Koranic schools), and the development of a more sophisticated agrarian economy through the introduction of new crops and agricultural methods.[18]

The *sénatus-consulte* was an ambitious attempt to transform the life of Algeria's native rural population completely, but it was not without precedent. Through it the French government sought to complete the process of replacing traditional lifestyles and indigenous agrarian practices so that the French could guide the Arabs to a greater degree of civilization. Though he welcomed the application of the *sénatus-consulte* and later, in 1873, was the author of a law bearing his name that extended its effects in Algeria, Dr Auguste Warnier was frank about its effects on the Arab population and its possibility of failure:

> When the time comes that an imperial decree orders the creation of private property among the Arab tribes, a complete social revolution will be decreed and it is not at all certain that the tribespeople accustomed to the yoke of their tribal leaders ... will not themselves repudiate the benefits of private property, in order to preserve the communism of collective ownership more in harmony with their nomadic lifestyle.[19]

Warnier's paternalistic diatribe betrays the fact that indigenous Algerians might have an interest in rejecting private property as proposed by the French authorities. Warnier was, in fact, one of the most prominent publicists of Algeria during the period. A colonist himself, he ceaselessly defended the rights of the settlers that he felt were neglected by Napoleon III's colonial administration. In his view, the interests of the colonists were sacrificed to those of the traditional Arab aristocracy, a group whose interests were to maintain their feudal control over the native population at the expense of the progress of colonialism. Therefore, he had no patience for alternative interpretations of colonial territory as represented by the *indigènes*. In the passage above, he accuses the entire population of a primitive form of communism and elsewhere he supposedly provided mathematical proof, based on official figures, that a colonist was worth ten natives.[20] The fact that such a proof rested upon agricultural production and taxes paid explains much about the interests of the settlers and the French government. The ideal colonial citizen, whether native or settler, grew a wealth of crops and paid his share of taxes, assuring the prosperity of the colony. Such a view is as simple as it is universal. It is founded on conceptions of production and society that, the author admits, were fundamentally foreign to at least a portion of the indigenous population. These notions are polemical and, when accompanied by the mathematical *proof* of the superiority of one group of humans over another, potentially dangerous.

In fact, the notions of property held by rural inhabitants of Algeria, both Arabs and Kabyles, were not so simple. Basically, three types of property existed in Algeria among rural populations, both Arab and

Kabyle: *Beylick*, or the domain of a *douar* or a tribe, *arch*, or collective property, and *melk*, something like private property in the sense that it belonged to a family and could be passed from generation to generation. This third category was most common in Kabyle societies, which was one reason this group was favoured by French intellectuals over the more nomadic Arab tribes.[21] In the texts of the *sénatus-consulte* and the instructions for its application, only the *Beylick* and *melk* forms of property are mentioned, with a single notable exception. Omission of the *arch* form constitutes turning a blind eye to one of the fundamental tenets of Arab culture, and worse. The 'Instructions générales pour l'éxecution du sénatus-consulte du 22 avril 1863 et du règlement de l'administration publique du 23 mai suivant' clarifies the intentions of this legislation. The constitution of individual property 'consists in putting an end to indivision in the colony by determining the respective rights of families that are property holders.'[22] It continues:

> This substitution of individual rights not commutable to the collective right of the *douar* on a portion of the *douar*'s own territory is a true revolution to set in motion in terms of the status of property laws among the Arabs; it is, in effect, the abrogation of the obscure Muslim property rights concerning land called *arch* or *sabega*.[23]

This honest admission of the French government's attempt fully to supplant Islamic law on the issue of collective property demonstrates that, far from aiding the Arabs in their quest for self-determination, this piece of 'Arab-friendly' legislation actually sought to undermine the legal codes and cultural practices of the Arabs native to the colony.[24] The need to 'stop indivision' through the administration of the *sénatus-consulte* had a double purpose for French colonialism in Algeria. On the one hand, the law sought to make members of *douars* or tribes into atomized individuals who would protect their own interests. This is nothing less than attempting to foist liberalism and individualism on traditional collectives by singling out individuals to make into landowners. Once an individual owns his own tract of land (only males need apply), he will naturally protect his interests over and above those of the collective. This pursuit is one that I cannot hope fully to analyse here, but it hinges upon France's self-imposed *mission civilisatrice* and is a demonstration of the Second Empire's obsessive fear of collectivization in any form. It was this sentiment that found expression in the previously analysed text by Warnier.

On the other hand, the advantage of making tribal lands into individual parcels was that it opened them up for French settlement. While the previous law of 1851 had held tribal lands apart from the market, the *sénatus-consulte* intended to distribute parcels to individuals who would then, acting in their own interests, sell the parcels to French colonists who sought to expand the colonial empire. In retrospect, this does not seem like a foolproof plan, since it assumes that the indigenous population of Algeria would immediately reproduce the individualistic interests of a French entrepreneur.

In the geographical writings of the 1860s pertaining to Algeria, the character of the colonial landscape was altered, leading to a conception of space as value. Whereas the earlier French geographers set out to classify, delimit, and, in so doing, synthesize the variegated territory of Algeria into comprehensible units, the works of Jules Duval sought to integrate such findings into the sphere of political economy. It was Duval who began his analysis of Algeria from the perspective of political economy and who eventually attempted to marry the information provided by geography to the systems of political economy in his theoretical work of 1863, *Des rapports entre la géographie et l'économie politique*.[25] Duval was something of a one-man intellectual force, serving as both the secretary of the *Société de la géographie* and as the director of *L'Économiste français*, and he also was one of the most prominent authorities on and boosters for Algeria. His essay 'Politique coloniale de la France, Algérie,' appeared in the *Revue des deux mondes* in 1859 and advocated what became Napoleon III's two central policy initiatives in Algeria in the 1860s: the privatization of tribal lands and the naturalization of native Algerians to France.[26] In brief, he was a uniquely significant figure for Algerian policy in Second Empire France who also articulated a theoretical application of geographical knowledge to economic issues.

Like Warnier, Duval was a *colon* who promoted the interests of the settlers in the French press, and in 1869 he collaborated on a book with Warnier;[27] but Duval's writings are, for the most part, less polemical. Duval was the first to articulate fully the colonial tactic of assimilation and to spell out what forms it would take in Algeria.[28] In *Des rapports entre la géographie et l'économie politique*, he makes an argument for the geographical determination of economic factors:

> Whether one discusses continents, portions of the world or less expansive regions, the contour exercises an influence that manifests itself in the

> destiny of its inhabitants: based upon whether it is whole or broken, angular or rounded, based on the respective proportion of these diverse traits, the political and economic effects will themselves be quite diverse.[29]

The use of the term 'contour' is self-consciously general and abstract, and therefore universally applicable. It is possible to divine that he refers to 'natural separations,' such as bodies of water and chains of mountains that were elaborated in previous geographical works on Algeria by authors such as Carette, Renou,[30] and Daumas.[31] Of course, the notion that innate geographical characteristics could affect the development of economics and politics would seem to belie the universalist claims of Duval's observation: an argument for attending to distinctions between places ('diverse traits') when analysing their economic and political development could undermine the undifferentiated formulas of political economy. However, Duval resolves this apparent contradiction by pointing to exchange as *the* universal condition of humans: 'In effect, exchange is the supreme sign of sociability in the material world. Certain animals work, only man exchanges and engages in commerce.' He continues:

> Society, in its turn, has instituted the diverse rules of exchange between the metropole and the colony, between people united by certain traits, etc. ...
>
> In this alliance of human forces, geography indicates the exchanges, commerce executes them, and political economy discovers the laws.[32]

While distinctions between countries exist and are the topic of geographical inquiry, exchange is the fundamental principle that connects these regions to one another. Commerce functions to assure relations through exchange and political economy studies this process and establishes laws of exchange. While I am in no position to evaluate the universal validity of political economy as it is articulated here, I want to point out the way spatial configurations are deprived of meaning in this schema. Even a relatively meaningless abstraction of space such as contours (of the earth? the earth as a body?) ceases to have importance in a world that is regulated by exchange that only political economy can properly understand. The 'laws' of political economy, since they express the patterns of commercial exchange, regulate the meaning of space because they cut across it. Regional distinctions are unified into a world economic picture in this framework and, more important, distinct places and cultures lose their meaning in the face of the laws of economic exchange. Not only are places deprived of their meaning; they become the spaces that commerce must traverse in order to achieve the goal of exchange. This line of reasoning is emblematic of abstract representations of space.

Such a system begins to have meaning in the context of Algerian colonization when, in a later work, Duval applies some of the laws of political economy to the colonial project. In 1866 he wrote, 'Between the surface expanse of a nation and the forces necessary to exploit it, there is a natural relation.' Further, 'It can be said that, to a great degree, the amount of budgetary expenses is proportional to the extent of spaces in all civilized countries.'[33] These two observations lead the author to insist upon the necessity for more settlers in Algeria, who need to be granted more land so that the territory can be more densely populated and thus more productive of revenues. The concern here is not so much with the policies articulated as with the way the territory of Algeria is rendered in such formulae. The idea that a natural relationship exists between the size of a country and the forces necessary to exploit it reduces the landscape to a measurement of space and reconfigures it as an abstract element (x) in a system governed by questions of productivity. In this equation, Algeria's regions become a codified space of measurement, a bounded terrain. Though people live in this space and are crucial in determining its value through the payment of taxes, the formula necessarily negates their particularity and any practices that did not yield direct economic results for the colonial administration. The second proposition informs us that, since the distance involved is great, it is also expensive for its governing body because it is necessary to cover this large space with public works, such as roads, artesian wells, and the like. The formula articulated here is: the more densely populated a space, the greater the return on expenditure since more people will contribute to its tax base. Though Duval actually employs the term spaces here, indicating that there are differences between them that force the writer to use the plural form, these spaces are so fully abstracted that they form one part of a mathematical equation.

These principles of political economy are new to the discourse of the colonial landscape. The reduction of the spaces of the colony to an abstract, quantifiable signifier was a significant step in the dematerialization of Algeria's terrain. Though this transformation occurred within the realm of the social sciences, it evidences a social metamorphosis in French culture, namely, the ability to denature a terrain completely, emptying it of any other meaning than its quantifiable numerical equivalent (14 million hectares). Based on this number, Duval advocated the adoption of particular policies in Algeria. The equations he employed allowed him to perceive the inhabitants of Algeria as distinct from the lands they occupied and thus he was able to render the terrain separate from those who resided on it. In essence, this was the task of the *sénatus-consulte*. Though this legislation offered tribal lands to the tribes and individuals within them, the real process of delimitation was to make formal the separation of each landholder from the piece of property whose deed he held.

The process of delimiting territory was the central administrative task of the *sénatus-consulte* and, in the context of the representation of the colonial landscape of Algeria, was the most ambitious project for reconfiguring the space of the colony. In this sense, the effects of the *sénatus-consulte* would have been similar to those achieved by the Haussmannization of Paris that occurred in the same period. The method for achieving this increased control of indigenous Algerians based upon spatial fragmentation – the distribution of private property to *douars* and individuals – was intended to inspire a respect for European (read civilized) values among Algeria's native population.

For the purposes of my inquiry, the application of the *sénatus-consulte* was significant because it remade the map of the colony, both literally and metaphorically. Even more striking is the way it attempted to replace traditional indigenous conceptions of place with the abstract concepts of both private ownership and parcels of land. The former was represented as a deed of title – words on paper – and the latter was delimited mathematically through surveying. Leaving aside the issue of whether the native population was able to understand the nature of such abstractions or whether they might have been hostile to such a transparent attempt by French authorities to undermine their way of life, it is clear that the administration of the law would lead to French domination in at least two ways. First, the second set of instructions guided the sub-commissions to study the tribes whose rights they were adjudicating with great care. In order to safeguard the interests of all, a full inquiry would have to be made about each tribe or *douar* whose property was to be delimited.[34] Of course, information gleaned from surveillance of tribes would lead to a greater degree of control over those tribes. Further, the delimitation of territory, literally fixing the area of each tribe or *douar* and parcelling it into pieces, represents the official triumph of French cartography. Obviously, the division of collective land requires a clear and decisive map so that the boundaries forged by the *sénatus-consulte* can be accurately traced and positively fixed. This map, called the 'Map of Algeria presenting current civil territory divided by communes and *douars* constituted by virtue of the *sénatus-consulte*' (figure 3.3) was finally produced in November 1870, just after the end of the Second Empire.

The map shows that, by the time the Second Empire fell, the administration had actually accomplished precious little in terms of privatizing tribal lands and opening them up for settlement. This map of Algeria is divided into three sections: civil territory (the only region available for colonial settlement), the *douars* in which property had been recognized as collective (*arch*), and the *douars* where property was not *arch*, but remained generally undivided. Looking at the map, it is clear that the colony is dominated by the last two categories. Inscriptions on the map spell out what these categories suggest. Out of hundreds of *douars* delimited, the inscriptions explain that the lands of only two have become part of civil territory (i.e., open to settlement), and private property has been established on only twenty-two others. Tribal autonomy appears to have been sustained in the last years of the Second Empire, despite the French government's attempt to impose the status of individual onto the native inhabitants of Algeria. However, the patchwork of coloured shapes that compose the territory of Algeria in this depiction reveal that the process of delimitation had proceeded successfully.

Compared with earlier French maps of colonial Algeria, the map of the *sénatus-consulte* speaks volumes about the clear, administrative division of territory as a result of this legislation. Maps are designed to organize information and to present it in a visual way that is immediately clear.[35] This map arranges the colony into abstract, visual units whose labels explain their significance. It was created in order to demonstrate the effects of the *sénatus-consulte*, and therefore its purpose of organizing space is paralleled by the activity of spatial delimitation it represents. In some sense, the *sénatus-consulte* was intended to make possible just such a representation of the colony because it sought to transform the tribes into administrative units, each occupying a specific territory. Michel de Certeau has discussed the way maps present information graphically in a way that erases the processes involved in their creation:

> The map thus collates on the same plane heterogeneous places, some *received* from a tradition [geometry] and others *produced* by observation ... The map, a totalizing stage on which elements of diverse origin are brought together to form a tableau of a 'state' of geographical knowledge, pushes away into prehistory or into its posterity, as if into the wings, the operations of which it is the result or the necessary condition. It remains alone on the stage. The tour describers have disappeared.[36]

While the *sénatus-consulte* did not lead to the intended privatization of indigenous lands, the map demonstrates that it did effectively redefine the colonial territory in abstract terms. In this representation, Algeria takes on the characteristics of a well-ordered colony and the activities that made it that way – the painstaking trouble of delimitation, the negation of indigenous conceptions of land and space – have been eliminated from the representation. This is the very visual representation of the abstraction of space achieved by the *sénatus-consulte* and theorized by Duval and Warnier. The proliferation of administrative divisions demonstrates the predominance of French methods of perceiving and organizing space on the surface of this landscape.

## Abstract Space as Landscape Painting

Turning to a consideration of the pictorial representations of Algeria during this period, it is noteworthy that the desert is the focus of landscape painting for the first time in history. As previously discussed, Heffernan has considered the symbolic aspects of the desert in the nineteenth century, which he has interpreted in the pictorial works of Guillaumet and those of Eugène Fromentin, the first artist to make an artistic subject of the Algerian Sahara.[37] Heffernan described the symbolism of the desert in the nineteenth century as two-sided. On the one hand, the desert was the place of ultimate desolation and, on the other, it represented the possibility of civilization and progress reclaiming this barren land and putting it to productive use.

Heffernan's symbolic interpretation of *The Desert* is focused on the tiny image of a group of mounted figures on the horizon. He admits that the image projected in this work is one of an 'entirely barren wilderness,' but points to the distant figures in an 'almost saintly light.' Heffernan writes that 'it is hard to avoid the assumption' that these figures, representing to him the possibility of salvation, are coming from the north.[38] While the symbolism of colonial salvation is clearly at stake in this image, the figures on the horizon are obscuring the light of the rising or setting sun and therefore could not literally be coming from the north. Yet there is a symbolic ambivalence here. As a viewer, one wonders if it is sunrise or sunset, if these figures are moving towards or away from the viewer, bringing salvation or abandoning the viewer to desolation. However, it is more difficult to read the symbolic message in a work that is nearly without figures. The skeleton of the camel in the foreground is a cliché, but its presence in the centre foreground of this composition makes it difficult to get beyond.

If one considers *The Desert* in relation to other paintings of the Algerian Sahara produced in the same period by Fromentin, it is possible to derive a sense of its unique power. There are a number of desert images in Fromentin's oeuvre, dating back to his first trip to Laghouat in 1853, but the most pertinent comparison is between Guillaumet's Sahara and Fromentin's two versions of *The Land of Thirst* (figures 3.4 and 3.5). In these two compositions made in the last years of the Second Empire (only the second is dated, to 1869), it is possible to compare an anecdotal representation of the desert to Guillaumet's extreme simplicity. As in many of his famous works, Fromentin's image is based on a story from one of his novels, in this case a narrative from the end of *Un Été dans le Sahara* (A Summer in the Sahara), originally published serially in 1856. These figures, abandoned in the desert, are literally expiring before us, and the power of the desert as a force of nature is paramount in this representation. While the figures add an element of human interest, Fromentin has provided them with realistic, as opposed to fantastic, dress, perhaps in order to make more forceful the actual tragedy the viewer witnesses. In the earlier composition (figure 3.4) the central figure reaches for the sky, in a gesture remarkably similar to that in Géricault's *Raft of the Medusa*.[39] In the second composition (figure 3.5), the artist has replaced this dramatic gesture with a number of vultures above the horizon. In both works, the placement of the figures is meant to appear natural, but is in fact artfully composed.

Besides the human interest these figures suggest, the desert appears quite distinct in these works. There is a landscape here, a place full of geographical features that provide the eye with a terrain to explore. There may not be any vegetation in sight, or any sign of human civilization, but the landscape itself has a clear structure, a set of rises and valleys that provides a sense of its rugged character and gives these pictures a sense of particularity. This specificity allows a viewer to put an interpretative framework in place and to read these pictures as a narrative. Whether it reflects the artist's view of imperial ideology, as Heffernan has suggested,[40] or the artist's response to the catastrophic drought that was raging in Algeria at this historical moment, the paintings convey a message through the landscape and the figures that populate it and provide a legible drama, a tableau of balanced pictorial elements – both figures and landscape forms – for the viewers to read.

Unlike Fromentin's two versions of *The Land of Thirst*, *The Desert* cannot be described as a tableau. This composition is not ordered, balanced, or self-conscious. Guillaumet, who had a rigorous academic training, turned his back on landscape conventions when he created this piece. Whereas other French painters of Algeria made use of landscape conventions in order to present the exotic terrain of Algeria as recognizable to a French audience, Guillaumet excerpted the desert in such a way that it appears abstract. *The Desert* cuts off the Sahara, arbitrarily, cleaving its apparent limitlessness into a comprehensible fraction. Further, the manner in which Guillaumet renders this plot of land is loose and evocative. The sensations of light and atmosphere which are the painting's most recognizable subject, lead the viewer to a more intimate and personal experience of this territory. Such a technique imposes the need for interpretation of the landscape upon the viewer because it denies the secure footing of landscape conventions. The landscape here needs to be translated by each individual who perceives it and, in that process, this piece of desert comes to mean something and belong to the viewer.

Perhaps the most relevant symbolic evocation of the desert to emerge in Guillaumet's *The Desert* is the sense of unlimited space. In this sense, *The Desert* departs most significantly from other contemporary manifestations of landscape painting in France. The few recognizable traces in the composition – the camel, the distant caravan, the few plants – do not measure space with the conventions of landscape paintings. There are no trees or figures to establish relative distances, and though a sense of atmosphere is palpable, a systematic use of aerial perspective is also absent. In the terms of landscape painting, *The Desert* is unmeasured. Beyond the absence of pictorial devices to measure space, there is the utter lack of any sign of human habitation or cultivation. The desert evoked is the place where human interaction with the terrain, in the form of agriculture, is impossible due to the nature of the place. It is literally a land without masters because humans could not squeeze an existence out of such a landscape. There is no hope of occupation, let alone agriculture, so the place is necessarily beyond the control of any individual or government.

Following this line of argument, the archetypal desert rendered by Guillaumet is a romanticization sharing little with the historical development of colonization traced earlier. In line with recent scholarship on Orientalism and the fantasies it conjures, one might be tempted to consider *The Desert* a mystification. Though Guillaumet travelled repeatedly to Algeria and had experience of various landscapes and settlements on the edges of the desert, one could argue that he represented the desert as an Orientalist fantasy of landscape. Just as Linda Nochlin has asserted that Gérôme's religious ethnographic art generated the appearance of an unthreatening Islam in contradistinction to historical realities,[41] one could argue that Guillaumet's archetypal desert distracts its viewers from the very real transformations the French government was effecting in the Algerian landscape. *The Desert* could be read as the very opposite of the map of 1870 because it provides a fantasy of a limitless space in the face of the application of the *sénatus-consulte*.

However, I am not certain that the landscape painting is fundamentally different from the map. Despite the evocation of limitless space it appears to proffer, the frame of the painting actually provides a boundary for the desert. Guillaumet delimited an enormous expanse of space in this work: he squeezed the entire Sahara into a frame of 110 by 200 centimetres! In *The Desert*, we see a synechdocal substitution: the painting renders this stretch of the Sahara and thereby lays claim to representing all of it. When a viewer perceives this painting, it is not this fragment of the Algerian Sahara that s/he gets. Rather the painting evokes the desert as an archetype. It acts as a magnet for received ideas because there are no particularities to dispel them. Nevertheless, if we think more literally of the frame and its function, the metaphorical conversion of part into whole takes on a different meaning.

Another effect produced by this sort of painting is that the location represented is similarly supplanted by the effect of it. The Sahara is what we might call a geographical fact. It is a desert in North Africa and it is big. In Guillaumet's painting, the Sahara is less a desert in Africa than the way it looks to a viewer perceiving it. In other words, if we consider the pictorial representation as a signifier and the desert as the signified, what becomes clear in this case is that, when a viewer confronts this painting, the signifier does not necessarily direct attention to the signified. Rather, the viewer is able to seize upon the effects captured by the artist, to be immersed in the impression conveyed by the painting without considering it as a representation of any place in particular. This place is transfigured into an abstract space that can be both measured and divided but only in the imagination of the colonial power. For what kind of fool would ever take possession of a desert? How can an artist make a landscape out of a limitless vacuity?

Guillaumet's *The Desert* frames the unlimited spaces at the edge of France's Algeria while conveying the effects of the desert in terms that can only be construed through the perceptual faculties of an individual's eye. This artist's flight from landscape conventions ultimately leads to an illustration of the colonial landscape whose terms are analogous to those of French social scientists and legislators of his epoch. *The Desert* does possess symbolic meanings, but more forceful is the lingua franca it intones that denudes the colonial landscape of its character and allows for its possession in the metropole. By making the desert appear abstract yet accessible through the terms of landscape painting, Guillaumet succeeded in framing the Sahara, France's empty Algerian frontier.

> As a picturesque description, as a graphic philosophy, dare I say of this once barbarous country today become a new France, the work of Guillaumet is a second conquest of Algeria, the conquest of art after the conquest of war.[42]

## NOTES

I would like to thank Vojtěch Jirat-Wasiutyński for organizing the conference and the volume, as well as the other conference participants who responded to this work with keen insights and helpful suggestions. An earlier version of this paper was presented in the geography department at the University of British Columbia, Vancouver, in the fall of 2000. Thanks to Derek Gregory and the department for their comments. Thanks to Jennifer Vanim for her help with the images. Unless otherwise noted, all translations are mine.

1 John Zarobell, 'Framing French Algeria: Colonialism, Travel and the Representation of Landscape, 1830–1870,' PhD dissertation, University of California, Berkeley, 2000.
2 Edward Said, *Orientalism* (New York: Vintage, 1978).
3 Charles-Robert Ageron, *Histoire de l'Algérie contemporaine,* 10th ed. (Paris: Gallimard, 1994), 25–32; and Charles-André Julien, *La conquête et les débuts de la colonisation (1827–1871)*, vol. 2, *Histoire de l'Algérie contemporaine* (Paris: Presses Universitaires de France, 1964), 396–415; and Annie

Rey-Goldzeiguer, *Le royaume Arabe: La politique algérienne de Napoléon III* (Algiers: Société Nationale d'Édition et de Diffusion, 1977).

4 Henri Lefebvre, *The Production of Space*, trans. Donald Nicholson-Smith (Oxford: Basil Blackwell, 1991), 288.

5 This reading follows that of Derek Gregory, who refers to a 'decorporalization of space' in the thought of Lefebvre. Derek Gregory, *Geographical Imaginations* (Cambridge, MA, and Oxford: Blackwell, 1994), 382–95.

6 Michael J. Heffernan, 'The Desert in French Orientalist Painting during the Nineteenth Century,' *Landscape Research* 16, 2 (1991): 41.

7 Ibid., 42.

8 Michèle Salinas has produced a remarkable graph charting the associations of Algeria with the desert presented by French writers. Michèle Salinas, *Voyages et voyageurs en Algérie, 1830/1930* (Toulouse: Privat, 1989), 136–7.

9 The sense of the term implied here derives from W.J.T. Mitchell, 'Gombrich and the Rise of Landscape,' in Ann Bermingham and John Brewer, eds, *The Consumption of Culture, 1600–1800: Image, Object, Text* (London: Routeledge, 1995), 103–18.

10 Donald A. Rosenthal, *Orientalism: The Near East in French Painting, 1800–1880* (Rochester, NY: Memorial Art Gallery, 1982), 89.

11 Philippe Jullian, *The Orientalists, European Painters of Eastern Scenes*, trans. Helga and Dinah Harrison (Oxford: Phaidon, 1977), 102.

12 Robert Rosenblum, 'L'Orientalisme,' in *Les peintures du Musée d'Orsay* (Paris: Nathan, 1989), 176.

13 Théophile Gautier, 'Le Salon de 1868,' *Le Moniteur universel*, 2 May 1868: 2.

14 See Gustave Guillaumet, *Tableaux algériens* (Paris: Plon, 1888).

15 'Sénatus-consulte de 22 avril 1863,' repr. in Rodolphe Dareste, *De la propriété en Algérie*, 2nd ed. (Paris: Lainé et Havard, 1864). Dareste is my source for the history of property law in Algeria during this period; he reprints in full the *sénatus-consulte* and the instructions for its application.

16 See Zarobell, 'Framing French Algeria,' Chapter 3. For a more complete discussion of Arab stereotyping, particularly by scholars working on Algeria, see Patricia Lorcin, *Imperial Identities: Stereotyping, Prejudice and Race in Colonial Algeria* (London: IB Tauris, 1995).

17 These are the critiques levelled by Warnier and Duval, among others, in several works that I will address below. An example of the emperor's favourable disposition towards Algeria's natives comes from a proclamation that he made in Algeria in 1865: 'You know my intentions; I have irrevocably assured the possession of the lands that you occupy; I have honoured your chiefs, respected your religion, I want to augment your

well-being, and to allow you to participate more and more in the administration of your country as one of the benefits of civilization.' Repr. in Florian Pharaon, *Voyage en Algérie de Sa Majesté Napoléon III* (Paris: Plon, 1865), 11.

18 Lorcin, *Imperial Identities*, 80.

19 Dr Auguste Warnier, *L'Algérie devant l'Empereur* (Paris: Challamel ainé, 1865), 25.

20 Ibid., x.

21 Warnier's text is an excellent example of this trend.

22 *'Instructions générales pour l'exécution du Sénatus-consulte du 22 avril 1863 et du règlement de l'administration publique du 23 mai suivant,'* reprinted in Dareste, *De la propriété*, 279.

23 Ibid.

24 A brief contemporary article sought to refute this point of view by rounding up Islamic scholars who lent their support to the *sénatus-consulte* by declaring it legal within the context of Koranic law. E. Vaysettes, 'La question de la propriété, jugée par les docteurs de la loi musulmane,' *Revue africaine*, 7th year n. 41 (September 1863): 353–6. In the same vein, Rey-Goldzeiguer describes the responses of Muslim tribal leaders to the legislation in strictly positive terms, even assuring us that the *bureaux arabes* sources she quotes did not just write such things for political reasons. Rey-Goldzeiguer, *Le royaume Arabe*, 249–53.

25 Jules Duval, *Des rapports entre la géographie et l'économie politique* (Paris: Arthus Bertrand, 1864). This work was excerpted from the *Bulletin de la société de géographie*, 1863, and was originally presented to the Society in that year. Duval's work remains unknown or considered insignificant by historians of geography and political economy, with the exception of Dominque Lejeune's recent work, *Les sociétés de géographie en France et l'expansion coloniale au XIXe siècle* (Paris: Albin Michel, 1993), 69–77. In this work, Lejeune mentions Duval's influence on the geographical society of Paris without discussing this figure in any detail. Otherwise, I have found only two brief bibliographies on Duval in recent literature: Roman d'Amat, ed., *Dictionnaire de biographie française*, vol. 12 (Paris: Librairie LeToucy et Ané, 1970), 979–80, and Rey-Goldzeiguer, *Le royaume arabe*, 120–1. The latter notes: 'Gautier's Orientalism of the bazaar rings just as false as the desiccated economic palaver of Jules Duval because, for one as much as the other, the idea was to integrate Algeria into a framework that was foreign to it' (121).

26 Jules Duval, 'Politique coloniale de la France, Algérie,' *Revue des deux mondes* 20 (15 April 1859): 891–930 and 22 (15 May 1859): 257–300.

27 Jules Duval and Dr Auguste Warnier, *Bureaux arabes et colons* (Paris: Challamel aîné, 1869).
28 Duval, 'Politique coloniale.'
29 Duval, *Des rapports*, 11.
30 E. Carette, *Recherches sur la géographie et la commerce de l'Algérie méridionale* and E. Renou, *Notice géographique sur une partie de l'Afrique septentrionale, Exploration scientifique de l'Algérie, Sciences historiques et géographiques II* (Paris: Imprimérie Royale, 1844).
31 M. le lieutenant-colonel Daumas, *Le Sahara algérien: Études géographiques, statistiques et historiques sur la région au sud des établissements français en Algérie* (Paris: Imprimérie de Crapelet, 1845).
32 Duval, *Des rapports*, 77 and 78.
33 Duval, *Reflexions sur la politique de l'Empereur en Algérie* (Paris: Challamel, 1866), 21 and 22.
34 'Instructions générales,' in Dareste, *De la propriété*, 282.
35 This is an oversimplification, of course. See J.B. Harley and David Woodward, eds, *The History of Cartography*, 3 vols. (Chicago: University of Chicago Press, 1992).
36 Michel de Certeau, *The Practice of Everyday Life*, trans. Steven R. Rendall (Berkeley and Los Angeles: University of California Press, 1984), 121.
37 For more on Fromentin's voyages to Algeria and the paintings he produced as a result, see James Thompson and Barbara Wright, *La vie et l'oeuvre d'Eugène Fromentin* (Paris: ACR Editions, 1987), Zarobell, 'Framing French Algeria,' and Roger Benjamin, *Orientalist Aesthetics: Art, Colonialism and French North Africa, 1880–1930* (Berkeley and Los Angeles: University of California Press, 2003), 11–32.
38 Heffernan, 'The Desert in French Orientalist Painting,' 40.
39 Thompson and Wright, *La vie et l'oeuvre*, 240.
40 Heffernan, 'The Desert,' 40.
41 Linda Nochlin, 'The Imaginary Orient,' *Art in America* 7, 5 (May 1983): 125.
42 Eugène Mouton, 'Introduction,' in Guillaumet, *Tableaux algériens*, 21.

# 4 The Untimely Classicism of Hans von Marées

ANDRÉ DOMBROWSKI

This, precisely, is the proposition the reader is invited to meditate upon: *the unhistorical and the historical are necessary in equal measure for the health of an individual, of a people and of a culture.*

Friedrich Nietzsche, *Untimely Meditations*

Of course modernist painters are always producing the problem of when and how to finish – the problem is modernism's lifeblood, and eventually its deathknell.

T.J. Clark, *Farewell to an Idea*

Writing about his travels in the Bay of Naples, Henry James formulated a double-edged definition of the late-nineteenth-century northern European fascination with Italy and its tradition.[1] Perpetually inspiring to artist and visitor alike, Italy was, James claimed, also overwhelming, even stifling, to any creative act. It was in equal measure welcoming and hostile to northern European modes of thought and representation. Writing about 'the classic, synthetic directness of the German passion for Italy,' James described the region's peculiar commingling of past and present, attraction and horror, as follows:

> The beauty and the poetry, at all events, were clear enough, and the extraordinary uplifted distinction; but where, in all this, it may be asked, was the element of 'horror' that I have spoken of as sensible? – what obsession that was not charming could find a place in that splendid light, out of which the long summer squeezes every secret and shadow? I'm afraid I'm driven to plead that these evils were exactly in one's imagina-

> tion, a predestined victim always of the cruel, the fatal historic sense. To make so much distinction, how much history had been needed! – so that the whole air still throbbed and ached with it, as with an accumulation of ghosts to whom the very climate was pitiless, condemning them to blanch for ever in the general glare and grandeur, offering them no dusky northern nook, no place at the friendly fireside, no shelter of legend or song.[2]

For James, these two sentiments in tandem – one life-affirming, the other thanatonic – constituted the fascination of Italy. As he and later Thomas Mann would have it, the former was not to be had in Italy without the latter. In the second half of the nineteenth century, many artists and visitors felt the suffocating presence of history ahead of its inspirational qualities. How does this morbidity and cultural pessimism, if we can call it such, make its presence felt within a nineteenth-century version of classical form? How do timeliness and timelessness, contemporaneousness and a sense of past write their contrary impulses into the making of a modernist artwork inspired by Italy? Such questions lie at the heart of what kept Italy fascinating for a whole range of artists during the rise of the painting of modern life in northern Europe.

The German painter Hans von Marées, who spent more of his life working in Italy than Germany, is certainly one of the best examples of the late-nineteenth-century fascination with Italy. He desperately tried to find through a new classicism a response to French modernist and German nationalist art, and painted, over and over again, nude bodies resting and interacting in an Arcadian landscape. But despite Arcadia's iconographic promise of equilibrium and stasis, Marées's paintings were perpetually unfinished and, according to his own testimony, never achieved the artistic expectations and aspirations he himself had set. Generations of artists and art historians since have agreed that the products of his brush are often painterly failures, convulsive and convoluted canvases born of a never-ending reworking process that at times took decades. He consistently sought, hesitantly and even obsessively, to forestall the moment of his paintings' completion. Most of his works hover on the brink of material and representational collapse: darkened and heavily cracked, they began to decay almost immediately after Marées abandoned them. His surfaces are endlessly built up, even an inch thick on occasion, and – not unlike James's Neapolitan air palpitating with history – filled with pictorial echoes of that which came before. The belaboured creation of his paintings is unflinchingly present in every move of the brush, in every gesture of their figures, in every aspect of their seemingly idyllic settings and compositions. Marées's paintings are thus not really incomplete or unfinished, but *over*-finished, with the extended *durée* of their tortured making visible on their surfaces. In their multiple, thick layers of paint, they chronicle an unusually wrenching artistic struggle.

This essay will examine the social and aesthetic valences of the problem of finish in Marées's oeuvre, in both its constructive as well as destructive aspects. Un-finish is destructive within Marées's project, as it quarrels with and renders temporal an ahistorical classical vision. But for Marées, a constant state of un-finish was also constructive, keeping alive an iconography not usually open to the particularity of everyday life. Iconography and technique had, for Marées, become separated, yet remained deeply responsive to one another, so much so that the fraught conjunction of Arcadia with Marées's overworked surfaces could only produce a sense of failure. Marées set himself the task to answer the question of how to keep the classical vision alive for the present, giving its claims to timelessness forms useful and negotiable for the here and now. The choice was between a dead Arcadia or a living one, a classicism able to acknowledge change or not. Marées sought to individualize, localize, and to some extent even gender and eroticize, the generality of Arcadia and classicism. Here, Marées's fascination with Italy is central for understanding how much contemporary history and politics (including, say, of Italy's unification) his work was willing and able to incorporate.

Much hinges, to be sure, on how we understand Marées's classicism, whether the classical for Marées was a fully stable category and averse to change, or able to accommodate a more modern understanding of the nature of reality as contingent. The term 'classical' was brought to bear on his art from early on, and used to define that which made Marées different from those modernist painters seeking modern life subjects.[3] Marées's bodies, faces, landscapes, gestures, and actions sought, it is said, not contemporaneity, but timelessness. At first glance, his scenes seem to have no traces of the industrial or the tourist age, no modern strictures or erotic charge in the representation of the naked body. Marées's paintings seem to have dreamed themselves back into a classical past, in the belief that here his painting could best escape the horrors of modernity, of capitalism and its destruction of an ancient vision of communal life. This definition of classicism is deeply hostile to modernity, and precisely for this reason, Italy was its chief fascination.

But Marées's outlook on what he perceived to be classical in fact had much in common with Henry James's version of Italy, and was much haunted by mixtures of past and present, of stability and flux. Note that Marées's classicism comes along, indeed could only come along, after modernity has done its work, and not before. Form, subject, and meaning seem to have been risked, and that risk welcomed, by a classicism trying to visualize an Arcadia in which life is not entirely separated from liveliness. As literary historian Frank Kermode put it:

> The doctrine of the classic as model and criterion entails, in some form, the assumption that the ancient can be more or less immediately relevant and available, in a sense contemporaneous with the modern – or anyway that its nature is such that it can, by strategies of accommodation, be made so. When this assumption is rejected the whole authority of the classic as model is being challenged, and then we have – whether in Alexandria or in twelfth- or seventeenth- or nineteenth- or twentieth-century Europe – the recurrent *querelle* between ancient and modern.[4]

The relevance of the classical for the modern seems to have been a particularly pointed issue for men like Winckelmann, von Marées, James, and Mann, men who projected onto the classical past a vision of a same-sex erotic utopia notably lacking in contemporary life.[5] For these men, the classical world and the dead hand of history carried, parodoxically, poignant liberating possibilities as well. Thus, their engagement with the past offered something of the urgency and passion of an emotional, not intellectual bond, a proto-politics of pleasure. When Marées left a classical picture unfinished, he did so in part to keep the conversation with the past alive, to resolutely refuse to make the past *past*, to enable a continued engagement with a source of passionate potential in his life. Here the open-endedness of his process is a kind of invitation to dream; to finish a utopia is to recognize it as such.

Born in 1837, Hans von Marées received his artistic training in the military and history painter Carl Steffeck's Berlin studio in the 1850s. Marées then spent most of his professional life in Italy – in Florence, Rome, and Naples – with few extended stays in Germany. Initially, the Munich art collector Baron von Schack employed him as a copyist. Soon dissatisfied with copying, Marées broke free from his commitments to Schack. In 1866 he met Conrad Fiedler in Rome, where the German philanthropist and art theorist agreed to support Marées for the rest of his life with a yearly stipend large enough to cover all his expenses.[6] Though their friendship grew strained during the 1870s and 1880s, Fiedler continued his support until Marées's unexpected death in 1887 at not quite fifty years of age. By freeing the painter from the burden of participating in the art market and from 'finishing' his paintings, Fiedler partly allowed him to live out an exceptional artistic identity. Although Marées continuously promised completed works, he also frequently misled Fiedler with empty promises. In part, Fiedler's uncompromising support for Marées was due to the fact that the painter seemed to come closest to the philanthropist and aesthetic theorist's own thought on the artwork as its own contingent reality, which he propounded in several essays published during the 1870s and 1880s. Fiedler and a small circle of mostly German artists and literati were certainly the main, private, if not the only, audience that Marées's paintings then received, although so many of them were made in large-scale public formats. Of the intended spaces and exhibition venues for Marées's creations we know little to nothing, except that Marées would have given them to Fiedler had he felt they were finished. Thanks to Fiedler's relentless promotion after the artist's death – Marées's work had never been publicly exhibited before he died[7] – the painter's reputation quickly grew in stature. In 1891 Fiedler donated the bulk of his works to the city of Munich, and in the spate of ensuing publications and exhibitions, Marées was nominated one of the leading figures of German modernism, especially in the installation of his paintings at the 1906 Deutsche Jahrhundertausstellung in Berlin.[8] By the early 1900s it became a commonplace to regard Marées as the closest German equivalent of Cézanne in France and as rivalling the modern French painters.[9] It was also due to Fiedler, who first publicly called Marées an artistic failure, that, alongside the general worship, Marées was never fully able to shake off the romantic image of an aesthetic seeker whose art bespoke doubt and that peculiarly romantic vision of ambitious, high-toned pessimism.[10]

Hans von Marées, to say the least, has always held a conflicted position within art history in Germany, hovering between early modernist genius and artistic failure. And although noted with curiosity and fascination by Richard Brettell in his recent *Modern Art, 1851–1929*, Marées has otherwise completely escaped Anglo-American art historical attention, unlike Adolph von Menzel.[11] Some of the reasons for this oversight are simple: due to Marées's aesthetic struggles, resulting in the sheer accumulation of unruly matter on his surfaces, most of his major works can never travel from their permanent home at the Neue

Pinakothek in Munich. Only here, where almost all of Marées's important works are grouped in one hauntingly somber, unparalleled ensemble, can the depth of Marées's achievement be appreciated.[12] Some of the other reasons for Marées's outsider position are more complicated. They have to do with the fact that our story of the rise of modernism in Western Europe simply cannot account for the doubt writ large on the surfaces of Marées's work. Except perhaps for Paul Cézanne's heavy contours and some of his bitter late struggles with portraiture (of his gardener Vallier in particular) whose function and position in modern painting are no less open for debate, we lack a convincing account of the unruly aspects of matter roaming freely and uncontrollably over the surfaces of paintings such as Marées's.[13]

Marées appears therefore to have been another Frenhofer, the main character of Balzac's *The Unknown Masterpiece*, or another Claude Lantier, in Zola's *L'Oeuvre*. Paint accumulates, wrinkles, and cracks on Marées's works, contours blur, and his paintings attract their own undoing. The legs of the male figure on the left in his *Praise of Modesty* (ca. 1879–85) stick out in their painterly convulsions like the legs in Frenhofer's otherwise illegible attempt at representation (figure 4.1). In most late-nineteenth-century avant-garde painting, every mark of the brush had to be precise, simple, and exact – not complex, multiple, and merging incoherently with its neighbours. Marées's angst-ridden, maladroit brushiness does not match the painterly surety and low-watt subject matter of Manet's single *Asparagus*, or even of the Impressionists at large. Marées's paintings do not perform an absolute economy of the brush and the subject – on the contrary, they belie this fiat so often made central to an understanding of the rise of the French avant-garde in the 1860s and 1870s.

We still require a language and an analytical apparatus that can fully take into account and make meaningful the failure and disintegration of form in Marées. How does such an overt painterly indecision operate, how does it produce meanings – about the nature of reality, say – rather than negate them? This is a slightly different question from the ones that have been brought to the problem of form versus content in Marées in the past. Marées scholarship has long been dominated by a formal account, initiated by Fiedler when he proclaimed in his obituary of the painter that Marées was seeking forms 'unconditioned by any kind of subject matter.'[14] Until after the Second World War, many Marées interpretations have maintained the modernist imperative that his choice of subject was nothing but secondary to his quest for autonomous forms or that his figures served, first and foremost, to structure his compositions and give them rhythm. Others, assuming a more moderate position, have emphasized the role of the human body and of narrative structures in Marées's painting. They have pointed to the repeated personal and biographical, or religious and mythological, content of many of his paintings.[15] This essay, like recent writings on the painter by Gerd Blum and others, seriously questions that a severance between form and content in Marées's body of work can be successfully maintained.[16] In this account, far from being separate entities, form and its disintegration pose aesthetic and ideological dilemmas keyed to the search for the classical body. That the undoing of paint and form was something Marées was ultimately unable to keep at bay, but that he also welcomed this disintegration as an agent of meaning into his work, is precisely the ambivalence that Marées's art invites its viewers to take seriously.

In what ways do notions of un-finish and over-finish operate in Marées's career? The question matters, for a painting's finish and a brush's economy, in a modernist universe, would always be an indicator of the painter's integrity and, by extension, of that of his subjects. Marées sometimes reworked a painting between fifty and eighty times, as he himself admitted.[17] Moreover, unlike many other artists who might have reworked their paintings just as often, he did not seek to erase the traces of his corrections. He simply added and added, building his canvases in certain areas to the height of a sculptural relief. In his palimpsestic paintings, succeeding layers of paint do not erase the ones underneath, but play with them, thus fossilizing Marées's indecision and self-doubt. The upper layers of paint are at times so translucent that the ones below peek through, creating an illusion of depth, but also of a painterly process of endless revision. In other parts of his paintings, where paint has accumulated to an extraordinarily high degree, deep wrinkles, crevices, and cracks have opened where paint has dried according to its own uneven logic, bringing too much attention to the paint's presence as material. Take, for instance, one of Marées's most acclaimed works, the *Hesperides-Triptych*, painted between 1884 and 1887 (figure 4.2).[18] Its three upper panels show gatherings of male and female nudes of all ages in orange groves, picking and holding oranges while posing for the viewer. Consider the deep crack in the chest of the centre left Hesperid in the middle panel: it exposes the countless layers of paint that, under their own weight and pressure, had no choice but to burst open (figure 4.3). The deep dark line that encircles her body seems to be carved out from layers of paint, pushing them up right and left, leaving the body with a demarcation both too literal and too inexact. The putti in the lower framing of the triptych, in contrast, are so flat and painted with such liquid paint that small streams run down the painting's wooden support. Sheer materiality helps to establish the hierarchy of a figure's overall importance within the composition.

To be sure, comparable manoeuvres have always held their place in French modernist painting, in Camille Pissarro's complexly layered technique for instance, but in Marées they appear more out of control, more unavoidable than fully intentional. Marées's unusual technique of layering oil and tempera paint, which he employed as a tribute to early Renaissance painters, clearly contributed to the often strange and uncomfortable effects of his surfaces. Marées was clearly inexperienced in this difficult and fairly incalculable technique, and many of his paintings are marked by the results of an uneven drying process, in which the tensions between the dried upper and the moist lower layers produced an unusual amount of wrinkles and cracks. Paint inscribes itself as an autonomous, unruly element into Marées's work, a symptom that his pupil Karl von Pidoll described in his reminiscences published three years after his teacher's death: 'Indeed, the material tends to revenge itself against any painterly carelessness.'[19] Some painters' manuals of Marées's day even warned of the concomitant use of oil and tempera paint, such as *Über die Grundsätze der Ölmalerei und das Verfahren der classischen Meister*, compiled in 1876 by Heinrich Ludwig, an art historian whose work Marées knew well.[20] Ludwig reminded artists of the complexities in combining water- and oil-based paint. Tempera, according to Ludwig, was hardly useful in creating strong illusions of light and shade, and it darkened quickly, so that a large amount of white was necessary to lighten certain areas. Problems occurred in particular when painting skin, the art historian concluded, an obstacle aggravated by tempera's tendency to dry fast. Marées, who knew such warnings, ignored them, and at least in part must have anticipated the final outcome.

It is equally possible that Marées was merely indifferent to his surfaces' physical appearance. Adolf von Hildebrand, one of his closest friends and pupils, insisted that the painter staked all on his paintings' conception and compositional 'arrangement,' which were always perfectly whole and finished, and that the 'so-called execution would not contribute anything substantive.'[21] Yet, Marées's own words easily belie such argumentation. Even after a long creative process of years, if not decades, Marées felt his paintings to be utterly unfinished. In his letters to his family, patron, and artistic friends, he obsessed about the moment of completion. In 1879 he wrote to Fiedler, doubting that finishing a painting would even be possible: 'I have caught myself believing that, each time I say this thing is done, I am never more than at the beginning. An artwork is never properly finished.'[22] A year earlier, he had mentioned to Fiedler that he was producing nothing but 'unfinished attempts.'[23] The formulation 'unfinished attempts' is a redundancy pointing to the heart of the problem: trying to finish that which by definition would not be the final result. At the same time, and despite the realization of the practically unfinishable nature of his art making, Marées felt himself close to what he was striving for, when he proclaimed to his brother Georg in 1884 that '[a]fter unspeakable efforts and a thousand hindrances I have finally succeeded. Tomorrow I will finish.'[24] Needless to add, such a tomorrow would never come. Already in 1880 he believed for a brief period of time that he had 'completed the epoch of trial.'[25] And in a letter to Fiedler of 1884 Marées proclaimed – in a distinction similar to the one Charles Baudelaire drew between 'fait' and 'fini' when describing Corot's work in his 'Salon of 1845': 'I continue focusing constantly on the main issue, and that is (not to *finish*) but to *complete* the painting at hand [*my emphasis*].'[26] Finishing here implies the simple act of stopping to paint at the moment where every brushstroke, necessary according to pre-established rules of technical accomplishment, is now in place. Completion, instead, implies more than technical bravura; for a painter to complete a painting, its state of technical finish is not necessarily the prime concern. It implies, rather, the capturing and preservation during the painterly process of the most eloquent unity among pictorial conception, composition, and technical ability.

There is arguably one body of works in Marées's oeuvre where such a balance of conception and technique has been achieved and where iconographic reference and technical effects are not separate. The fresco cycle at the Stazione Zoologica di Napoli, executed between May and November 1873, has often been rightly considered Marées's most finished and accomplished body of work and provides a test case as to how much reality, contemporaneity, history, and even politics Marées's classicizing style can and wants to accommodate (figures 4.4, 4.5, 4.6). Part of this success was, of course, due to technical reasons, as Marées had only eight days of retouches: 'To paint al fresco ... would today do good to all painters, there is frightful, eternal correction everywhere,' claimed Hildebrand.[27] The cycle has always been regarded as a mix of a-historicity with specific biographical and regional references. The scenes depict a classicized life of fishermen, as well as a group portrait of the intellectuals involved in the zoological institute, the first aquarium in Europe built in the early 1870s.[28] Two of the main scenes show fishermen at work, departing for or returning from the sea. There is a scene of idyllic garden work and one of leisurely repose. In aggregate, the frescoes seem to suggest a reflection on states of work like starting, finishing, and resting.

This cycle of frescoes is the only case in Marées's career in which he had to face a certain degree of collaborative and scientific correction, as the room was part of a larger complex of natural history study. Anton Dohrn, who, along with Fiedler, commissioned both Marées and Hildebrand, was one of the leading zoologists of his day, and a student of Ernst Haeckel.[29] After much debate, the sole room singled out for fresco decoration was initially used as a music and entertainment room, dedicated to non-scientific pleasure. It still comes somewhat as a surprise that the final frescoes, covering the upper parts of all four walls, betray so little of their scientific context.

Although Marées mentioned in a letter to Fiedler of 1873 that '[t]he subject is completely taken from life,' the life he meant was certainly not the professional one of the scientists around him, except for the tavern scene on the east wall where his acquaintances have gathered (figure 4.4).[30] Here we see Dohrn himself, seated to the left, hat still in hand as if he had just arrived. Behind him Nicolaus Kleinenberg, another zoologist and student of Haeckel, Charles Grant, an English journalist and writer seated in the middle, and Marées, almost hidden behind the blond Hildebrand to the right.[31] These men were active, publishing scientists at the time Marées and Hildebrand lived with them, but to find traces of their Darwinian work on embryology and evolution or on the fauna and flora of the gulf of Naples in the frescoes themselves seems almost impossible.[32]

The frescoes instead describe a Neapolitan fisherman's existence, anachronistically depicted in the nude, trapped between routine realism and heroic display. Some pensive faces, some attempts to communicate, interrupt the rhythms of work (figure 4.5). These scenes are meant to read as topographically specific – had there been any contemporary recognition of the work before the start of the twentieth century, viewers would have certainly been able to recognize the cliffs and orange groves of nearby Sorrento early on.[33] The group of scientists and artists, looking over to the fishermen with all the social and class distance that this look implies, were nonetheless taking part in Neapolitan everyday life. The owner of the inn at the Palazzo Donn'Anna, where they used to gather, joins them on the steps; and a poor fish vendor – inspired by Titian's *Presentation of the Virgin at the Temple* – has spread out her meagre catch in the right corner. Despite the local colour, there is an air of isolation or remove in the immediate environment of these men – there is no Italian scientist or cultural critic among them. In fact Marées, in his entire correspondence, never wrote to a single Italian artist, intellectual, or friend; indeed, he hardly ever mentioned one and instead remained entirely entrenched in Fiedler's and Hildebrand's cultural circles in Germany. Charles Darwin and Karl Ernst von Baer, an early German embryologist, appear as busts set into the frescoes, the only emblems of the natural historical function of the building. But these are Hildebrand's busts, not Marées's, left to do that job. Marées's and Hildebrand's frescoes are trying, desperately, to keep the Italy where they lived, the modern Italy, out of the picture; the native figures do not seem to resemble the Neapolitan fishermen and orange pickers of Marées's day. And still, Marées thought that his subjects were 'completely taken from life' – but an Italian life lived as if modernity had not happened, nor ever would.

What was at stake, of course, was the loss of the utopia that was Italy and an acknowledgment of the processes of modernization. Marées seemed to betray a truly German desire, from Winckelmann and Goethe on, to keep Italy safeguarded from modernity – even Jacob Burckhardt called Italy 'modernitätsmüde' (too tired to modernize) and a 'stilles wunderbares Grabmonument' (quiet wonderful grave monument).[34] Marées's is a desperate vision of an unspoiled Italy, a vision entirely born of modernization. But his work spoke too deeply of its motive force, and his fetishization of the surface trapped time and its corporealization in an unstable social world. In Marées's art, a peaceful gathering of nudes was no longer an expression of a truly harmonious form of community, but was ridden with desire, eroticism, and the failure to communicate. The alienating forces of modern experience have, in Marées's work, fully entered Arcadia and transformed it.

Through his permanent refuge in Italy, it might seem that Marées tried to escape German history entirely at a time when most of his fellow countrymen celebrated their national unification and military strength. The 'philistines,' to use the term Nietzsche flaunted again and again in the face of the newly founded German Kaiserreich in the early 1870s, were most satisfied with the new state of things, not interested in change. Marées's paintings of the 1870s and 1880s can easily be read as counterweights to such celebratory cultural monuments as the Berlin Victory Column, inaugurated in 1874 and decorated with a historical and allegorical mosaic frieze by the Prussian court painter Anton von Werner. Nothing of that is found in Marées, it would seem, no instrumentalized classicism coded to contemporary Germany and its newfound glory. His paintings – at least in their subject matter – deliberately evoked a realm outside of history, and Italy offered, not specifically, but ideologically, the perfect background. For most of Marées's career, his works never speak of a specific modernity or a specific history.

Italy, in the 1870s and 1880s, was the place for Germans where such escapism was still possible, even traditional. Yet, Italy's own national development was deeply entangled in the process of German unification, on which its own political future depended. In 1870 German and Italian efforts at unification were established in mutual assistance at the same moment in history. Rome, the last Italian bastion in French hands, was finally taken by the Italian army in 1870 when Napoleon III had to withdraw his army from Italy for use in the Franco-Prussian War. France's declaration of war against Prussia was therefore one of the leading causes for the final founding of the unified Italian nation. The members of the intellectual circle of the Stazione were certainly aware of these facts and their political resonance. They frequently read and communicated with German cultural and political critics and historians like Ferdinand Gregorovius or Heinrich von Treitschke, who, in his famous study on Camillo Cavour, advocated a parallel between the German and Italian national unifications.[35] Such a line of argument had become popular since the early 1860s, intensified during the Prussian-Austrian disagreement over Italy in 1866, and reached its pinnacle in 1870/1. Italy's and Germany's new-found yet age-old national brotherhood – the two were frequently called 'old hostile *sisters*' in the press – was described by Gregorovius as follows: 'As both great nations had, for centuries, faced a similar misfortune, they both arose, at the same time, to full freedom and unity. They helped each other up, the one aiding the other, in the bitter battle for their national renewal.'[36] After

1870/1, one country's historical fate was inevitably and consequentially linked to that of the other. But as a result, Germany had to renegotiate its image of Italy, acknowledging it as a contemporary political entity. Tellingly, Marées left for Italy, almost permanently, in the early 1870s.

This history was meaningful and important to German expatriates in Italy in the years after 1871, and especially to Marées, who was himself a soldier in the Prussian army during the war, stationed in Cologne. His brother had been severely wounded in battle.[37] When Marées modelled the two women in the orange grove on the south wall so clearly after Johann Friedrich Overbeck's famous 1828 painting *Italia and Germania*, he could not have been unaware of the new resonance of this painting for his own political moment (figure 4.7).[38] If these are Italia and Germania in intimate conversation in Marées's fresco (figure 4.6) – one blond, one dark-haired, in an embrace similar to that in Overbeck's painting – then these figures speak to the recent development in German and Italian political relations. The union between the two national allegories suggests that this union is necessary to provide a potential for a *new* Arcadia and a *new* classicism, one engendered by Germans and Germany *for* Italy. The frescoes' harmonious, classicizing vision of the rural working class could only have been made possible, Italia and Germania suggest, *because* the two nations are now linked – Germany's unification process enabling Italy's and bringing it to a close. This, then, was Marées's challenge: to find expression for the pull between the new shifting historical conditions and the dream of an ancient immutable stability that led to Italy in the first place. Trying to speak political specificity *and* immutability is the trap that Marées's modern classicism ran into, or the task it set itself to resolve.

As Manfredo Tafuri has argued, the 'disintegration of the concept of form corresponded to the formation of a new metropolitan universe, located in Paris and elsewhere.'[39] Yet, for Marées, paradoxically, disintegration of form was a staple ingredient of classicism in marked opposition to metropolitan modernism. Marées confessed in a letter some years after the frescoes' completion that he wanted to remove one fresco, which he, fortunately, never did. There has been speculation about which one – he did not specify – ever since.[40] Maybe he meant the two women, since their Arcadian setting and romantic idyllicism could too easily be assimilated to a political reading that the entire cycle worked to forestall. But this episode shows just how difficult it had become, by the early 1870s, to paint parts of Europe as if untouched by history and political change – because they were not, nor could have been.

To be sure, by the latter half of the nineteenth century, the question of a painting's finish had emerged as one of the hot-button issues of the day, and the line between sketch and painting was anything but firmly drawn. Still, Marées, as an artist torn so completely between the two camps, remains a unique figure within nineteenth-century art. Marées felt the tension between his hopes for completion and his realization that his aesthetic practice could not allow for a finished product. In fact, he exploded, willingly or not, the categories of finish as such. 'Always at the right moment, someone should take my pictures away from me.'[41] The surfaces of Marées's paintings seem to testify to a lack of the restraint and confidence necessary to discipline his material. Shortly after Marées's death, many writers took the unfinishedness as a sign of more than just technical difficulty and, lending an ethical dimension to the debate, declared the artist lacking in will and moral strength. To them, he was the 'willing, struggling type of artist who would never reach his greatest promise and fulfilment.'[42] Such statements also imply that his will was not firm enough to ensure painterly success. And according to Karl von Pidoll, another of Marées's zealous students, it was not just his will that was not secure enough for the difficulties of his profession, but its very source, his masculinity: 'As noble as his instrument was, it was as difficult for him to learn to use it. It did not suit him in this endeavour to make use of his entire manhood with all its physical, spiritual, and moral forces.'[43]

Marées, in his constant search for finish, is understood as either a mere searcher unable to find or a fighter unable to win – a process he himself called his 'Don Quixoterie.'[44] He undoubtedly had the highest and most rigid moral expectations of his artistic identity, to live by the highest codes of honourability and integrity. He had equally high expectations of his masculine identity, so high, in fact, that the norm he envisioned for himself was far beyond his reach and thus left him constantly tormented. He was, in short, a man striving for a proper blend of masculine normativity and artistic control – and failing: 'It remains most desirable at the end of one's career, to know that one has fulfilled one's task as a man ... A self-sufficient artist can only be a man who has dominated over all prejudices.'[45]

The fraught relationship between masculinity and finish was emblematized by a vision of masculinity forestalled. This aesthetic adolescence was not just centrally thematized in Marées's painting, but was also a common trope within the writings of Marées's and especially Fiedler's Leipzig literary circle. In fact, in several short stories, we find main characters that echo Marées's own existential and artistic struggles. In Max von Schlägel's 'Torso,' a short artist's novel published in 1873 in *Der Salon für Literatur, Kunst und Gesellschaft*, the protagonist, Robert Pfeil, is an unsuccessful, thinly talented young artist called 'Torso,' because he cannot finish his paintings: '"You call me Torso jokingly because I can't finish anything ... Ideas, which threw me into a true ecstasy of creation, exploded underneath my fingers towards formlessness and monstrosity, or shrank into a shadowy grimace."'[46] Despite his professional difficulties, Torso is nevertheless considered a very moral character. Unable to watch the love of his youth grow more and more unhappy in her marriage to an old wealthy banker, Torso makes her – publicly and in front of her husband – face her unhappiness, though not entirely selflessly. Her divorce is – according to the author – the only morally justifiable decision, and Torso is credited with bringing it about. After marrying her himself and confirming his moral strength, Torso writes a book, is finally productive and turns into a 'complete' man: 'And here, we would like to end – since Torso died with the emergence of his creativity – Robert Pfeil, lives on as a *complete*, enviable man [*my emphasis*].'[47]

Another literary character who thought himself 'incomplete' is Fridolin, the main character in Adolf Wilbrandt's 1875 novel *Fridolin's Mystical Marriage*. In a conversation with his former student Leopold on the topic of marriage, Fridolin admits that he is already secretly married to his 'inner' female half. During the course of the novel, the art historian and philanthropist Fridolin falls in love with both men and women – first with the niece of his housekeeper, Ottilie, and later with her brother Ferdinand, whom he calls 'Ottilius.' But, as Fridolin explains, he will never have a gratifying relationship, since his second half – the one momentarily not in love – steps back into his conscience and intervenes. Always already internally married, yet always looking for a real-life partner, he is destined to fail, despite the fact that he has attained the highest level of civil achievement and a secure public post: 'Fridolin sighed with whimsical sentimentality. "While I, at forty, am not my own physician, have not finished my moral training, and have not mastered my profession! I am utterly incomplete – incapable of completion."'[48]

Thus, there seems to be a then current equation between the successful development of a masculine and moral self and the ability to finish or complete professional obligations. Marées seems to have believed, along with some of his contemporaries, that he was not morally equipped, which is to say not man enough, to finish his work. Yet at the same time, Marées seems to have carried this defining crisis to such extremity as to unmask the ideological equivalence among morality, manliness, and the ability to finish.

In this moralizing universe, a painting's finish, finally, had ethical and sexual consequences and evoked existential fears beyond the reach of an artist's brush. No painterly fantasies that sought what Marées sought – not a fossilized but a living, breathing Arcadia – would be able to shore the masculine artistic self under pressure from the destabilizing forces of life and its desires that these same fantasies unleashed. To paint an animated Arcadia thus required a firm manhood that the very aspiration to it foreclosed. Yet un-finish was also in some form or other a guarantee that this Arcadia would remain alive, evolving in the present. The price to pay for such a Mephistophelean bargain was self-doubt, born of a loss of control over the artist's materials and, concomitantly, his manliness.

Marées's whole career courted destabilization under the pressure of a need to complete, a will to complete, a not-being-able-to-complete, and a not-wanting-to-complete, which his critics sensed early on. The uneven surfaces of Marées's paintings, 'ruinous' as they were often called, played heavily into the hands of these critics and into the rhetoric of unfinishedness surrounding Marées's work shortly after his death. Paint supposedly rested on his canvases like 'cushions,' applied by a 'trowel.'[49] Adolf von Hildebrand drafted the following devastating verdict about Marées's abilities in an 1885 letter to Fiedler: 'An impossibly hideous technique, his things in horrible condition and saved merely by their decorative effects. Gagged up in effort and despair, gnawed off to the skeleton of a conception.'[50] The cracks and wrinkles were perhaps particularly unsettling for early viewers because they affected the human figure most. As Heinrich Ludwig predicted, Marées would have immense difficulty painting skin. His bodies, like those in the *Hesperides* protruding from their surroundings, are built up much higher than the rest of the image, a sign that the human form was of particular importance to Marées, but that it also produced notably more painterly anxiety. Marées, in his early critics' eyes, painted – amidst seemingly classical, stable, and timeless landscapes – a humanity that was visually scarred and decrepit. Despite the Elysian fields, a green shade of skin, a complexion of sickness, and the signs of aging make their round in Arcadia. And solid flesh appears as mere projection or shadow, held together not by signs of its materiality, but by effects on the bodies' surfaces. Heinrich Wölfflin, who wrote a brief essay on Marées in 1891, described this discrepancy between idyll and sickness as follows:

> What was striking here is the following: the most genuine beauty was paired with laughable deformity; the most magnificent movements, but the limbs here and there completely stunted; deep, saturated colours in the background that resign all effects to the glowing bodies, but the bodies themselves painted over again and again in a morbid manner so that whole cushions of paint rested on single parts and attracted all attention in an untoward manner.[51]

Such a feeling of morbidity in Arcadia extended far beyond Marées's technical inconsistencies. As Wölfflin intimates, movements, interactions, gestures, and even whole compositions were equally affected. Observe not just the deep crack in the left Hesperid's chest, but try to decipher the strange gestures of her companions. They are offering fruit and breasts at once, raising arms, extending hands to no particular avail – addressing no one, directly, inside or outside the painting's visual field. There is no narrative cohesion to this scene, or to this triptych, just an uncertainty about what there might be to convey. Similarly, in Marées's *The Golden Age II*, painted between 1880 and 1883, we see a gathering of male and female nudes in an Arcadian landscape (figure 4.8). There seems to be hardly any narrative structure to this allegorical painting, no communication between the protagonists, just some shyly exchanged glances and gestures. Bodies are too composed, hips and shoulders too bent, to bespeak naturalness and comfort. The naked body is merely put on display here, in its canonical and erotic dimensions.

Yet, this is a largely empty eroticism, expurgated and distanced from what we know as the workings of human desire, though not completely: beyond the erotic platter including offerings of breasts as fruit, there are even naked bodies conjoined, yet unresponsive, genitals to an equal degree exposed and covered, children partaking in the same erotic teasing as their grown-up counterparts.[52] This is an Arcadian eros, playful and innocent, distanced from the sweat and odour of the human form, the rawness of desire. But it nonetheless opens onto a prospect of sexual desires unwelcome in other nineteenth-century painting, desires like homoeroticism.[53] (Marées himself has often been said to have had homoerotic inclinations towards his pupils, to say the least, especially toward Adolf Hildebrand. Marées never married and the few times he courted a woman, such as Melanie Tauber, he did so in exceedingly formalized and non-committal terms.) In Marées's *Three Male Youths under Orange Trees* of 1875–80, three young, naked men point or even stare at each other's crotches, while picking fruit or simply resting (figure 4.9). Genitals, again, can be both carefully covered, or fully exposed, gestures and gazes empty or meaningful. Marées is intent on showing us a world innocent enough to stand completely apart from the modern world and the metropolis, yet aware of modernity's dense investment in erotic and sexual imagery.

The utter composure and strange purposelessness of the naked figure in Marées's art surely added to the perception that his bodies were 'classical' and bereft of incident, but then, in the same measure, also not human. In the words of many critics, his figures showed an antique, 'classical' existence, freed from history, vicissitude, the social and personal. At first glance, Marées's painting seems the perfect 'Existenzmalerei' or 'Existenzbild' – 'painting of existence' – as Jacob Burckhardt called it in his 1855 *Cicerone* when describing Venetian painting like that of Veronese.[54] He meant to describe a type of painting that sought the underlying structures of life, not its distracting narrative, incident, or expression. For Fiedler, this quality was Marées's attempt to achieve an 'illusion of life.'[55] Fiedler meant to suggest an ontological exploration of the essence of existence, the deep structure of all human relation expressed in classical forms of permanent stability. Yet Marées tried for more, if not the impossible: to write the classical in forms that also bespoke a more modern sense of the contingency of reality and desire. But if bodies blur and look strangely uncomfortable, then the paintings' deep humanism can never be fully successful. The classical landscape and the classical body that Marées set out to recover seem to be in a state of development, like the paint itself, revealing their incomplete construction rather than stable essences. Over- or un-finish supplements Marées's humanist scenes, constantly haunts the idyll. The supposedly natural state of nakedness in Arcadia reveals its artificiality, because its painful painterly production is left too overtly visible.

A similar contradiction between the processual and the stable nature of the artwork marks Marées's relation to the aesthetic theories of his patron and mentor Conrad Fiedler. Fiedler's neo-Kantian aesthetics, which he propounded in essays written during the 1880s like 'Modern Naturalism and Artistic Truth' and 'The Origin of Artistic Activity,' influenced such important late-nineteenth-century texts as Adolf von Hildebrand's *The Problem of Form* published in 1893.[56] In his writings, Fiedler proved to be less interested in the final artwork and its interpretation than its creative process. Analytically, at least, Fiedler always favoured the artistic individual and his perceptual capacities over the importance of inspiration or even the final product those faculties had wrought. To be sure, theory and practice never fully cooperate, and a painter's working methods were far from Fiedler's preoccupations: an artist's cognition, not hands, concerned him. On the topic of Fiedler's influence on Marées, and vice versa, scholars are therefore anything but united, claiming for Marées a residue of mimeticism and illusionism that was foreign to Fiedler's postulates of art's autonomy as its own reality.[57] In Fiedler's early essay 'On Judging Works of Visual Arts' of 1876, art is said *not* to be a reproduction of reality, but reality itself. Art, in this theory of cognition, is a genuine vector of human experience – 'a self-realizing reality. In that it equals language,' to quote Gottfried Boehm, who has written extensively and most persuasively about Fiedler.[58] Fiedler himself formulated his proposition most succinctly in 'Modern Naturalism':

> If, for ages, two major principles – that of the imitation and that of the transformation of reality – have fought over the right to be considered the true expression of the nature of artistic activity, then a settlement of the dispute seems possible only if we replace these principles by a third: the principle of the creation of reality. Because art is one of the primary means by which humanity produces reality.[59]

Fiedler thus concluded, very much in Marées's spirit, that the artwork could only replicate processes of 'becoming' – like nature and reality itself – rather than represent and freeze a completed 'being' that existed outside of art. Because nature, life, and reality – as emblems of the world's contingency – were Fiedler's models, the artwork was destined to an eternal doing and undoing, ultimately unfinishable and as circumstantial as the real:

> The realization that our entire possession of sensory reality is limited to events of perception and conception which do not represent a steady condition, but are composed of becoming and disappearing, of growing

> and dying – this realization leads us to believe that in reality, we perceive not just a fugitive, but also an underdeveloped or atrophying construction.[60]

If our conception of reality is thus defined as one of eternal flux, growth, and development, art, similarly, is rendered a sphere of comparably autonomous, yet unceasing *production*, not *re-production*. But what exactly *is* the work of art, then, and what are its new norms and resistances, if not entirely self-imposed? If art should *be* nature and not be *like* nature, then the artwork was also structured by the very principles of reality that governed the world at large and from which even the artwork's autonomy offered no relief. Marées called this the 'turmoil of modern jumble.'[61] Art had to risk its own undoing, lose its boundaries and definitions, for, as Fiedler insisted, reality, any reality, was by necessity changing and in perpetual flux. No wonder Fiedler shied away from establishing more accurately what such an art object would actually look or *be* like. Marées, paradoxically the artist of the classical past, of Arcadian idyll, became for Fiedler the artist who might – at least at the outset of their partnership – create a painterly response to his understanding of reality as contingency.

If a painting's state of completion, by extension, cannot even be realized theoretically, it can, in practice, only be deferred *ad infinitum* and never reached. 'Failure thus becomes a historical necessity.'[62] Wölfflin, for instance, found a contradiction in Marées's work and pointed directly to his necessary failure. On the one hand, he claimed that Marées sought 'the normal and general. In the composition of his figures, as well as in their movements, he avoided the special, the exceptional.'[63] On the other, alluding to Marées's convulsive surfaces, he declared his figures painted in a 'sickly manner.'[64] Wölfflin thus evacuated any possible connection Marées might have hoped for between his subjects and his paint handling.

In Marées's understanding, a possible version of a modern classicism might be one that declared a continuous, autonomous painterly process – art *as* its own reality and nature – as a substitute for, or correlate to, classicism's claim to the 'natural' body or the 'natural' landscape. This new classicism, although Fiedler never called it such, would use a rhetoric of art – in subject matter and technique – *as* nature, rather than *like* nature. Unlike Fiedler, who would not venture to make such connections between theme and handling, Marées would continue to hope that the classical could be communicated *both* through the application of paint and through Arcadian compositions. He continued to paint the *Hesperides*, or a *Golden Age*, and never let go of subject matter altogether. The 'lively' layers of paint on his surfaces were always to some extent autonomous from, yet linked to, what they were seeking to describe and define. Yet, Marées did not seem to fully realize, or was unable to control, the fact that his paint's autonomy was somehow at odds with his subjects. Reality's flux and Arcadia's essence were written in different temporal frames – in Marées's paintings, process and timelessness quarrel rather than unite. Nature in Marées's works seems to promise both an underlying essence *and* an unending process of becoming. But perhaps the point of his art making can best be described as follows: in order to give the classical idiom a modern form, Marées permitted it the contamination of the temporal. But the advent of the temporal in the classical inaugurates its annihilation.

The classic spirit will probably always be crosscut with hopes and aspirations that the classical can, one day, be truly reborn. But it will also bear the utter pessimism that the past is forever lost *in* the past and that a modern classicism would amount to nothing but an awakening of ghosts better left sleeping. Or even worse: the pleasures of the classical and its pledge of harmony are too premised on containment. As Henry James testified, it was precisely through its double-edged fascination for northern Europeans that Italy offered itself up to a new generation of German cultural pessimists like Thomas Mann and many more. It was a space where the cultural losses of modernity's rise could be all the more keenly felt and therefore all the more theatrically mourned. Italy was beautiful *and* tragic after all, northern Europe's lure and horror. Classicism, at least in the manner Marées conceived of it, was a modernization of artistic form out to halt modernity in its tracks, yet unsure and internally conflicted as to how much of the modern – and its presentness, change, alienation, and disintegration – it could actually assimilate.

## NOTES

In addition to the conference in Toronto that provided the occasion for this anthology, a different version of this paper was presented at the College Art Association annual conference in Chicago on 3 March, and at the University of California, Berkeley, on 13 April 2001. I am grateful not only to Vojtěch Jirat-Wasiutyński and the co-organizers of the Toronto symposium, but also to the audiences at these three events; all their responses have helped to strengthen the arguments of this essay. I would like to thank Andreas Beyer, Whitney Davis, Christiane Groeben, Katherine Kuenzli, Thomas Laqueur, and Monika Wagner for sharing their thoughts on Marées with me and for providing helpful critique to earlier incarnations of the manuscript. In particular, my gratitude belongs to Jonathan D. Katz, without whose continued stimulating conversations on the topics of Marées, Germany, sexuality, and failure, as well as editorial guidance, this essay would not have been possible. All translations from the German are my own.

1 The literature on American and northern European artists in Italy is vast. For recent over-views of the field, see *The Lure of Italy: American Artists and the Italian Experience, 1760–1914*, ed. T.E. Stebbins, exh. cat., Museum of Fine Arts (Boston, 1992). For a comprehensive study and bibliography on the artistic circle central to this essay, see *'In uns liegt Italien.' Die Kunst der Deutsch-Römer*, exh. cat., Haus der Kunst (Munich, 1987–8) and *Arnold Böcklin e la cultura artistica in Toscana, Hans von Marées, Adolf von Hildebrand, Max Klinger, Karl Stauffer-Bern, Albert Welti*, exh. cat., Palazzina Mangani (Fiesole, 1980).

2 Henry James, 'The Saint's Afternoon and Others (1900–1909),' in James, *Italian Hours*, ed. J. Auchard (University Park: Pennsylvania State University Press, 1992), 306, 311–12.

3 See, for instance, Karl Heinz Herke, 'Hans von Marées und die Zukunft des klassischen Ideals,' *Hochland* 18, 1 (1920–1): 59–66. For a critical investigation of the uses of the term classicism in early Marées criticism, see Anne-S. Domm, *Der 'klassische' Hans von Marées und die Existenzmalerei Anfang des 20. Jahrhunderts*, PhD dissertation, Eberhard-Karls-University Tübingen, 1987 (Munich: Neue Schriftenreihe des Stadtarchivs, 1989). On Marées's alleged classicism, cf. also Alfred Neumeyer, 'Hans von Marées and the Classical Doctrine in the Nineteenth Century,' *Art Bulletin* 20, 1 (1938): 291–311; Neumeyer, 'Hans von Marées' Arcadia,' in P. Bloch, T. Buddensieg, A. Hentzen, and T. Müller, eds, *Intuition und Kunstwissenschaft: Festschrift für Hanns Swarzenski zum 70. Geburtstag am 30.8.1973* (Berlin: Gebr. Mann, 1973), 559–69; and L.D. Ettlinger, 'Hans von Marées and the Academic Tradition,' *Yale University Art Gallery Bulletin* 33, 3 (1972): 67–84.

4 Frank Kermode, *The Classic: Literary Images of Permanence and Change* (1975) (Cambridge, MA: Harvard University Press, 1983), 16. Cf. also chapter 3, 'Strange Classicism: Aesthetic Vision in Winckelmann, Nietzsche, and Thomas Mann,' in Harold Mah, *Enlightenment Phantasies:*

*Cultural Identity in France and Germany, 1750–1914* (Ithaca, NY: Cornell University Press, 2003), 71–115.

5 In art history, recent scholarship on Winckelmann in particular has explored the relationship among art, art history, and homoeroticism. See Whitney Davis, 'Winckelmann Divided: Mourning the Death of Art History,' in *Gay and Lesbian Studies in Art History*, ed. W. Davis, *Journal of Homosexuality* 27, 1–2 (1994): 141–59; and Alex Potts, *Flesh and the Ideal: Winckelmann and the Origins of Art History* (New Haven, CT: Yale University Press, 1994). On the Mediterranean as fertile ground of homoerotic fantasy and projection, cf. Robert Aldrich, *The Seduction of the Mediterranean: Writing, Art and Homosexual Fantasy* (New York, London: Routledge, 1993).

6 On Fiedler's philanthropy and his generous support of Marées, see Peter Hirschfeld, *Mäzene: Die Rolle des Auftraggebers in der Kunst* (Munich: Deutscher Kunstverlag, 1968), 237–47.

7 Even friends were rarely admitted to Marées's studio, and critical opinion written during the artist's lifetime is therefore extremely scarce.

8 Cf. Georg Fuchs, *Deutsche Form: Betrachtungen über die Berliner Jahrhundertausstellung und die Münchner Retrospektive* (Munich, Leipzig: Georg Müller, 1907), 313–32. See also, among many other examples, Ferdinand Avenarius, 'Marées als Mode,' *Der Kunstwart* 22, 2 (June 1909): 371–2. For a comprehensive bibliography of the early criticism on Marées, see *Hans von Marées*, ed., C. Lenz (Munich, 1987–8), 363–76; Uta Gerlach-Laxner, *Hans von Marées: Katalog seiner Gemälde* (Munich: Prestel, 1980), 236–8.

9 For an early comparative study of Marées and Cézanne, see Oskar Hagen, 'Marées und Cézanne,' *Ganymed: Blätter der Marées Gesellschaft* 1 (1919): 60–71. Cf. as well *Hans von Marées und die Moderne in Deutschland*, exh. cat., Kunsthalle Bielefeld, Kunstmuseum Winterthur, 1987–8; Gert Schiff, 'Hans von Marées and His Place in Modern Painting,' *Yale University Art Gallery Bulletin* 33, 3 (1972): 85–102; and Werner Hofmann, 'Courbet et Marées,' *Revue de l'art* 45 (1979): 31–6.

10 Conrad Fiedler, *Hans von Marées* (1889), ed. H. Uhde-Bernays (Munich: Nymphenburger, 1947).

11 Richard R. Brettell, *Modern Art, 1851–1929* (Oxford, New York: Oxford University Press, 1999), 114–16. *Adolph Menzel, 1815–1905. Master Drawings from East Berlin*, ed. P. Betthausen, exh. cat., Frick Collection (New York, 1990). *Adolph Menzel, 1815–1905: Between Romanticism and Impressionism*, ed. Claude Keisch, exh. cat., National Gallery of Art (Washington, 1996–7). And, most recently, Michael Fried, *Menzel's Realism: Art and Embodiment in Nineteenth-Century Berlin* (New Haven, CT: Yale University Press, 2002).

12 This does not hold true, though, for his accomplished drawings, which are also virtually unknown outside Germany. Cf. the following German exhibition catalogues: *Hans von Marées: Zeichnungen*, exh. cat., Pfalzgalerie, Kaiserslautern, 1982; *Hans von Marées: Zeichnungen*, exh. cat., Von der Heydt-Museum, Wuppertal, 1987; *Hans von Marées: Zeichnungen. Eigener Bestand*, exh. cat., Staatliche Graphische Sammlung, Munich, 1987–8.

13 For two recent accounts of the complex interplay between autonomous matter/painterly logic and representational/experiential illusionism in Cézanne, see T.J. Clark, 'Phenomenality and Materiality in Cézanne,' in T. Cohen, ed., *Material Events: Paul de Man and the Afterlife of Theory* (Minneapolis: University of Minnesota Press, 2001), 93–113; and Kathryn A. Tuma, 'Cézanne and Lucretius at the Red Rock,' *Representations* 78 (Spring 2002): 56–85.

14 'Indem Marées seinem künstlerischen Ausdrucksbedürfnis eine Form suchte, die von keinerlei gegenständlichem Inhalt bestimmt war, tat er einen neuen Schritt'; Fiedler, *Hans von Marées*, 43. Compare: 'Marées's pictures offer no interest in subject matter.' Heinrich Wölfflin, 'Hans von Marées' (1891), in Wölfflin, *Kleine Schriften (1886–1933)*, ed. J. Gantner (Basel: Benno Schwabe, 1946), 78.

15 This tendency in Marées scholarship is best exemplified by the contributions to the catalogue of the large Marées retrospective of 1987–8 in Munich: *Hans von Marées*, ed. C. Lenz (Munich, 1987–8).

16 Gerd Blum, '"Symbolische Akte": Zum Mittelbild des Hesperidentriptychons von Hans von Marées,' *Münchner Jahrbuch der bildenden Kunst* 47 (1996): 147–66. See also Gerd Blum, *Hans von Marées: Autobiographische Malerei zwischen Mythos und Moderne* (Munich: Deutscher Kunstverlag, 2005).

17 Marées in a letter from Rome to Fiedler, 24 June 1883. Hans von Marées, *Briefe*, ed. A.-S. Domm (Munich, Zurich: R. Piper, 1987), 260. On Marées's technique, cf. Hubertus Falkner von Sonnenburg, 'Die Maltechnik des Hans von Marées,' in *Hans von Marées*, ed. C. Lenz (Munich, 1987–8), 105–26. See also Uta Gerlach-Laxner, 'Notizen zum Problem des technischen Zustandes im Werk Hans von Marées,' in H. Althöfer, ed., *Das 19. Jahrhundert und die Restaurierung: Beiträge zur Malerei, Maltechnik und Konservierung* (Munich: Georg D.W. Callwey, 1987), 198–201.

18 For the most recent, extensive treatment of the *Hesperides*, see Frank Schmidt, *Fresken malen ohne Wände: Zur Funktion, Genese und Bedeutung der Triptychen Hans von Marées'* (Weimar: VDG, 2003), 25–52.

19 'Auch pflegt sich das Material für Übereilungen zu rächen.' Karl von Pidoll, *Aus der Werkstatt eines Künstlers: Erinnerungen an den Maler Hans*

*von Marées aus den Jahren 1880–81 und 1884–85* (Luxembourg: V. Bück, Leo Bück, 1890), 74.

20 See especially the chapter 'Die Wasserfarbentechnik zur Zeit des van Eyck, in Beziehung zur Technik der Oelfarben.' Heinrich Ludwig, *Über die Grundsätze der Ölmalerei und das Verfahren der classischen Meister* (1876), 2nd ed. (Leipzig: Wilhelm Engelmann, 1893), 7–38. In his letters, Marées mentioned Ludwig, who published a monumental study on Leonardo da Vinci in 1882, several times. See Marées, *Briefe*, 134–5, 138. Vis-à-vis Marées's technique, cf. also Pidoll, *Aus der Werkstatt eines Künstlers*, 65–80; Lorenz Dittmann, 'Zur Klassizität der Farbgestaltung bei Hans von Marées,' in J. Meyer zur Capellen and G. Oberreuter-Kronable, eds, *Klassizismus: Epoche und Probleme. Festschrift für Eric Forssman zum 70. Geburtstag* (Hildesheim, Zurich, New York: Georg Olms, 1987), 99–117; and Stefan-Maria Mittendorf, *Farbe Bekennen: Tizian – Rembrandt – Marées. Versuch über die Farbe an Münchner Werken zur Bestimmung ihres Stellenwertes in der Kunst Hans von Marées'* (Frankfurt am Main: Peter Lang, 1997).

21 '[D]ie sogenannte Ausführung würde nichts Wesentliches beitragen'; Adolf von Hildebrand in *Beilage der Münchner Neuesten Nachrichten*, 9 January 1909. Cited in Julius Meier-Graefe, *Hans von Marées: Sein Leben und sein Werk*, 3 vols. (Munich, Leipzig: R. Piper, 1909–10), 3: 336. The most comprehensive account of Hildebrand's career is Sigrid Braunfels-Esche, *Adolf von Hildebrand* (Berlin: Deutscher Verlag für Kunstwissenschaft, 1993). See also Bernhard Sattler, ed., *Adolf von Hildebrand und seine Welt: Briefe und Erinnerungen* (Munich: Georg D.W. Callwey, 1962).

22 'Auf etwas habe ich mich ertappt, dass ich jedes Mal, wenn ich von einer Sache sage, sie ist fertig, ich mich eigentlich erst am Anfang befinde. Eigentlich fertig wird ein Kunstwerk nie'; from Rome to Fiedler, 11 June 1879. Marées, *Briefe*, 190; for similar formulations, see 185, 200, 202, and 256.

23 '[M]eine unfertigen Versuche'; from Rome to Fiedler, 27 July 1878. Ibid., 180.

24 'Nach unsäglichen Mühen und tausend Hindernissen ist mir dies endlich gelungen. Morgen schliesse ich definitv ab'; from Rome to his brother Georg, 21 May 1884. Ibid., 274.

25 '[M]it der Probirepoche [*sic*] abgeschlossen'; from Rome to Georg, 27 September 1880. Ibid., 223.

26 'Ich behalte indessen immer die Hauptsache im Auge, d. i. das Vorliegende zunächst (nicht fertig zu machen) sondern zu vollenden'; from Rome to Georg, 19 December 1884. Ibid., 283. Charles Baudelaire, 'The Salon of 1845,' in Baudelaire, *Art in Paris, 1845–1862: Salons and*

*Other Exhibitions*, ed. J. Mayne (Ithaca, NY: Cornell University Press, 1981), 1–32, here 24. Compare the insightful comments on Marées's problems of finishing by Walter Seitter, *Hans von Marées: Ein anderer Philosoph* (Graz, Vienna: Droschl, 1993), 18–24.

27 'Fresco malen, im Großen mit der Form hantieren, thät [*sic*] heut allen Malern gut, es ist ein ängstliches, ewiges Corrigieren [*sic*]'; from Florence to Fiedler, 23 June 1881. Günther Jachmann, ed., *Adolf von Hildebrands Briefwechsel* (Dresden: Wolfgang Jess, 1927), 154. See also Magdalena Droste, *Das Fresko als Idee: Zur Geschichte öffentlicher Kunst im 19. Jahrhundert* (Münster: Lit, 1980).

28 On the Stazione Zoologica, see Karl Josef Partsch, *Die Zoologische Station in Neapel: Modell internationaler Wissenschaftszusammenarbeit* (Göttingen: Vandenhoeck & Ruprecht, 1980); Domenico De Masi, 'La Fabrica della scienza,' *Rivista IBM* 1 (1987): 1–16; and *The Naples Zoological Station at the Time of Anton Dohrn*, ed. C. Groeben, I. Müller, exh. cat., Stazione Zoologica (Naples, 1975). And on the fresco cycle, cf. Christiane Groeben, *Der Freskensaal der Stazione Zoologica Anton Dohrn: Biographie eines Kunstwerkes* (Naples: Macchiaroli, 1995); Bernhard Degenhart, *Hans von Marées: Die Fresken in Neapel* (Munich: Prestel, 1958); Laura Giusti, 'Hans von Marées alla Stazione Zoologica di Napoli: Tecnica esecutiva e interventi di restauro,' *ON – OttoNovecento* 3 (1999): 30–4; Karlheinz Nowald, '"Das ungeheure Drama des Lebendigen" – Hans von Marées' Neapler Fresken,' in U. Bischoff, ed., *Romantik und Gegenwart: Festschrift für Jens Christian Jensen zum 60. Geburtstag* (Cologne: DuMont, 1988), 165–73; Roswitha Siewert, 'Die Neapler Fresken des Hans von Marées in der Auseinandersetzung zwischen Bayern und Preußen,' *Jahrbuch Preußischer Kulturbesitz* 21 (1984): 293–354; Hans Wille, 'Vorzeichnungen zu den Neapler Fresken im Wuppertaler Skizzenbuch des Hans von Marées,' *Wallraf-Richartz-Jahrbuch* 21 (1959): 227–34. The proceedings of an international symposium on Marées, recently published, also deal at length with the Naples frescoes: Lea Ritter Santini and Christiane Groeben, eds, *Arte come autobiografia. Kunst als Autobiographie: Hans von Marées* (Naples, Stazione Zoologica Anton Dohrn and Gaetano Macchiaroli, 2005). This essay was written, however, before this collection was published.

29 For the most extensive account of Anton Dohrn's career (1840–1909), see Theodor Heuss, *Anton Dohrn* (1940) (Stuttgart, Tübingen: Rainer Wunderlich, Hermann Leins, 1948). See also Alfred Kühn, *Anton Dohrn und die Zoologie seiner Zeit* (Naples: Stazione Zoologica di Napoli, 1950).

30 'Der Gegenstand ist ganz aus dem Leben gegriffen'; from Naples to Fiedler, 20 July 1873. Marées, *Briefe*, 101.

31 Charles Grant's (1841–89) *Stories of Naples and the Camorra* (London: Macmillan) were published in 1896. On Grant, see Alice Sieben's brief biographical postscript in Charles Grant, *Peppiniello* (Ulm: Aegis, 1947), 104–6.

32 Anton Dohrn published, among many other publications, *Der Ursprung der Wirbelthiere und das Princip des Functionswechsels: Genealogische Skizzen* (Leipzig: W. Engelmann, 1875). Kleinenberg's evolutionary publications at the time of his contact with Marées included *Hydra: Eine anatomisch-entwicklungsgeschichtliche Untersuchung* (Leipzig: Wilhelm Engelmann, 1872). See Irmgard Müller, 'Der "Hydriot" Nikolai Kleinenberg, oder: Spekulation und Beobachtung,' *Medizinhistorisches Journal* 8 (1973): 131–53; and Gunter Mann, 'Hans v. Marées' Ölstudie des "Hydrioten" Nikolai Kleinenberg zu den Fresken der Zoologischen Station in Neapel, 1873,' *Medizinhistorisches Journal* 10 (1975): 146–50. Christiane Groeben has also edited Dohrn's important correspondence with the leading scientists and evolutionists of his day: Christiane Groeben, ed., *Charles Darwin–Anton Dohrn. Correspondence* (Naples: Macchiaroli, 1982); Groeben, ed., *Correspondence. Karl Ernst von Baer–Anton Dohrn* (Philadelphia: American Philosophical Society, 1993). On portraying friends, and on the importance of friendship in Marées's paintings, see Christian Lenz, 'Im Zentrum der Kunst. Ein Freundschaftsbild von Marées,' in S. Michalski, ed., *Martin Gosebruch 1919–1992, TU Brunsvigensien* 22 (Technische Universität Braunschweig, 2000): 32–77; Roman Zieglgänsberger, *Hans von Marées als Bildnismaler* (Frankfurt am Main: Peter Lang, 2001), 45–53.

33 See Marées in a letter from Naples to Melanie Tauber, 18 July 1873. Marées, *Briefe*, 99. Cf. Helmut Börsch-Supan, 'Das "Orangenbild" von Hans von Marées in der Berliner Nationalgalerie,' in T. Buddensieg and M. Winner, eds, *Kunsthistorische Studien: Hans Kauffmann zum 70. Geburtstag 1966* (Berlin: Bruno Hessling, 1968), 1–9.

34 Quoted in Jens Petersen, *Italienbilder–Deutschlandbilder: Gesammelte Aufsätze* (Cologne: SH–Verlag, 1999), 103.

35 See the essays in Petersen, *Italienbilder–Deutschlandbilder,* especially the essay on Gregorovius, 35–59, and 'Risorgimento und italienischer Einheitsstaat im Urteil Deutschlands nach 1860,' 90–119. See also Heinrich von Treitschke, 'Cavour' (1867), in von Treitschke, *Historische und politische Aufsätze: Neue Folge,* 2 vols. (Leipzig: S. Hirzel, 1870), 1: 349–494. Cf. also Ernst Portner, *Die Einigung Italiens im Urteil liberaler deutscher Zeitgenossen: Studie zur inneren Geschichte des kleindeutschen Liberalismus* (Bonn: Ludwig Röhrscheid, 1959).

36 '[W]ie beide großen Nationen Jahrhunderte lang ein ähnliches Mißge-

schick erduldet haben, so erstanden sie auch in gleicher Zeit zu ihrer vollen Freiheit und Einheit. Sie richteten sich auf, die eine durch Hilfe der andern, … in dem harten Kampf um ihre nationale Erneuerung.' Letter to Ritter Venturi, 27 August 1872, quoted in Petersen, *Italienbilder–Deutschlandbilder*, 45.

37 See Marées's letters written between July 1870 and January 1871. Marées, *Briefe*, 59–66.

38 The influence of the painting on Marées's fresco has been noted many times. See Christian Lenz, 'Die Fresken von Marées in Neapel,' in *Hans von Marées*, 60–2. On Overbeck's painting, cf. *Johann Friedrich Overbeck, Italia und Germania*, exh. cat., Staatliche Graphische Sammlung (Munich, 2002).

39 Manfredo Tafuri, *The Sphere and the Labyrinth: Avant-gardes and Architecture from Piranesi to the 1970s* (Cambridge, MA: MIT, 1987), 15. Marées visited Paris in July 1869 and saw some examples of the modern French school – he was not impressed. Which paintings exactly he saw is unknown. Letter from Paris to Hildebrand, 23 July 1869. Marées, *Briefe*, 53–4.

40 Cf. Lenz, in *Hans von Marées*, 60.

41 'Einmal sagte er in bezug auf sein häufiges Übermalen: "Man müsste mir die Bilder immer zur rechten Zeit wegnehmen."' This statement is quoted in the reminiscences of Artur Volkmann, Marées's student. Artur Volkmann, *Vom Sehen und Gestalten: Ein Beitrag zur Geschichte der jüngsten deutschen Kunst* (Jena: Eugen Diederichs, 1912), 37.

42 'Typus des wollenden, ringenden, nie zur letzten Erfüllung und Abrundung gelangenden Künstlers'; Max Osborn, *Meisterwerke der Kunst: Eine kurzgefaßte Geschichte der Kunst* (Berlin, Vienna: Ullstein, 1909), 414.

43 'So edel das Instrument, so schwierig erschien ihm aber auch die Erlernung seines Gebrauches und er stand nicht an, zu diesem Geschäfte das ganze Mannesleben mit allen seinen physischen, geistigen und sittlichen Kräften in Anspruch zu nehmen'; Pidoll, *Aus der Werkstatt eines Künstlers*, 84–5.

44 Marées, *Briefe*, 39, 57, 69, and 133. Marées also believed that if he continued to search for strength, the results of his efforts to paint would improve. Ibid., 41, 82, 174, and 179.

45 'Das Wünschenswertheste [*sic*] bleibt immer am Ende seiner Laufbahn das Bewusstsein haben zu können, seiner Aufgabe als Mann nachgekommen zu sein … Ein selbständiger Künstler (in anderen Fächern wird es eben so sein) kann nur ein Mann sein, der über alle hergebrachten Vorurtheile [*sic*] Herr geworden ist'; letter to Fiedler, mid-January 1878. Ibid., 174.

46 '"Ihr nennt mich spottweise Torso, weil ich nichts fertig bringe … Eine

Idee, die mich in einen wahren Schöpfungstaumel stürzte, schwoll unter meinen Fingern auf zum Formlosen, Ungeheuerlichen, oder schrumpfte zusammen zur schattenhaften Fratze."' Max von Schlägel, 'Torso,' ed. E. Dohm and J. Rodenberg, *Der Salon für Literatur, Kunst und Gesellschaft* 7 (Leipzig, ca. 1873): 41. Hans Marbach, a novelist that Marées knew and appreciated, also published in this literary journal read by Fiedler's Leipzig literary circle. See Marées's letter from Florence to Georg, 11 April 1874. Marées, *Briefe*, 117.

47 'Und hier wollen wir enden – denn mit dem Entstehen dieser Werke ist Torso gestorben – und es lebt nur noch ein ganzer, beneidenswerther [*sic*] Mann – Robert Pfeil'; Schlägel, 'Torso,' 59.

48 'Fridolin seufzte, mit sentimentalischem Humor. "Und ich, mit vierzig Jahren, bin weder als Selbstarzt, noch als Charakter, noch als Berufsmeister fertig. Ich bin die Unfertigkeit. Ich bin das Niefertigwerden."' Adolf Wilbrandt, *Fridolin's heimlich Ehe: Nach Erinnerungen und Mittheilungen* (Vienna: L. Rosner, 1875), 43. English quote taken from Adolf Wilbrandt, *Fridolin's Mystical Marriage: A Study of an Original Founded on Reminiscences of a Friend* (New York: William S. Gottsberger, 1884), 45. On the novel, see James W. Jones, *'We of the Third Sex.' Literary Representations of Homosexuality in Wilhelmine Germany* (New York, Frankfurt: Peter Lang, 1990), 115–28. Marées and Wilbrandt knew one another, as Marées mentioned their meeting in Rome in 1879 when writing to Fiedler: 'Der Dichter Wilbrandt war einige Zeit hier und ich habe mich sehr gut mit ihm unterhalten; er ist doch ein feiner, liebenswürdiger und intelligenter Mensch, von dem man wünschen möchte, dass er in eine richtige Bahn gelangte.' Marées in a letter to Fiedler, 11 December 1879. Marées, *Briefe*, 200–1.

49 'Kissen,' 'Maurerkelle.' Otto Krebs, 'Hans von Marées,' *Pan* 5 (1899): 116. See also Hermann Becker, *Deutsche Maler: Von Asmus Carstens an bis auf die neuere Zeit – in einzelnen Werken kritisch geschildert* (Leipzig: Carl Reissner, 1888), 238.

50 'Eine unmögliche scheußliche Technik, die Sachen in schrecklichstem Zustand und nur die decorative [*sic*] Wirkung gerettet. Zusammengewürgt mit Mühe und Verzweiflung, abgenagt bis zum Gerippe einer Vorstellung'; from Florence, 5 January 1885. G. Jachmann, ed., *Adolf von Hildebrands Briefwechsel mit Conrad Fiedler* (Dresden: Wolfgang Jess, 1927), 219–20.

51 'Was auffallend dabei war: die lauterste Schönheit war gepaart mit lächerlicher Mißbildung; die herrlichsten Bewegungen, aber die Glieder teilweise ganz verkümmert; tiefe, satte Farben im Grund, die alle Wirkung

den leuchtenden Körpern zuleiteten, die Körper selbst aber in krankhafter Weise so überstrichen und wieder überstrichen, daß ganze Kissen von Farbe auf den einzelnen Teilen lagerten und die Aufmerksamkeit in widriger Weise auf sich zogen'; Wölfflin, 'Hans von Marées,' 75. See also Susanne Anderson-Riedel, 'Heinrich Wölfflin, Hans von Marées and the Principles of Art,' *Pantheon* 57 (1999): 151–60.

52 On Marées's depiction of children see Werner Schnell, 'Das Kind als Ziel. Hans von Marées' Suche nach den Anfängen,' *Wallraf-Richartz-Jahrbuch* 50 (1989): 219–49.

53 There is evidence of homoeroticism in both Marées's correspondence and his art, but a full account of the relation between his sexuality and his work is still outstanding. Cf. Aldrich, *The Seduction of the Mediterranean*, 138–41. See also David Getsy, 'Behind Formalism: Obscured Eroticism in Adolf von Hildebrand's Problem of Form,' unpublished lecture, 1998. I thank David Getsy for allowing me to read his compelling manuscript. Marees's courtship of Melanie Tauber is well documented in several letters. See Marées, *Briefe*, 158–66. Cf. Alexandra Pätzold, 'Die Knabenliebe, der Antikendiskurs und das Nicht-Gesagte,' in I. Lidner, S. Schade, S. Wenk, and G. Werner, eds, *Blick-Wechsel: Konstruktion von Männlichkeit und Weiblichkeit in Kunst und Kunstgeschichte* (Berlin: Dietrich Reimer, 1989), 41–8.

54 Jacob Burckhardt, *Der Cicerone: Eine Einleitung zum Genuß der Kunstwerke Italiens* (1855), ed. E. Schaeffer (Leipzig: Alfred Kröner, 1927), 908–35. Cf. Domm, *Der 'klassische' Hans von Marées*, 60–2.

55 'Illusion des Lebens'; Fiedler uses this phrase in his obituary of Marées. Fiedler, *Hans von Marées*, 46.

56 See Conrad Fiedler, *Schriften zur Kunst*, ed. G. Boehm, 2 vols. (Munich: Wilhelm Fink, 1991). Gottfried Boehm's introduction to these two volumes has greatly informed my understanding of Fiedler's thought. Adolf von Hildebrand, *Das Problem der Form in der bildenden Kunst* (1893) (Strasbourg: J.H. Ed. Heitz, 1905). Although some of Fiedler's writings have recently been translated into French (Besançon: Éditions de l'Imprimeur, 2002; and Paris: Éditions École normale supérieure, 2003), only one of Fiedler's essays on aesthetics has, to my knowledge, been translated into English, and that many years ago (there are, curiously, some translations of his writings on architecture): Conrad Fiedler, *On Judging Works of Visual Art*, ed. H. Schaefer-Simmern (Berkeley, Los Angeles: University of California Press, 1949).

57 See esp. Gottfried Boehm, '"Sehen lernen ist Alles" Conrad Fiedler und Hans von Marées,' in *Hans von Marées*, ed. C. Lenz (Munich, 1987–8), 145–

50; Andreas Beyer, 'Anatomie einer Entzweiung. Über Konrad Fiedler und Hans von Marées,' in S. Majetschak, ed., *Auge und Hand: Konrad Fiedlers Kunsttheorie im Kontext* (Munich: Wilhelm Fink, 1997), 223–36; and Gerd Blum, 'Geltung und Grenzen von Fiedlers Urteil über Hans von Marées: Von den *Lebensaltern* zu den *Hesperiden*,' in Majetschak, ed., *Auge und Hand*, 237–62. And on the intellectual friendship among Marées, Fiedler, and Hildebrand, cf. Elisabeth Decker, *Zur künstlerischen Beziehung zwischen Hans von Marées, Konrad Fiedler und Adolf Hildebrand: Eine Untersuchung über die Zusammenhänge von Kunsttheorie und Kunstwerk*, University of Basel, 1966 (Dudweiler: Klein, 1967); Hubert Faensen, *Die bildnerische Form: Die Kunstauffassungen Konrad Fiedlers, Adolf von Hildebrands und Hans von Marées* (Berlin: Akademie-Verlag, 1965); and Max Imdahl, 'Marées, Fiedler, Hildebrand, Riegl, Cézanne. Bilder und Zitate (1963),' in Imdahl, *Reflexion, Theorie, Methode: Gesammelte Schriften*, vol. 3, ed. G. Boehm (Frankfurt a. M.: Suhrkamp, 1996), 42–113.

58 '… eine *sich selbst realisierende Realität*. Darin gleicht es der Sprache'; Gottfried Boehm, 'Die Logik des Auges. Konrad Fiedler nach einhundert Jahren,' in Majetschak, ed., *Auge und Hand*, 36. See also Gottfried Boehm, 'Hildebrand und Fiedler im Florentiner Kontext,' in *Storia dell'arte e politica culturale interno al 1900: La fondazione dell'Istituto Germanico di Storia dell'Arte di Firenze* (Venice: Marsilio, 1999), 130–41.

59 'Wenn von alters her zwei große Prinzipien, das der Naturnachahmung und das der Umwandlung der Wirklichkeit, um das Recht gestritten haben, der wahre Ausdruck des Wesens der künstlerischen Tätigkeit zu sein, so scheint eine Schlichtung des Streites nur dadurch möglich, daß an die Stelle dieser beiden Prinzipien ein drittes gesetzt wird, das Prinzip der Produktion der Wirklichkeit. Denn nichts anderes ist die Kunst als eins der Mittel, durch die der Mensch allererst die Wirklichkeit gewinnt.' Conrad Fiedler, 'Moderner Naturalismus und künstlerische Tätigkeit,' (1881), in Fiedler, *Schriften über Kunst*, ed. H. Eckstein (Cologne: DuMont, 1996), 128–9.

60 'Die Einsicht, daß sich unser gesamter sinnlicher Wirklichkeitsbesitz auf Wahrnehmungs- und Vorstellungsvorkommnisse beschränkt, die nicht einen gleichmäßig dauernden Zustand, sondern ein Kommen und Gehen, ein Entstehen und Verschwinden, ein Werden und Vergehen darstellen – diese Einsicht führt uns dazu, in der Wirklichkeit nicht ein flüchtiges, sondern auch ein vielfach unentwickeltes oder verkümmertes Gebilde zu erkennen.' Conrad Fiedler, 'Der Ursprung der künstlerischen Tätigkeit,' (1887) ibid., 162. On Fiedler's further statements on unfinishedness, see his letter to Hildebrand from Munich on 27 December 1882. Jachmann,

*Adolf von Hildebrands Briefwechsel*, 193–5. Or his letter to Anton Dohrn, written from Leipzig on 29 March 1873. See Marées, *Briefe*, 382–3.

61 '"Getümmel des modernen Wirrwarrs"'; Fiedler, *Hans von Marées*, 30.

62 'So wird das Scheitern zur historischen Notwendigkeit'; Boehm, in *Hans von Marées*, ed. C. Lenz (Munich, 1987–8), 148.

63 'Dabei leitete ihn sein Sinn durchaus auf das Normale und Allgemeine. Sowohl in der Bildung seiner Figuren wie in ihrer Bewegung vermied er das Besondere, den Ausnahmefall.' Wölfflin, 'Hans von Marées,' 79.

64 '[I]n krankhafter Weise.' Ibid., 75.

# 5 A Politicized Pastoral: Signac and the Cultural Geography of Mediterranean France

ANNE DYMOND

Nineteenth-century cultural geography often divided the French nation into dichotomous pairs such as Paris and 'la province,' or North and South, with the Mediterranean south often perceived as pre-modern and backward. Despite this dominant perception, an alternative cultural geography existed, which saw traditions of liberty and social accord as concomitant with Mediterranean France's naturally harmonious landscape. Neo-Impressionist painter Paul Signac drew on this idea of the Mediterranean and appropriated the conventions of classical pastoral painting to his anarchist goals to envision a utopian future that would be situated on the southern coast. His immense manifesto painting, *In the Time of Harmony: The Golden Age Is Not in the Past, It Is in the Future* (figure 5.1), which measures more than three by four metres, significantly reconfigured traditional associations between the political right and the classical tradition of idealized, orderly, and harmonious landscapes of the Mediterranean. In this and other major works of the 1890s, Signac claimed the Mediterranean coast as a site for politically critical, avant-garde art of the left.

In the decades before 1880, avant-garde painters rarely depicted France's southern shore due, in part, to the cultural affiliation between southern France and academic classicism, in turn linked with cultural and political conservatism.[1] Not until the 1880s did avant-garde Parisian artists, such as Auguste Renoir and Claude Monet, begin to visit France's Mediterranean coast in significant numbers, while the most famous visitors of the 1880s, Vincent Van Gogh and Paul Gauguin, were attracted to the inland town of Arles.[2] Neo-Impressionists were among the first avant-garde painters to reside on the coast. Henri-Edmond Cross, who would adopt the Neo-Impressionist technique in 1891, wintered around Monaco from 1883 to 1891, before settling in Saint-Clair in 1892.[3] And in 1892, Signac was the first Parisian artist to settle in Saint-Tropez, then a small fishing village on the recently 'discovered' Côte d'Azur that might still be called 'off the beaten track.'[4]

The correlation between the Midi, classicism, and conservatism persisted and even found new impetus in the 1890s, when rising French nationalism and anxiety over French cultural identity led to increasing calls from many quarters for a return to classical landscapes, in the tradition of Claude Lorrain and Nicolas Poussin, thought to express the truly French characteristics of clarity and order.[5] Moreover, James Herbert has shown that the link between the classical ideal and the Mediterranean landscape would be appropriated by the political right in the twentieth century to represent their 'call to order.'[6] Nonetheless, as I will show, in the 1890s the classical landscape and the allied Mediterranean heritage were invoked to represent an opposing view: the anarchist ideal of natural order and harmony that would be found in the golden age to come. After moving to Saint-Tropez in 1892, Signac, a committed anarchist, began to paint politicized pastorals, juxtaposing north and south and promoting a left-wing vision of the Mediterranean shore.[7]

I begin by differentiating the pastoral tradition from the classical landscape as a mode that invokes comparison and juxtaposition, features that Signac would use to full advantage. I subsequently examine the cultural construction of the Mediterranean as linked to a tradition of liberty in the literary works of Stendhal and Guy de Maupassant, and as the perfect milieu for the development of a well-balanced society by anarchist geographers Élisée Reclus and Pierre Kropotkin. Signac invoked these ideas of the Mediterranean when he used the conventions of pastoral landscape painting to radicalize seemingly innocuous depictions of the region. His manifesto piece *In the Time of Harmony* (figure 5.1), thus initiates a modern, left-wing tradition of picturing the Mediterranean that relies on an anarchist cultural geography that differentiated north and south. Furthermore, I suggest that its pastoral form inherently suggests the juxtaposition of the idyllic south with the north as it had been pictured in earlier Neo-Impressionist representations. Thus, I argue a formative role for Neo-Impressionism in the iconography of the Mediterranean shore: Signac and his Neo-Impressionist colleagues created a radical association for the classical tradition and the Mediterranean coast.

My interpretation relies on a definition of pastoralism that implies a potential for radicalism.[8] The pastoral landscape tradition employs many of the same compositional signifiers as the classical landscape, or *paysage composé*, such as a structured, harmonious landscape marked by its unity and completeness. It also generally employs Arcadian themes, rather than historic or mythological subject matter. Yet, as Leo Marx has persuasively asserted, pastoralism's deeper essence is defined not by composition or subject matter, but by the juxtaposition of dichotomies such as real and idyllic, urban and rural, and, as I will suggest, north and south.[9] Marx shows that the pastoral is a sophisticated representation that mediates two conflicting ways of life: social complexity and natural simplicity.[10] Moreover, while such juxtapositions may have been explicit in early pastoral landscapes – for example, by the inclusion of a distant town that contrasts with the idyllic country life in the foreground – the formal structure that signifies pastoralism in painting comes to evoke such juxtapositions even when they were no longer made explicit.[11] As David Rosand has shown, certain conventions, such as a dominant sheltering tree, acquire their own 'expressive momentum,' eventually signifying pastoralism and the sense of conflicting ways of life now recognized as inherent in the mode. With this understanding of pastoralism, I argue that when Signac moved to the Mediterranean shore and used this pictorial paradigm, he was relying on the formal conventions of the painted pastoral to invoke comparisons between north and south, between his work and other representations, and to envision a better future that contrasted with the present.

## Situating the South in the Nineteenth Century

The nineteenth-century cultural geography of the French nation emanating from the capital imagined the south as a region distinct from the heart of the French nation. The nineteenth-century historian Jules Michelet emphasized this sense of southern otherness when he wrote of 'the true France, the France of the North.'[12] Throughout the nineteenth century, social scientists increasingly traced geographic, economic, racial, and cultural differences across a divide running between Geneva and Saint-Malo; while they noted unequal development, however, they did not agree about which side of the divide had the advantage.[13] The construction of the Midi as backward and other was countered within Provence by the myth that the south was the most Latin, and thus most truly French, region within the nation.[14] Interpretations of southern culture by the writers Stendhal and Maupassant (both favourites of

Signac), and the anarchist geographers Reclus and Kropotkin as well, inventoried differences between north and south; more important, however, their accounts accentuated the perceived freedom of life in the south and, in the case of Reclus, highlighted the region's special role in an anarchist-inspired harmonious future. These constructions of the south as freer and more harmonious would have been particularly attractive to Signac and his Neo-Impressionist colleagues.

Stendhal, whom Signac saw as a libertarian *avant la lettre*,[15] described the south as a place of freedom where the worst faults of capitalist society were less entrenched than in the north. Signac certainly knew Stendhal's accounts of the south and, in an article describing his voyage from the Atlantic to the Mediterranean on his sailboat *Olympia*, even quoted Stendhal's assessment that the region was more beautiful than Italy.[16] In *Memoirs of a Tourist*, Stendhal's fictional account of a businessman's travels, the southerner is described as having a joy, a 'brio,' absent in northerners.[17] Stendhal wrote that there could hardly be a greater contrast between a northern and southern man; in the south freedom is highly valued as an essential part of life, in contrast to Paris, where freedom is necessarily relinquished in order to get ahead in society. Briefly describing the restrictions in Parisian society, Stendhal's narrator concludes, 'Even a vision of this kind of life would make a Marseillais grow pale. For him his life is all freedom and movement.'[18] Describing the region as free from the constraints of polite society, Stendhal also suggests the southerner's healthier relation to money:

> The South of France is in the same situation as Spain and Italy. Its natural *brio*, its vivacity, keeps it from being 'Englished' like the North. A man of the Midi ... is not made for the civilization that has reigned since 1830: money and the shrewd and legitimate ways of getting it ...
>
> 'But do you think of money every two minutes?' they [Northerners] answer him.
>
> 'You sacrifice wines to the interest of iron,' he says.
>
> There is no answer to that.[19]

Stendhal links the south of France to other 'Latin' countries that are also outside 'civilized' societies' concern for money. Signac's similar disdain for a culture that chooses financial gain over other considerations is indicated by his selection of Stendhal's aphorism 'The exclusive love of money is what most spoils human beings,' for publication in the anarchist journal *La Revue Libertaire* in 1894.[20] This portrayal of the vivacious southerner (who, free from the constraints of civilization, seems to belong to an earlier time that predates capitalism and modernity) would certainly have appealed to escapist bourgeois fantasies of 'authentic' life. Yet it also resonated with Signac's anarchist belief in a natural way of life that was harmonious, free, and not found under modern capitalism.

In a somewhat different fashion, Maupassant mythologized the south as a place of freedom where individuals had the time to pursue intellectual concerns, which would also resonate with Signac's view of an anarchist future. Despite Maupassant's ironic nostalgia, his vivid description of the beauty of the Mediterranean coast, published as *Sur l'eau* in 1888, has long been recognized as a likely influence on Signac's choice of locale.[21] There is more than beauty in Maupassant's account, however, that would have attracted Signac. Maupassant was caught in the typical tourist dilemma: he knew that the authenticity he sought no longer existed, and perhaps never had, but he still wanted to see the region as savage and wild. Consequently, his account veers between knowing irony and nostalgia. For example, while emphasizing the exotic isolation and wildness of the region, Maupassant simultaneously underlined how far this stereotype was from reality, as he humorously reported attempts to create *stations hivernales* (winter resorts) along the *côte de maures*.[22] Along this isolated coast, he explains, one finds planned roads named after famous painters cutting through the empty landscape: 'boulevard Ruysdael, boulevard Rubens, boulevard Van Dyck, boulevard Claude Lorrain. One wonders why all these painters? Ah! Why? It's the banks, it is said, like God himself before lighting the sun: "This will be an artist's resort (station d'artistes)!"'[23]

When Maupassant turns to describe Saint-Tropez, he directly confonts the stereotype of the supposedly savage region. His narrator sympathizes with the miserable life of the office workers of Saint-Tropez as they leave for their lunch breaks, for whom 'all the days, the weeks, the months, the seasons, the years resemble each other ... They give themselves up as prisoners for eight hours of the day; the prison is open from six in the morning, until the night falls.'[24] He laments: 'Oh liberty! liberty! Only source of happiness, only hope and only dream!'[25] He draws a parallel between his own quest for freedom and that of the office clerks, concluding, 'We remain free despite all the strangleholds.'[26] Maupassant thus asserts an indomitable individualism that survives despite modern society's efforts to crush it, even in supposedly isolated Saint-Tropez. This is followed by the narrator's account of local conversations that 'reorganized the army and the magistrature, reformed laws and the Constitution, defined an ideal Republic.'[27] In its entirety, Maupassant's account of Saint-Tropez would have appealed to Signac for its description of physical beauty but, more important, because of its tribute to individual liberty, which persisted despite all attempts to suppress it. Maupassant described a world where workers were able to consider such intellectual concerns as the structure of the ideal Republic, and he made it clear that these individuals were part of the modern French nation. This description of freedom-loving, intelligent workers (as opposed to primitive peasants) clearly resonates with Signac's choice of locale and his representations of the locals made only a few years after the publication of *Sur l'eau*.

**Reclus and Kropotkin: Latin Culture and Anarchism**

Élisée Reclus and Pierre Kropotkin, as both anarchists and geographers, also contributed to the development of the myth of the Mediterranean in ways that would have appealed to Signac.[28] Indeed, Signac later cited Reclus's description of the region as one of the sources that had interested him in the south.[29] Both Reclus and Kropotkin believed in the power of geographic location to shape social and political institutions, and both advocated a decentralized political system. Kropotkin saw the peoples of the Mediterranean basin as more naturally sympathetic to anarchism than German peoples.[30] He believed that Germanic peoples responded to the Paris Commune by supporting the authoritarian socialism of Marx, while Latin peoples responded with sympathy to the anarchism of Bakunin.[31] Critiquing the German Social Democratic Party and socialism as espoused by Karl Marx and Friedrich Engels, Kropotkin wrote that the German socialists began to favour

> not the kind of state that might be termed the highest type among those existing today, namely the *federated* state, but the Roman type, unitary, indivisible and centralized in the Roman manner.
>
> Against this Germanic spirit, therefore, the Latin peoples had to defend the very right to revolutionary agitation. They had to wage a difficult struggle against their governments and against the socialists of the German school.[32]

Kropotkin's idiosyncratic definition of Latin and German culture associates centralized political authority with the Germanic spirit and with the tradition of the Roman Empire. He distinguished Latin culture as opposing centralization and seeking anarchist revolution. Kropotkin repeatedly characterized anti-Marxist anarchists as Latin, for example, when he explained the split between the anarchists and socialists. He wrote, 'the Latin federations, Spanish, Italian, Belgian and Jurassic (French could not be represented) constituted among themselves a Federal union which broke entirely with the Marxist general council of the International.'[33] As Kropotkin included both Belgians and Swiss in the category, his definition of Latin seems to be those who support anarchism.

Reclus similarly condemned Germanic culture and praised some aspects of Latin culture.[34] Reclus believed in progress, which he defined as the spread of emancipation.[35] While not anti-German, Reclus criticized the current state of German culture for its regression in terms of emancipation and for its nationalism, militarism, and expansionism.[36] Yet he found the current state of Latin culture even more ambiguous. He recognized the elasticity of the term 'Latin,' which could apply to any civilization that had been part of the ancient Roman world. Nevertheless, of all the invasions of France, he believed that the Latin one had been the most significant because of its impact on the French language.[37] It was because of the Latin characteristics of the language, he wrote, that 'the French spirit took an essentially classical turn.'[38] Thus, Reclus emphasized the classical elements within French culture and linked them to a Latin heritage.

Reclus had long advocated a decentralized state as the best social structure, and he linked this to traditions in southern France.[39] For Reclus, the ideal political structure would be independent and self-administering local units, based on 'natural' associations. He contrasted this decentralized model with the artificial hierarchies of centralized states, which he argued had been 'a tool of despotism, especially in France.'[40] Examples of natural units could be found in the south, Reclus wrote, where most of the small landowners resided within the local town so they could effectively take part in its decision-making processes.[41] In the small villages of Provence and the Mediterranean region of France, he suggested, '[t]he great privilege of being able to discuss public interests has, traditionally, changed everyone into urban dwellers. The call of the agora, as in Greece, of municipal life in Italy, attracts inhabitants towards the central square, where they debate communal affairs.'[42] Anarchism, Reclus noted, was most entrenched where this kind of communal decision making was combined with a tradition of freethinking, where 'the spirits have for a long time been liberated from religious and monarchical prejudices, where revolutionary precedents have loosened the faith in the established order, where the practice of communal franchises has better accustomed men to dispense with a master, where disinterested study developed thinkers outside every coterie.'[43] Reclus thus recognized that historical tradition alone did not guarantee progress. He stated that in the Middle Ages the south 'unquestionably represented the most advanced part of the nation,' but regretted that in the present it combined advanced and regressive elements.[44] On the positive side, he cited the strong political support for *radicale* or *radicale-socialiste* parties, which called for the separation of church and state, and the 'peasants who deliberately enter into co-operative, even communist arrangements.'[45] On the negative side, he noted a reactionary element within the regionalist movement. He lamented the irony that southern towns had rallied their municipal spirit against the central government only to assert their cultural right to bullfighting, which he saw as barbaric.[46] Nevertheless, Reclus saw the tradition of local self-governance as the best form of governance, and he associated it with the Latin culture of the Mediterranean south.[47]

In tourist guides Reclus similarly positioned the Mediterranean as geographically separate from the north. Like others, he suggested that, with the Spanish coast, it constitutes 'a distinct part of the world where the transition between Europe and Africa takes place.'[48] Since it was a crossroads between north and south, 'France historically became the place where the races of the north were united with the south, where the Mediterranean civilization came to intersect with elements of Celtic and German culture.'[49] The nation, and particularly its southern part, was therefore uniquely situated; as a crossroads, it would bring about a fusion of all races to create a universal brotherhood. In contrast to those who saw the south as having declined since the age of the troubadours, Reclus argued that Provence still had a role to play in the future of humanity: '[H]istory has not at all deserted the shores of the Mediterranean.'[50] Thus, both Kropotkin and Reclus associated anarchism with some aspects of Latin culture, and Reclus's vision of the future of the Midi would have further contributed to the attraction of the region for Signac.

## Situating Signac in Saint-Tropez

Signac had travelled to the south of France and painted its coastline at Collioure in 1887 and Cassis in 1889, before taking a second home in

Saint-Tropez in the summer of 1892.[51] He chose Saint-Tropez after lengthy correspondence with his friend Henri-Edmond Cross, a recent convert to Neo-Impressionism who spent 1891 in nearby Cabasson on Signac's suggestion that he visit that part of Provence.[52] In turn, Signac asked Cross if it was too hot to paint there and where he might find a good port for his yacht, *Olympia*, before finally announcing his intention to instal himself in the south, 'provided I can find a little corner in which to make my nest and a good anchorage for *Olympia*, that's all I ask: a sky, the sea, the setting sun. Less and less I seek the motif.'[53] While Signac was obviously drawn by the physical beauty of the south, his letter indicates that he was in search of more than new motifs to paint. Cross first saw the Midi when visiting his uncle, who lived in the already fashionable resort of Monaco, and he would later settle on the coast at Saint-Clair because of his health problems.[54] These two Neo-Impressionists thus exemplified the changing tourist trends in the Midi, which had previously attracted mainly wealthy convalescent tourists in winter but was increasingly drawing more fashionable and active year-round tourists seeking an alternative to urban life. They also exemplify the wider trend, both artistic and touristic, of travel from the nation's centre to its peripheries in search of new motifs and new cultural encounters, seen, for example, in van Gogh's choice of Arles and Gauguin's trips to Brittany, Arles, and overseas. The artistic trend may be partially attributed to Georges Seurat's *A Sunday Afternoon on the Island of La Grande Jatte* (figure 5.2), which Fred Orton and Griselda Pollock have argued made the definitive statement on modern urban life, closing the Parisian landscape as a subject for vanguard painters and leading ambitious artists to find new spaces of representation.[55] Yet it also corresponds to larger cultural trends and, in the Neo-Impressionist case, represented a deliberate and anarchist-inspired rejection of Parisian culture in favour of the potential of Mediterranean culture.

After Signac's arrival in Saint-Tropez, his art underwent a rapid and significant change.[56] Until his move to the south, Signac had generally avoided pastoral images and landscapes that included prominent figures. His three previous major figure paintings – *The Milliners* (figure 5.5), *The Dining Room, Opus 152* (1886–7, 90 × 117 cm, Kröller-Müller Museum, Otterlo, FC 136), and *Sunday* (1888–90, 150 × 150 cm, private collection, FC 197) – had been set indoors.[57] His landscapes (including those of Collioure and Cassis) had been largely unpopulated. Moreover, most of Signac's landscapes were not on a grand scale: indeed, his only large-format works had been the three aforementioned figure paintings. Once ensconced on the coast, however, Signac showed a new interest in situating figures in large-scale, classically inspired landscape settings, as indicated in a letter written to Camille Pissarro shortly after his arrival in Saint-Tropez in May 1892. 'I'm thinking of a large canvas, with figures,' he wrote. 'Here I will avoid falling into my eternal seascape.'[58] A sketch from this first summer in Saint-Tropez (figure 5.3) seems to be the earliest incarnation of what would become two large-scale multiple-figure landscapes exhibited as *Young Provençal Women at the Well: Decoration for a Panel in Half-Light* (figure 5.4) and *In the Time of Harmony: The Golden Age Is Not in the Past, It Is in the Future* (figure 5.1). At more than two by one-and-a-third and three by four metres respectively, both works are significantly larger and more ambitious than anything Signac had painted previously. Both also relate to the revived interest in the 1890s for a decorative public art – seen in the critical acclaim given Pierre Puvis de Chavannes and in the mural works of the Nabis – that could be considered the modern inheritor of the classical tradition. Moreover, both of Signac's works accord with Cross's suggestion that they begin to paint the harmonious, anarchist future: 'Until now, the pictures dealing with the theme of anarchy always depicted revolt either directly or indirectly, through scenes of poignant misery. Let us imagine instead the dreamed-of age of happiness and well-being and let us show the actions of men, their play and their work in this era of general harmony.'[59] In the first half of the decade, Signac was primarily occupied with these works, which makes his attachment to the region and his politicized version of the pastoral very clear.

## The Locals in the Landscape

*Young Provençal Women at the Well*, of 1892, uses the eminently classical motif of two local women gathering water at a communal well, while another carries her water up a hill and into the distance.[60] The view conflates several sites, sacrificing realism for the idealism associated with the classical tradition.[61] Signac's portrayal of daily life in Saint-Tropez reveals the anarchist belief that rural culture was more likely to embrace the ideal of mutual aid, which Pissarro also depicted in the early 1890s.[62] The women at the well seem to assist each other in their task; the figure on the left swings her jug, as if to move it up to the ledge, while the figure on the right draws the water.[63] More important, the well is communal, not private. This representation of communal living accords with Kropotkin's ideals of 'mutual aid' and communal property. Indeed, Kropotkin noted that 'a peasant commune, no matter where, even in France, where the Jacobins have done their best to destroy all communal usage,' shares resources, including water.[64]

The sketches in which Signac worked out the final composition reveal that the motif of two women together at the well was a virtual constant.[65] The significance of this representation of mutual aid is made clear by comparison with Signac's previous figural works – showing relations in the north – in which social interaction is consistently depicted as stilted or formal. Neither *The Milliners* (figure 5.5) nor *Sunday* portrays any exchange between the figures. In *The Dining Room* the man and woman at the table show no signs of interaction. The only implied interaction is one of servitude – the maid approaches the woman of the house – in a relation that runs counter to the anarchist ideal of individual liberty.[66] The chosen motif in *Young Provençal Women at the Well* instead embodies the anarchist ideal of a communal society in which individuals share communal resources and assist each other willingly.[67]

Signac's portrayal of regional women in this painting stands out in contrast to that of other artists of the day, such as Jules Breton, Vincent van Gogh, Paul Gauguin, or Émile Bernard. The figures have neither the sturdy body types nor the so-called traditional regional costume (a tradition invented in the nineteenth century) that normally mark locals as peasants.[68] In contrast, many works by van Gogh and Gauguin in Arles (or a host of artists visiting Brittany) clearly designate their subjects as locals by both body type and costume. In Gauguin's *The Night Café* (1888, Pushkin State Museum of Fine Arts, Moscow), the women in the bar wear what is clearly meant to signify traditional Arlésienne clothing. Their identity is summarized by their costume in a stereotypical response that reduces individuals to types.[69] Signac, however, conveyed an aspect of the everyday life of local women, avoiding the by-now standard depiction of the peasant hard at work in the fields *à la* Jean-François Millet or Breton. He used the grandeur of a decorative, classicizing composition but did not archaize the scene by putting the women in identifiably regional clothing. Indeed, Signac's work refuses the oft-made distinction between the modern and the provincial, a distinction that van Gogh had positively remarked on in Émile Bernard's *Breton Women in a Meadow* (1888, private collection). Describing the painting, van Gogh noted the importance of women's clothing as signifiers of their relation to modernity: 'I have seen a Sunday afternoon in Brittany by him [Bernard], some Breton peasant women, children,

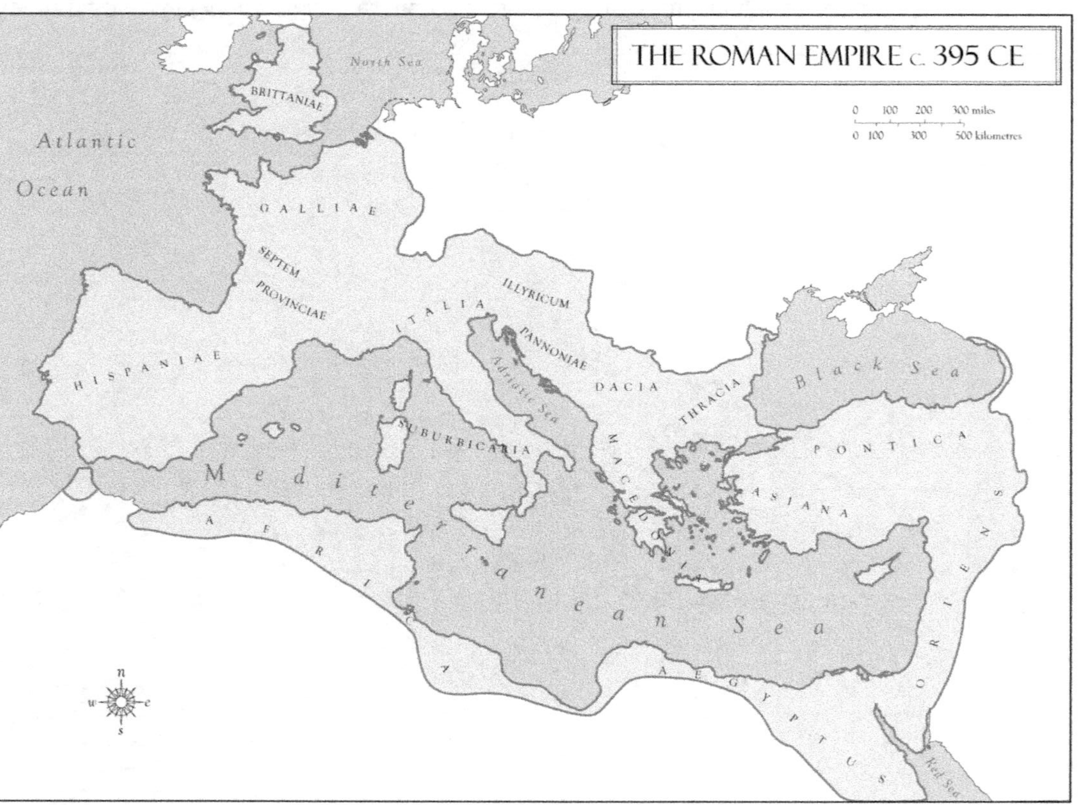


Figure 1.1 Map of Roman Empire, late 4th century CE (design Jennifer Grek Martin).

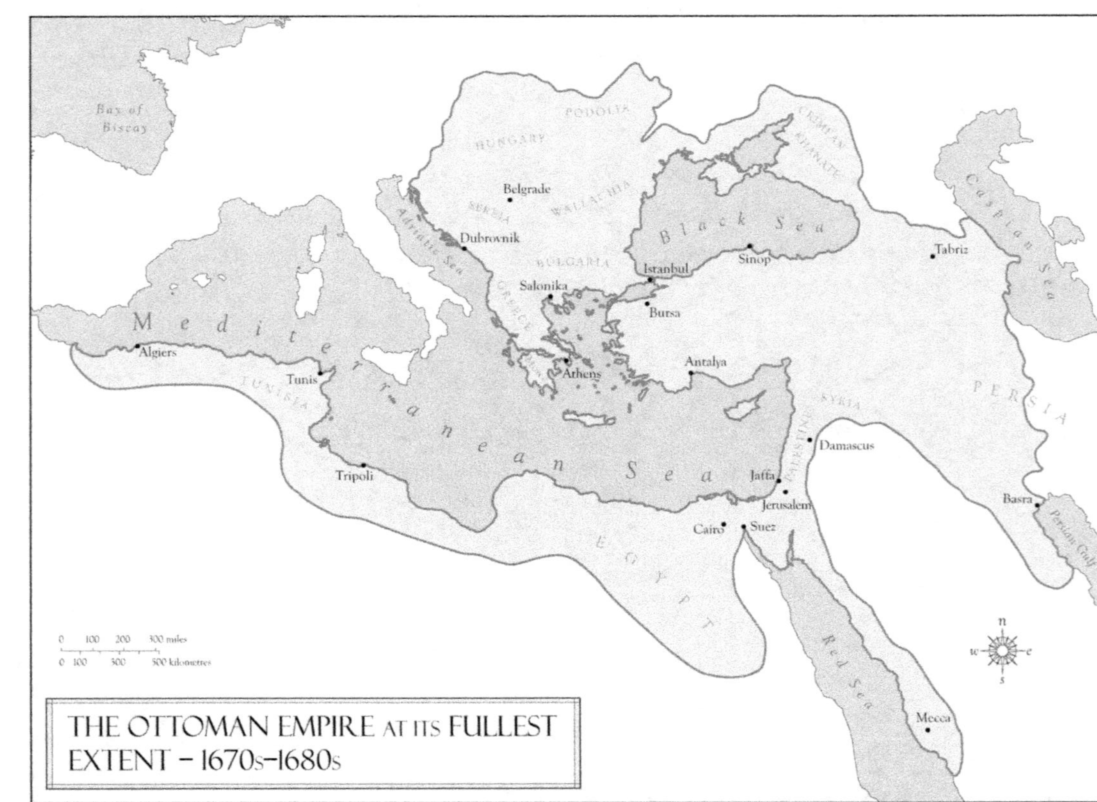


Figure 1.2 Map of Ottoman Empire, late 17th century CE (design Jennifer Grek Martin).

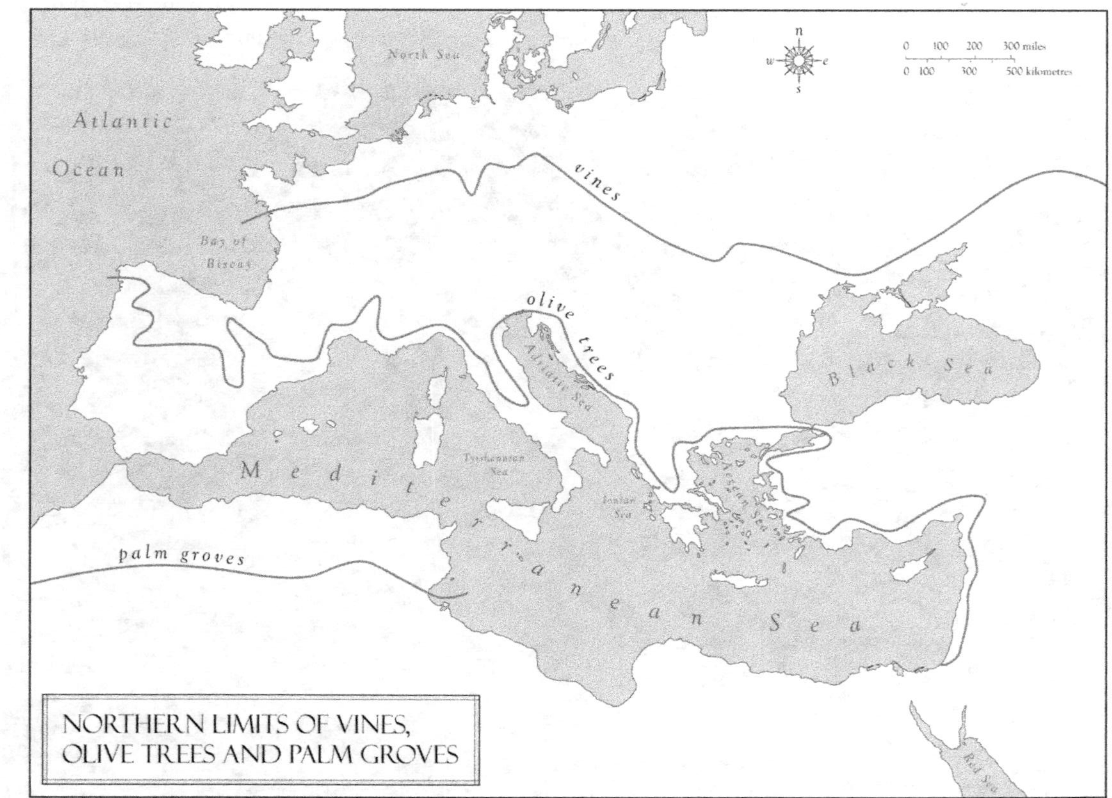


Figure 1.3 Map of Mediterranean showing range of olive trees, vines, and palm groves (design Jennifer Grek Martin).

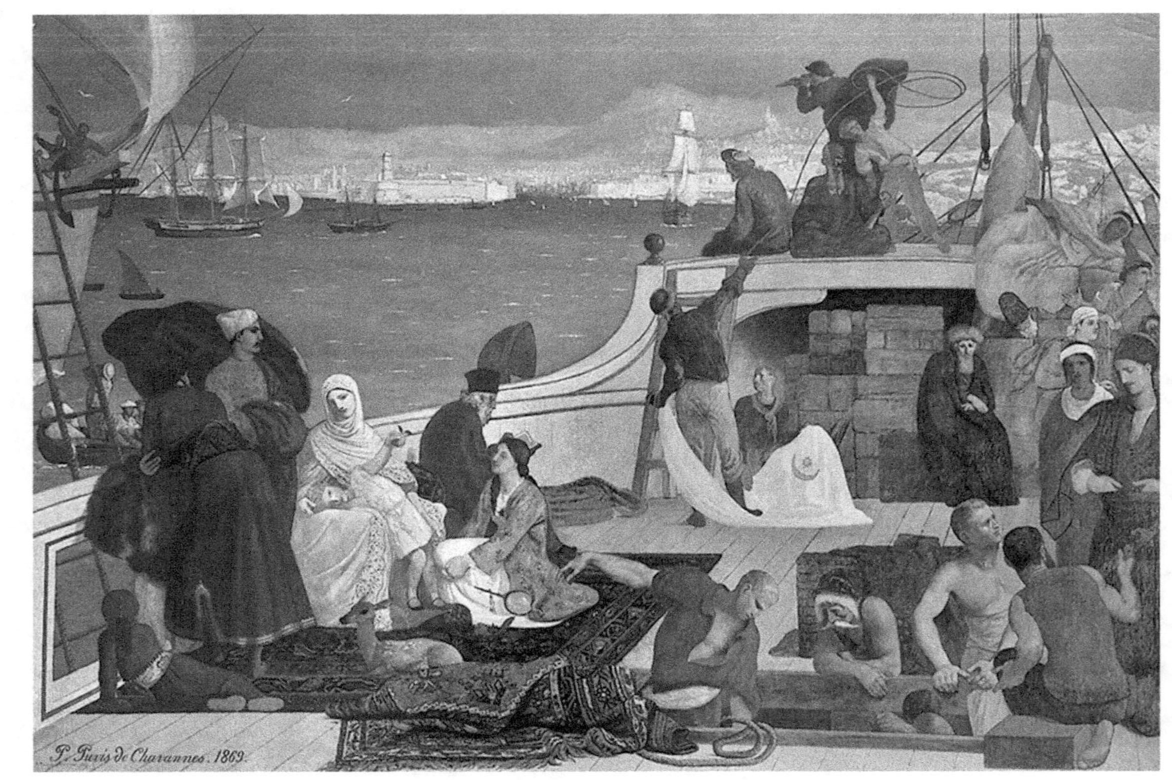


Figure 1.4 Pierre Puvis de Chavannes, *Marseille Porte de l'Orient*, 1869, oil on canvas. Musée des Beaux-Arts, Marseille (photograph Jean Bernard).

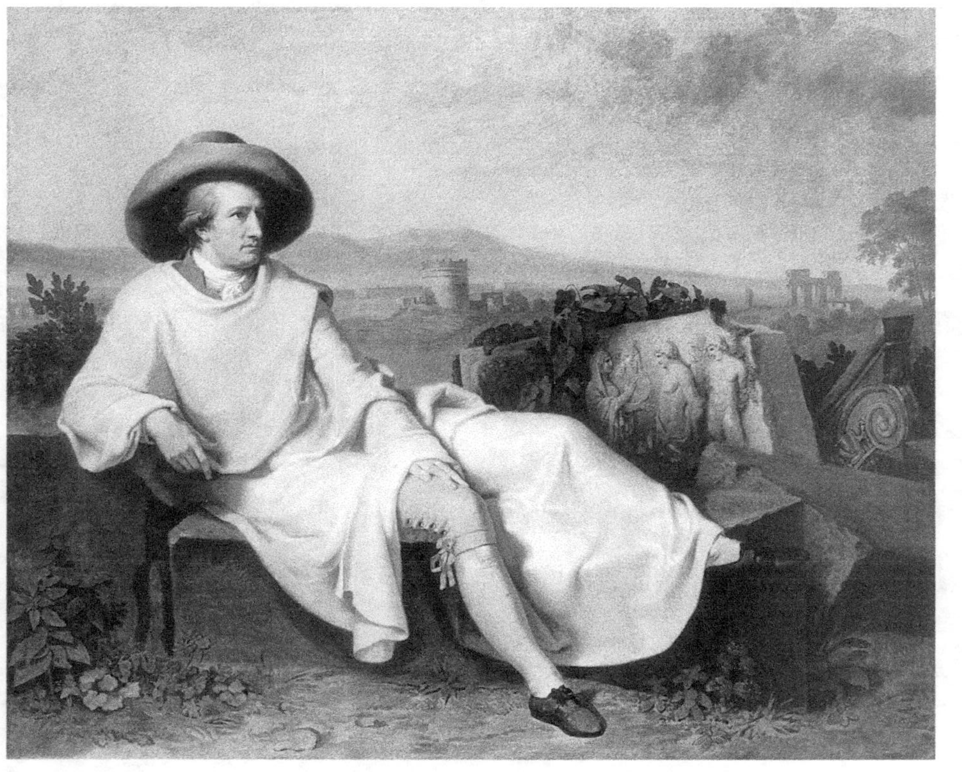

Figure 1.5 Wilhelm Tischbein, *Goethe in the Roman Campagna*, 1787, oil on canvas, 164 × 206 cm. Staedel Kunstinstitut, Frankfurt (photograph Ursula Edermann).

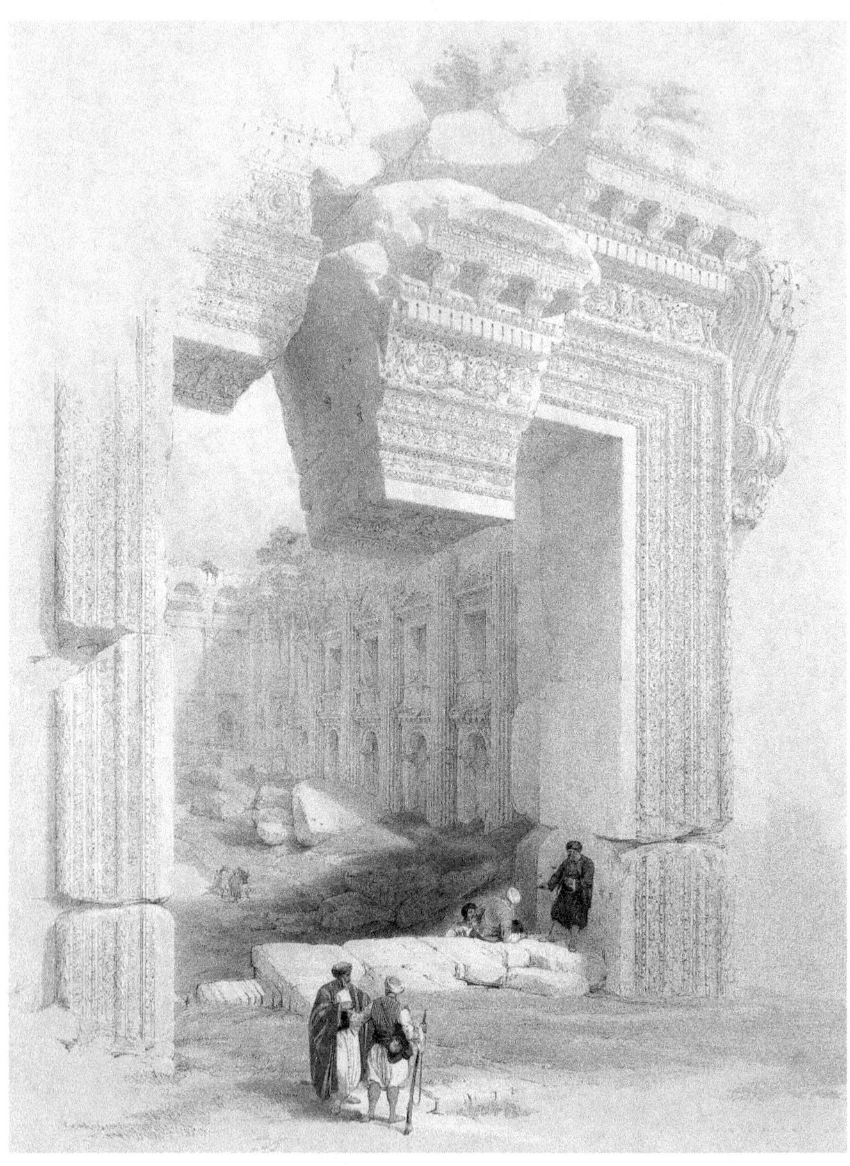

Figure 1.6 *Gateway to the Great Temple at Baalbec*, lithograph from David Roberts, *The Holy Land: Syria, Idumea, Arabia, Egypt and Nubia* (London 1842–9), vol. 2 (Typ 805.42.7492PF). Department of Printing and Graphic Arts, Houghton Library, Harvard College Library, Cambridge, Mass.

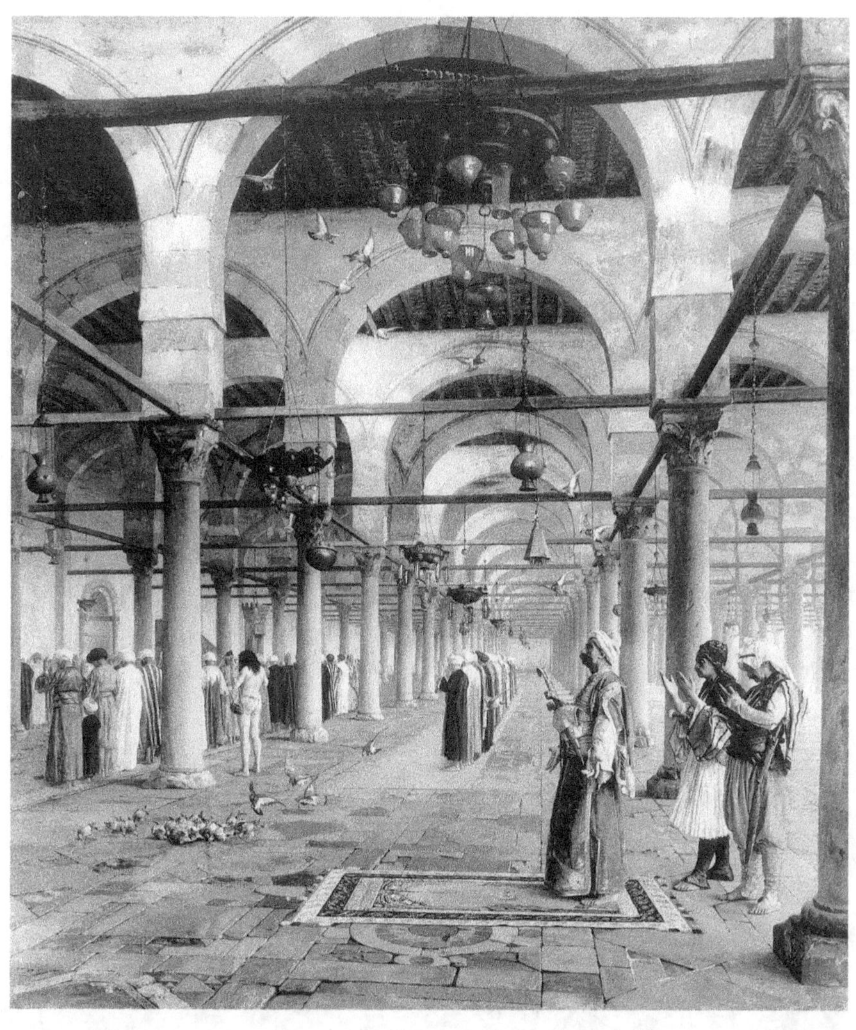

Figure 1.7 Jean-Léon Gérôme, *Prayer in the Mosque of 'Amr*, ca. 1872, oil on canvas, 88.9 × 74.9 cm. The Metropolitan Museum of Art, Catharine Lorillard Wolfe Collection, Bequest of Catharine Lorillard Wolfe, 1887 (89.15.130), New York (photograph, all rights reserved, The Metropolitan Museum of Art).

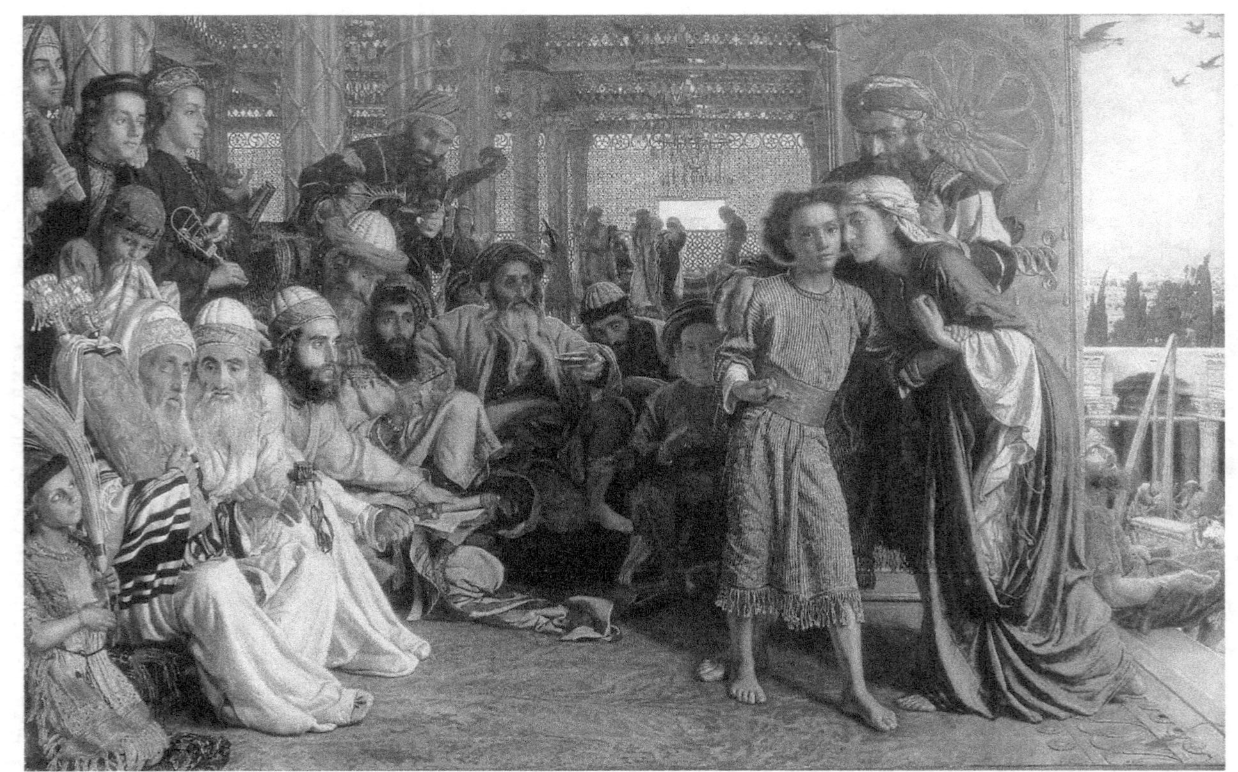

Figure 1.8 William Holman Hunt, *Finding of the Saviour in the Temple*, 1854–60, oil on canvas, 45.5 × 70 cm. Birmingham Museum and Art Gallery.

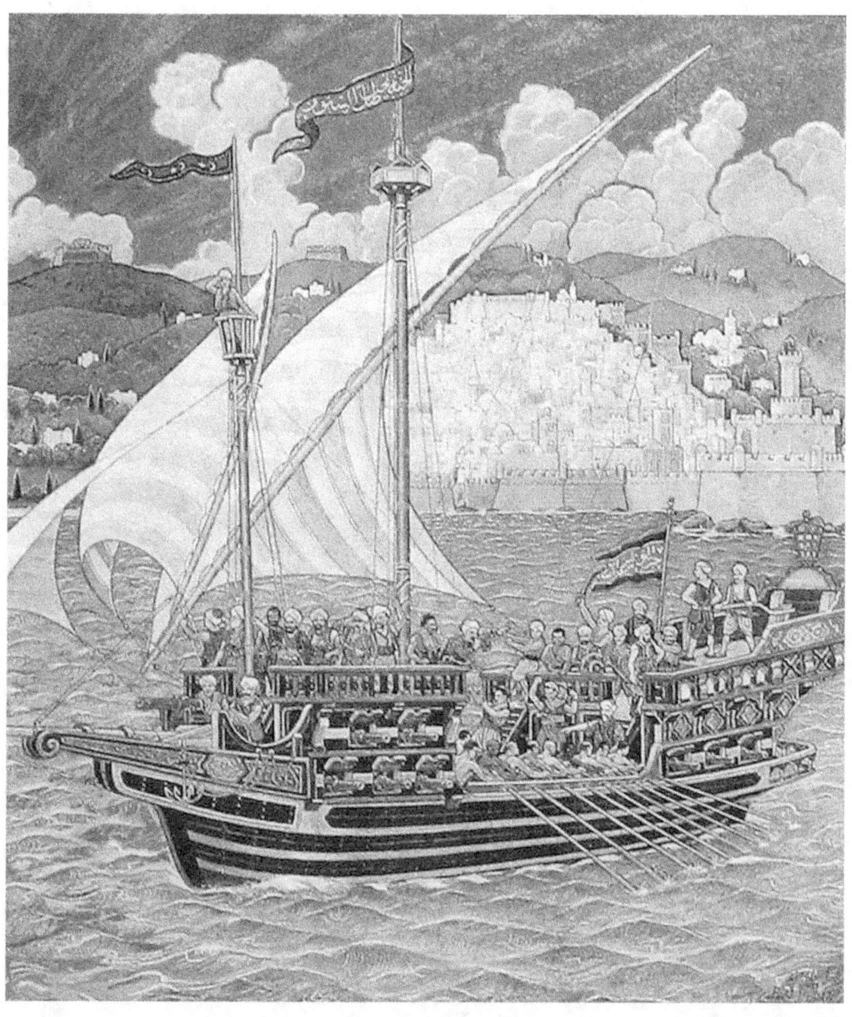

Figure 1.9 Mohammed Racim, *Corsairs before at-Djezira*, ca. 1931, gouache on paper, 18.5 × 13.5 cm. Present whereabouts unknown (reproduced from *Mohammed Racim, miniaturiste algérien* (Paris: Arts et Métiers Graphiques, 1972).

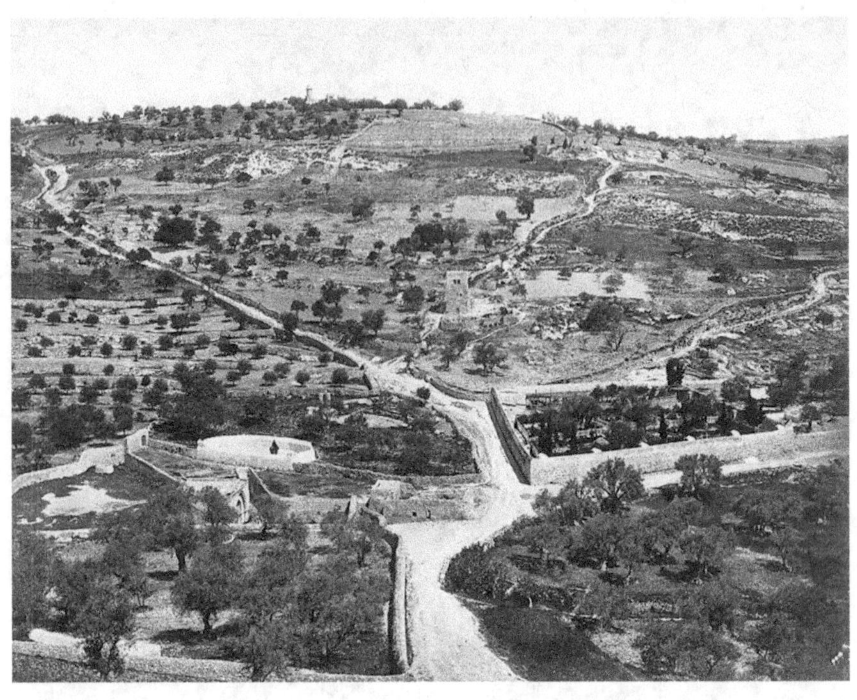

Figure 1.10 *The Mount of Olives and Garden of Gethsemane from Jerusalem*, albumen print on paper from glass collodion plate, ca. 1856. Allen Emery collection, Fine Arts Library Visual Collections, Harvard University, Cambridge, Mass.

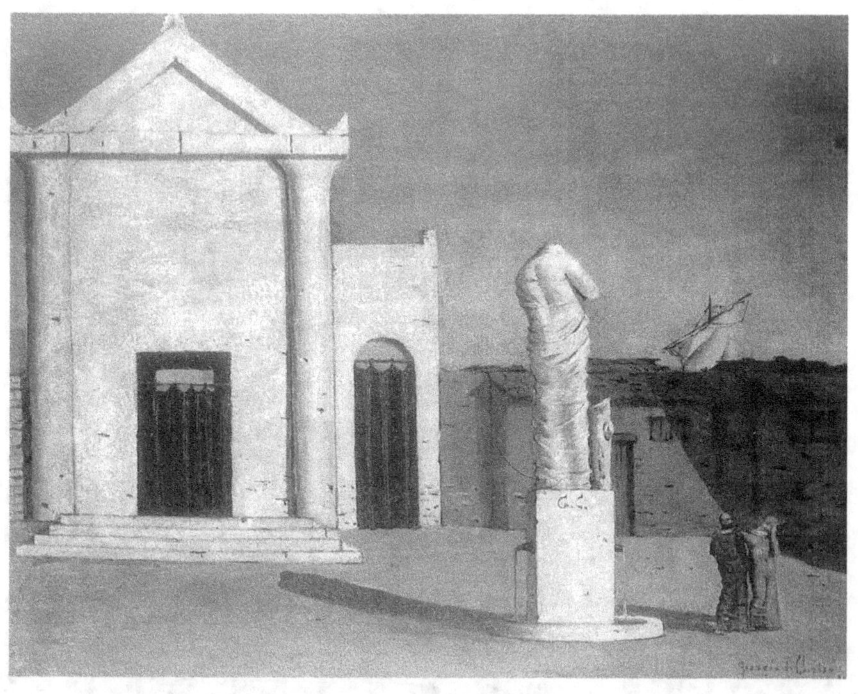

Figure 2.1 Giorgio de Chirico, *L'énigme d'un après-midi d'automne*, 1910, oil on canvas, 45 × 60 cm. Private collection, Buenos Aires. Estate of Giorgio de Chirico/SODRAC (2005).

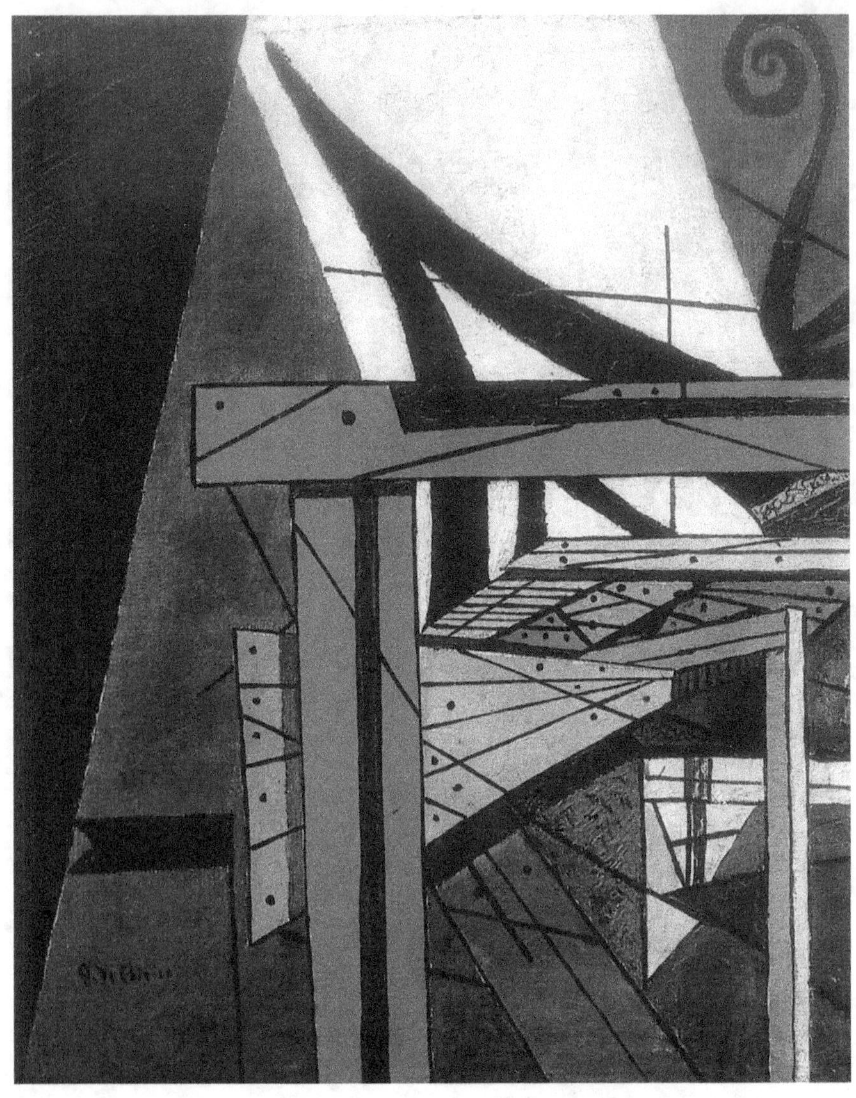

Figure 2.2 Giorgio de Chirico, *Composizione metafisica*, 1916, oil on canvas, 35 × 26 cm. Private collection, New York. Estate of Giorgio de Chirico/SODRAC (2005). Photograph provided by Museum of Modern Art, New York/Art Resource, NY.

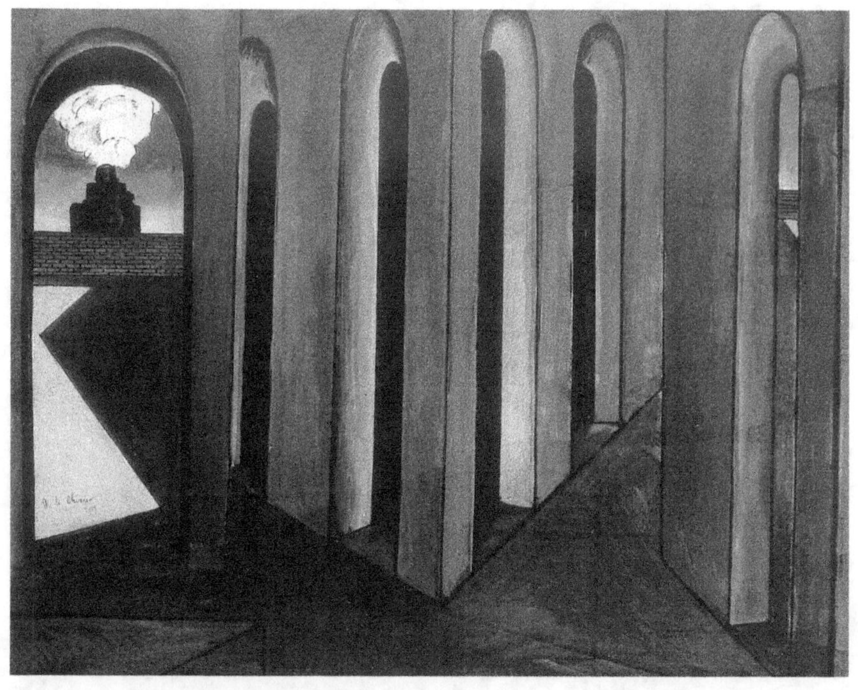

Figure 2.3 Giorgio de Chirico, *Le voyage émouvant*, 1913, oil on canvas, 74.4 × 107 cm. Museum of Modern Art, New York. Estate of Giorgio de Chirico/SODRAC (2005). Image © The Museum of Modern Art/SCALA/Art Resource, NY.

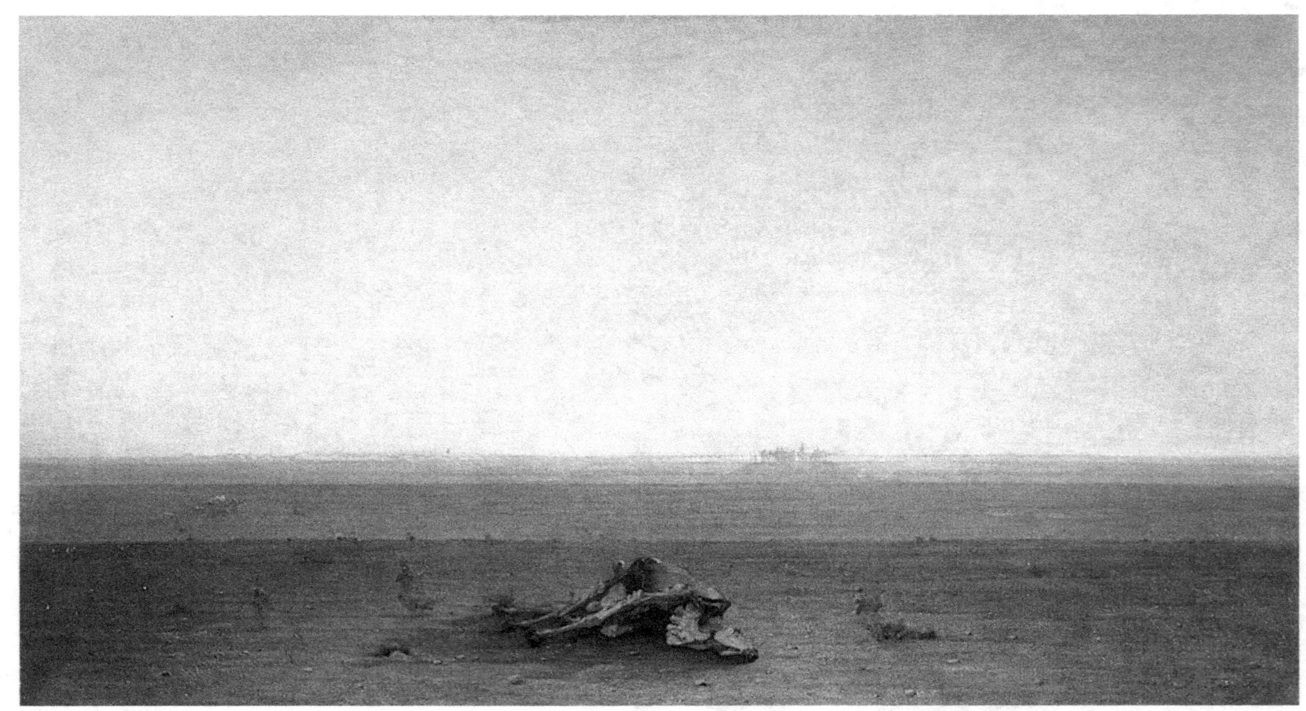

Figure 3.1 Gustave Guillaumet, *The Desert*, Salon of 1867, oil on canvas, 110 × 200 cm. Musée d'Orsay, Paris.

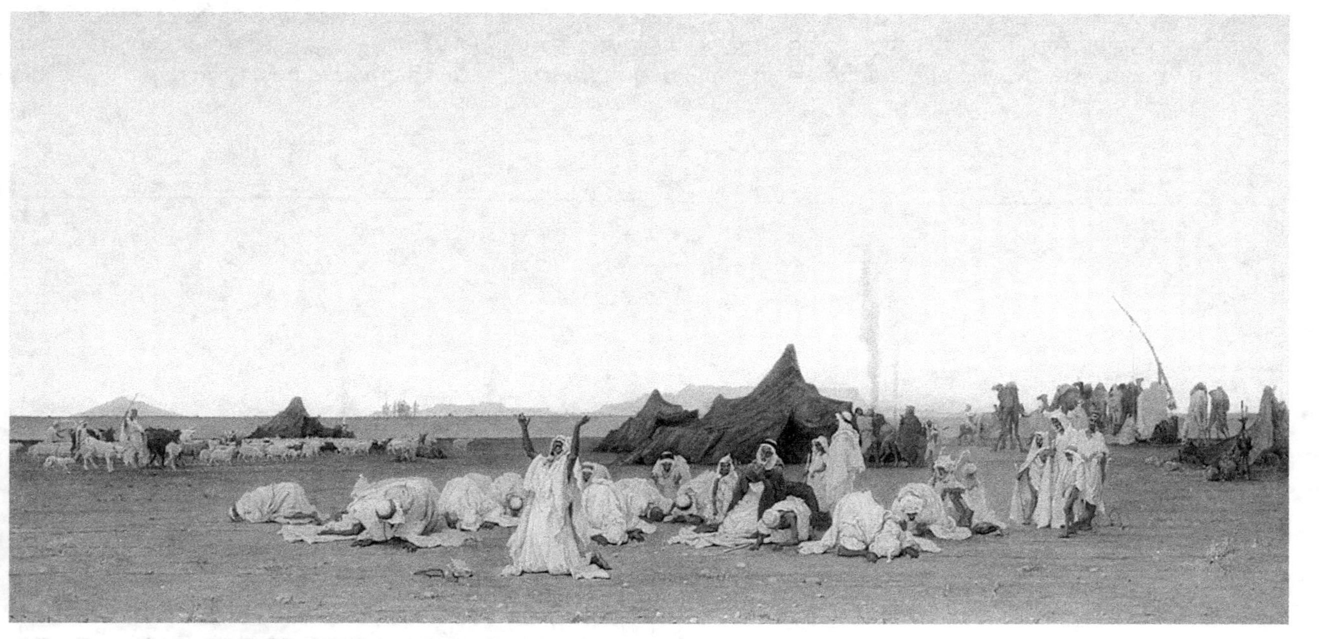

Figure 3.2 Gustave Guillaumet, *Evening Prayer in the Sahara*, Salon of 1863, oil on canvas, 137 × 285 cm. Musée d'Orsay, Paris.

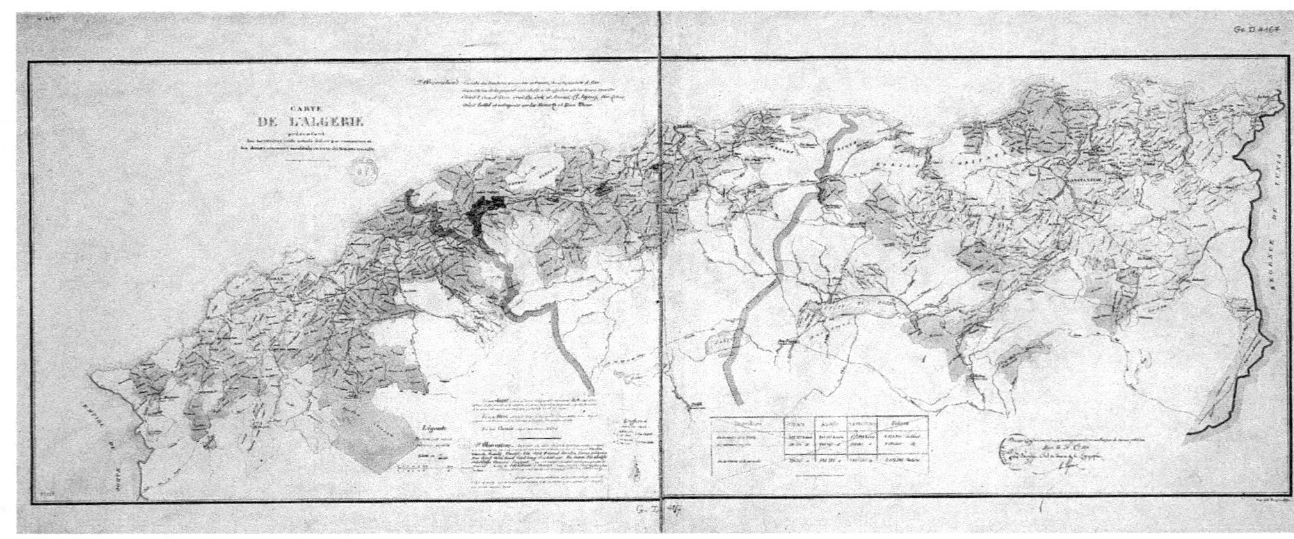


Figure 3.3 'Map of Algeria presenting current civil territory divided by communes and *douars* constituted by virtue of the *sénatus-consulte*, 1870,' 125 × 44 cm (Algiers: Imp. Lith. Bouyer, 1870). Bibliothèque nationale de France, Département des cartes et plans, Ge D.4167.

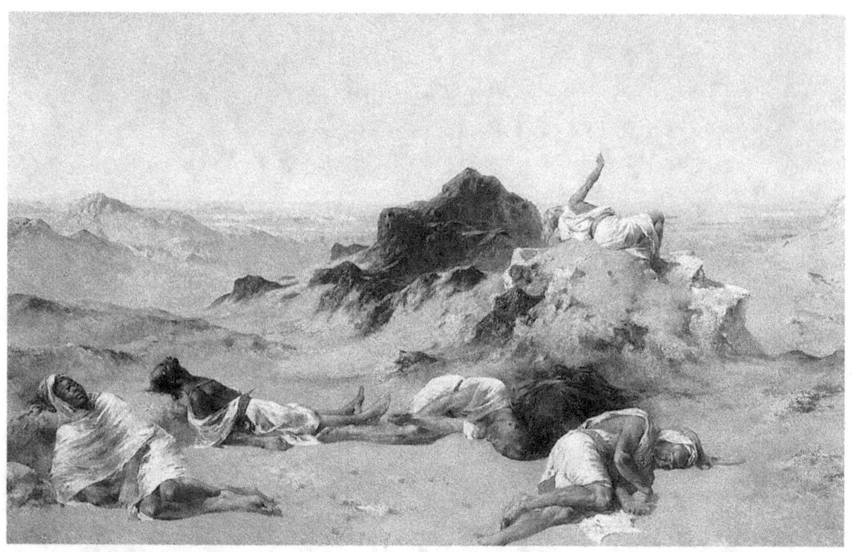

Figure 3.4 Eugène Fromentin, *The Land of Thirst*, undated, oil on canvas, 103 × 143.2 cm. Musée d'Orsay, Paris.

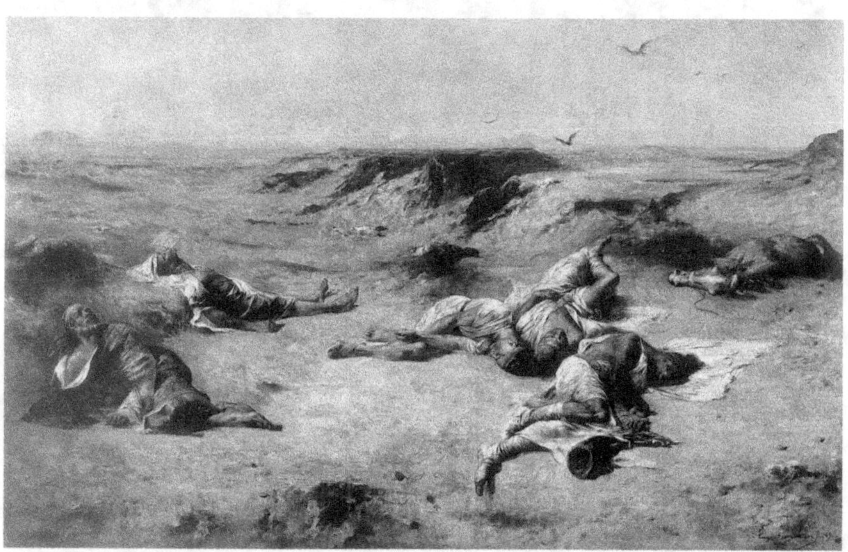

Figure 3.5 Eugène Fromentin, *The Land of Thirst*, 1869, oil on canvas, 103.5 × 144 cm. Musées Royaux des Beaux-Arts de Belgique, Brussels.

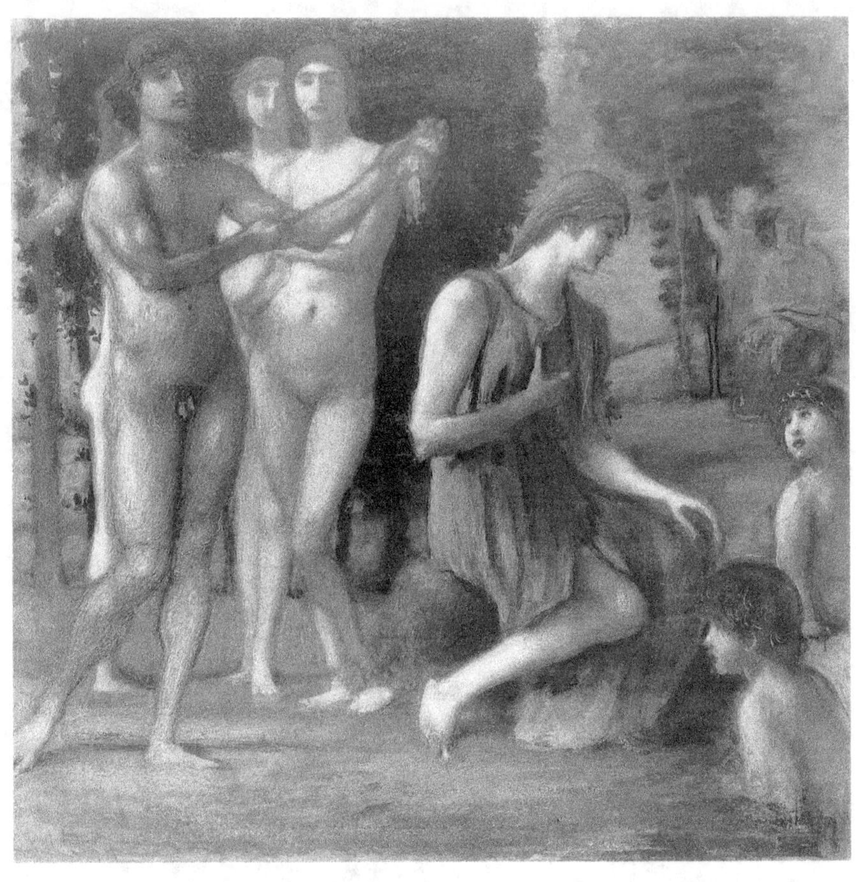

Figure 4.1 Hans von Marées, *Praise of Modesty*, ca. 1879–85, mixed media on wood, 113.5 × 115 cm. Bayerische Staatsgemäldesammlungen, Neue Pinakothek, Munich, Inv. 7859.

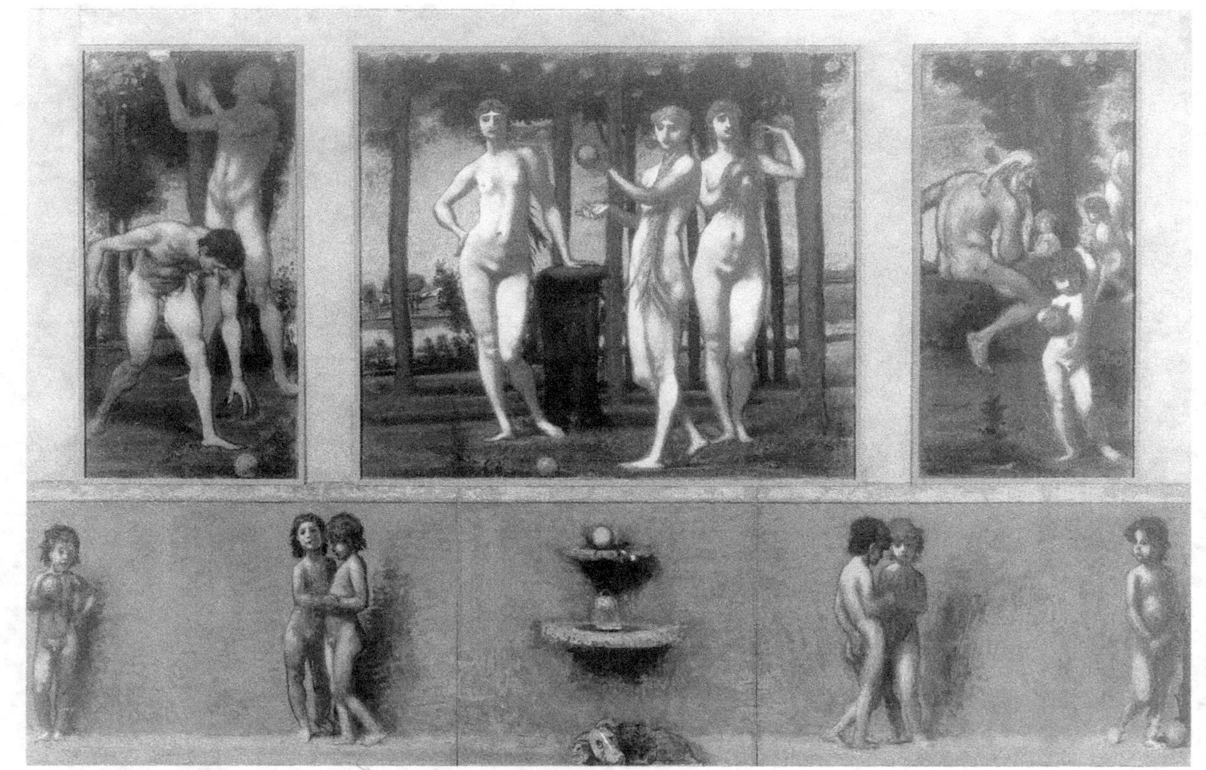

Figure 4.2 Hans von Marées, *Hesperides II*, ca. 1884–7, mixed media on wood, 341 × 482 cm. Bayerische Staatsgemäldesammlungen, Neue Pinakothek, Munich, Inv. 7854a–f.

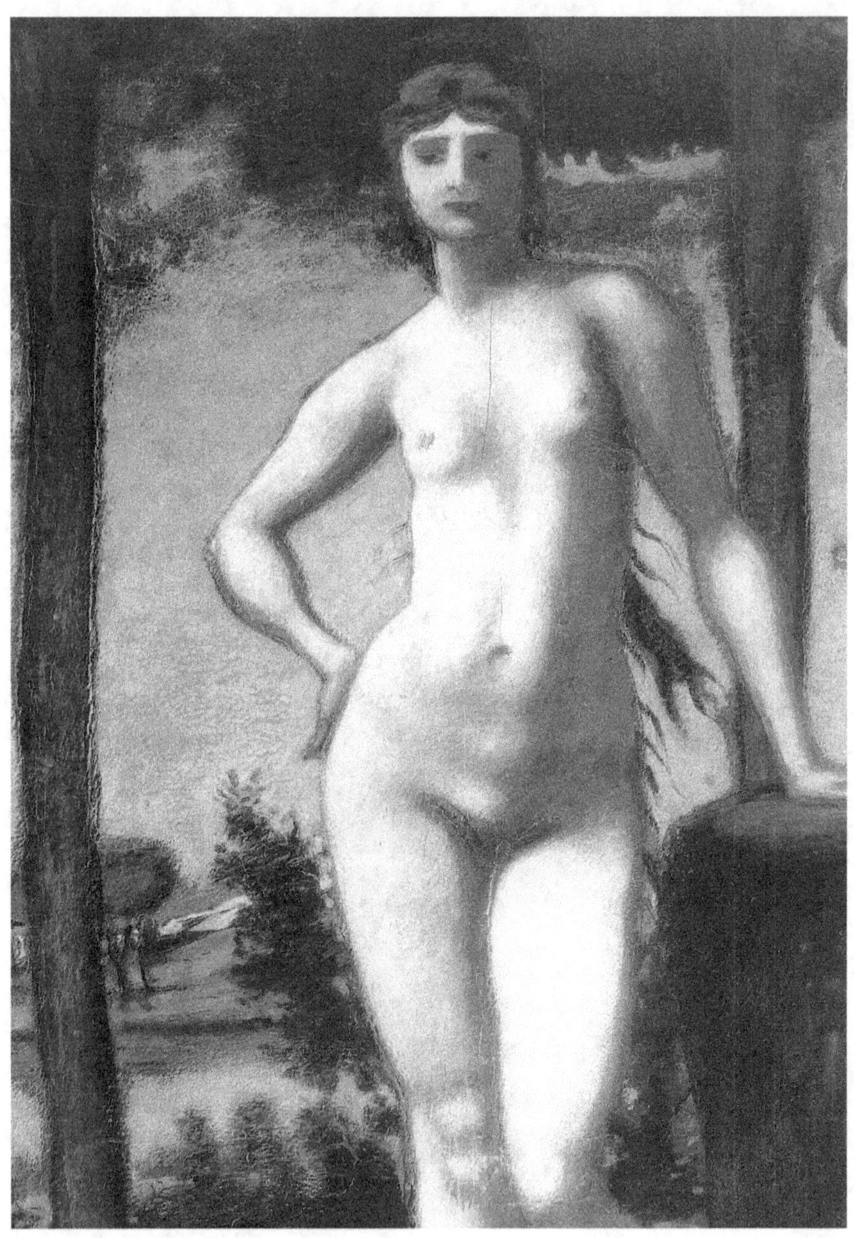

Figure 4.3 Detail of Figure 4.2, central panel.

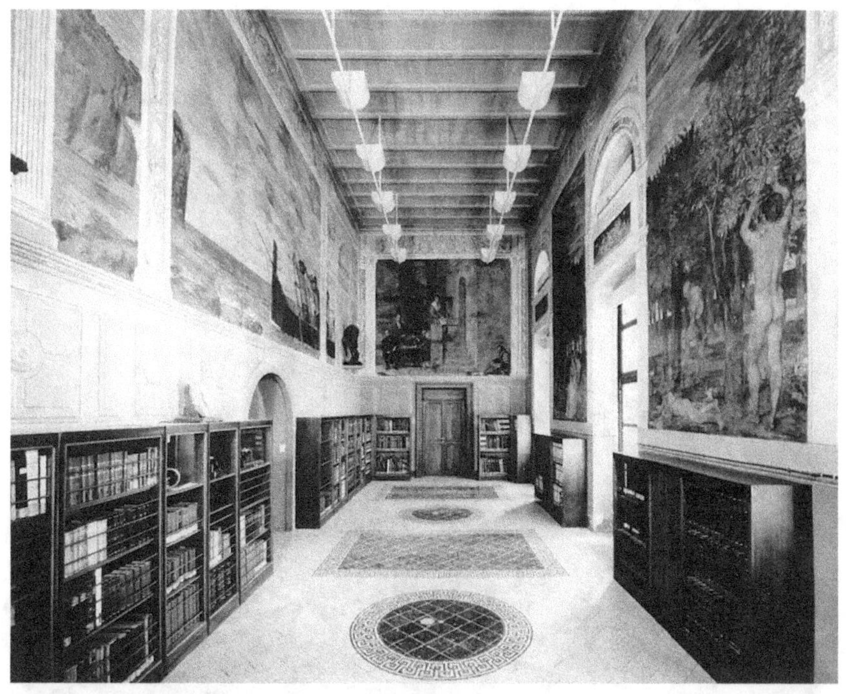

Figure 4.4 Hans von Marées, Adolf von Hildebrand, 'Fresco Room,' 1873, 13.5 m long, 7.5 m high, 5 m wide, view looking east. Naples, Stazione Zoologica Anton Dohrn, Historical Archives. Photograph by Luciano Pedicini, 2002.

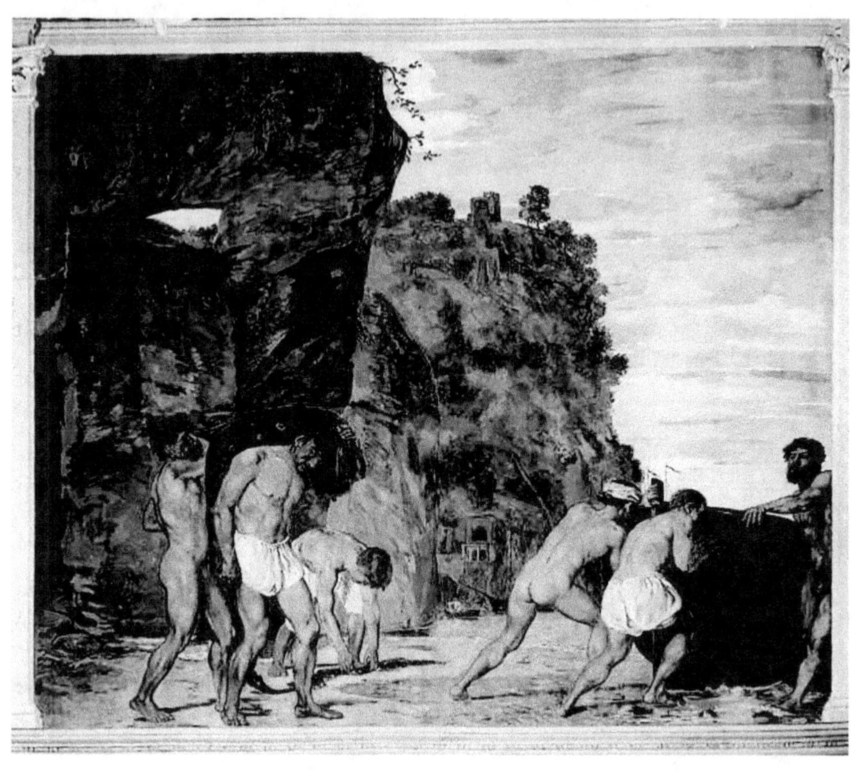

Figure 4.5 Hans von Marées, Adolf von Hildebrand, 'Fresco Room,' 1873, 350 × 500 cm, west wall. Naples, Stazione Zoologica Anton Dohrn, Historical Archives. Photograph by Luciano Pedicini, 2002.

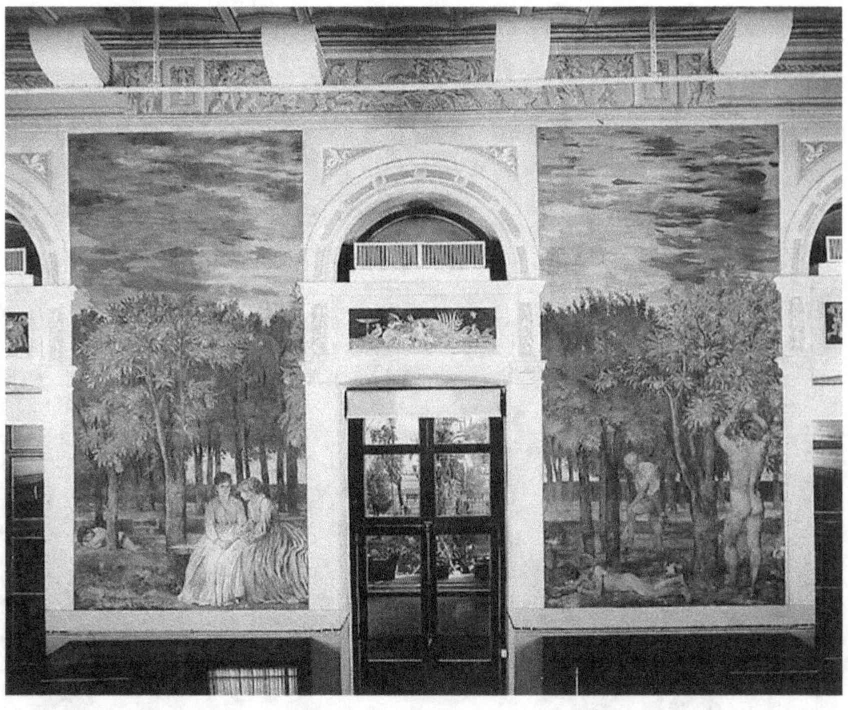

Figure 4.6 Hans von Marées, Adolf von Hildebrand, 'Fresco Room,' 1873, 470 × 1350 cm, view towards south wall. Naples, Stazione Zoologica Anton Dohrn, Historical Archives. Photograph by Luciano Pedicini, 2002.

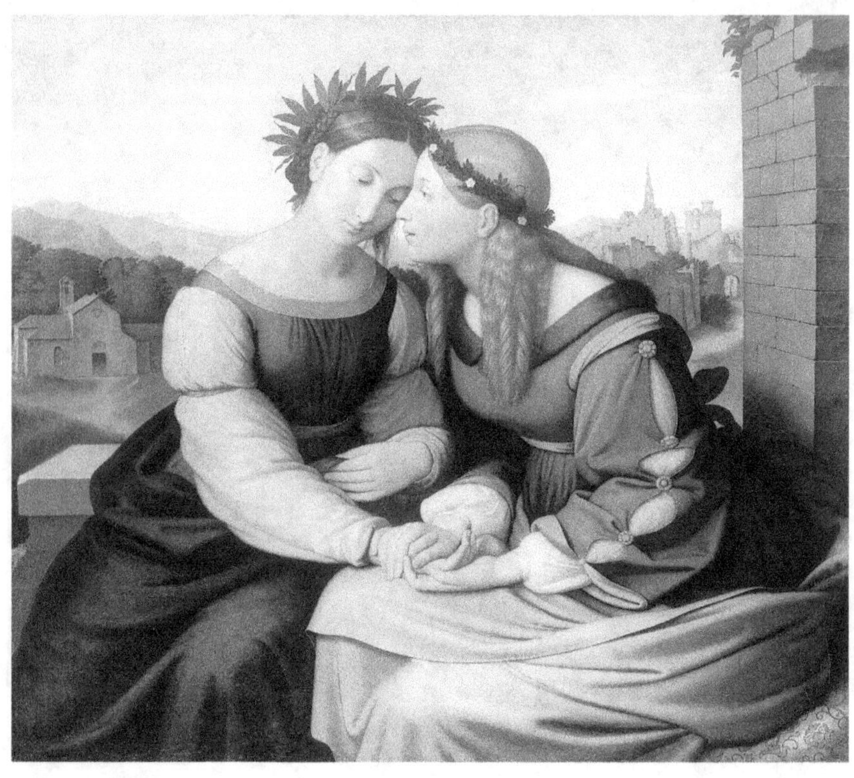

Figure 4.7 Johann Friedrich Overbeck, *Italia and Germania*, 1828, oil on canvas, 94.5 × 104.7 cm. Bayerische Staatsgemäldesammlungen, Neue Pinakothek, Munich, Inv. WAF 755.

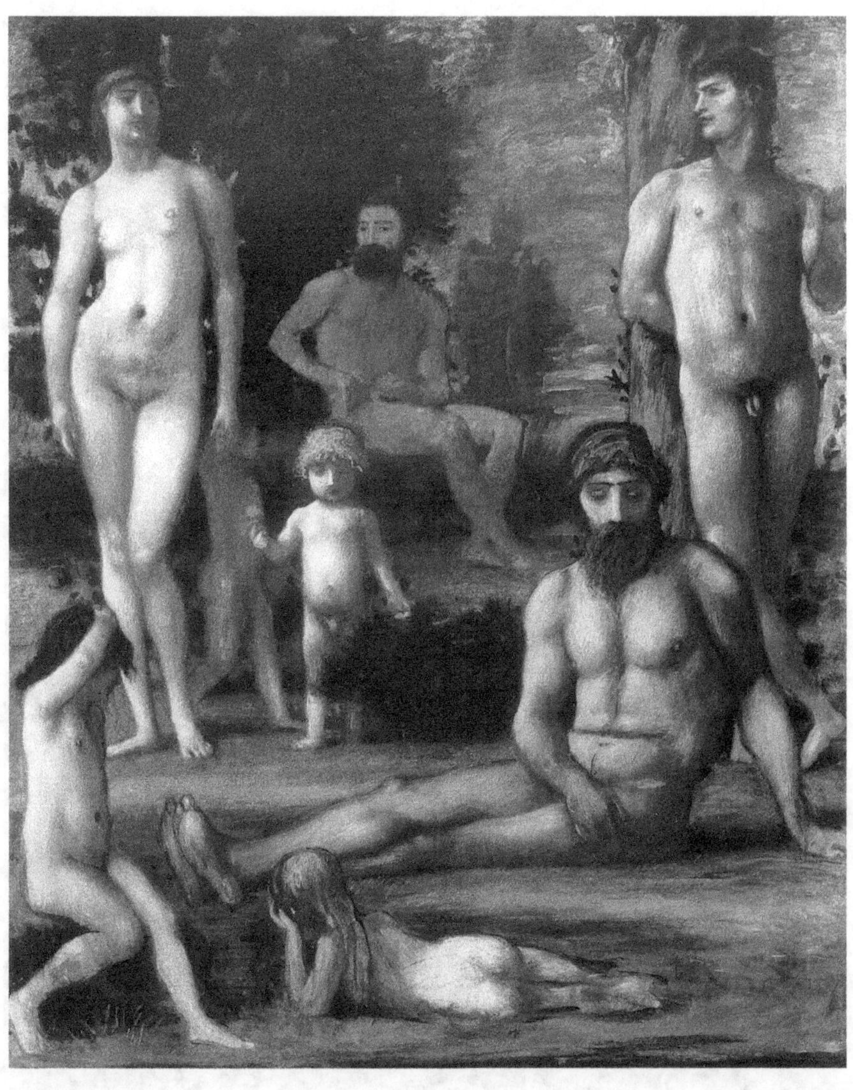

Figure 4.8 Hans von Marées, *Golden Age II*, ca. 1880–3, mixed media on canvas, 187.4 × 145 cm. Bayerische Staatsgemäldesammlungen, Neue Pinakothek, Munich, Inv. 7861.

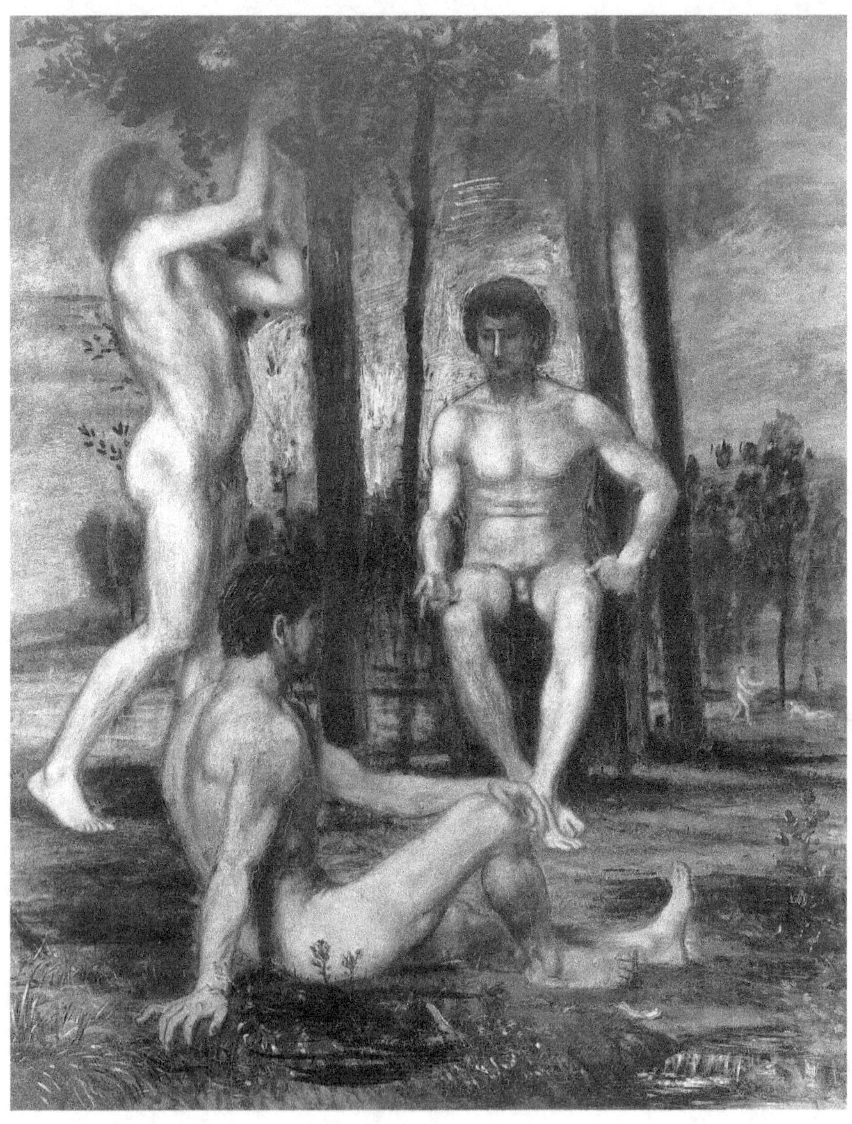

Figure 4.9 Hans von Marées, *Three Male Youths under Orange Trees*, ca. 1875–80, mixed media on wood, 187 × 145 cm. Bayerische Staatsgemäldesammlungen, Neue Pinakothek, Munich, Inv. 7863.

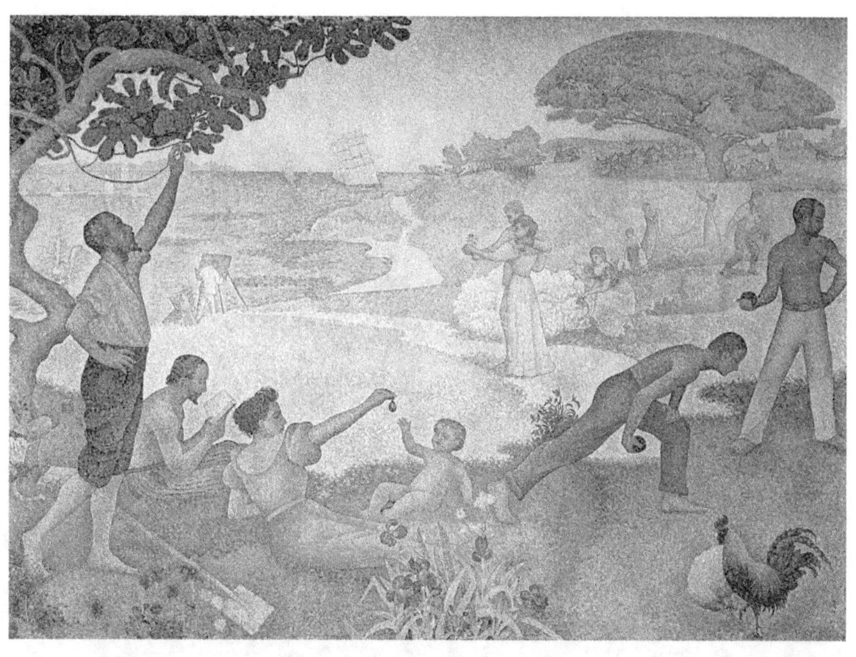

Figure 5.1 Paul Signac, *In the Time of Harmony: The Golden Age Is Not in the Past, It Is in the Future*, 1893–5, 300 × 400 cm. Montreuil, Mairie (photo: image © Erich Lessing / Art Resource, New York).

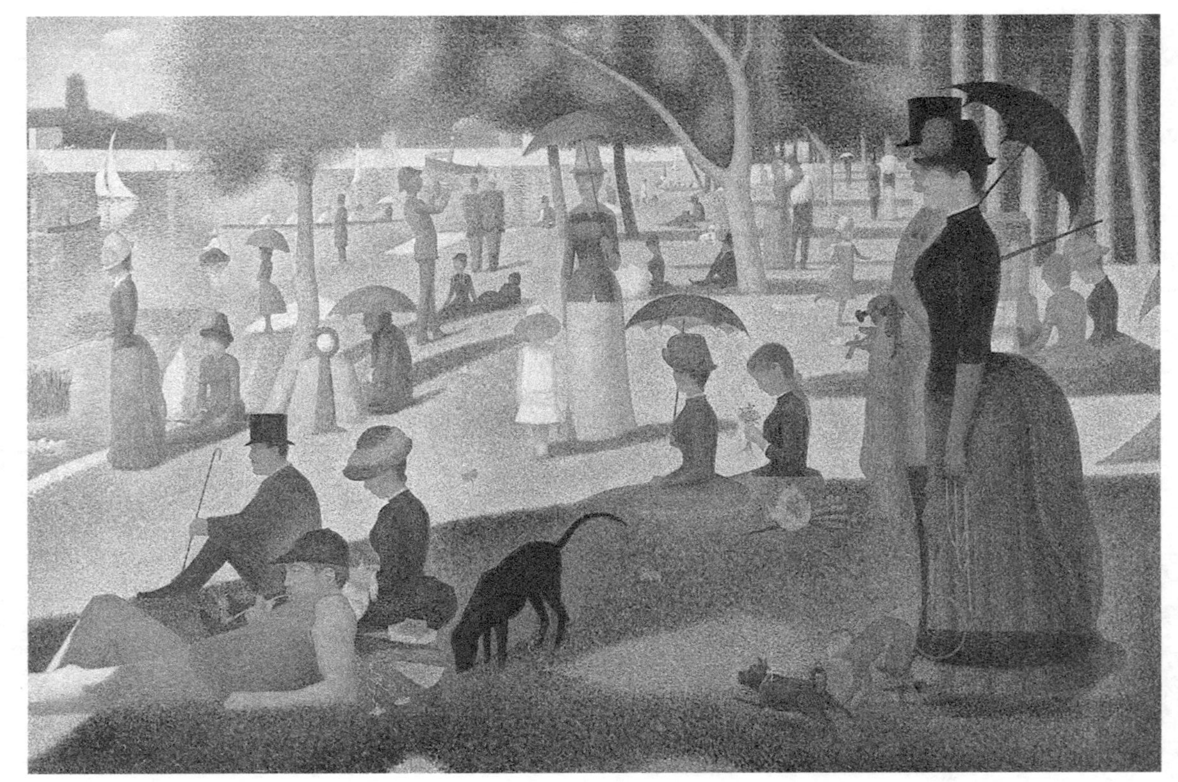

Figure 5.2 Georges Seurat, *A Sunday Afternoon on the Island of La Grande Jatte*, 1884–6, 207.5 × 308 cm. Art Institute of Chicago, Helen Birch Bartlett Memorial Collection (photo: image © The Art Institute of Chicago).

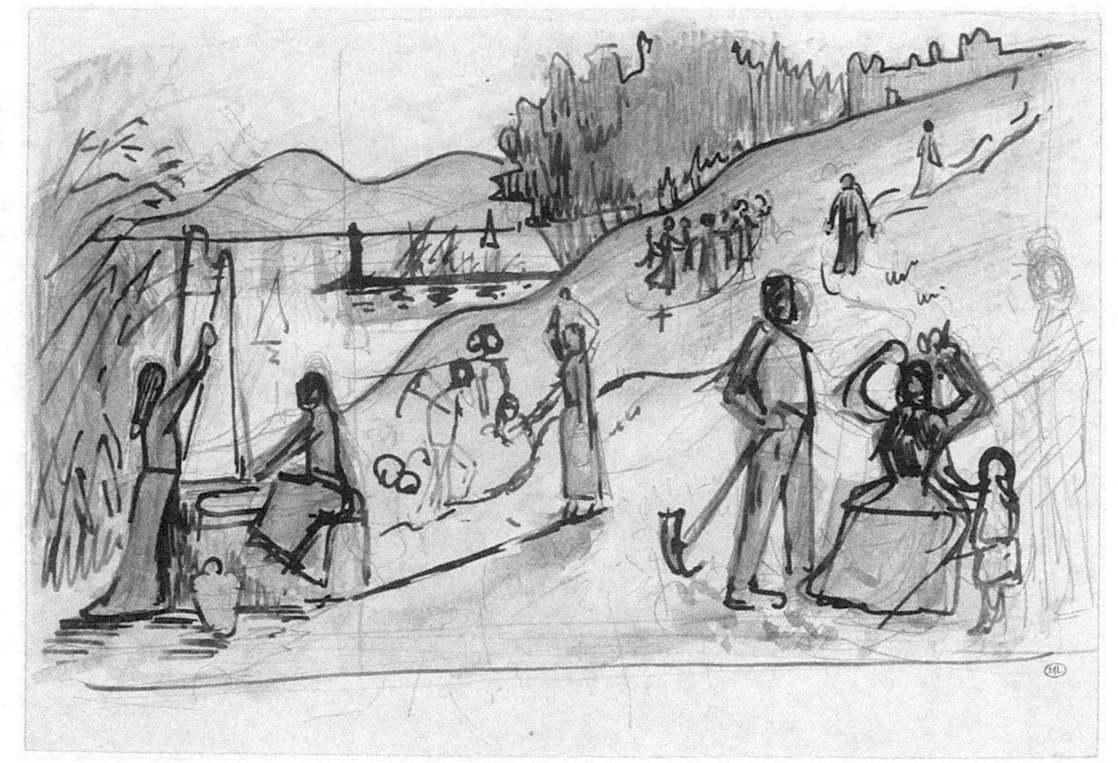

Figure 5.3 Signac, Study for *Young Provençal Women at the Well*, 1892, graphite, ink, and watercolour on paper, 19.6 × 28.7 cm. Paris, Musée du Louvre, Cabinet de Dessins, RF 37071 (photo: Réunion des Musées Nationaux / Art Resource, NY).

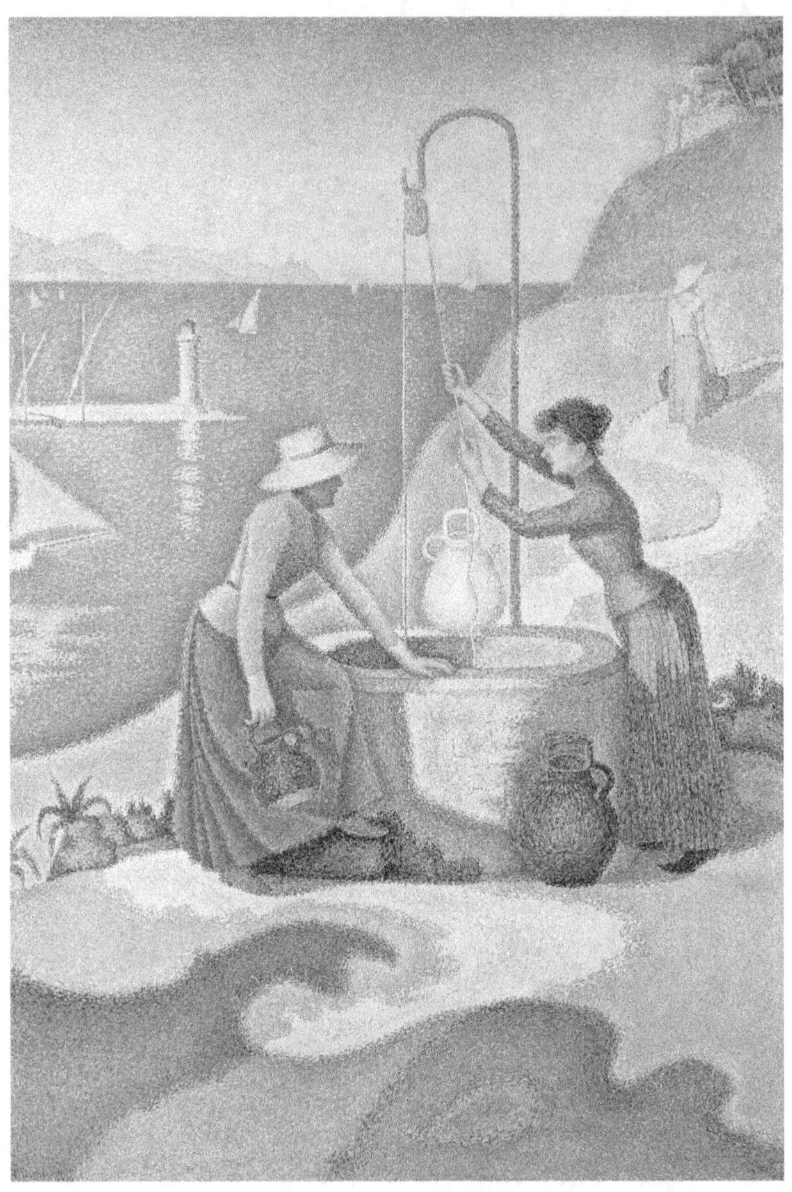

Figure 5.4 Paul Signac, *Young Provençal Women at the Well: Decoration for a Panel in Half-Light*, 1892, 194.8 × 130.7 cm. Paris, Musée d'Orsay (photo: image © Erich Lessing / Art Resource, NY).

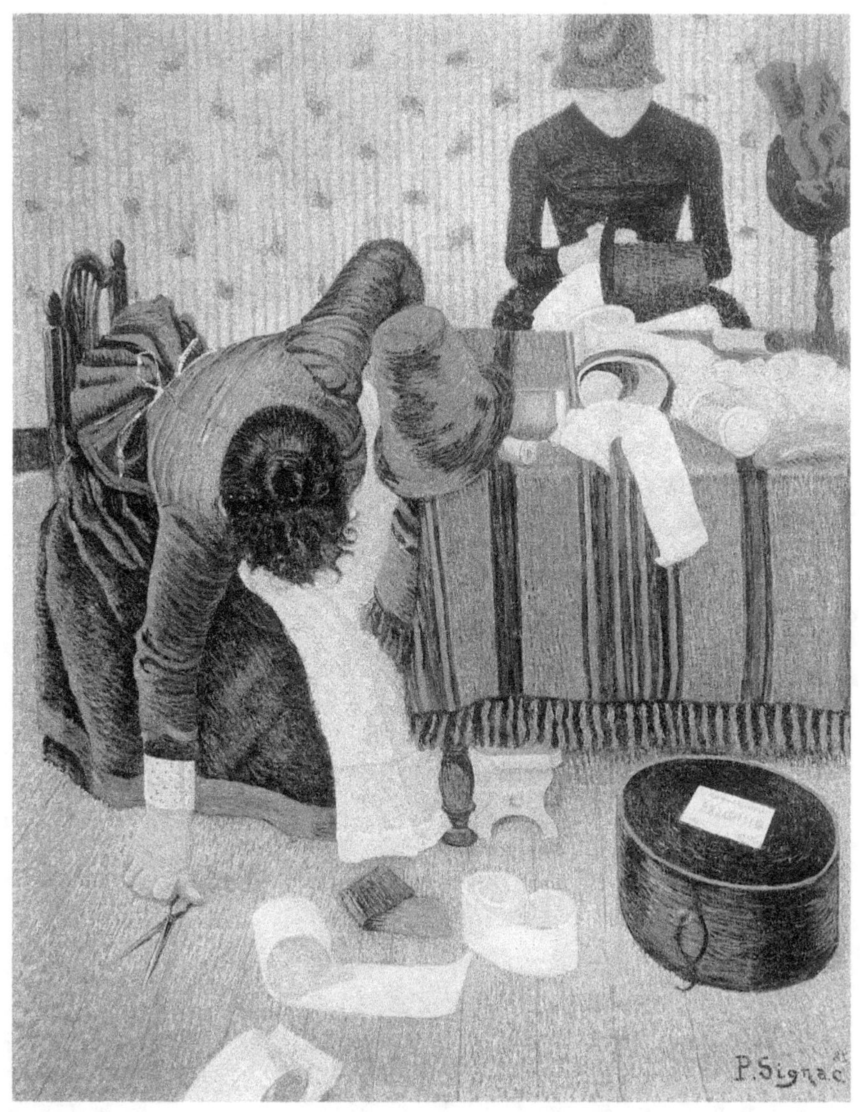


Figure 5.5 Paul Signac, *The Milliners,* 1885–6, 118 × 88 cm. Zurich, Fondation E.G. Bührle.

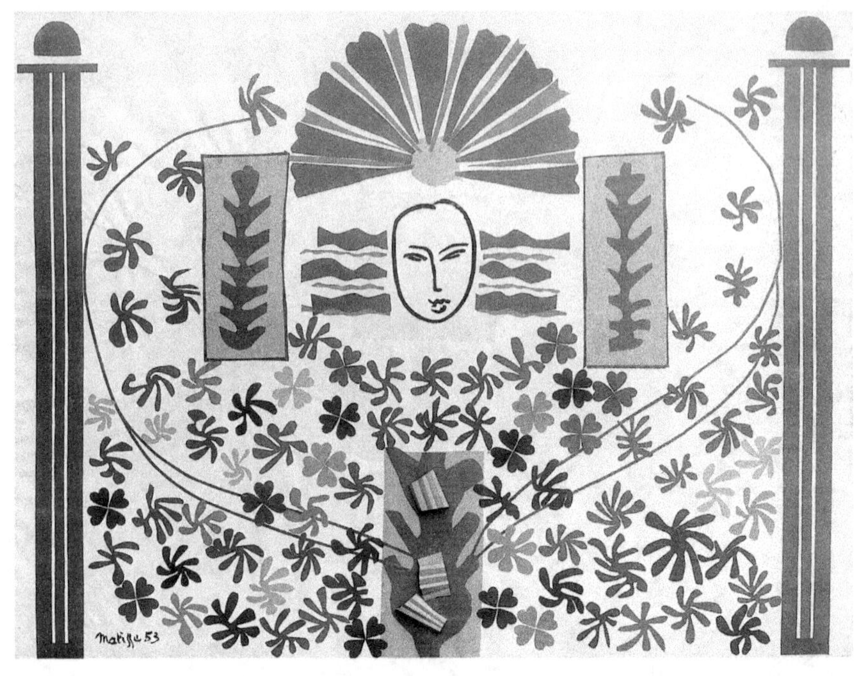


Figure 6.1 Henri Matisse, *Apollo*, 1953, gouache and ink on paper, cut and pasted on paper, 327 × 423 cm. Moderna Museet, Stockholm.

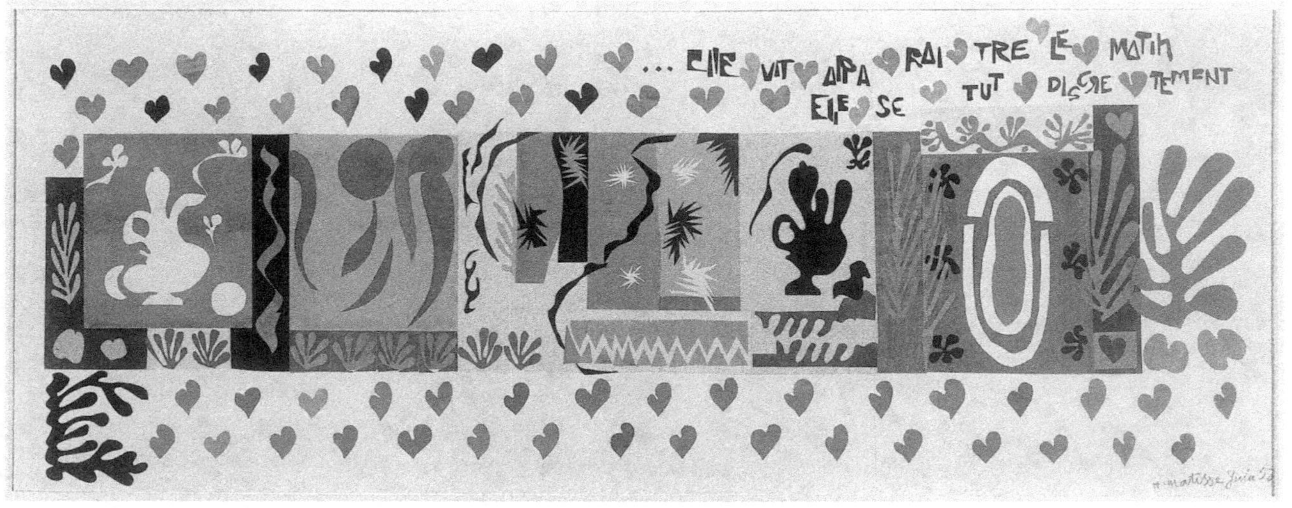


Figure 6.2 Henri Matisse, *The Thousand and One Nights*, 1950, gouache on paper, cut and pasted on paper, 140 × 374 cm. Carnegie Museum of Art, Pittsburgh; acquired through the generosity of the Sarah Mellon Scaife Family.

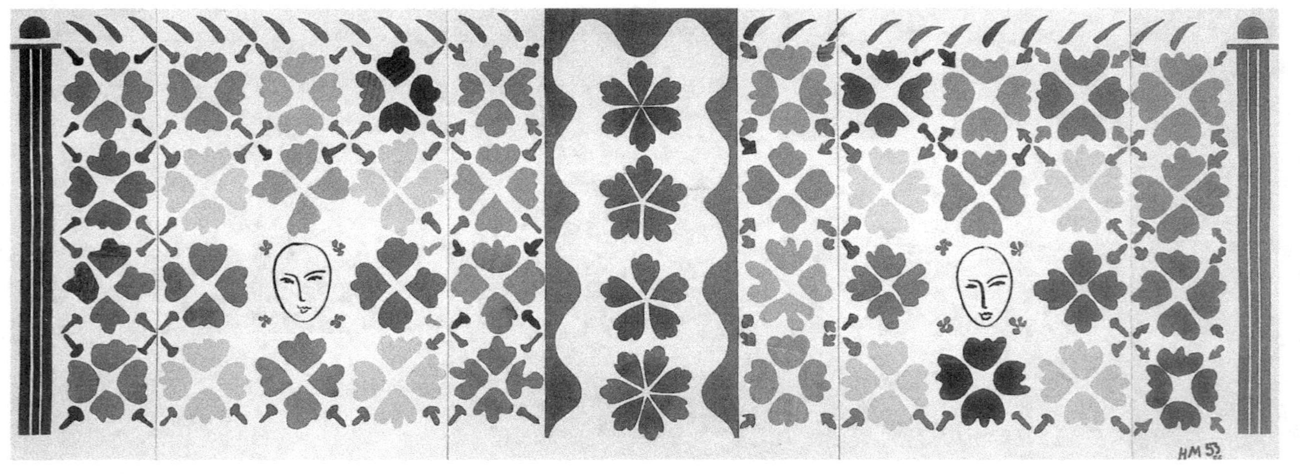


Figure 6.3 Henri Matisse, *Large Decoration with Masks*, 1953, gouache and ink on paper, cut and pasted on paper, 353.7 × 997 cm. National Gallery of Art, Washington, Ailsa Mellon Bruce Fund.

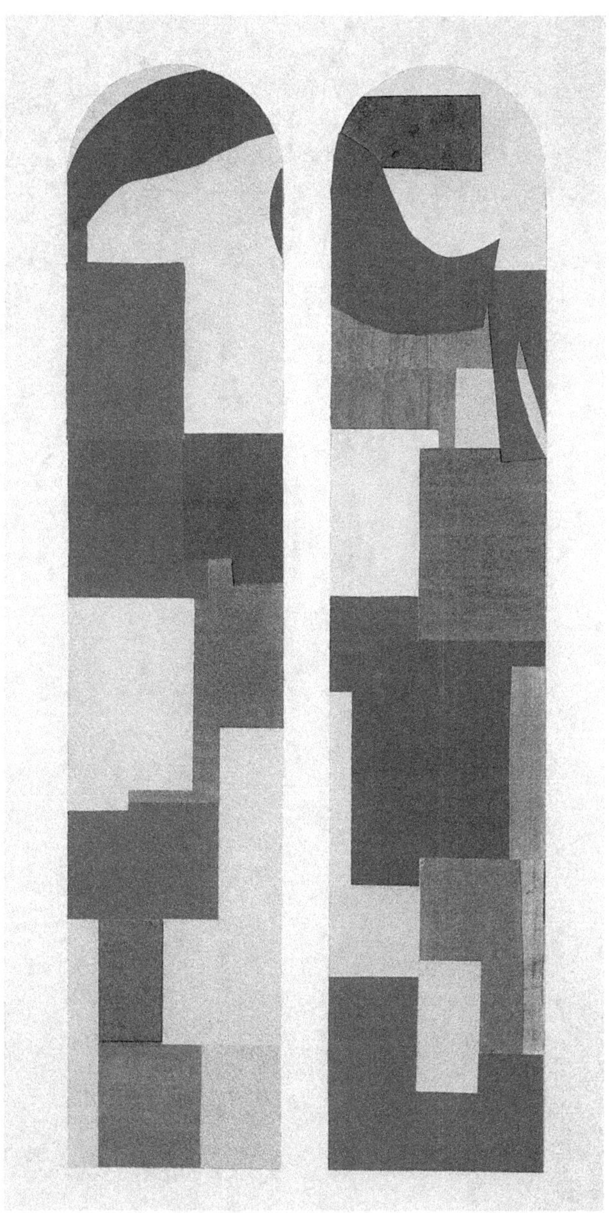

Figure 6.4 Henri Matisse, *Celestial Jerusalem*, 1948, gouache on paper, cut and pasted on paper, 270 × 130 cm. Vatican Museums, Vatican City State.

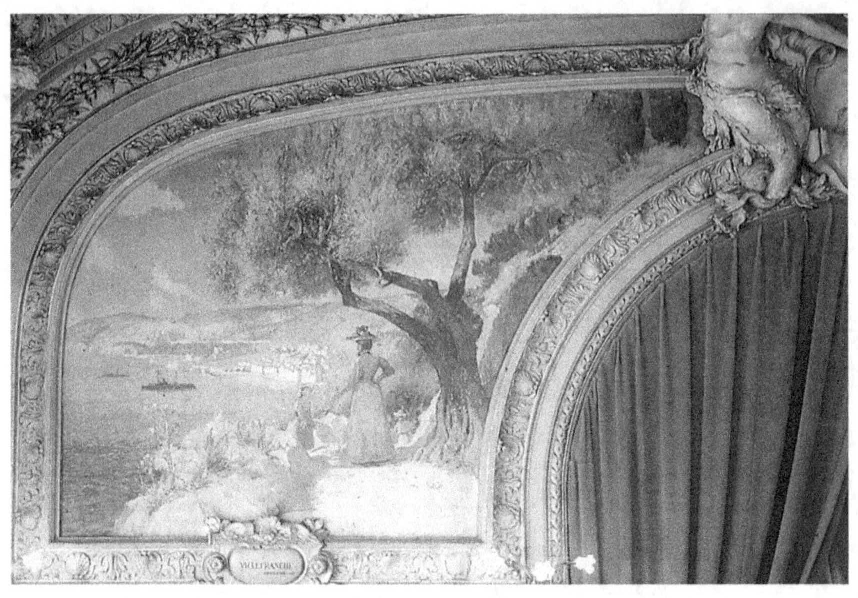

Figure 6.5 Frédéric Montenard, *Villefranche*, 1901, oil on canvas, glued to wall, 305 × 430 cm (approx.). Restaurant 'Le Train bleu,' Gare de Lyon, Paris.

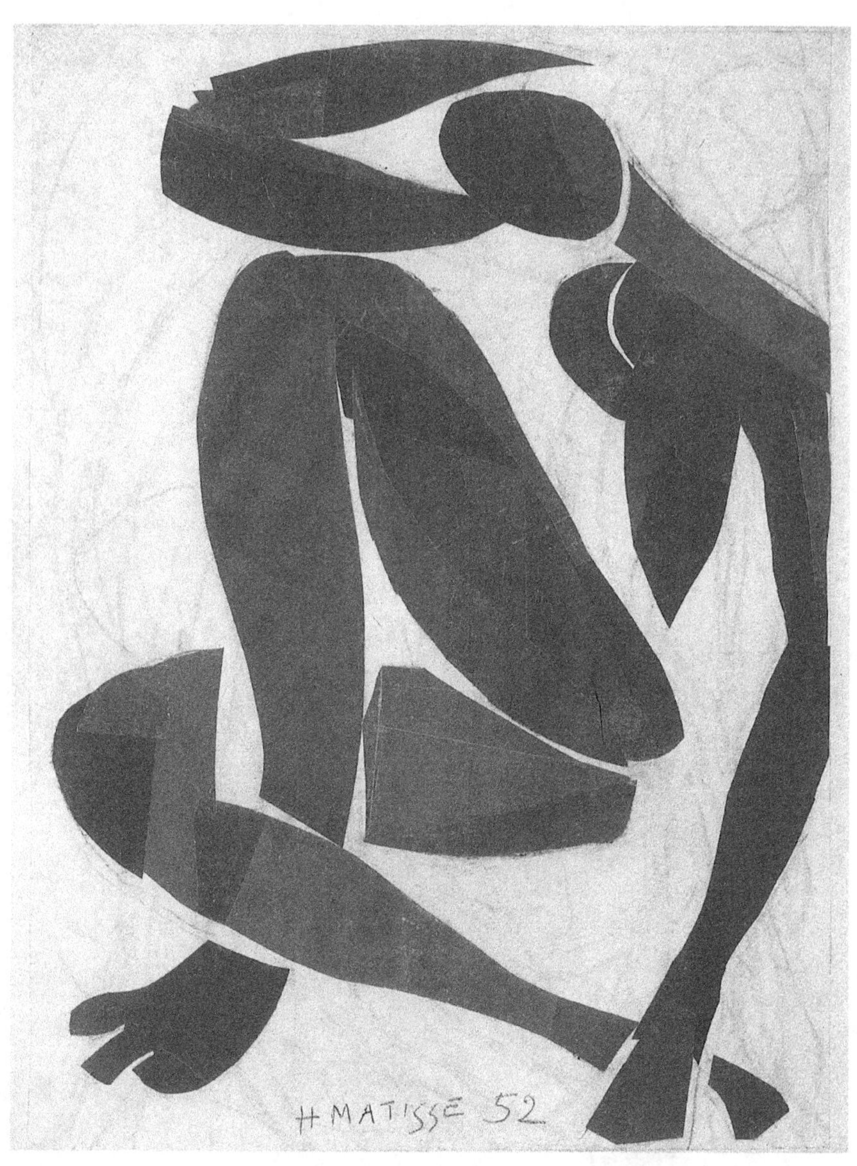


Figure 6.6 Henri Matisse, *Blue Nude IV*, 1952, charcoal on paper and gouache on paper, cut and pasted on paper, 102.9 × 76.8 cm. Musée Matisse, Nice.

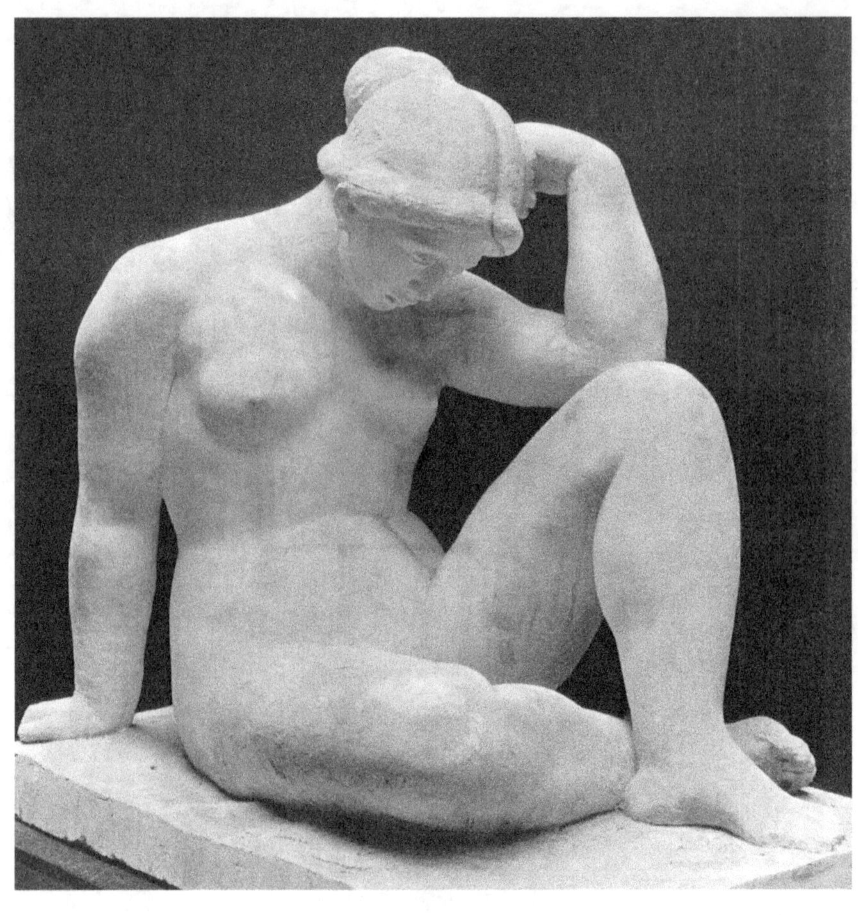

Figure 6.7 Aristide Maillol, *The Mediterranean*, 1900–5, plaster, 110 cm high. Private collection.

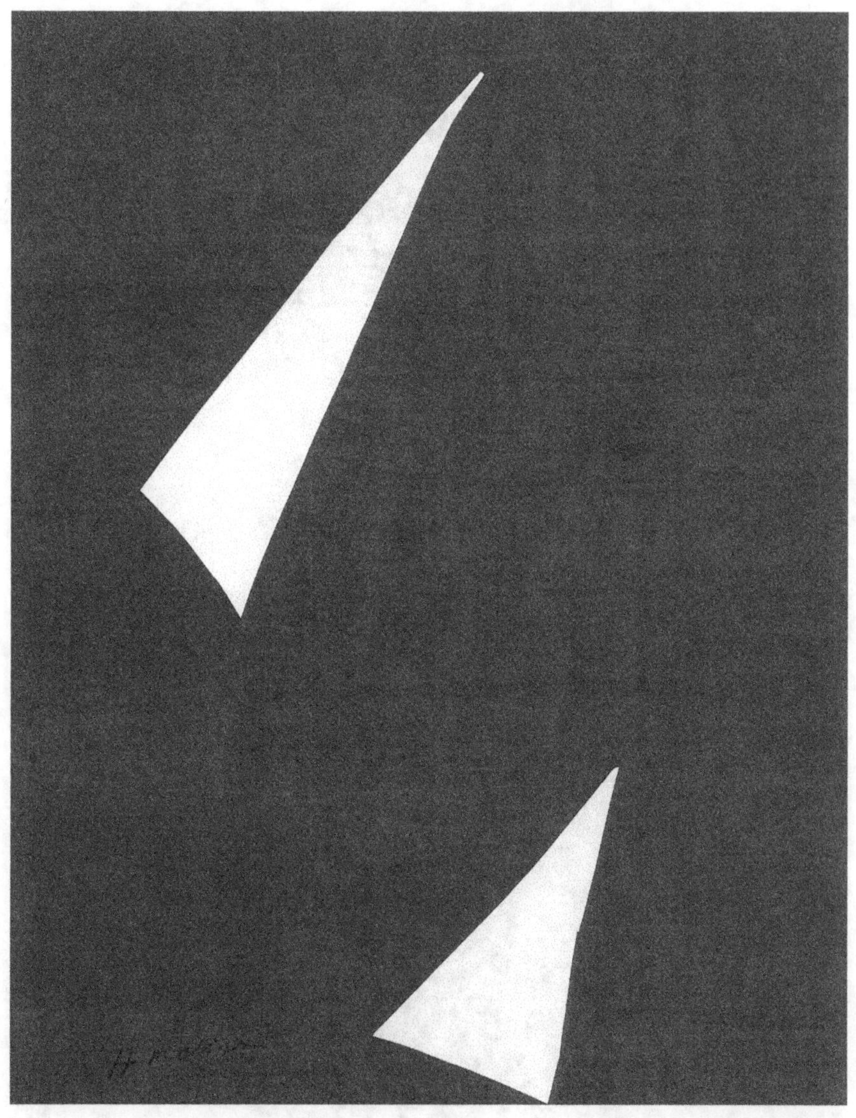

Figure 6.8 Henri Matisse, *The Sails*, 1952, gouache on paper, cut and pasted on paper, 72 × 60 cm. Private collection.

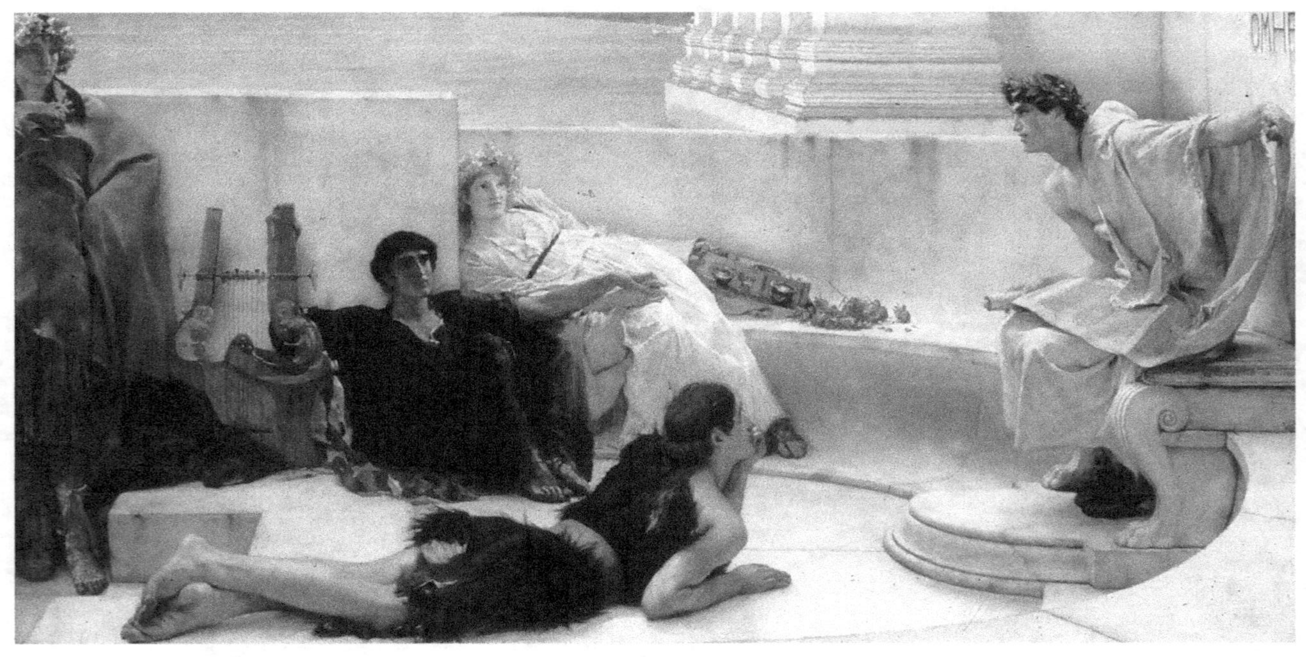

Figure 7.1 Lawrence Alma-Tadema, *A Reading from Homer*, 1885, oil on canvas, 91.4 × 183.8 cm. Philadelphia Museum of Art, George W. Elkins Collection.

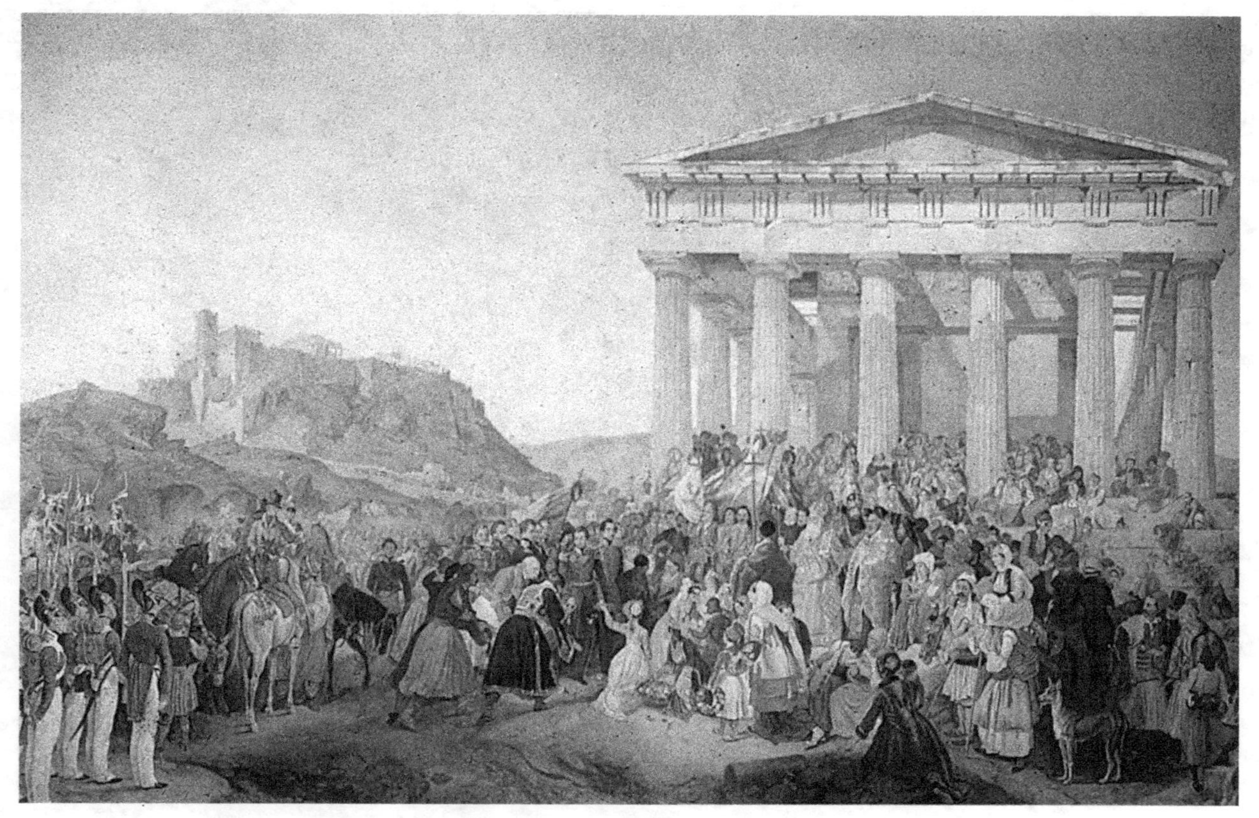

Figure 7.2 Peter von Hess, *Arrival of Otto in Athens*, 1839, oil on canvas, 273 × 416 cm. Neue Pinakothek, Munich.

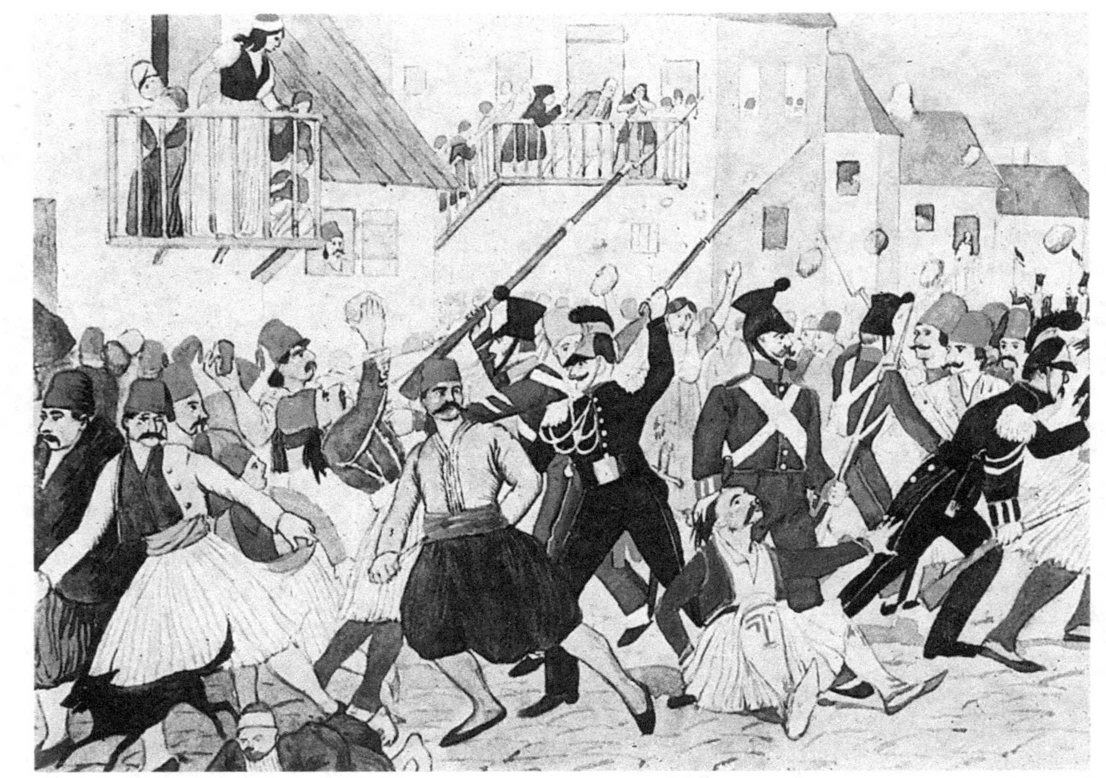

Figure 7.3 Ludwig Köllnberger, *Bavarian Troops against Greek Insurgents*, watercolour, 24 × 13.5 cm, copy from original by Hans Hanke, 1909. National Historical Museum, Athens.

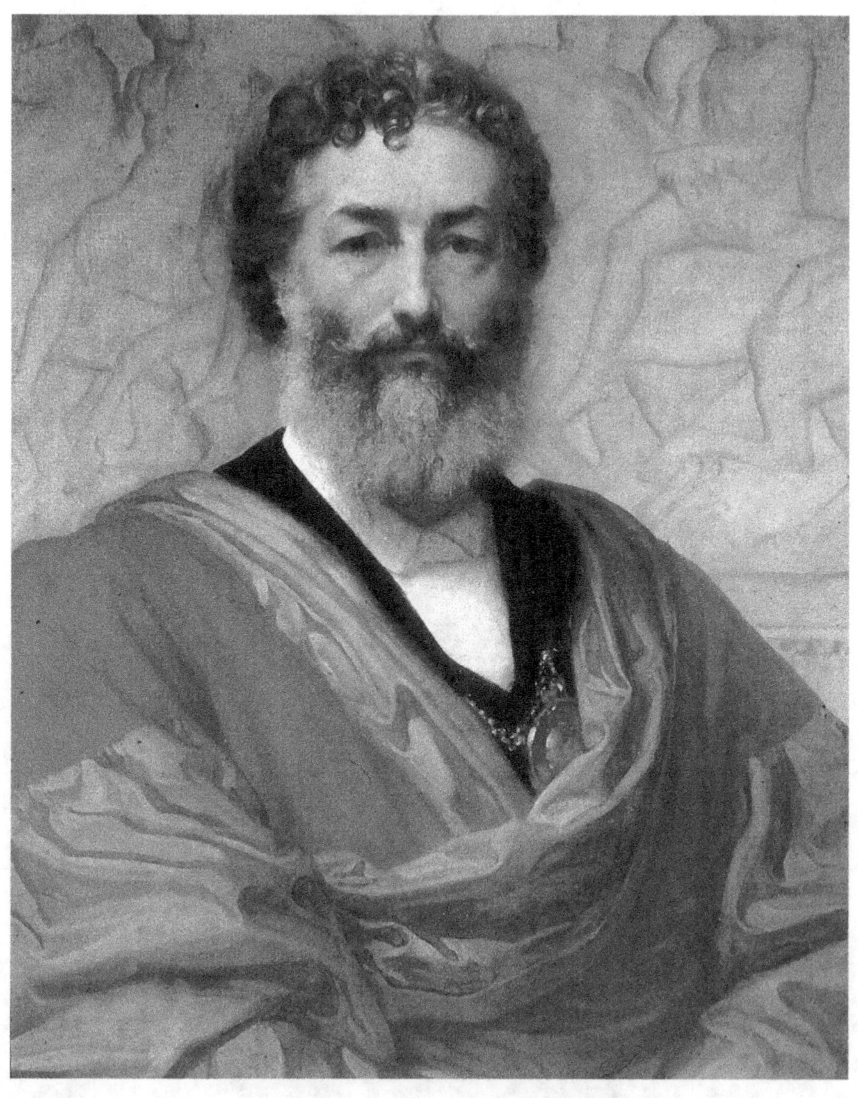

Figure 7.4 Frederic Leighton, *Self-Portrait*, 1880, oil on canvas, 76.5 × 64 cm. Galleria degli Uffizi, Florence.

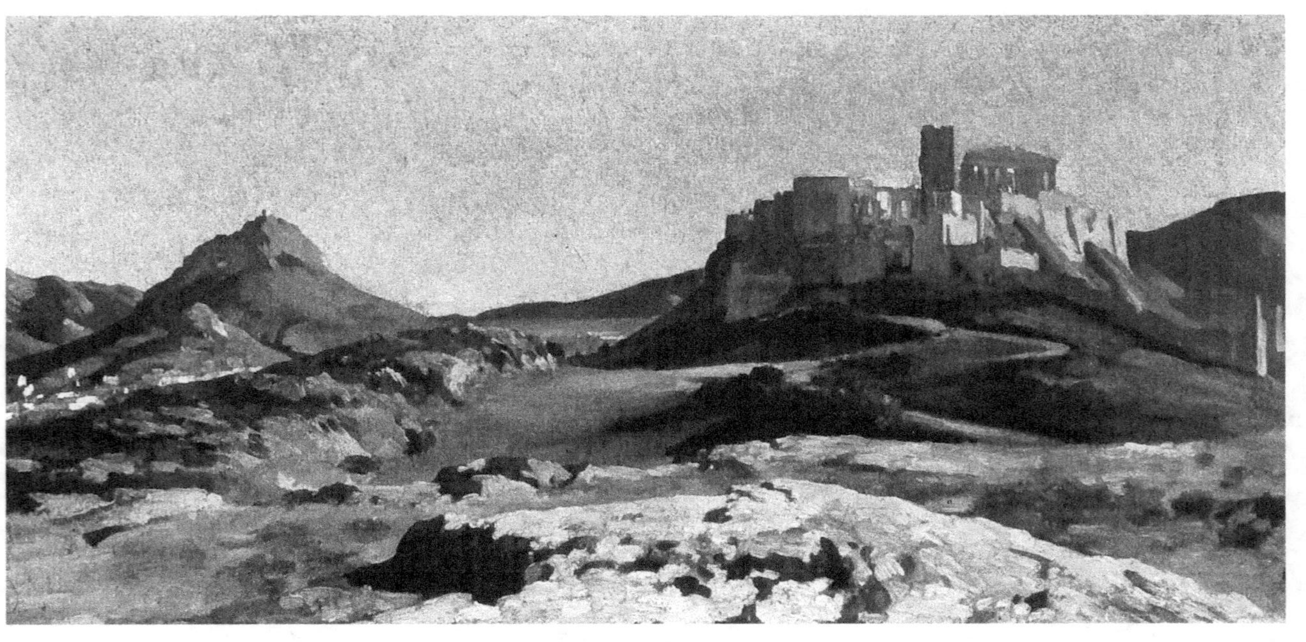

Figure 7.5 Frederic Leighton, *The Acropolis in Athens with the Genoese Tower*, 1867, oil on canvas, 18.5 × 39.4 cm. Private collection.

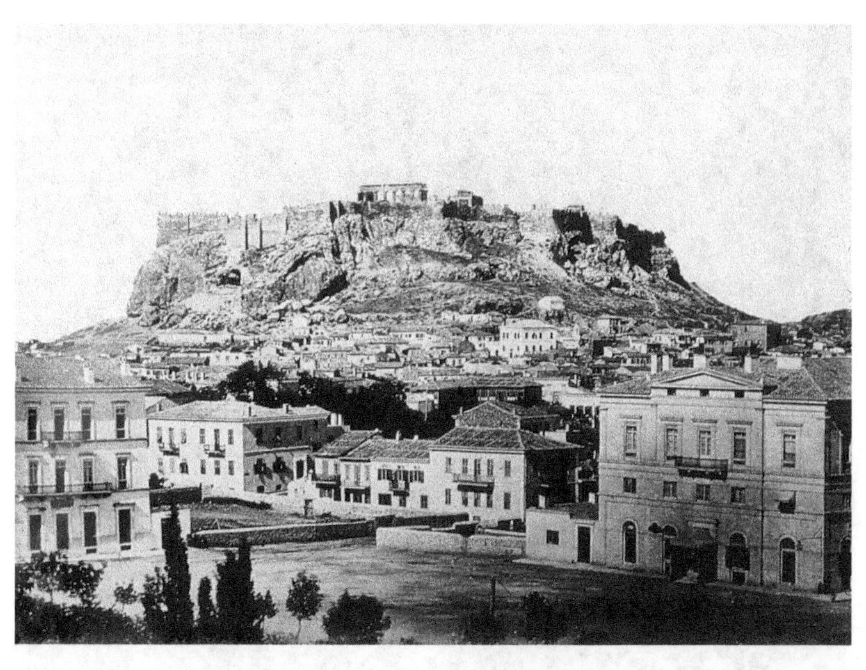

Figure 7.6 Dimitrios Constantinou, ‘View of Athens,’ 1859–60, photograph, 18 × 24 cm.

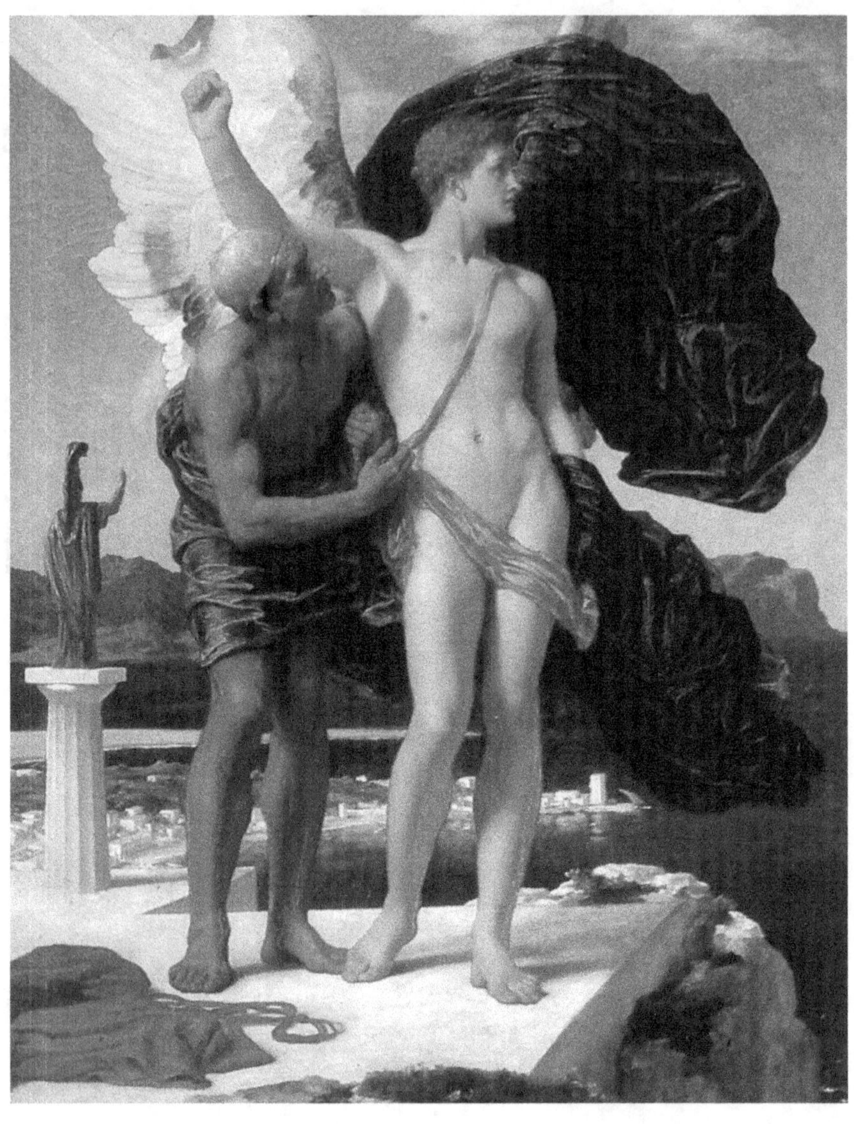

Figure 7.7 Frederic Leighton, *Daedalus and Icarus*, 1869, oil on canvas, 138.2 × 106.5 cm. Buscot Park, England, The Farrington Collection.

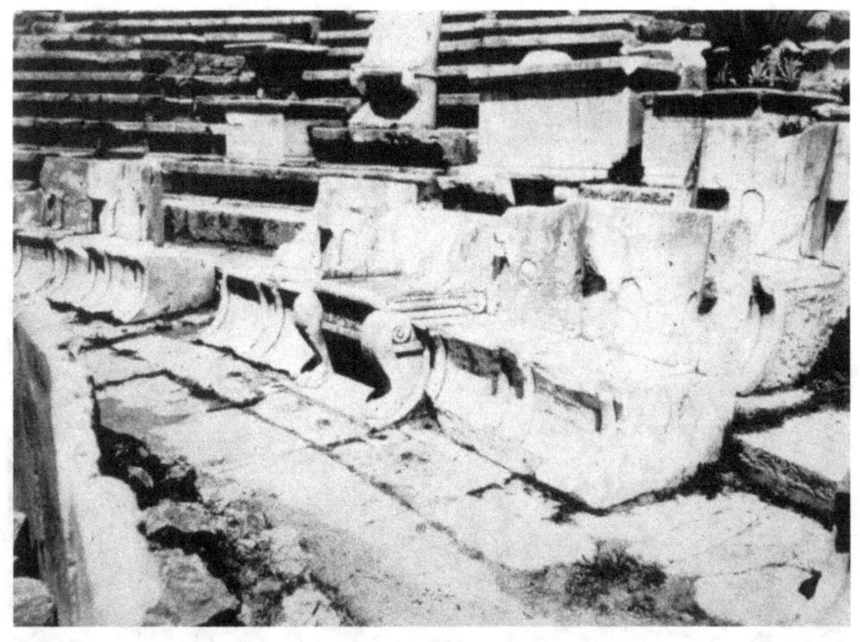

Figure 7.8 Félix Bonfils, 'Athens, Seats from the Theatre of Dionysus,' photograph, 1872, 18 × 24 cm. Special Collections, Birmingham University, England.

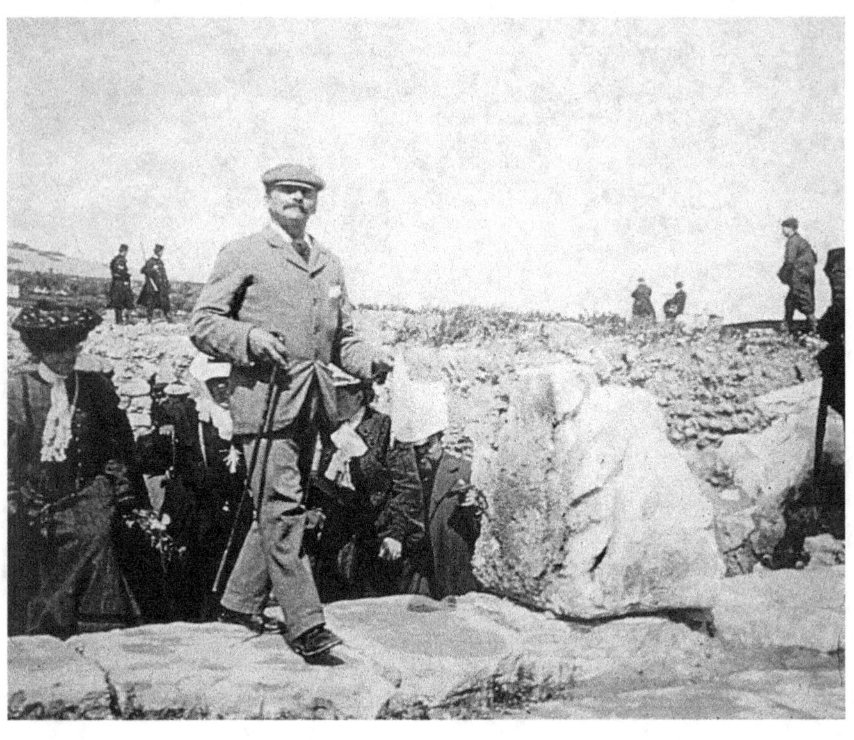

Figure 7.9 Sir Arthur Evans leads a tourist group in Cnossos, Crete, ca. 1900, photograph, 18 × 24 cm.

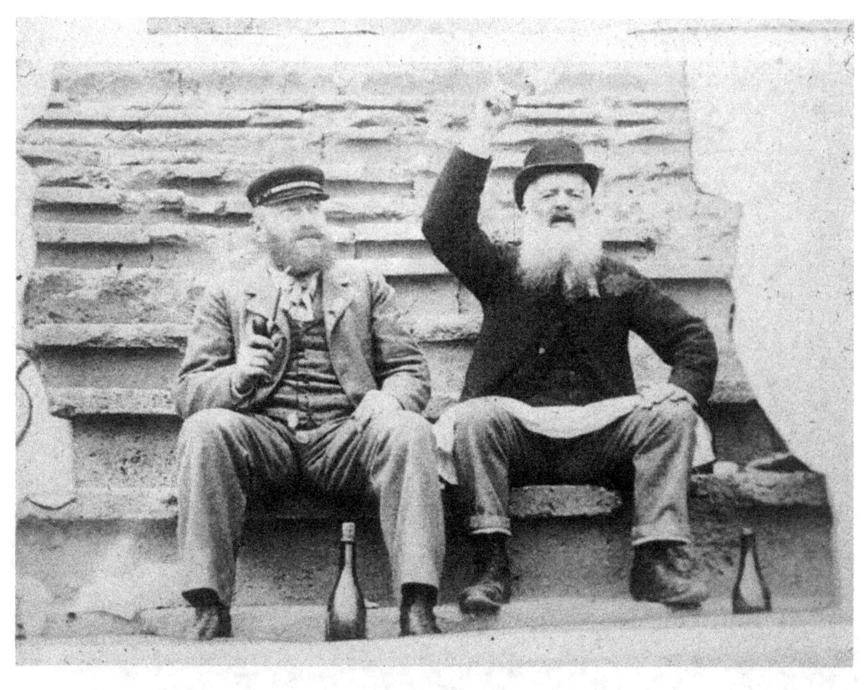

Figure 7.10 Lemoyne, 'Tourists at the Theatre in Delphi,' ca. 1900, photograph, 18 × 24 cm.

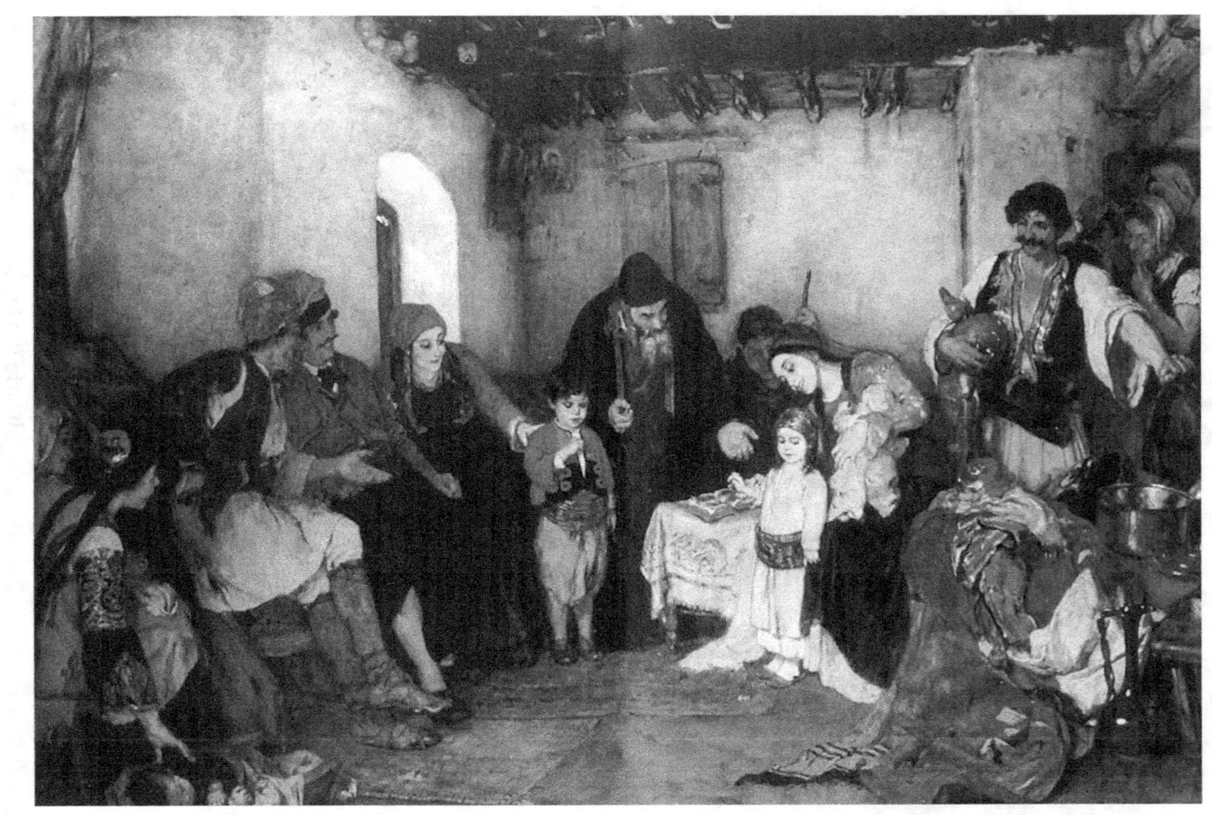

Figure 7.11 Nicolaos Gyzis, *Children's Betrothal*, 1877, oil on canvas, 103 × 155 cm. National Gallery, Athens.

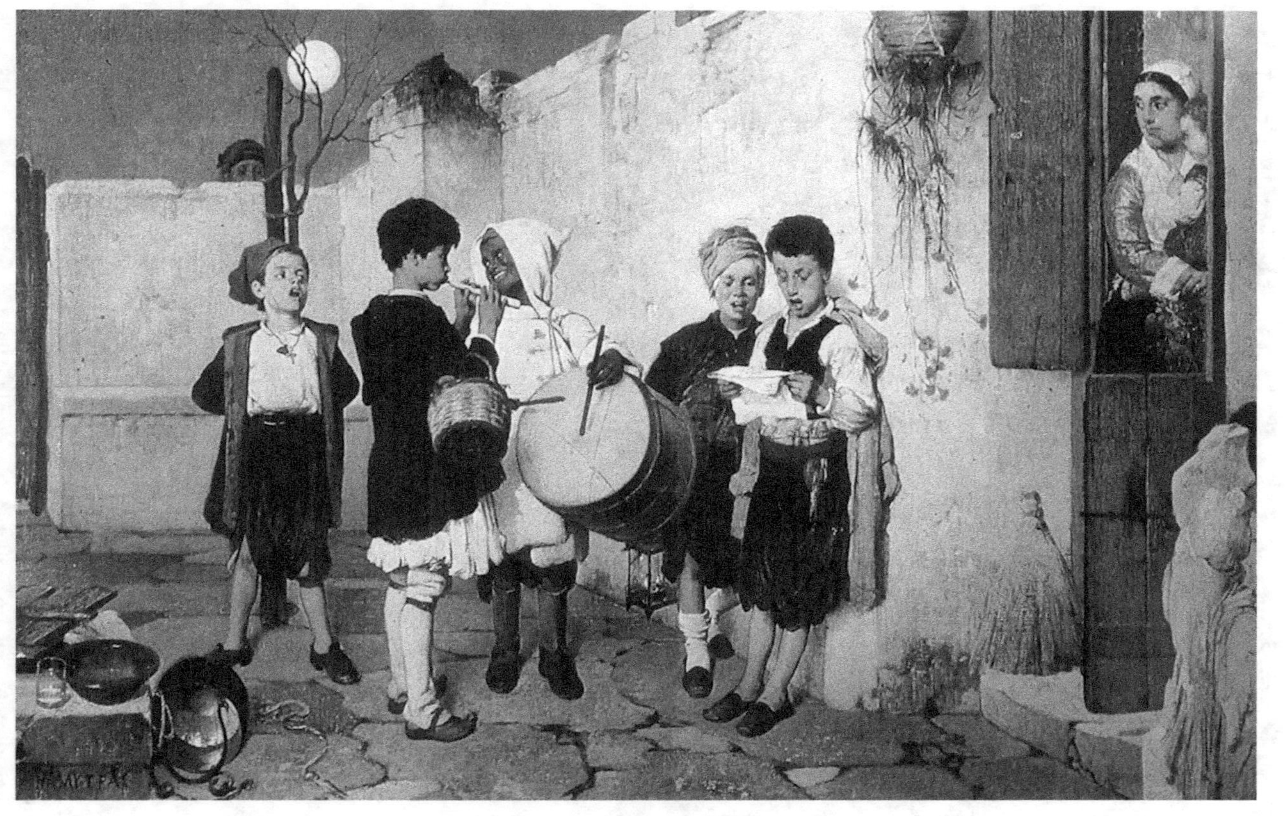

Figure 7.12 Nikiphoros Lytras, *Ta kalanda* (New York's Carols), 1870s, oil on canvas, 58 × 87 cm. National Gallery, Athens.

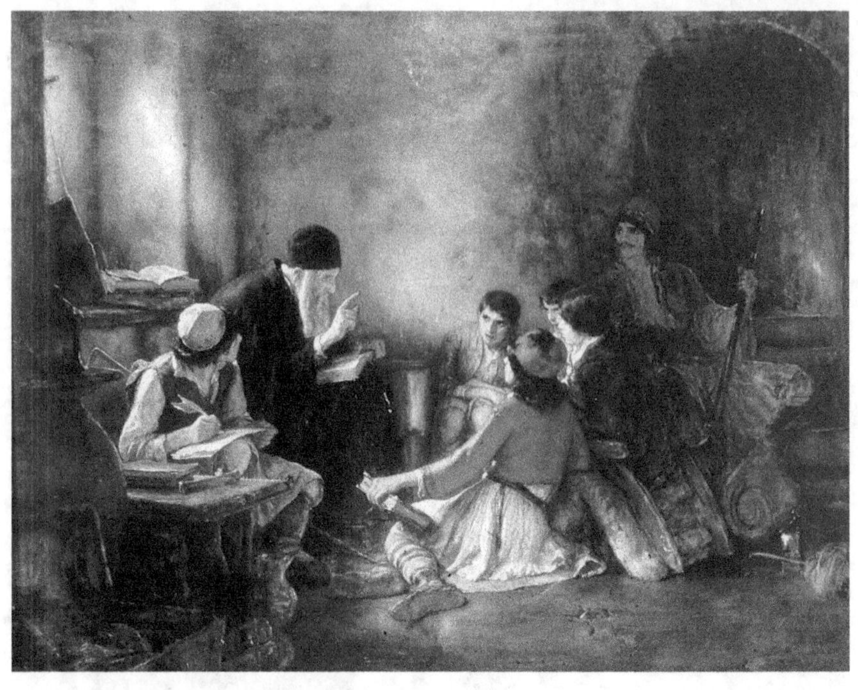

Figure 7.13 Nicolaos Gyzis, *To krypho scholio* (The Secret School), 1885, oil on canvas, dimensions unavailable. National Gallery, Athens.

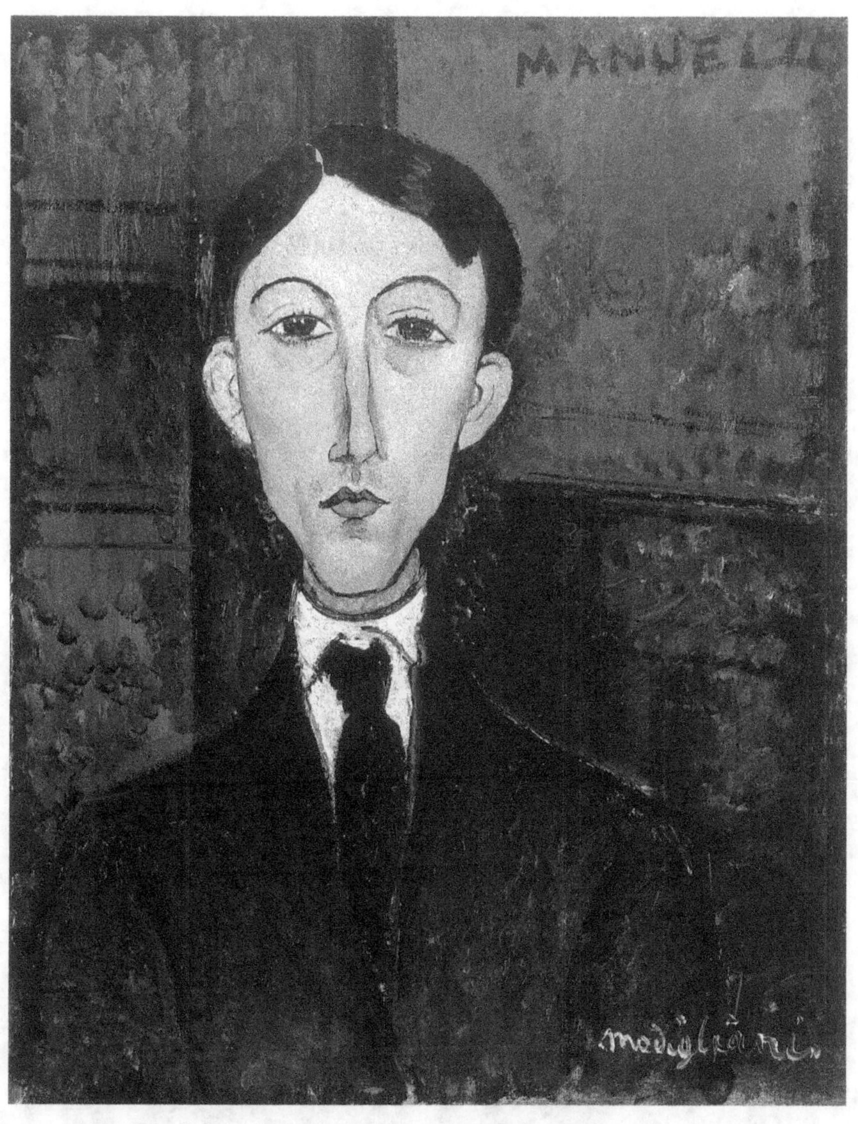


Figure 8.1 Amedeo Modigliani, *Portrait of Manuello*, ca. 1916, oil on canvas, 66 × 51 cm. Los Angeles County Museum of Art, Gift of Mr and Mrs William Wyler (51.22).

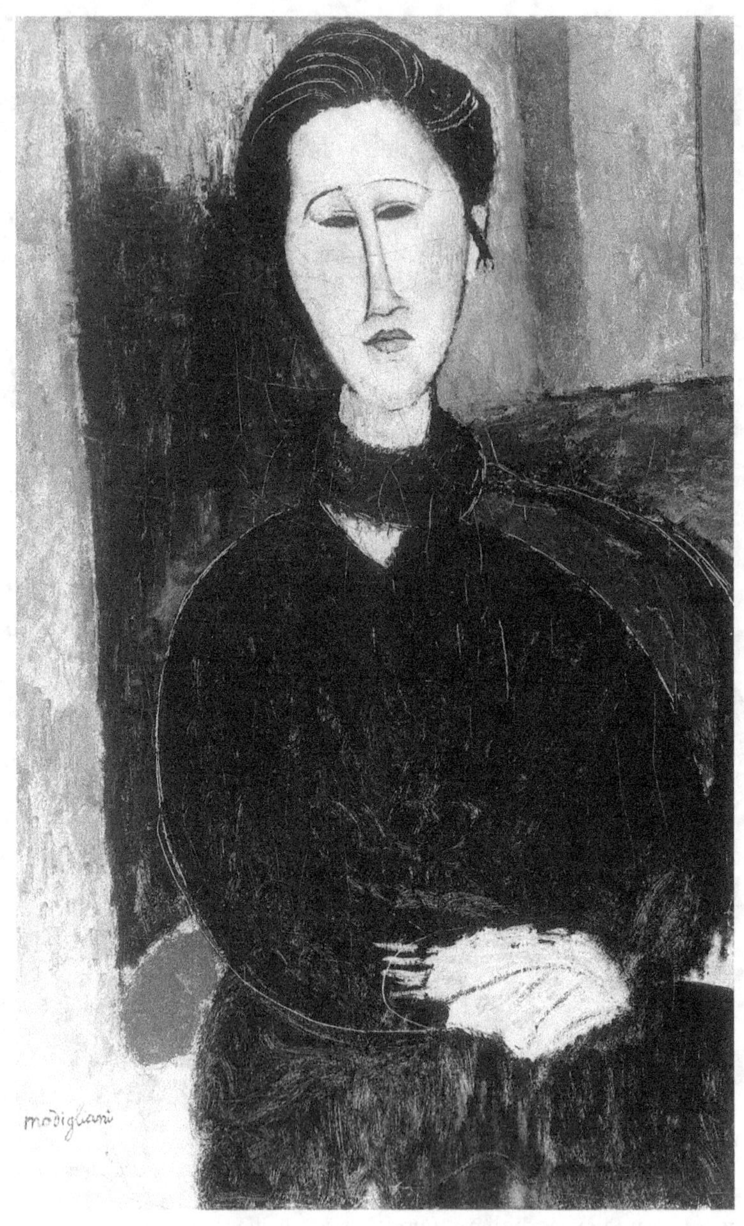


Figure 8.2 Amedeo Modigliani, *Portrait of Anna (Hanka) Zborowska*, 1916, oil on canvas, 76.2 × 45.1 cm. The Alex Hillman Family Foundation Collection.

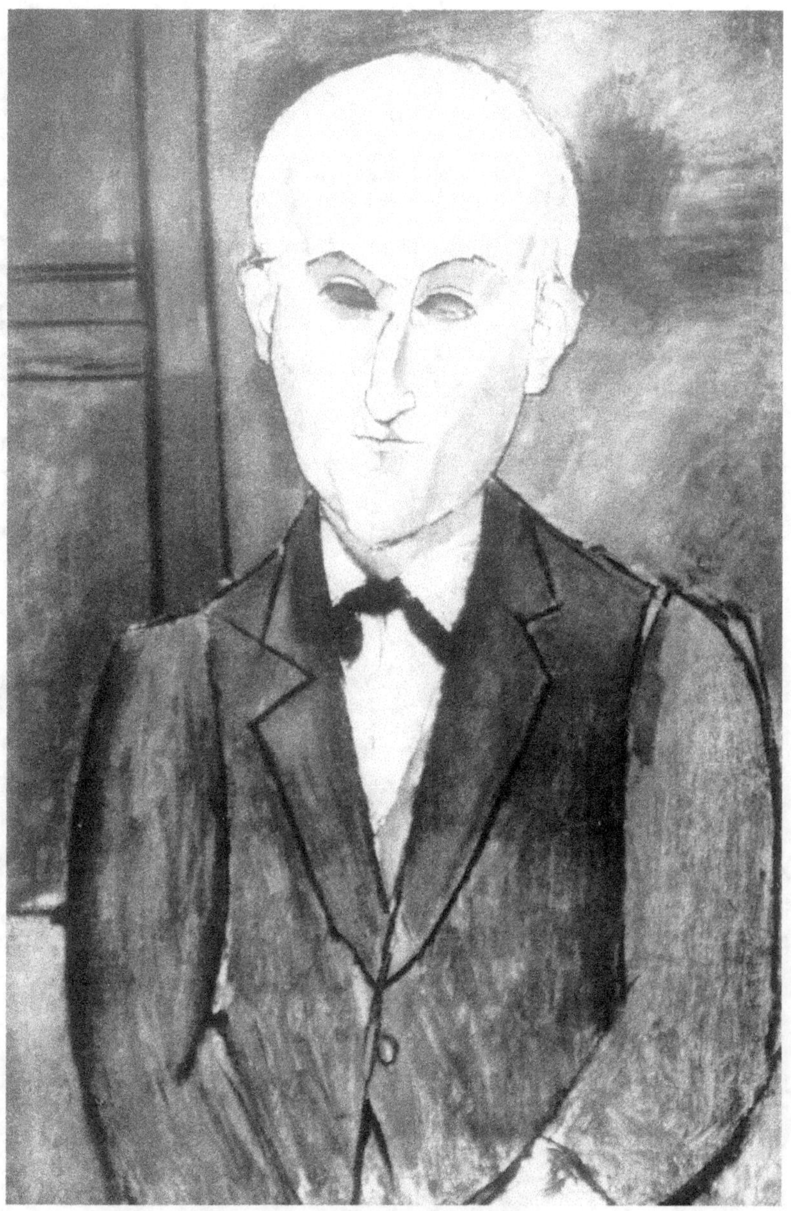

Figure 8.3 Amedeo Modigliani, *Portrait of Max Jacob*, ca. 1920, oil on canvas, 93 × 60 cm. Cincinnati Art Museum, Gift of Mary E. Johnston (1959–43).

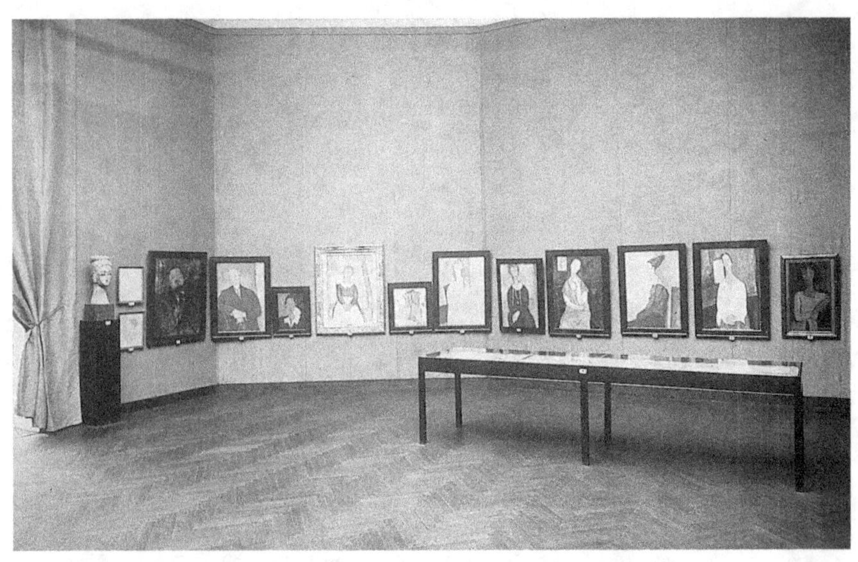

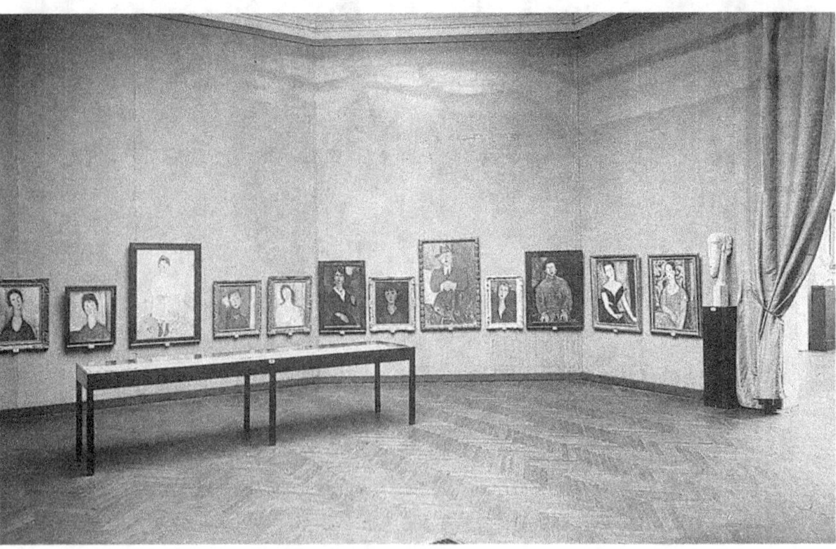

Figure 8.4 and 8.5 Installation views of the Modigliani Room (Sala 31) at the XVII Esposizione Internazionale d'Arte di Venezia, 1930.

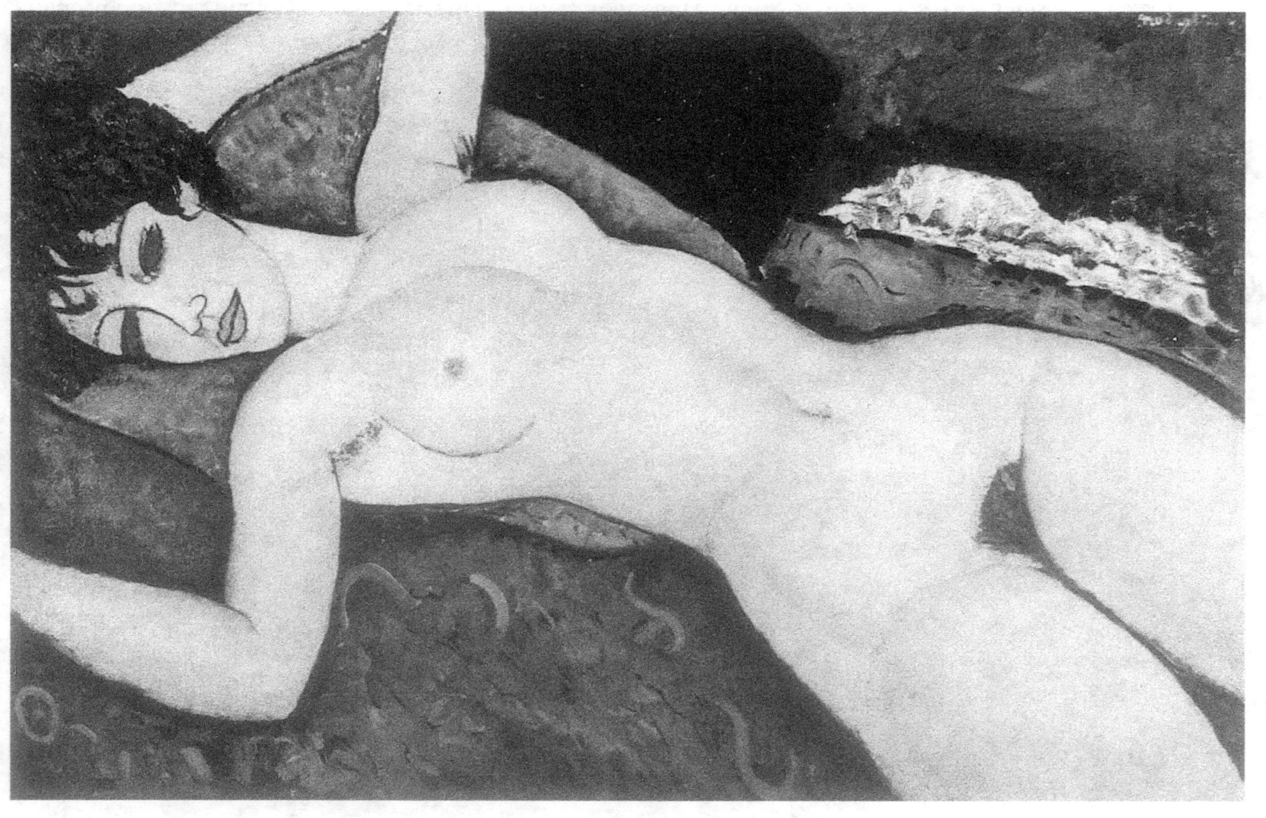

Figure 8.6 *Nude* (*Nu couché, les bras ouverts*); also known as *The Red Nude*, 1917, oil on canvas, 60 × 92 cm. Private collection.

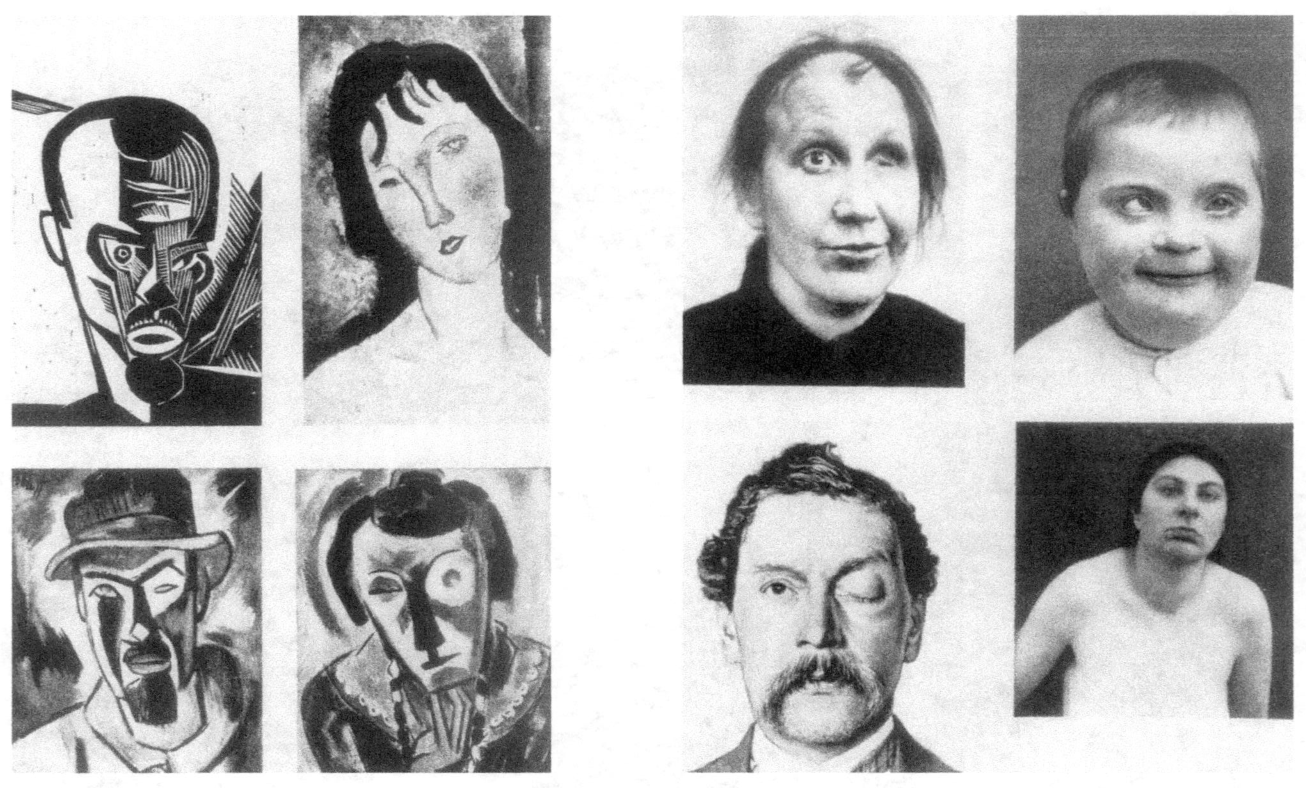

Figure 8.7 Modigliani's *Portrait of a Young Woman* (*Ragazza*) (second column, top), juxtaposed with works by Karl Schmidt-Rotluff and photographs of facial deformities, from Paul Schultze-Naumburg's book *Kunst und Rasse* (1928).

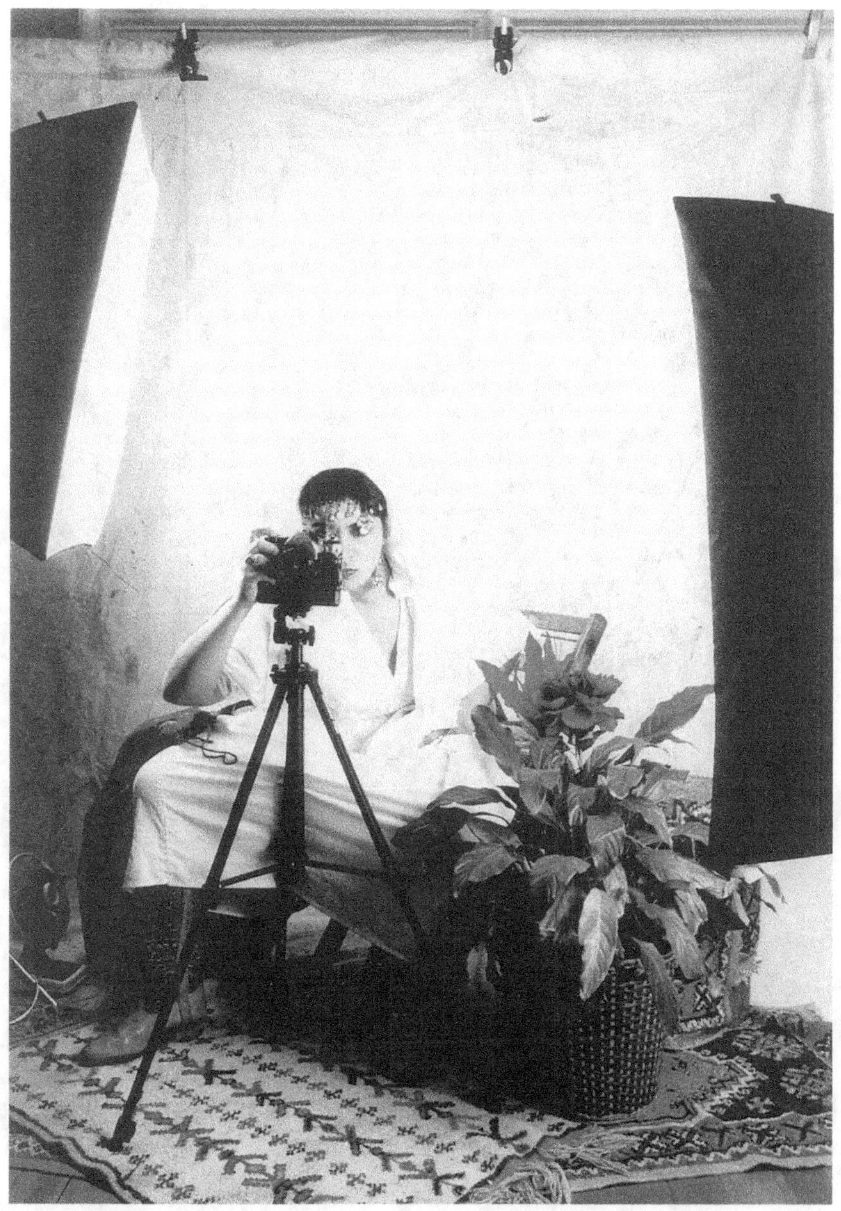

Figure 10.1 Yasmina Bouziane, 'Untitled, Self Portrait,' 40 × 50 cm, C-print (courtesy of Yasmina Bouziane).

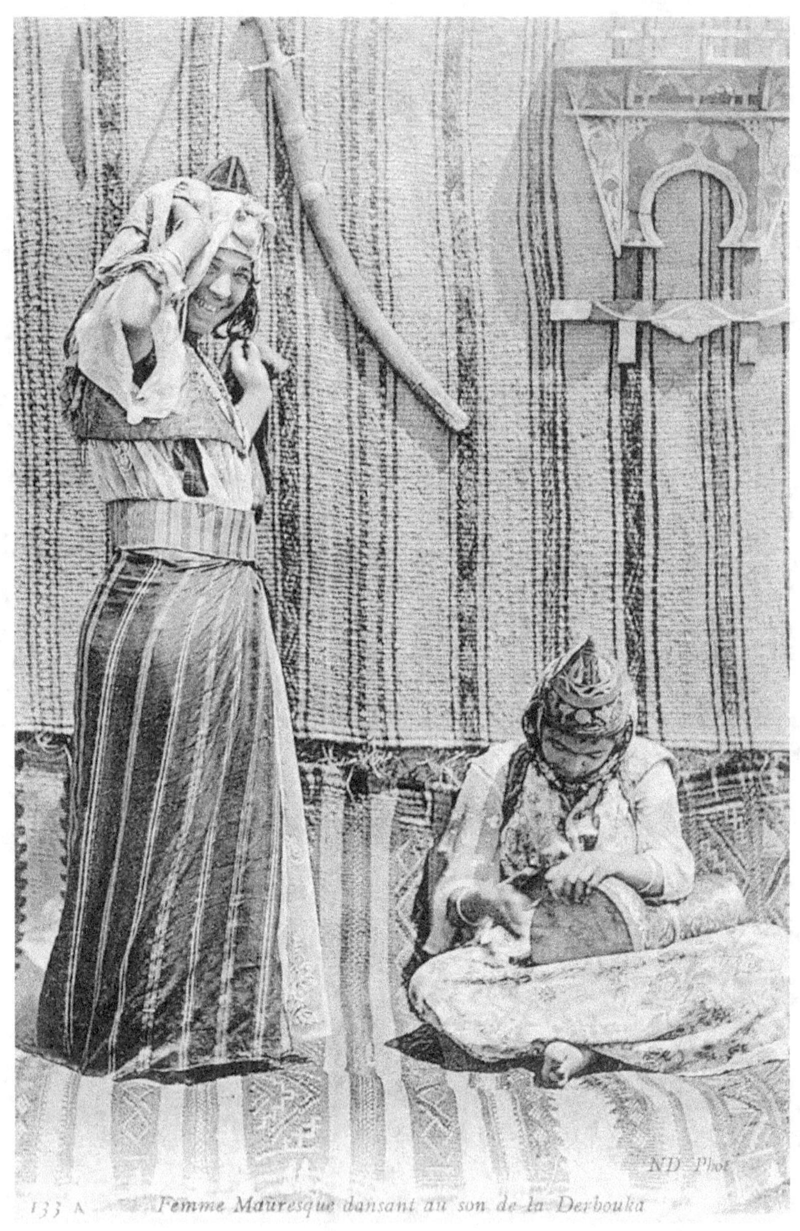


Figure 10.2 '133A Femme Mauresque dansant au son de la derbouka,' ND Photo, early 20th century, postcard (collection of the author).

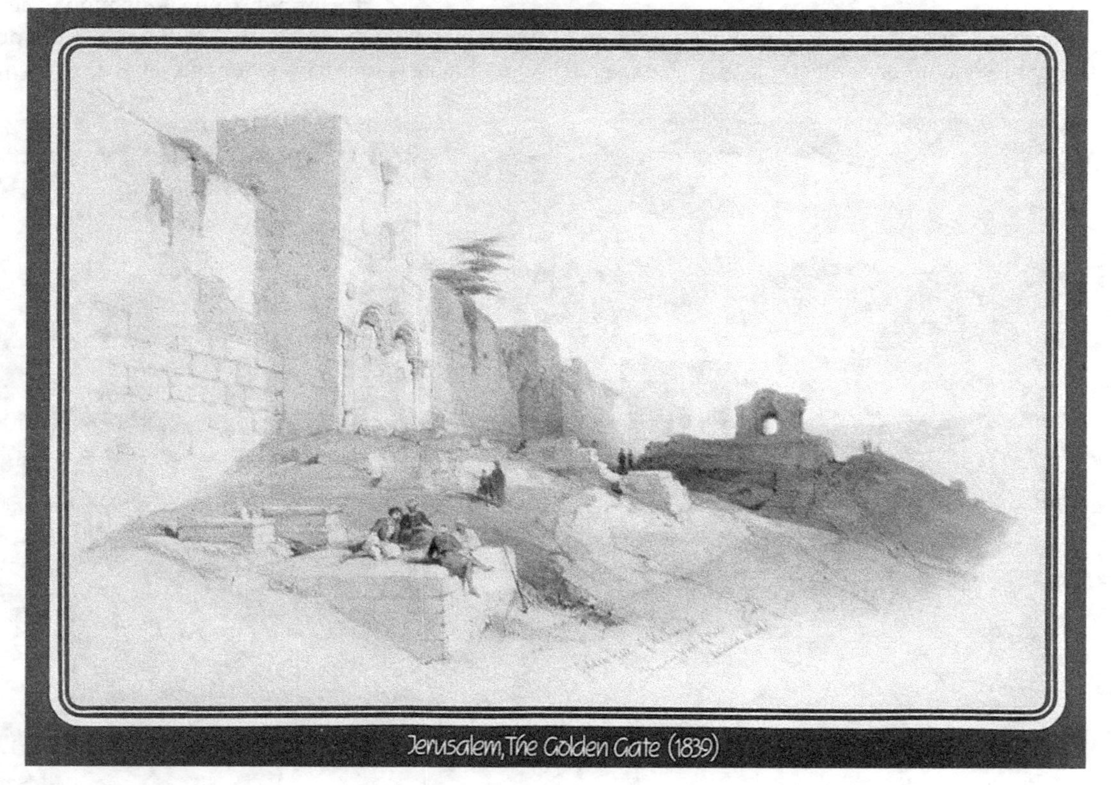


Figure 10.3 David Roberts, 'Jerusalem, the Golden Gate (1839),' postcard reproduction published by Palphot, Israel (collection of the author).

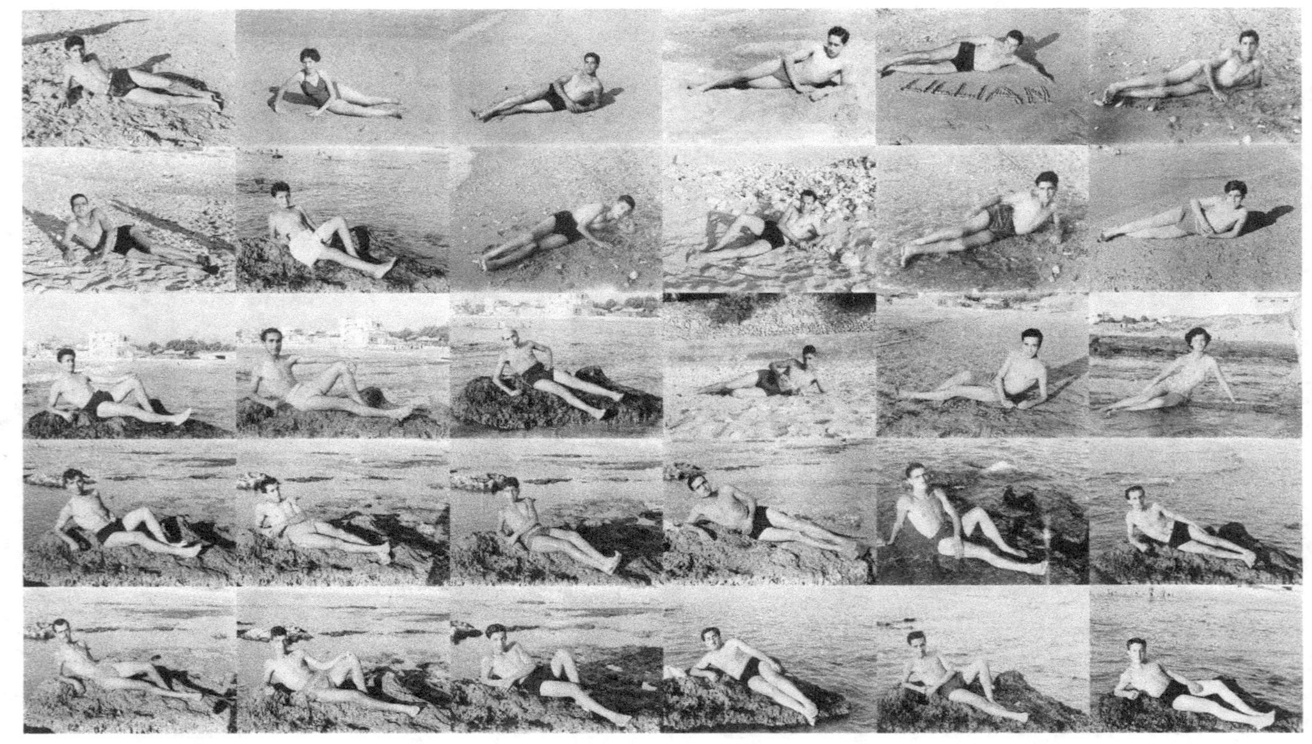

Figure 10.4 Hashem el-Madani, 'Beach series–reclining,' Saida, Lebanon, 1949–55, wall-sized montage of 30 large-format black and white photographs from Arab Image Foundation collection for the exhibition 'Mapping/Sitting' (courtesy of Arab Image Foundation and Walid Raad).

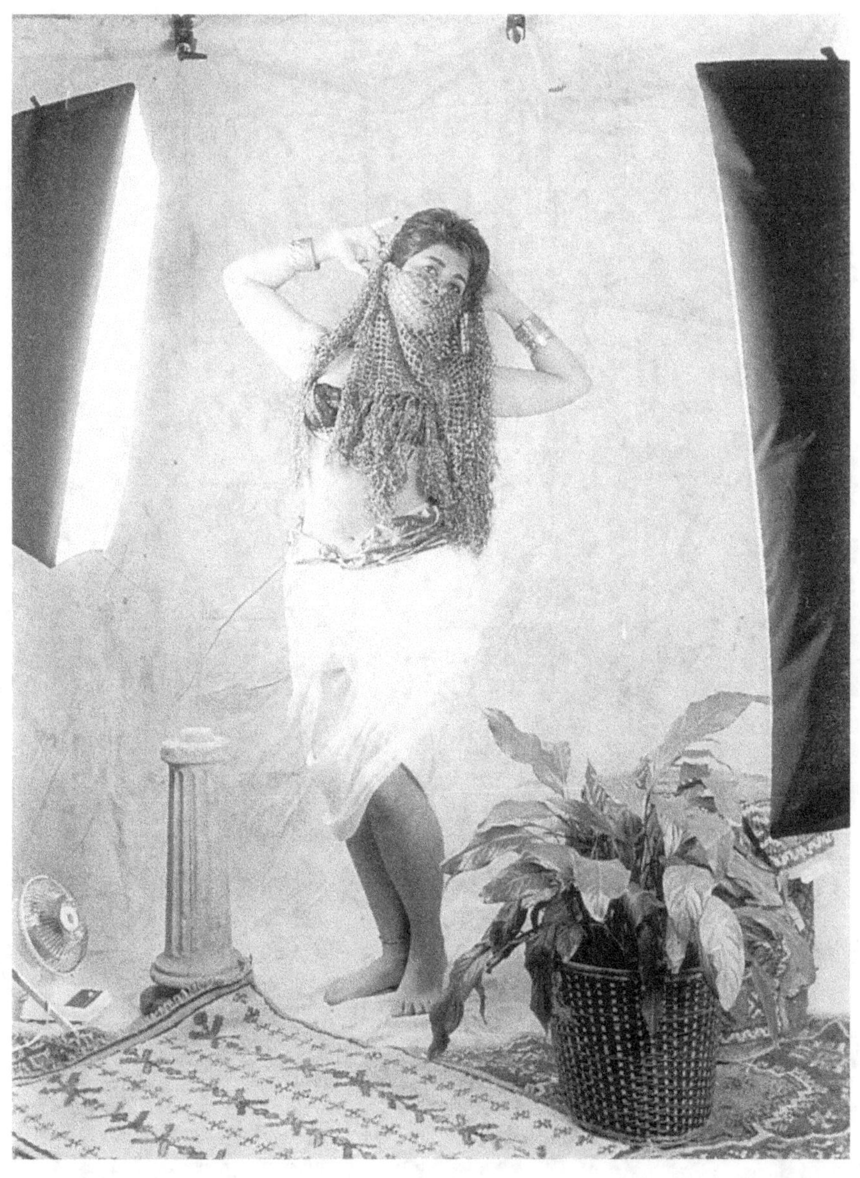

Figure 10.5 Yasmina Bouziane, 'Untitled, Self Portrait 10,' 40 × 50 cm, C-print (courtesy of Yasmina Bouziane).

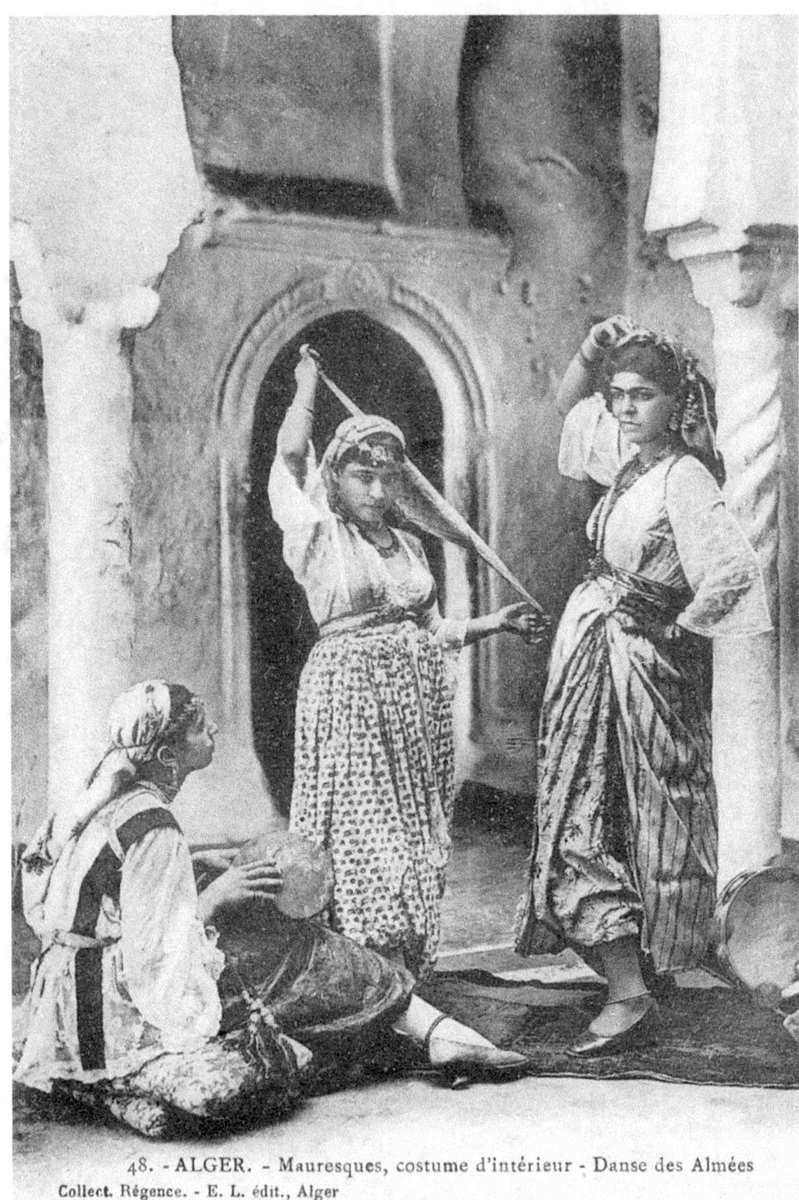


Figure 10.6 48 'Alger. Mauresques, costume d'intérieur. Danse des Almées,' Collection Régence, early 20th century, postcard (collection of the author).

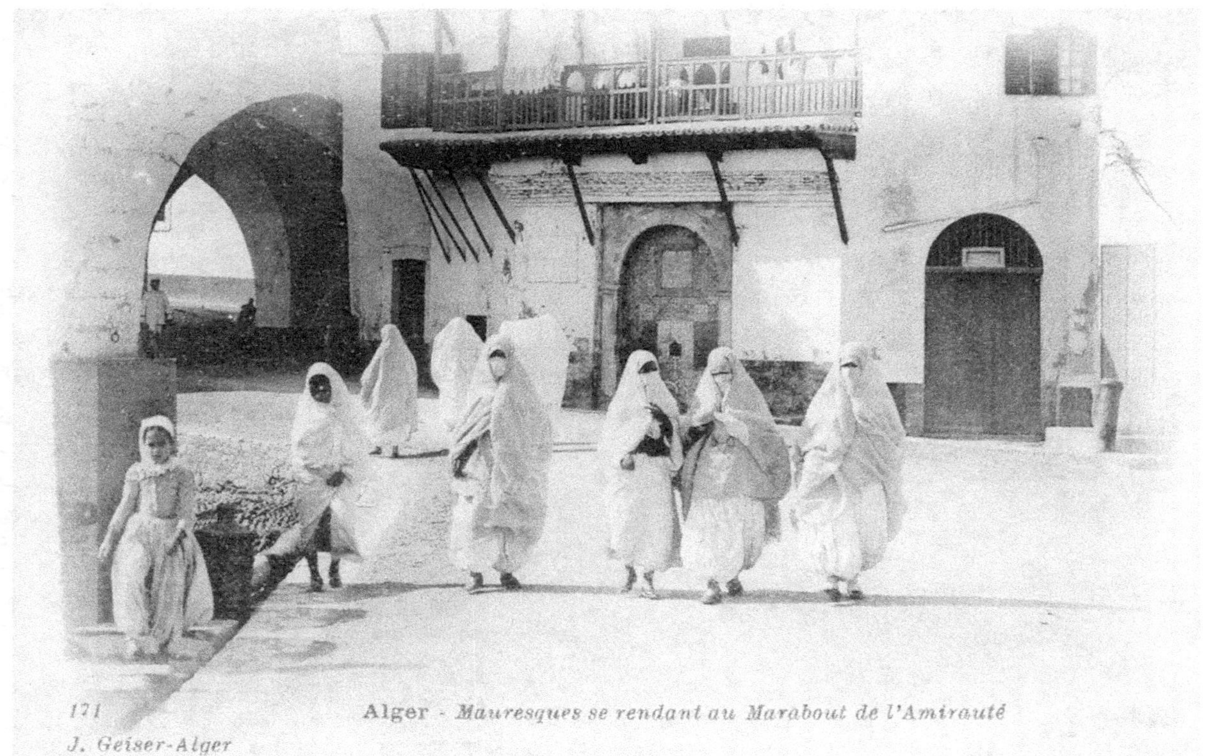


Figure 10.7 171 'Alger. Mauresques se rendant au Marabout de l'Amirauté,' J. Geiser, early 20th century, postcard (collection of the author).

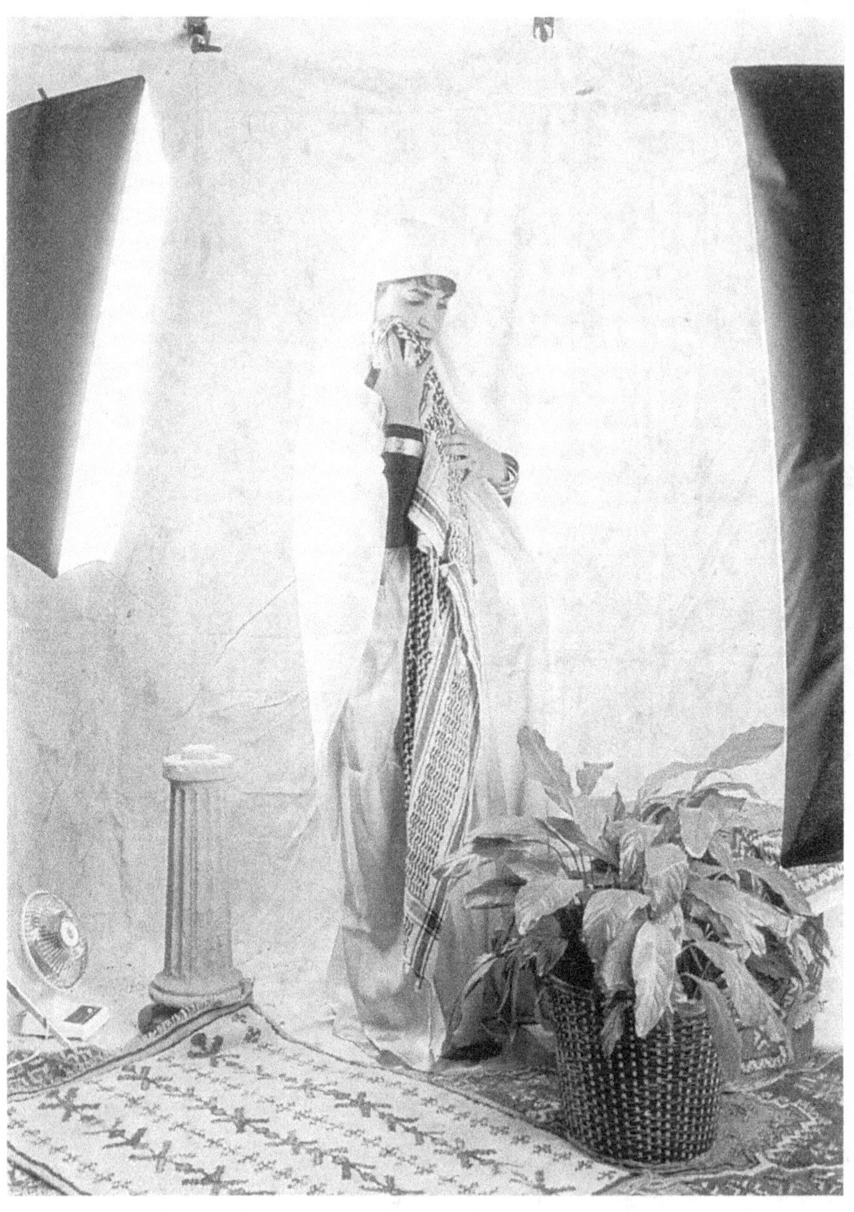

Figure 10.8 Yasmina Bouziane, 'Untitled, Self Portrait 8,' 40 × 50 cm, C-print (courtesy of Yasmina Bouziane).

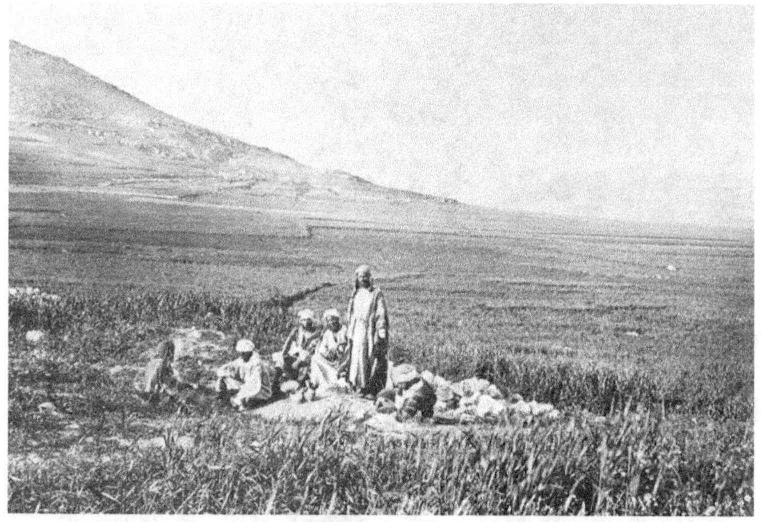

Figure 10.9 F.M. Good, 'Jacob's Well,' c. 1868, postcard reproduction from the exhibition 'Photographic Heritage of the Holy Land, 1839–1914,' published by Tel Aviv Museum, 1980 (collection of the author).

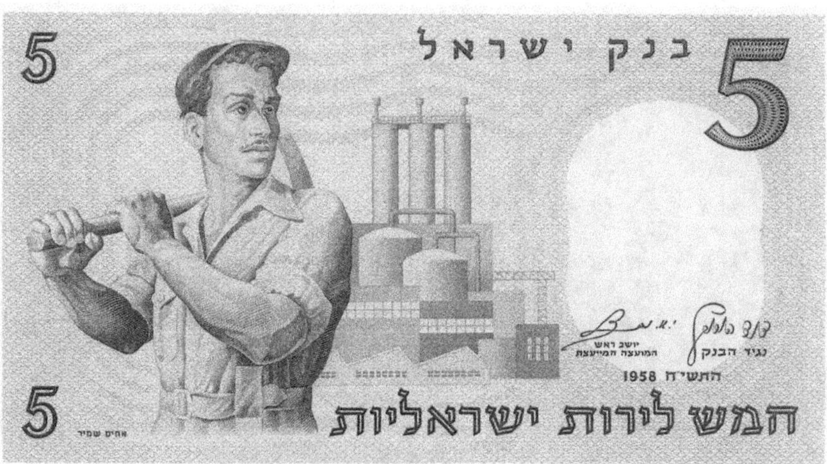


Figure 10.10 'Hebrew Labourer,' postcard reproduction of Israeli 5-pound banknote, second series, 1958–71 (collection of the author).

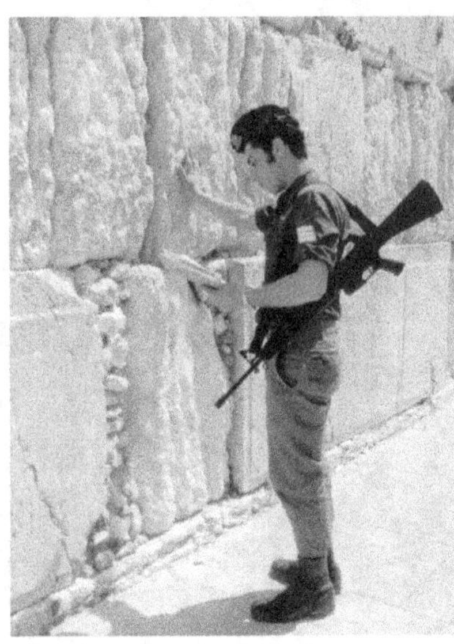

Figure 10.11 'Jerusalem, Soldier by the Western Wall,' Palphot, Israel, postcard (collection of the author).

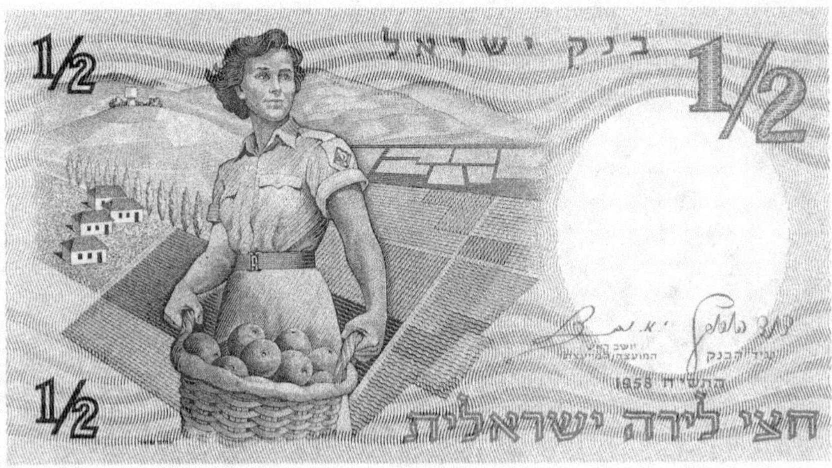


Figure 10.12 'Woman Soldier of the "Nahal,"' postcard reproduction of Israeli ½-pound banknote, second series, 1958–71 (collection of the author).

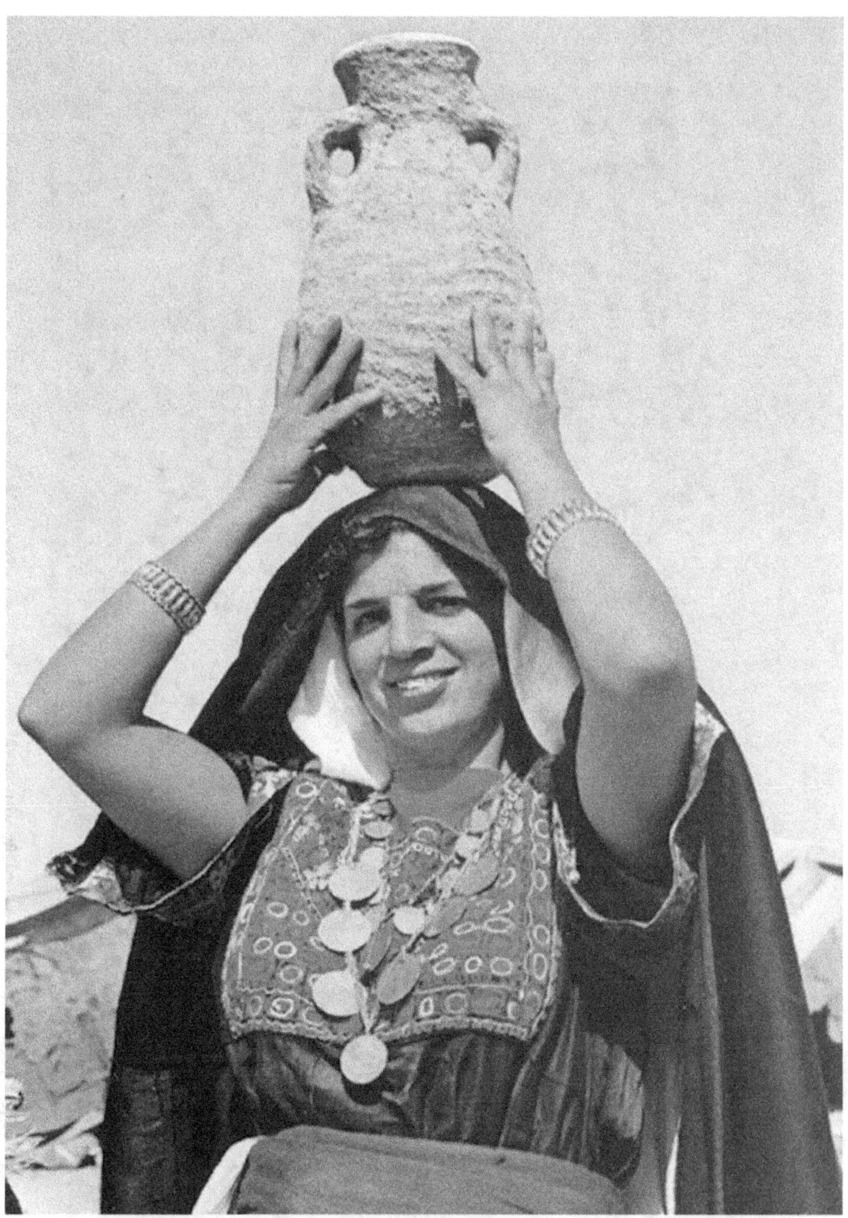

Figure 10.13 'Beduin Women [*sic*] with Her Water Jar on Her Head on the Way from the Water Well,' Palphot, Israel, postcard (collection of the author).

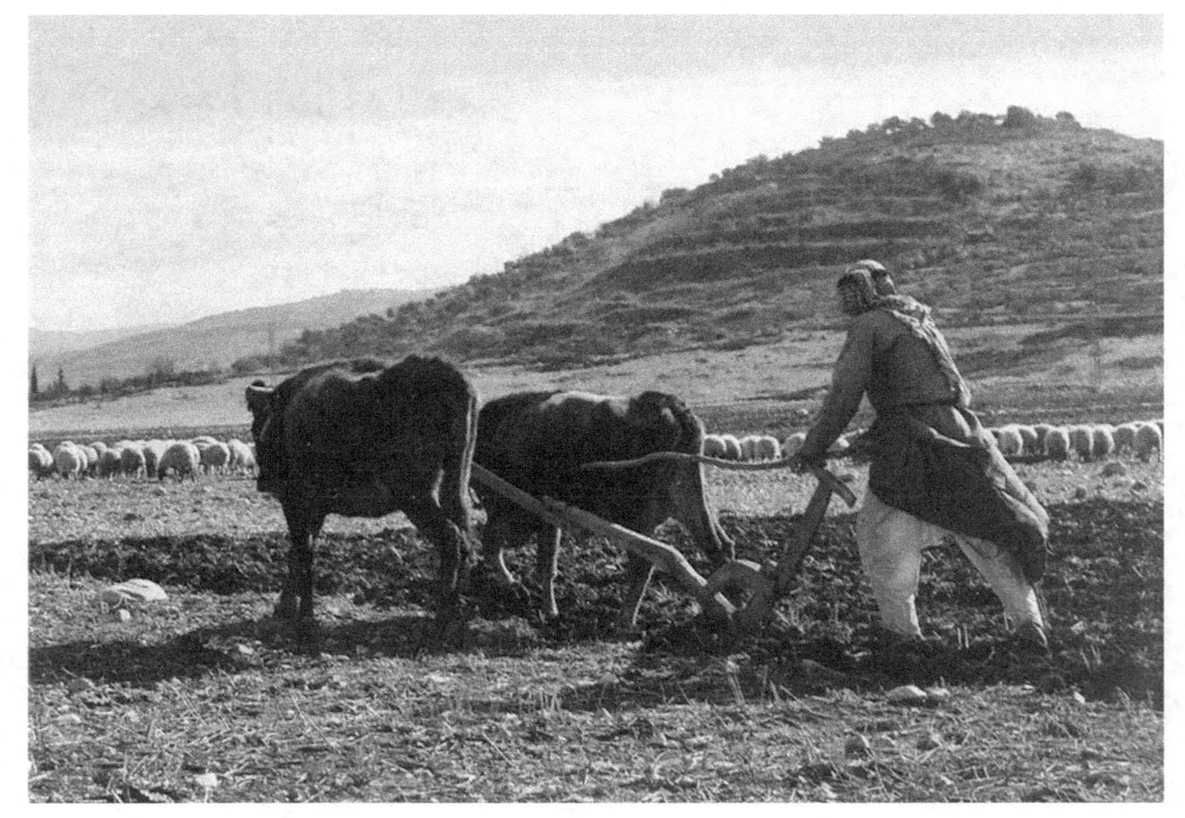

Figure 10.14 'Plowing the fields as in biblical times,' Palphot, Israel, postcard (collection of the author).

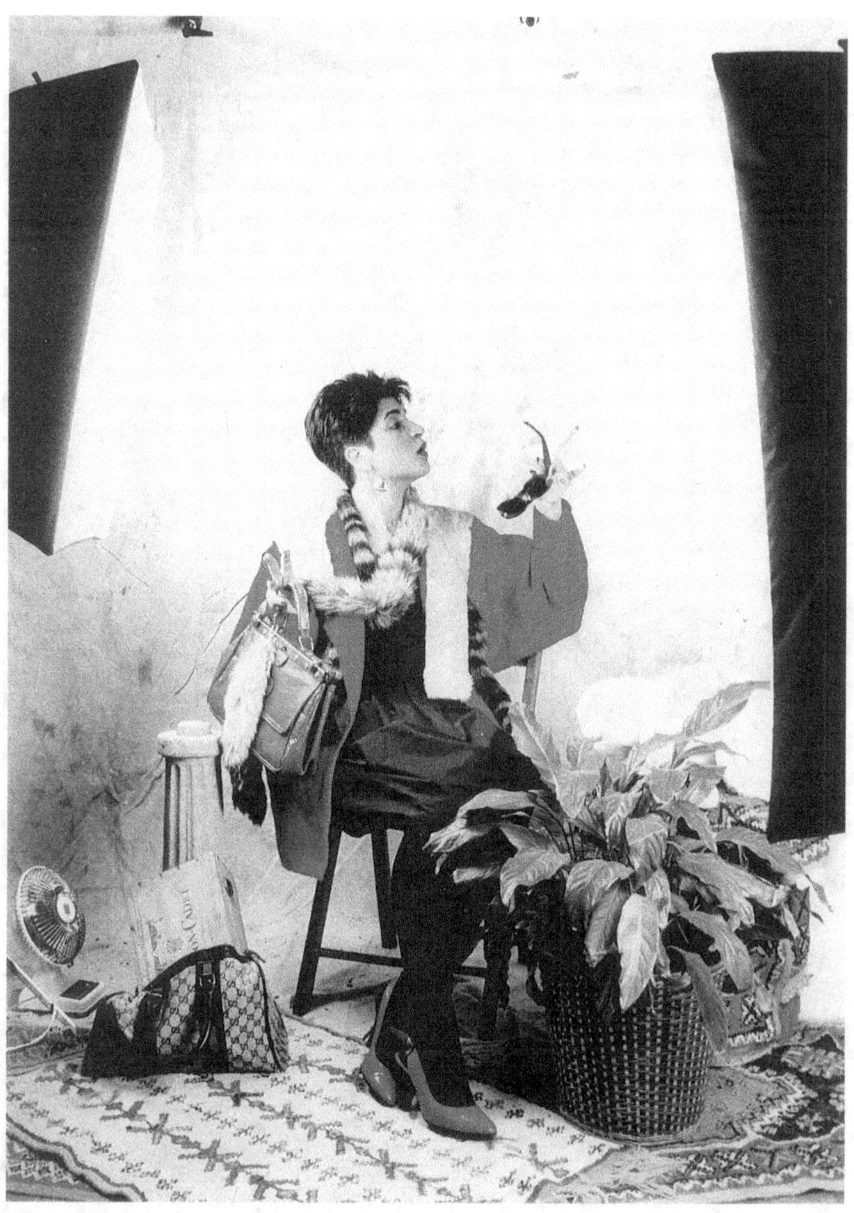

Figure 10.15 Yasmina Bouziane, 'Untitled, Self Portrait 11,' 40 × 50 cm, C-print (courtesy of Yasmina Bouziane).

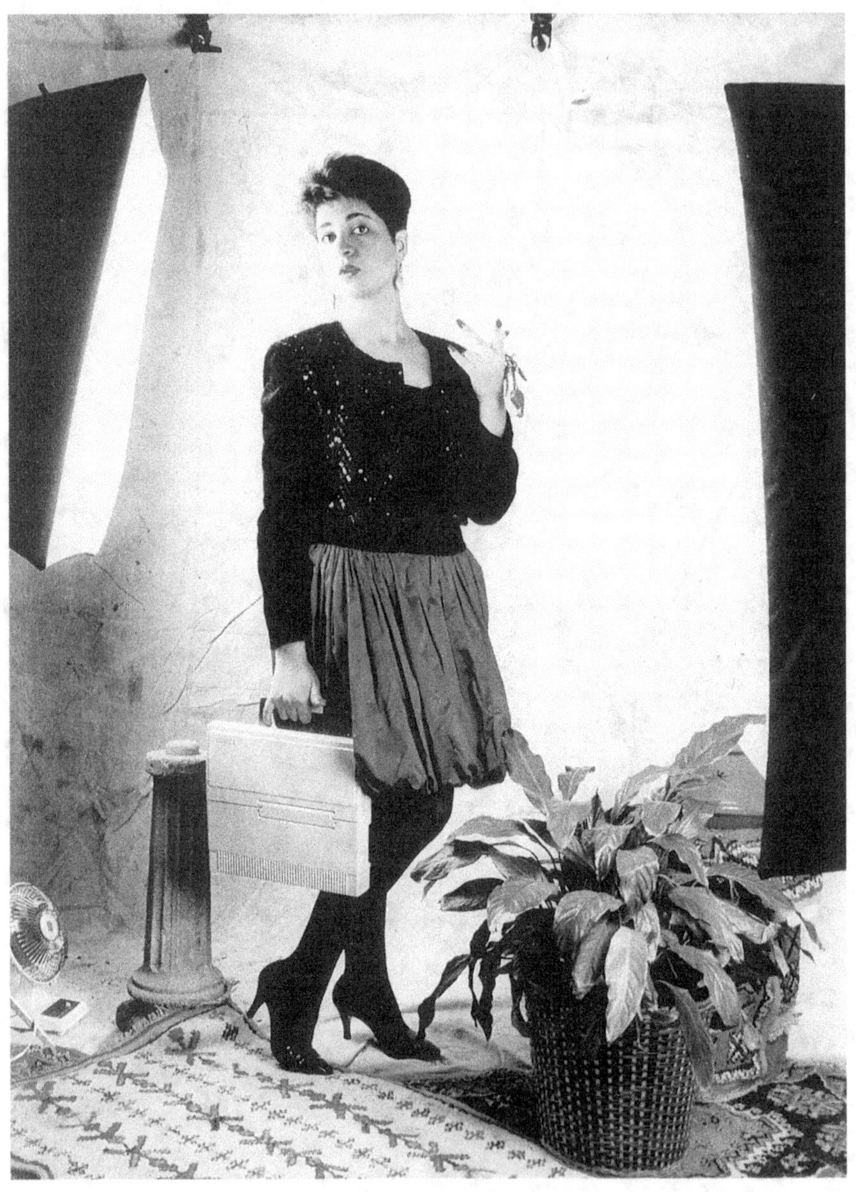

Figure 10.16 Yasmina Bouziane, 'Untitled, Self Portrait 6,' 40 × 50 cm, C-print (courtesy of Yasmina Bouziane).

peasants, dogs, walk about in a very green meadow, the costumes are black and red and the coiffes are white. But in this crowd there are two ladies, one in red, the other in bottle green, who make it a very modern thing.'[70] In contrast, in Signac's painting the viewer is forced to recognize that the women exist in the present and are, at the same time, Provençal. This is a distinction most other artists would not or could not make,[71] but that Maupassant's account of the office workers of Saint-Tropez had emphasized.

Signac thus avoided the facile primitivizing that so often characterized sympathetic portrayals of rural life at the end of the nineteenth century, and this, too, may relate to Kropotkin's theories. Kropotkin noted that artists' depictions of field workers were 'not true to life, nearly always merely sentimental,'[72] and asked how a depiction could be truthful if the painter 'only knows it as a bird of passage knows the country he soars over in his migrations.'[73] Kropotkin's view, well known in anarchist circles, that artists should avoid sentimentalizing peasants or workers by not depicting them until they had lived among them and understood them may be a reason why Signac's earlier landscapes were largely depopulated and why he generally represented his own social class in bourgeois interiors.[74] It may also explain why Signac's paintings from his earlier summer travels, such as *Cap Lombard, Cassis* (1889, Gemeentemuseum Den Haag, FC 182), had fewer figures than those from milieus with which he was more familiar, such as *Le Passage du Puits Bertin, Clichy* (1886, location unknown, FC 118). While figures took on a prominent role once Signac settled in Provence, they are not the stereotypical fisherman or herdsman nor the sentimental field worker. In *Young Provençal Women at the Well*, Signac simultaneously invoked the idealizing, classical tradition and certain anarchist precepts to represent the communal traditions of the harmonious Provençal town, while explicitly avoiding the suggestion that this harmony does not belong in the modern world.

## An Anarchist Pastoral

Signac again linked classical conventions, the Mediterranean south, and anarchist ideals in his next major work, *In the Time of Harmony: The Golden Age Is Not in the Past, It Is in the Future* (figure 5.1).[75] The manifesto painting proclaims an anarchist utopia that would be situated in a rural, Provençal landscape, and it uses the conventions of the pastoral to contrast this ideal with the urban north. The massive size of the work, which was not made for a particular buyer or location, suggests its importance in Signac's oeuvre as a very public statement of personal belief.[76] We can read his personal engagement in his inclusion of a self-portrait in the figure of the painter at the easel and a portrait of his wife Berthe, who modelled for the woman in the foreground.[77] The commitment is further suggested by his intention that *Harmony* be the first in a series of paintings to show the idyllic future and the stages of transformation necessary to reach it.[78] I begin by examining the ways in which the painting is simultaneously marked as classical, anarchist, and Provençal before turning to explore how its pastoralism inevitably juxtaposes north and south by recalling the absent referent, Seurat's *A Sunday Afternoon on the Island of La Grande Jatte* (figure 5.2).

Classical and pastoral conventions are clearly evident in *Harmony*. The painting's monumental scale emphasizes its connection to the classical landscape, as does the broad panoramic view of the Mediterranean bay.[79] The repoussoir tree in the foreground providing shelter for the group below is one of the key signifiers of pastoral landscape.[80] The obvious idealization of the generalized, yet southern, scene, the sense of unity and completeness of the vision, the disposition of the figures throughout the clearly constructed, orderly landscape with its alternating patches of sunlight and shadow, and the path that leads us through that landscape all invoke the classical tradition.[81]

Simultaneously, however, the painting recodes traditional pastoral imagery to picture the anticipated anarchist future.[82] In a letter to Cross written in the summer of 1893, Signac described the painting, and made its relation to anarchism clear.

> Great news! On your advice, I'm going to try a large canvas! ... The boules player is becoming a minor figure of: in the time of anarchy (title to be determined). In the foreground, a group at rest ..., man, woman, child ... under a large pine an old man tells stories to the young kids ... on a hillside ... the harvest: the machines smoke, work, lessen the drudgery: and around the haystacks ... a farandole of harvesters ... in the centre, a young couple: free love![83]

Although Signac ultimately dropped the term anarchy from the title, Albert Boime points out that its substitute, 'harmony,' hardly disguises the point, since this term was widely used with reference to the ideal anarchist society.[84] The man reading, in the left foreground, evokes the Arcadian image of the shepherd reciting poetry in days of old. He bears a double message, however, since he also indicates the anarchist belief in the importance of education for all.[85] Situated on the path that winds into the middle distance, an embracing couple signifies 'free love,' as Signac put it, which was both a common motif in the pastoral and widely espoused by anarchists. Signac referred to the setting as the harvest; yet, since the irises indicate spring, the image underlines the region's bounty by emphasizing that it may have two annual harvests. Moreover, the fig tree, so prominently displayed, is a traditional symbol of plenty because of its many seeds and because it can produce two crops per year. In the background, a tractor relieves much of the human labour formerly necessary for harvest, allowing for the leisurely life depicted elsewhere in the painting; it invokes the anarchist belief that modern machinery would improve the lot of humanity.[86] In Signac's image and anarchist ideology, utopia is not cut off from the modern world but, instead, will arrive once we have harnessed the benefits of industrialization and shared them with all of society.

The embracing couple signifies another important, albeit less obvious, aspect of the anarchist future.[87] They contemplate a flower, which they hold in outstretched arms. The pose is repeated in the woman seated by the sea and in several other significant Neo-Impressionist works, including Signac's *Portrait of Félix Fénéon*.[88] It seems to signify aesthetic contemplation, which is an important aspect of both traditional pastoral poetry and anarchist harmony. Kropotkin saw aesthetic appreciation as an elevated goal, but one that would be available only after baser needs were satisfied. He wrote of humankind: 'As soon as his material wants are satisfied, other needs, which, generally speaking may be described as of an artistic character, will thrust themselves forward.'[89] Signac concurred, stating, 'When the society that we dream of exists, when rid of the exploiters who exhaust him, the worker will have time to think and to learn. He will appreciate all the qualities of a work of art.'[90] Signac included an artist at his easel, which is a traditional signifier of aesthetic appreciation, the implication being that once the anarchist future has arrived, others will also appreciate beauty.

In several documents Signac indicated that he related the classicism so evident in *Harmony*'s composition to anarchist thought. In a letter to his friend the Belgian Neo-Impressionist Théo van Rysselberghe, Signac revealed his awareness of the classical referents behind his approach to the work: 'started the sketch [esquisse] for "In the time of Harmony." Every morning, gymnastics for half an hour: sketches [croquis] after Raphael, Puvis, Andre de Sarto [*illegible word*] – excellent training.'[91]

The composition often invokes comparison to the work of the most classical of contemporary artists, Puvis de Chavannes, whom Signac linked to anarchism.[92] When beginning the large painting, Signac thanked his friend Jean Grave, the anarchist writer and publisher, for his latest book, writing that Grave had succeeded in conveying 'the hope of this near future where, finally, for the first time, all individuals will be free. In the great poetic decor, *à la* Puvis, – of Kropotkin, what solid memorials, practical and livable, you erect! How well one breathes there.'[93] In this succinct statement, Signac linked the anarchist philosophies of Grave and Kropotkin to the large-scale classical mural compositions of Puvis. The intellectual and idealizing tendencies of classical compositions, their harmony and order, conveyed to Signac hope for the ideal future.

The picture contains several identifiably Provençal features, which are also linked to anarchist ideology within the picture.[94] Led by a drummer, a group of women performs the traditional dance of Provence, the *farandole*, under the shelter of the umbrella pine in the background. Their joyous gestures are echoed in the motion of the women folding laundry in the middle ground, suggesting the anarchist ideal of unalienated labour in which work and leisure need not be so different. The *boules* players in the foreground are similarly signifiers of both Provence and the similarity of work and leisure, since one player's gesture is echoed by the sower, a common anarchist motif, behind him.[95] The vegetation, especially the characteristic umbrella pine set before the beautiful bay, indelibly marks the Mediterranean location. I would suggest, however, that the southern location takes on additional significance when it is understood as implicitly juxtaposed to the painting that 'every vanguard artist ... had to come to terms with' after 1886: Seurat's *La Grande Jatte* (figure 5.2).[96]

## *Harmony* and *La Grande Jatte*

As others have noted, *Harmony* recalls *La Grande Jatte* in several ways.[97] The paintings are compositionally similar: both depict a sunlit shoreline, using alternating patches of sunlight and shadow, with small groupings of figures mainly engaged in leisure activities. Signac evidently drew on Seurat's work and, in doing so, he juxtaposed urban and rural, capitalism and anarchism, and north and south.

This was not the first time that Signac had responded to *La Grande Jatte*. At the eighth Impressionist exhibition, where Seurat exhibited it in

May 1886, Signac showed *The Milliners* (figure 5.5).[98] The painting depicts two women finishing hats, illustrating the labour involved in the contemporary fashion industry. Signac reworked the painting with the divisionist technique after seeing Seurat's work, indicating the painting's engagement with the formal qualities of *La Grande Jatte*.[99] However, its subject matter also responds to Seurat's work.[100] We can surmise that Seurat was deliberately concerned with contemporary fashion in *La Grande Jatte*, since sketches give evidence that in the final version he increased the already exaggerated size of the bustle of the woman on the right. If nothing else, the alteration seems to gently mock bourgeois women's elaborate clothing styles.[101] Signac chose as his subject the contemporary labourers who created these fashions, taking Seurat's critical observation to the level of class analysis.

The garment industry gave rise to much debate on the plight of the working poor, women's labour, and industrialization in the late nineteenth and early twentieth centuries.[102] Needleworkers became 'the very image of poverty'[103] in the late nineteenth century. Most were too poor to purchase sewing machines and did piecework in their homes by hand, as is likely depicted in Signac's painting. As Seurat had done, Signac specified the location: the rue de Caire, a street in Paris's second *arrondissement* where rents had become particularly expensive after the reconfiguration of Paris directed by Baron Georges-Eugène Haussmann, and where the working classes were finding it increasingly difficult to make ends meet.[104] Thus, while Seurat portrayed the suburban recreation of the middle classes, Signac pictured working-class life in the city; while Seurat ambiguously rendered the signifying clothing of modern, suburban recreation, Signac showed the inexpensive labour on which the modern fashion industry relied. Signac's representation of behind-the-scenes labourers in the fashion world affirms that he entered into a dialogue with Seurat's paintings from his first foray into Neo-Impressionism, and that he took that dialogue in a direction that was more unequivocally antibourgeois than Seurat's ambiguous imagery would ever allow.

There is strong evidence that Seurat's painting continued to be relevant for Signac. In December 1894, while he was at work on *Harmony*, Signac went to see *La Grande Jatte* in Seurat's mother's apartment.[105] Moreover, when *Harmony* was exhibited in 1896 in Brussels, Signac ensured that it hung in the same position that *La Grande Jatte* had occupied nine years earlier.[106] Signac's aspirations are also indicated by the painting's size: *Harmony* measures 300 by 400 cm, considerably larger than *La Grande Jatte* (207.5 by 308 cm). But they differ significantly in their depictions of human interaction, labour, class, and, most important, in terms of place.

The contrasting overall tenor of the two paintings comes largely from the figures.[107] Seurat's figures are stiff and hieratic, resisting interaction, which Linda Nochlin has argued signifies modern alienation.[108] She quotes a critic of the day: '[O]ne understands the stiltedness of the Parisian promenade, stiff and distorted; even its recreation is affected.'[109] If Nochlin's conclusion that the picture is an anti-utopian allegory does not fully recognize the work's ambiguity, most historians agree that the picture engages 'the viewer in a dialogue of cohesion and separateness ... Here we have nothing other than the dilemma of modern urban people under industrial capitalism.'[110] In contrast, despite their equally evident stylization, Signac's figures play and work together in harmonious interaction, inverting Seurat's mockery of Parisian mores.[111] Where Seurat's stylization underlines the lack of interaction between the figures, Signac's stylization often links the figures together in rhythmic patterns. For example, the undulating pattern created by the movement from left to right in the foreground figures is so stylized that it emphasizes how each figure is connected to the next. While the meaning of Seurat's painting and its figures remains ambiguous and open to debate, Signac's figures are clearly meant to convey harmonious relations.

The figures also point to the issue of class. Seurat's figures are dressed in contemporary fashions, which may signify the intersection of differing classes in modern recreation, but are certainly common indicators of socio-economic difference. In contrast, Signac's figures wear much simpler clothing that avoid such markers of class as parasols and top hats. The clothes of the women working are not markedly different from those of the women at leisure. Similarly, one cannot identify class from the clothing of the male figures. The bare-chested men in the foreground enact both characteristically lower-class activities (playing boules) and upper-class ones (reading), signifying the lack of hierarchy in the society to come.[112] Indeed, Seurat's title points out that the painting depicts a day of leisure – a defining feature of work under modern capitalism – yet, as discussed above, work and leisure take place side by side and are not so very different in Signac's *Harmony*.

The animals extend the juxtapositions. The prominently depicted hen and rooster form the brightest spot in the foreground, as they are encircled by an aureole of light.[113] More than just a foreground space filler, as Henry van De Velde suggested, the hen and rooster wittily juxtapose rural anarchist harmony and suburban anomie by analogy with Seurat's much-debated woman with a monkey.[114] Signac's use of the rooster as an anarchist symbol takes on particular significance in the early 1890s, when the French government enacted the so-called *lois scélérates*, which criminalized any kind of anarchist propaganda and led to the Trial of the Thirty, in which Signac's friends Maximilien Luce, Jean Grave, and Félix Fénéon were charged.[115] As Marina Ferretti-Bocquillon points out, Signac's journal entry of 7 August 1894 linked the rooster with these political events in the entry: 'Drew the rooster. Beginning of the Trial of the Thirty.'[116] Further evidence of the rooster's currency as an anarchist symbol comes from an article published serially in 1893 by Élie Reclus, an anarchist and the brother of Élisée. 'Mythologie populaire: Le coq' appeared in *La Société Nouvelle* throughout the fall of 1893, when Signac was working on *Harmony*.[117] Reclus saw the cock as a symbol of the revolution, since it will fight until it wins or dies, and consequently as a symbol for the 'rights of man.'[118] Describing a drawing of a cock beating its wings over the globe, Reclus concluded: 'It represented, no doubt, the triumph, still far off, of universal Liberty, Equality and Fraternity. "Here is," I thought, "the glorious decoration that the Arc de l'Étoile will receive when the French Revolution has succeeded."'[119] For Reclus the crowing rooster signals the dawn of the anarchist future; Signac's rooster, who rests peacefully, is a symbol of the anarchist battle won.

The hen and rooster can also be seen as a visual and symbolic reference to the strutting couple with the monkey in *La Grande Jatte*.[120] The rooster's plumage echoes the monkey's tail in Seurat's painting; in turn, the monkey's tail echoes the Parisian woman's bustle. At least one critic of the day referred to Seurat's woman as a *cocotte*, or prostitute, and Signac has paralleled her with the rooster and a real *cocotte*, or hen.[121] Élie Reclus noted the similarity between a rooster's flamboyant plumage and contemporary fashion, stating that in France 'our stylish people copy the physique and morals of the sultan of the henhouse, imitate his gestures, manners and attitudes, his posture and his costume.'[122] The utopian theorist Charles Fourier saw the rooster and hen as a sign of good marital relations between the sexes, which heightens *Harmony*'s contrast with *La Grande Jatte*.[123] Signac's poultry thus contrast with Seurat's elegant couple in numerous ways: they invoke the juxtaposition of natural and artificial, make a verbal pun on *cocotte*, and simultaneously show Fourier's ideal of harmonious relations between the sexes.

The most significant juxtaposition, however, is that of place. Where

Seurat's work is set in a park – a representation of nature emblematic of modern, urban life – Signac's is set in the open countryside. Furthermore, Signac has transposed the setting from the northern suburbs, so irrevocably linked to Neo-Impressionism by *La Grande Jatte*, to an archetypal southern village. It is precisely the kind of village applauded by Kropotkin for sustaining the anarchist ideal of mutual aid and by Élisée Reclus for maintaining a tradition of public culture in which villagers are not disenfranchised from decision making.[124] Signac believed that the artist's ability to create harmony was stronger in a harmonious setting.[125] Indeed, he encouraged his friend van Rysselberghe to leave Paris, stating, 'I believe that the environment where an artist lives has a big influence on him.'[126] In addition, in another letter thanking Grave for his latest book, Signac linked the anarchist future to the contemporary Provençal setting: 'I will read it in the shadow of a pine tree, by the sea, and in the beauty of this setting, I naturally recall the life of goodness and harmony that you allow us to hope for. One breathes freely in your book, as under this tree, in the breeze off the open sea.'[127] For Signac, then, the environment of Saint-Tropez enabled a vision of a better life. It is here, in a decentralized, independent, and southern society, that Signac located the anarchist future. It is not, in Signac's image and anarchist ideology, part of the modern metropolis, but neither is it cut off from the modern world. He reconfigured the Mediterranean pastoral to express his political vision, taking advantage of the pastoral's ability to juxtapose the ideal and the real. Signac's pastorals indicate that, in the 1890s, the Latin heritage so closely allied to the Midi could have associations other than those of the political right.

The idea of the Mediterranean, bound to the legacy of classicism, was a potent myth in late nineteenth-century France, and I have argued that the anarchist left did not abdicate control of this construct;[128] instead, they continued to invoke its legitimating power through a reconfigured classical tradition that relied on an alternative cultural geography. Paul Signac reconfigured the Mediterranean pastoral, taking advantage of its ability to evoke an ideal – in this case, the anarchist myth of the south that envisioned it as a harmonious land with a tradition of communal life – and to heighten the contrast between the ideal and the real by juxtaposition. Signac's pastorals indicate that, around the turn of the century, the Latin heritage so closely allied to the Midi could have associations other than with the political right, and Signac made these other associations palpable in his art. Like most potent ideologies, the myth of Mediterranean classicism could be used by both left as well as right, to look forward as well as back.

NOTES

A longer version of this essay appeared in the *Art Bulletin*. I am grateful to Patricia Leighten, Mark Antliff, Vojtěch Jirat-Wasiutyński, Perry Chapman, Leslie Dawn, and the anonymous *Art Bulletin* readers for their comments, and to Françoise Cachin for her permission to quote from Signac's letters in the Getty Research Center. Research for this article was supported by , a Bader Fellowship from Queen's University, a Social Sciences and Humanities Research Council of Canada Doctoral Fellowship, and the University of Lethbridge. Unless otherwise noted, translations are mine.

1 On the nineteenth-century association of the south and the classical landscape as 'all but an absolute,' see Richard Thomson, *Monet to Matisse: Landscape Painting in France, 1874–1914*, exh. cat., National Galleries of Scotland (Edinburgh, 1994), 78, 17, 22–7, 77–87.
2 On artists visiting the southern coasts see Françoise Cachin, *Méditerranée: De Courbet à Matisse*, exh. cat., Galeries Nationales du Grand Palais (Paris, 2000). On Cézanne, see Nina Athanassoglou-Kallmyer, *Cézanne and Provence: The Painter in His Culture* (Chicago: University of Chicago Press, 2003).
3 Cross's family wintered at the home of his uncle Dr Soins, in Monaco; Cachin, *Méditerranée*, 48.
4 For a critique of the construction 'off the beaten track' see James Buzard, *The Beaten Track: European Tourism, Literature and the Ways to Culture, 1800–1918* (Oxford: Clarendon Press, 1993). The term Côte d'Azur was coined with the publication of Stéphen Liégeard's *La Côte d'Azur* (Paris: Maison Quantin, 1887), although it did not come into widespread use until into the twentieth century. For current bibliography on Signac, see Françoise Cachin, *Signac: Catalogue raisonné de l'œuvre peint*, with Marina Ferretti-Bocquillon (Paris: Gallimard, 2000); references to catalogue entries in this book will be noted as FC, followed by the catalogue number; M. Ferretti-Bocquillon et al., *Signac 1863–1935*, exh. cat., Metropolitan Museum of Art (New York, 2001). On his Saint-Tropez period, see M. Ferretti-Bocquillon, ed., *Signac et Saint-Tropez, 1892–1913*, exh. cat., Musée de l'Annonciade (Saint-Tropez, 1992); and Françoise Cachin, 'L'arrivée de Signac à Saint-Tropez,' ibid., 11–15.
5 See Margaret Werth, *The Joy of Life: The Idyllic in French Art, circa 1900* (Berkeley and Los Angeles: University of California Press, 2002); Jennifer L. Shaw, *Dream States: Puvis de Chavannes, Modernism, and the Fantasy of France* (New Haven, CT: Yale University Press, 2002). Thomson, *Monet to Matisse*, 24, 78, persuasively argues that classicism was never fully extin-

guished and was so widespread a construction that it belonged to no one affiliation.

6 See James D. Herbert, *Fauve Painting: The Making of Cultural Politics* (New Haven, CT: Yale University Press, 1992), 124–9.

7 On the relationship between Neo-Impressionism and anarchism, see Robert L. Herbert and Eugenia W. Herbert, 'Artists and Anarchism: Unpublished Letters of Pissarro, Signac and Others,' pts. 1 and 2, *Burlington Magazine* 102 (Nov. 1960): 473–82, and (Dec. 1960): 517–22; and John G. Hutton, *Neo-Impressionism and the Search for Solid Ground: Art, Science, and Anarchism in Fin-de-Siècle France* (Baton Rouge: Louisiana State University Press, 1994). On the relation of this politics to Neo-Impressionist landscape see Robyn Roslak, 'Organicism and the Construction of a Utopian Geography: The Role of Landscape in Anarcho-Communism and Neo-Impressionism,' *Utopian Studies* 1, 2 (1990): 96–114, and 'The Politics of Aesthetic Harmony: Neo-Impressionism, Science, and Anarchism,' *Art Bulletin* 73, 3 (1991), 381–90; on the politics of the department of the Var, especially as related to changing concepts of the decorative, see Peter J. Flagg, 'The Neo-Impressionist Landscape,' PhD diss., Princeton University, 1988, 160–236.

8 On the parallel debate in left-wing circles over the politics of utopian imagery – condemned as compensatory and thus diverting revolutionary potential, or praised as anticipatory and thus furthering the cause – see the excellent overview in Werth, *Joy of Life*, 86–7 and passim.

9 Leo Marx, 'Does Pastoralism Have a Future?' in *The Pastoral Landscape*, ed. John Dixon Hunt, exh. cat., National Gallery of Art (Washington, 1992), 213.

10 Ibid., 212–13.

11 David Rosand, 'Pastoral Topoi: On the Construction of Meaning in Landscape,' in *The Pastoral Landscape*, ed. Hunt, 9; Rosand, 'Giorgione, Venice and the Pastoral Vision,' in *Places of Delight: The Pastoral Landscape*, ed. R. Cafritz, L. Gowing, and D. Rosand, exh. cat., Phillips Collection (Washington, 1988), 50; and Thomson, *Monet to Matisse*, 77–87. The view of pastoral as a play of contrasts is maintained in Thomas Crow's assessment of its relevance in contemporary art, 'The Simple Life: Pastoralism and the Persistence of the Genre in Recent Art,' *October* 63 (Winter 1993): 47–8.

12 Jules Michelet, *Tableau de la France*, 1831; quoted in Maurice Agulhon, 'Conscience nationale et conscience régionale en France de 1815 à nos jours,' in *Histoire vagabonde*, vol. 2, *Idéologies et politique dans la France du XIXe siècle* (Paris: Gallimard, 1988), 156.

13 Roger Chartier, 'The Two Frances: The History of a Geographical Idea,'

in *Cultural History: Between Practices and Representations*, trans. Lydia G. Cochrane (Cambridge: Polity Press, 1988), 172–200.

14 Eugen Weber, 'Nos ancêtres les gaulois,' in *My France: Politics, Culture, Myth* (Cambridge, MA: Belknap Press, 1991), 35.

15 Cachin, *Signac*, 75.

16 Paul Signac, 'D'océan en Méditerranée par les canaux,' *Le Yacht* 15, 759 (1892): 352. Evidence of Signac's continuing interest in Stendhal is found in 1894 (as in n. 20), and in 1914, when Signac published anonymously a pamphlet on the writer; Cachin, *Signac*, 75.

17 Stendhal, *Memoirs of a Tourist*, trans. and ed. Allan Seager (Chicago: Northwestern University Press, 1962), 263.

18 Ibid., 274.

19 Ibid., 302.

20 Cachin, *Signac*, 75.

21 Françoise Cachin, *Paul Signac*, trans. Michael Bullock (Greenwich, CT: New York Graphic Society, 1971), 56, notes Maupassant's description of the Saint-Tropez bay in her explanation of Signac's attraction to the south and notes further evidence of Signac's admiration in the painting *Nature morte: Livre, oranges* (1885, Nationalgalerie, Berlin, FC 83), which prominently includes Maupassant's book *Au Soleil*.

22 Guy de Maupassant, *Sur l'eau* (Paris: Gallimard, 1993), 120; Jacques Dupont, Preface, ibid., 42 n. 2, describes the rampant financial speculation on Côte d'Azur land, noting that the financial group Société Foncière de Cannes et du Littoral had specifically created resort towns starting in the 1880s, although as we have seen artists did not travel there in significant numbers until the 1890s.

23 Ibid., 120.

24 Ibid., 125.

25 Ibid., 123–4.

26 Ibid., 128.

27 Ibid., 129.

28 The importance of milieu in Reclus's and Kropotkin's works is convincingly argued in Roslak, 'Organicism,' 100–4. The connection between Reclus's science and his anarchism is convincingly argued by Marie Fleming, *The Anarchist Way to Socialism: Élisée Reclus and Nineteenth-Century European Anarchism* (London: Croom Helm, 1979).

29 Cachin, *Méditerranée*, 108, cites a 1932 letter from Signac to Georges Besson, which states that Signac encouraged Cross to settle there based on Reclus's descriptions of the region. Given his general immersion in anarchist circles from around 1888, Signac would have known the work of

Kropotkin, as shown by Herbert and Herbert 'Artists and Anarchism,' 477; and around 1893 he refers directly to Kropotkin's work (ibid., 519).

30 Caroline Cahm, *Kropotkin and the Rise of Revolutionary Anarchism, 1872–1886* (Cambridge: Cambridge University Press, 1989), 8.

31 Ibid.

32 Peter Kropotkin, *The Conquest of Bread and Other Writings*, ed. Marshall Shatz (Cambridge: Cambridge University Press, 1995), 215.

33 Ibid., 242.

34 For Reclus, cultural characteristics were determined by environment, history, and education, and so they were not immutable; see Fleming, *Anarchist Way*, 239–44; on Reclus's concept of race and his assertion of the importance of education in determining national characteristics, ibid., 153.

35 Ibid., 39 and passim.

36 Reclus, *L'homme et la terre*, vols. 5–6 (1905–8; repr. Paris: Fayard, 1990), 169–70, recognized that Germany had made much material progress, but as for its 'march toward a future of equality and justice ... the same assessment cannot be made.'

37 Élisée Reclus, *Nouvelle géographie universelle: La terre et les hommes*, vol. 2, *La France* (Paris: Librairie Hachette, n.d.), 50.

38 See Reclus, *L'homme et la terre* (1990), 169–70.

39 Fleming, *The Geography of Freedom: The Odyssey of Élisée Reclus* (Montreal: Black Rose Books, 1988), 64, summarizes Reclus's ideal political structure as one that 'would take the form of small groups or associations whose relationship to existing communes would depend on the people involved. While each association would be independent and self-administering, the people of one, acting out of a sense of brotherly love rather than competition, might well join the people of another to form a larger association, and these would vary in size'; on his decentralist ideas in general, see ibid., 63–5, 115.

40 Ibid., 64.

41 Élisée Reclus, *L'homme et la terre*, excerpted and ed. Béatrice Giblin, 2 vols. (Paris: François Maspero, 1982), 2: 46.

42 Ibid.

43 Reclus to Georges Renard, 2 June 1888, quoted in Fleming, *Anarchist Way*, 153.

44 Reclus, *L'homme et la terre* (1990), 146.

45 Ibid., 146–7.

46 Ibid., 147.

47 This positive view of Latin culture is emphasized in the illustration for Élisée Reclus, *L'homme et la terre*, 6 vols. (Paris: Librairie Universelle,

1905–8) by František Kupka, also an anarchist, entitled *Latins et Germains*, which is reproduced in Gary S. Dunbar, *Élisée Reclus: Historian of Nature* (Hamden, CT: Archon Books, 1978), 117.

48 Élisée Reclus, *Les villes d'hiver de la Méditerranée et les Alpes Maritimes* (Paris: Librairie Hachette, Collection des Guides Joanne, 1864), iii.

49 Reclus, *Nouvelle géographie*, 4.

50 Reclus, *L'homme et la terre* (1990), 114.

51 See Cachin, *Signac*, 43–9; Ferretti-Bocquillon, ed., *Signac et Saint-Tropez;* Cachin, 'L'arrivée de Signac'; and Anne Distel, *Signac au temps d'harmonie* (Paris: Découvertes Gallimard and Réunion des Musées Nationaux, 2001), 65–74.

52 Henri-Edmond Cross to Signac, 4 Nov. 1891, quoted in Cachin, 'L'arrivée de Signac,' 13.

53 Signac to Cross, 21 Nov. 1891, quoted ibid., 14.

54 Cross regularly visited the Monaco home of his uncle Dr Soins from 1883 until 1891, when he ventured to the less frequented Cabasson, the year before building his house in nearby Saint-Clair; see Françoise Baligand et al., *Henri-Edmond Cross, 1856–1910*, exh. cat., Musée de la Chartreuse de Douai (Douai, 1999), 13–14, 25.

55 Fred Orton and Griselda Pollock, 'Les données Bretonnantes: La prairie de répresentation,' *Art History* 3, 3 (1980): 331–2.

56 On the significant changes in Neo-Impressionist style that would occur throughout the 1890s – enlarged brushstrokes, increased interest in the decorative, move away from realism to idealism – see Cachin, *Signac*, 56–62; and Flagg, 'Neo-Impressionist Landscape,' 14.

57 Claire Frèches-Thory, 'Paul Signac, Acquisitions récentes,' *Revue du Louvre et des Musées de France* 33, 1 (1983): 38. Although some of his landscapes include figures, such as *Le Passage du Puits Bertin, Clichy* (1886, location unknown, FC 118), they are not usually the focus of his outdoor compositions. See also Frèches-Thory, 'La donation Ginette Signac,' *Revue du Louvre et des Musées de France* 28, 2 (1978): 107–12. The lack of figures may be due both to Signac's lack of formal training and the difficulties of the Neo-Impressionist technique, since it becomes more pronounced after his adherence to the style.

58 Signac to Camille Pissarro, May 1892, quoted in Frèches-Thory, 'Paul Signac,' 38; Signac's new interest in the 'Claudian idiom' is discussed by Richard Thomson, 'Signac,' exhibition review, *Burlington Magazine* 143, 1180 (2001): 444, and Thomson, *Monet to Matisse*, 24–5 and 77–80.

59 Cross to Signac, n.d., as translated in Ferretti-Bocquillon et al., *Signac 1853–1935*, 196.

60 Marina Ferretti-Bocquillon, 'Paul Signac au temps d'harmonie, 1892–1913,' in *Signac et la libération de la couleur de Matisse à Mondrian*, exh. cat., Musée de Grenoble (1997), 58, suggests that this work, consciously or not, recalls Seurat's *Le cirque*. On the work in general, see Frèches-Thory, 'Paul Signac'; Flagg, 'Neo-Impressionist Landscape,' 208–15; Ferretti-Bocquillon, ed., *Signac et Saint-Tropez*, 32–9; Martha Ward, *Pissarro, Neo-Impressionism, and the Spaces of the Avant-Garde* (Chicago: University of Chicago Press, 1996), 214–15; Ferretti-Bocquillon et al., *Signac 1863–1935*, 181–3; and Werth, *Joy of Life*, 93–103, which also includes an analysis of the significant use of the term *décoration* in the subtitle of *Young Provençal Women* and its relation to anarchist thought.

61 Ferretti-Bocquillon et al., *Signac 1863–1935*, 181.

62 For a consideration of other Neo-Impressionist images that idealize peasant life as evidence of Kropotkin's ideology of mutual aid, see Roslak, 'Organicism,' 101–3; see also Ward, *Pissarro*, 174. Signac specifically refers to the work of Kropotkin in a letter to Jean Grave dated about 1893, in Herbert and Herbert, 'Artists and Anarchism,' 519. Kropotkin's *The Conquest of Bread* was published serially in *Le Révolté* and *La Révolte* and as a book in 1892.

63 Werth, 'Le Bonheur de Vivre: The Idyllic Image in French Art, 1891–1906,' PhD diss., Harvard University, 1994, 152, sees them as gossiping.

64 Kropotkin, *Conquest of Bread*, 61–2.

65 Of the seven known preparatory works, only the two sketchiest renditions (FC 236 recto and verso), which depict two separate wells, do not show the women working together.

66 Ferretti-Bocquillon et al., *Signac 1863–1935*, 149–50, sees *Sunday* as evidence of Signac's bleak, sterile view of bourgeois marriage; Thomson, 'Signac,' 444, disagrees, since figures facing 'different directions hardly adds up to a damning critique of marriage.' However, Ferretti-Bocquillon et al., 125–6, suggest the possibility of a more positive reading of *The Dining Room*, as the older man on the right is a portrait of Signac's supportive grandfather. Regardless, the contrast between the total lack of interaction depicted in these works and the interaction depicted in his two major canvases from Saint-Tropez is notable.

67 For an alternate reading see Roslak, 'Organicism,' 108.

68 I thank Perry Chapman for alerting me to the importance of body types. On the so-called traditional costume, see Pascale Picard-Cajan, ed., *Arlésienne: Le mythe?* exh. cat., Museon Arlaten (Arles, 2000).

69 On van Gogh's interest in cataloguing portraits by 'types' see Vojtěch Jirat-Wasiutyński, 'Vincent van Gogh's Roulin: Radical Republican and

Socratic Type,' in Craigen Bowen et al., eds, *Dear Print Fan: A Festschrift for Marjorie B. Cohn* (Cambridge, MA: Harvard University Art Museums, 2001), 167–73; and Carol Zemel, *Van Gogh's Progress: Utopia, Modernity, and Late-Nineteenth-Century Art* (Berkeley and Los Angeles: University of California Press, 1997), 102–4.

70 Vincent van Gogh, quoted in Orton and Pollock, 'Données Bretonnantes,' 332–3.

71 Ward, *Pissarro*, 215, makes a similar point.

72 Kropotkin, *Conquest of Bread*, 104.

73 Ibid., 103. For a differing interpretation of the relation between artists and anarchist theories of art, see Herbert and Herbert, 'Artists and Anarchism,' 478.

74 Michael F. Zimmermann, *Seurat and the Art Theory of His Time* (Antwerp: Fonds Mercatur, 1991), 205.

75 For a comprehensive bibliography, see Cachin, *Signac*, 215–16; the most thorough accounts with extensive use of unpublished sources are Ferretti-Bocquillon, ed., *Signac et Saint-Tropez*, 50–9, and Ferretti-Bocquillon et al., *Signac 1863–1935*, 195–200; Flagg, 'Neo-Impressionist Landscape,' 215–27; Linda Nochlin, 'Seurat's *Grande Jatte*: An Anti-Utopian Allegory,' *Museum Studies* 14, 2 (1989): 140–1; Hutton, *Neo-Impressionism*, 135–48; Werth, *Joy of Life*, 83–142; Ferretti-Bocquillon, 'Paul Signac,' 57–61; and Marie-Pierre Salé, 'Le mythe de l'Âge d'or et le retour à la nature,' in *1900*, exh. cat., Galeries Nationales du Grand Palais (Paris, 2000), 314–19.

76 Signac wanted to donate the work to a site that had sufficient viewing space for a large work and that would also be appropriate ideologically; he negotiated to donate it to a *maison du peuple* (socialist workers' building) being designed by Victor Horta in Brussels. Acceptance of the gift was delayed, resulting in Signac caustically asking if it would be more easily accepted if he changed the name to 'In the Time of the Socialist Deputies'; Ferretti-Bocquillon et al., *Signac 1863–1935*, 199.

77 Ibid., 195.

78 Ibid., 198. It is unknown when Signac first envisioned the series, which is mentioned in his unpublished diaries of 1896. It was to have included other panels depicting boat haulers, wreckers, and builders; apparently only *The Wrecker* (1897–9, Nancy, Musée des Beaux-Arts, FC336) was completed.

79 For Neo-Impressionism and the changing concept of the decorative in the 1890s and this work, see ibid., 2001, 198; Flagg, 'Neo-Impressionist Landscape,' 195, 208, and passim; Werth, *Joy of Life*, 97–100; and Ward, *Pissarro*, 210–22.

80 Rosand, 'Pastoral Topoi,' 169; the motif of the sheltering tree is repeated in the background.
81 Werth, *Joy of Life*, 105, notes the importance of totality in this work; because of its emphasis on the future rather than the past, she categorizes it as utopian with pastoral components; 'Bonheur de Vivre,' 134.
82 Hutton, *Neo-Impressionism*, 135–7, is primarily concerned with the anarchism of the image; see also Werth, *Joy of Life*, 103–16.
83 Translated, but retaining ellipses from Ferretti-Bocquillon, ed., *Signac et Saint-Tropez*, 52.
84 Albert Boime, 'Georges Seurat's "Un dimanche à la Grande-Jatte" and the Scientific Approach to History Painting,' in E. Mai and A. Repp-Eckert, eds, *Historienmalerei in Europa: Paradigmen in Form, Funktion und Ideologie* (Mainz: Phillip von Zabern, 1990), 316; on the subtitle, taken from anarchist writer Charles Malato, see Salé, 'Mythe de l'Âge d'or,' 314–15.
85 Kropotkin, *Conquest of Bread*, 18.
86 The fruit-bearing fig tree could also be a symbol of plenty, since it can have two crops per year; I thank Hayden Maginnis for pointing out the variety of seasons indicated in the picture. See also Werth, 'Bonheur de Vivre,' 166.
87 For a different reading of this couple and the role of sexuality in this work, see Werth, *Joy of Life*, 108.
88 The full title is *Portrait of Félix Fénéon (Against the Enamel of a Background Rhythmic with Beats and Angles, Tones and Tints)* (1890–1, Rockefeller Collection, New York, FC 211). Fénéon appears to be gazing beyond the flower; a similar pose is used in Signac's *Portrait of My Mother* (1892, private collection, FC 228); in Cross's *The Evening Air* (1893–4, Musée d'Orsay, Paris), discussed in Werth, *Joy of Life*, 113; and in one of the seated girls in Seurat's *La Grande Jatte*.
89 Kropotkin, *Conquest of Bread*, 94.
90 Signac, ca. 1902, in Herbert and Herbert, 'Artists and Anarchism,' 479.
91 Paul Signac to Théo van Rysselberghe, Van Rysselberghe Archive, 870355, Getty Research Institute, Special Collections, Los Angeles: 'Commencé l'esquisse de "Au temps d'harmonie." Tous les matins gymnastique d'une ½ heure: croquis d'après Raphael, Puvis, Andre del Sarto [*illegible word*] – excellent entrainement.'
92 See Werth, *Joy of Life*, 128–9; Ferretti-Bocquillon et al., *Signac 1863–1935*, 195–6; as Werth, ibid., 21–35 and passim has shown, Puvis's classicism was applauded by all camps in the period; see also Shaw, *Dream States*, 2 and 187–90; and Ward, *Pissarro*, 204–22. On other Neo-Impressionists' attitudes towards Puvis de Chavannes, see Hutton, *Neo-Impressionism*, 119–22.

93 Signac to Jean Grave, ca. 1893, in Herbert and Herbert, 'Artists and Anarchism,' 519.
94 See Ferretti-Bocquillon, ed., *Signac et Saint-Tropez*, 58–9.
95 Although boules is widely played, it was associated with Provence; see, for example, B. Durand, 'Le Joueur de Boules,' in *Les Français peints par eux-mêmes: Encyclopédie morale du dix-neuvième siècle*, vol. 2 (Paris: L. Curmer, 1840), 294. On the sower as an anarchist symbol, see Salé, 'Mythe de l'Âge d'or,' 316; and Werth, 'Bonheur de Vivre,' 164.
96 Orton and Pollock, 'Données Bretonnantes,' 332.
97 See Hutton, *Neo-Impressionism*, 136–7, who notes that the first to compare the two paintings was Sally S. Medlyn, 'The Development of Georges Seurat's Art with Special Reference to the Influence of Contemporary Anarchist Philosophy,' MA thesis, University of Manchester, 1976; see also the extended comparison by Werth, *Joy of Life*, 103–9; and John Leighton, 'Out of Seurat's Shadow: Signac, 1863–1935, An Introduction,' in Ferretti-Bocquillon et al., *Signac 1863–1935*, 15–16.
98 The work was exhibited as *Apprêteuse et garnisseuse (modes), rue de Caire*; see Cachin, *Signac*, 171.
99 This is reported by Seurat in his letter to Fénéon asserting his primacy over Signac in the invention of the technique; see Robert L. Herbert et al., *Georges Seurat: 1859–1891*, exh. cat., Metropolitan Museum of Art (New York, 1991), 383.
100 Ward, *Pissarro*, 66–7 analyses the painting in relation to similar formal elements in Pissarro's paintings; Cachin, *Paul Signac*, 26, notes that 'the pleasure or interest aroused by the picture ought to come simply from the lines, the contrast of values and colors ... This is a deliberately stylized and, as it were, dehumanized version of a "genre scene"'; Herbert et al., *Georges Seurat*, 175, discusses its primitivizing features.
101 For a judicious assessment of the literature see Herbert et al., *Georges Seurat*, 170–9 and 425; and Herbert, *Seurat and the Making of La Grande Jatte*, exh. cat., Art Institute of Chicago (2004), 152–69.
102 See Judith G. Coffin, *The Politics of Women's Work: The Paris Garment Trades, 1750–1915* (Princeton: Princeton University Press, 1996).
103 Ibid., 4.
104 On high rent in this district, see Lenard Berlanstein, *The Working People of Paris, 1871–1914* (Baltimore: Johns Hopkins University Press, 1984), 32, 191.
105 Paul Signac, 'Extraits du journal inédit de Paul Signac,' ed. John Rewald, *Gazette des Beaux-Arts*, 6th ser., 36 (July–Sept. 1949): 171.
106 Werth, *Joy of Life*, 104.

107 For another comparison of their figures, see ibid., 161–73.
108 Nochlin, 'Seurat's *Grande Jatte*,' 147.
109 Henry Fèvre, 1886, quoted ibid., 140.
110 Herbert et al., *Georges Seurat*, 177.
111 Hutton, *Neo-Impressionism*, 137.
112 In contrast, see Werth, *Joy of Life*, 110–11, who argues that work can be divided into a left half, identified with intellectual and artistic pursuits, and a right half, associated with rural labour and peasants, primarily stemming from the male foreground figures; however, in my reading of the picture, a man instructing children in the background right fails to follow this division.
113 Ferretti-Bocquillon, ed., *Signac et Saint-Tropez*, 54, suggests this is 'a nod' to Seurat's painting; Nochlin, 'Seurat's Grande Jatte,' 140, notes that the 'hen and rooster play out the theme of mutual aid and interaction spelled out by the work as a whole'; Salé, 'Mythe de l'Âge d'or,' 316, states the rooster is an anarchist symbol.
114 Henry van De Velde, 'Les expositions d'art,' *La Revue Blanche* 10 (1896): 284–7.
115 See Hutton, *Neo-Impressionism*, 46–52; and Jean Maitron, *Le mouvement anarchiste en France*, vol. 1, *Des origines à 1914* (Paris: Gallimard, 1975), 206–61. Paul Reclus, nephew of Élisée, was also charged.
116 Ferretti-Bocquillon et al., *Signac 1863–1935*, 198.
117 See Élie Reclus, 'Mythologie populaire: Le coq,' parts 1–3, *La Société Nouvelle* 106 (Oct. 1893): 470–82; 107 (Nov. 1893): 587–602; and 108 (Dec. 1893): 700–15. Eugenia W. Herbert, *The Artist and Social Reform: France and Belgium, 1885–1898* (New Haven, CT: Yale University Press, 1961), 155, notes that *Le Coq Rouge* was the name of the Belgian edition of the anarchist journal *Les Temps Nouveaux* in 1895.
118 Élie Reclus, 'Mythologie populaire,' 472.
119 Ibid., 715.
120 Richard Thomson, *Seurat* (Oxford: Phaidon, 1985), 123, argues that the term *singesse* (monkey) was slang for prostitute and thus supports his assertion that the woman represents a prostitute; Herbert et al., *Georges Seurat*, 176, rejects this identification, arguing that the monkey's tail only mocks 'the pretentiousness of this elegant couple.'
121 Anonymous critic, likely George Moore, in *The Bat* (25 May 1886), 186, quoted in Thomson, *Seurat*, 123.
122 Élie Reclus, 'Mythologie populaire,' 600.
123 Charles Fourier, *Oeuvres complètes de Ch. Fourier*, vol. 6, *Le nouveau monde industriel et sociétaire* (Paris: Librairie Sociétaire, 1845; repr. Paris: Éditions

Anthropos, 1966), 464: 'The rooster reveals the opposite character, the courteous man who, without mastering women, knows how to maintain his rank among them: he is the man of good spirits.'

124 Kropotkin, *Conquest of Bread*, 61–2; Reclus, *L'homme et la terre* (1982), 2: 46; and as discussed above.

125 On the importance of harmony in anarchist and Neo-Impressionist thought, see Roslak, 'Politics of Aesthetic Harmony.' This belief is also present in the theories of Charles Henry; in 'Rapporteur esthétique et sensation de forme,' pt. 1, *Revue Indépendante* 7, 18 (1888): 90, which Signac recommended to van Gogh, Henry stated that better art is produced in more harmonious societies, where artists are better able to sense the universal harmony, and he concluded, 'It is not the schools, but the outstanding social states as one saw in Greece or in the Renaissance that produce the great periods of art.'

126 Signac to Théo van Rysselberghe, Wednesday, 18 November [no year], Van Rysselberghe Archive (see n. 91) criticizes Maurice Denis's influence over van Rysselberghe and urges him to move, stating: 'Je crois le milieu où vit un artiste a sur lui une grande influence.'

127 Signac to Jean Grave, n.d., in Herbert and Herbert, 'Artists and Anarchism,' 521.

128 For an opposing view, see J. Herbert, *Fauve Painting*, 124–9.

# 6 Inventing Mediterranean Harmony in Matisse's Paper Cut-Outs

JOHN KLEIN

Although Henri Matisse is one of the best-known twentieth-century artists of the Mediterranean, this has been acknowledged primarily through his Fauve painting in Saint-Tropez and Collioure, his Moroccan canvases of the early teens, and the theatrical performance of a trans-Mediterranean blend of the Côte d'Azur and North Africa in his so-called Nice period, roughly from the end of the First World War to the close of the 1920s. Less attention has been paid in this respect to the innovative works of art Matisse made in Nice in a late-career flowering – his paper cut-outs. These often large-scale collages of flat, decorative colour and bold composition have of course attracted considerable admiration and study, but their iconography has in general not been thoroughly analyzed.[1] All made in the Mediterranean ambience, the cut-outs of the late 1940s and early 1950s feature 'timeless,' harmonious subjects that intertwine the two major French figurations of the Mediterranean, the oriental and the classical. Moreover, Matisse frequently inflected this thematic axis with his epiphanic experience of Tahiti, a contemporary version of an idea of earthly paradise that so often motivated modern artists and writers to render idealized images of escape through 'a certain permeability of site,' in the words of Kenneth Silver, superimposing one exotic vision over another.[2] Matisse's cut-outs are also, to a great degree, projections of this overdetermined Arcadia to the audience with a growing role in the patronage of his work after the Second World War, in the United States.

If after the horrors of the war the Atlantic Ocean, with the United States on the other side, promised a cleansing of France's wounds, the Mediterranean was unavoidably dirty. Layered with history, fraught with nationalist and colonial conflict, culturally miscegenetic, the Mediterranean was thoroughly implicated in what many observers earlier in the century perceived as the growing impurity of French culture, a hotbed of jazz-age decadence. Yet during the war of 1939 to 1945 pressure from the north, in the form of Germany's invasion and occupation of the greater part of the French *hexagone*, gave the Mediterranean region new significance as the centre of the Free Zone, looking across to North Africa, from which the initial hope of liberation would come in the Allied victories over Rommel in Tunisia. Under the Vichy government the conservative view of France's decadence resurfaced with a vengeance. For Matisse and other French artists of the period, the Mediterranean took on a new role as a refuge, an escape from wartime oppression, a promise of a return to a more idealistic past, and even perhaps a source of solace as a place of suspension from time and history.[3] Following the war, when Matisse's cut-outs flourished, he invested heavily in ideas and themes of the classical and the oriental for images of plenitude, luxury, and salvation (figures 6.1, 6.2). Throughout the turbulent post-war period, Matisse continued to make images of timelessness and serenity, derived from both East and West, insisting on a heterogeneous but harmonious Mediterranean as the source of his ultimate goal in art. The comprehensive decoration he sought, an art that would offer an environmental experience to the viewer, would also reconcile the fruitful antinomies that had characterized his work throughout a long career – oppositions between drawing and colour, figure and field, flatness and depth, identity and anonymity. Such reconciliation was also implicitly a means to restore through art a wholeness that had eluded a region long in conflict.

With extended stays or residence in Ajaccio, Saint-Tropez, Collioure, Biskra, Cavalière, Tangier, Nice, Vence, and other locations, Henri Matisse spent much of his career making art in the Mediterranean region. He is often regarded as the quintessential modern painter of the Côte d'Azur, retailing its pleasures and luxuries, all bathed in the golden light he spoke of so frequently, light being always one of the first things that impressed him about a new place. When he travelled in 1930 to New York and Tahiti, he was fascinated by the difference in the light between those places and the light of Nice. Though Mediterranean light was long familiar, perhaps even taken for granted, his travels elsewhere confirmed his preference for that setting. Of course his sense of the Mediterranean was larger than what is encompassed by the view from the French coast and the caressingly illuminated forms that fill his paintings. In its hybridity, Matisse's Mediterranean *seems* to embrace what one study of the region has called its 'dense fragmentation,' in which the geographic unity of the littoral area has been historically undercut by competing cultural and political claims.[4] This fragmentation was plain in the mid-twentieth century. The period in which Matisse made his celebrated paper cut-outs, during and after the Second World War up to the end of his life in 1954, was a time of considerable tension and instability in the Mediterranean, first in its domination by the Axis powers and subsequent liberation by the Allies; then, after the war, as murderous reprisals against collaborators were carried out, the French colonies of the Maghreb lurched violently towards independence, the new nation-state of Israel was brought into existence, and the Mediterranean overall became a highly contested theatre of the Cold War.

It is no surprise that none of these conflicts is reflected in the subject matter of Matisse's cut-outs. Nor is there a contemporary reference of any kind in these works of art. He was not in that sense an artist of contemporary public life or political engagement, as were Picasso and Léger in the same period. The imagery of his paintings and drawings during the Second World War and after is severely restricted, consisting for the most part of still lifes and compositions of female figures, largely domestic subjects in his salon and studio. These had been his reliable themes since he had first permanently moved to the region in the late teens. The paper cut-outs are another matter. There we find a proliferation of diverse subject matter to challenge the formal potential of his innovative but essentially simple technique of arranging pieces of coloured paper, cut into discrete shapes with scissors, into a composition, sometimes on a very large scale.[5]

In many cases, the mural-size paper cut-outs were essentially proposals or maquettes for decorative projects that were to be realized by skilled craftsmen in other, more durable (and traditional) media, especially ceramic tile (figures 6.1, 6.3), stained glass (figure 6.4) and various fabrics, including tapestry, linen, and woven carpets. Only subsequently (though almost immediately) did Matisse consider the cut-outs as independent works of art, comparable in ambition and effect to his paintings. It was through the cut-outs and the settings for which these designs were conceived that Matisse most avidly renewed his career-long goal of a modern decoration, a hoped-for equivalent of the Roman wall painting, Byzantine mosaics, Renaissance frescoes, and nineteenth-century French mural ensembles that he admired so much, and that are such prominent features of the art history of the Mediterranean region.[6] He most fully realized his ambitions in this respect in the Chapel of the Rosary at Vence, in which he controlled nearly every aspect of the design of both the building and its decorative embellishment, but his desire for a lasting achievement in the context of architectural decoration is clear in many other of his works in cut paper. The emphasis in Matisse's cut-outs on timeless, harmonious, and even idyllic imagery is thus thoroughly in keeping with the ideas of duration and stability on which the tradition of architectural decoration is predicated.

Classical versus Oriental is one of the great generative oppositions in modern culture.[7] It is perhaps second in importance in the modern visual arts only to another productive dichotomy, that between the classical and the primitive, to which it is sometimes closely related. In modern art, the classical/Oriental opposition is most frequently expressed in the pictorial realm; the classical/primitive polarity is an issue mainly in the sphere of sculpture. The opposition of the classical and the primitive in sculpture is resolved in abstraction or archaism. The opposition of the classical and the Oriental in two dimensions is resolved in decoration. Decoration was equivalent to reconciliation.

The question to be posed here is, Was Matisse's decoration, culminating in the paper cut-outs, predominantly classical or Oriental? Or neither, if the reconciliation of the classical and the Oriental in Matisse's work ultimately required the superimposition of his Tahitian experiences in order for it to be rendered as decoration? And yet another answer is suggested in some of the last and simplest of Matisse's Mediterranean images, in which his goal seems to be not to create a decoration, an ornamental work of art with environmental capabilities, but to distil an idea of the Mediterranean into timeless signs.

The extent of Matisse's engagement with Mediterranean sites over his long career needs little rehearsal here. From Corsica in the 1890s, Saint-Tropez on the Côte d'Azur and Collioure in Basque country in the Fauve period, Algeria and Morocco in 1906, 1912, and 1913, to his extended residence in Nice beginning in the late teens – he rendered Mediterranean France and North Africa in landscapes, urban views, figure studies, and imaginary pastoral scenes. When he first went to the Midi from his *pays natal* in the sugarbeet plains of the north, he said, as he so often did to explain his reasons for travel, that he was motivated by the prospect of seeing a new kind of light.

And painting in the strong Mediterranean light proved to be difficult.

Since Delacroix had gone to Morocco in the 1830s, the challenge of representing Mediterranean light in paint had bedevilled many French artists. Renoir and other Impressionists lightened their entire palette into a blond haze of close-valued hues. Van Gogh's and Gauguin's approach in Arles, by contrast, was to saturate colours, striving in their juxtaposition to achieve an equivalent of the intensity of meridional light. The Fauves, led by Matisse, made paintings of small floating areas of often vivid (but just as often pastel) colour, pictorial mosaics whose reticulations were the pure white of the ground plane. In these Fauve paintings light is not so much represented as it is a product of a pictorial structure that insists on the integrity of the surface on which a scene in nature is rendered to the eye as a bright pattern.

In his late decorative ensembles Matisse returned to this pattern of reticulated light, most literally and dramatically in the carved door of the confessional in the Chapel of the Rosary at Vence (a strong echo of the lace-like Moorish fabric hanging that was such a prominent feature of his studio), but also in such large-scale paper cut-outs as *Large Decoration with Masks* of 1953 (figure 6.3), one of four designs he proposed for a commission from a Los Angeles collector. Here symmetrical quatrefoil units are repeated in alternating colours and interpolated with smaller clove-bud shapes that punctuate the white space between the quatrefoils, forming two grids on either side of the central, also symmetrical arrangement of floral motifs. The whole is flanked by fluted and capped columns; the fields of stylized coloured blossoms are crowned with sprouting flecks that radiate to each side from the centre. The overall impression is of bright colour but also of extreme whiteness. Light is never represented in the cut-outs; it is completely ambient, dialectically inseparable from the coloured design because the light is the inverse of the colour, its absence. Paper cut-outs such as these are the brightest, most luminous works of art Matisse made in his career.

The qualities of Matisse's large paper cut-outs as decoration – the respect for the surface, the ambition on the scale of architecture, the commensurability of figure, field, atmosphere, and illumination – can also be found in the works of other artists who sought to create large-scale decorative ensembles in the Mediterranean ambience. Here too the Mediterranean themes of the classical and the Oriental are in play. The archetype for this kind of modern decoration in the Mediterranean context is the pair of murals by Pierre Puvis de Chavannes, showing ancient Marseille as a Greek colony and modern Marseille as the gateway to the Orient (see figure 1.4), commissioned for the grand staircase of the Marseille museum on the occasion of the opening of the Suez Canal in 1869, at a moment of high hopes for a new integration of France with the Levant. In Puvis's murals, a decorative aesthetic, of which he was the most significant practitioner of his time, is used to allegorize the contributions of classical antiquity and modern trade with the East to the heritage and continuing vitality of France through its principal southern port.

For the Impressionists and the Post-Impressionists, the Mediterranean as a subject of decorative mural painting had strong Arcadian or pastoral associations. With the exception of Renoir, these late-nineteenth-century artists largely ignored the Oriental elements of Mediterranean culture in favour of emphasizing the classical heritage of the region. Timelessness, stability, and harmony in the Mediterranean are the themes of Paul Signac, who integrated the classical and the contemporary in his pastoral composition *In the Time of Harmony* (see figure 5.1 and the essay by Anne Dymond), expressing the hope of an ideal future time. The Nabis Bonnard, Denis, and Roussel, without the overt anarchist politics of their contemporary Signac, nevertheless projected in large-scale decorations an Arcadian vision that evoked the mythic Mediterranean of Daphnis and Chloë. Nor was the attraction of the south for northern, specifically Parisian, audiences always merely implicit. In other contemporary mural paintings, Mediterranean motifs rendered as decoration could even be intended as frank advertising for the region, as in the turn-of-the-century mural ensemble by Frédéric Montenard for the station restaurant at the Gare de Lyon in Paris, the gateway for travel to southern France and the Mediterranean coast. Montenard's *Villefranche* (figure 6.5) idealizes one of the destinations of the Chemin de Fer du Midi, promising to the holiday-bound Parisian an idyllic experience far removed from anything resembling actual fin-de-siècle France.

In his own early integration of Mediterranean themes and a decorative aesthetic, Matisse came down firmly on the side of the classical in his mix of Arcadian dream and a contemporary family on a picnic in such paintings as *Luxe, calme et volupté* of 1904 (Musée d'Orsay, Paris), a composition made very much under the sign of Signac in both style and temperament, and in fact destined for the dining room of Signac's house in Saint-Tropez, to form part of an integrated décor. Signac, of course, was not the source of Matisse's interest in classicism. The classical as a reference point was part of Matisse's lifeblood as an artist, especially as an artist of the human figure, which he had drawn from antique statuary as a student.[8]

Soon enough, though, Matisse would enlist both classical and Oriental motifs in his decorative aspirations. In the ceramic mural commissioned in 1907 by the German collector Karl Osthaus, Matisse reworked the classical theme of the nymph and satyr, a violent narrative that he would distil to a decorative essence repeatedly throughout his career. In several large and ambitious paintings from around this time he represented a profusion of Oriental patterning in Turkish rugs, figured textiles, and framing devices derived from Persian miniatures, as in *The Artist's Family* of 1911 (Pushkin Museum, Moscow). His interest in the decorative capacities of non-figurative Islamic art was more recent than his long-standing training in the classical. He eagerly saw two important exhibitions of Islamic art in Paris (1903) and Munich (1910), whose impact can be seen in his subsequent immersion of his own painted figures in a profusion of patterned colours for a series of large decorations, of which *The Artist's Family* is an example. Soon after, his transformative journeys to Morocco in 1912 and 1913 reinforced his earlier direct exposure to the Islamic world in Algeria in 1906. Thus, a number of developments in this period contributed to the enduring legacy of the Oriental in Matisse's art.[9] And for a while, the Oriental would dominate the classical in his figural representation.

In his so-called Nice period, when he took up residence on the Côte d'Azur for the first time in the late teens, Matisse spun out variation after variation on the theme of the 'femme orientale' in a sumptuously decorated hothouse interior, but always using French or Italian models as his ersatz odalisques, in a patently artificial evocation of the harem, wittily skewered by his friend Pierre Bonnard, who struck a pose himself in Matisse's fake seraglio décor, as if replacing the model during her rest period or smoke break. For Matisse, the 1920s was an orientalizing period, as his odalisques fused his own devotion to the nude female figure to a satisfying vision of French domination of its supine colonial territories in the Mediterranean. At the end of the decade the classical re-enters his repertoire of motifs in the form of impressively monumental sculptures of the nude female figure and in his illustrations for Mallarmé's poems. In many ways the 1930s saw in his work a return to an engagement with the antique, and in fact this period has been called Matisse's classical decade.

By the end of the 1930s, therefore, Matisse had behind him a long and deep affiliation with both cultural visions of the Mediterranean. What is more, he had begun to integrate these eclectic cultural interests with his ambition to design for the wall, for the table, and for the theatrical stage, in a variety of commissions and personal initiatives for mural paintings, tapestries, costumes, set designs, and even a glass vase for the Steuben company in New York. By this time, too, he had already begun to use the technique of the paper cut-out as a design medium, first for the tripartite mural *Dance* for the Barnes Foundation, then for the covers of special issues of the avant-garde journals *Cahiers d'Art* and *Verve* and for the costumes and front curtain for the Massine ballet *Rouge et Noir*. The simple technique of cutting shapes out of coloured paper was beginning to show an enormous potential not only for transforming Matisse's working practice, but for realizing his ambition of a decorative art of disarming simplicity and profound effects.

The beginning of the Second World War in 1939 brought any hope of wholeness or harmony under immediate threat. The next time he made substantial use of the cut-out technique, it was to design *Jazz*, which, for all its celebrated innovation and upbeat aura, contains numerous images of peril, fear, fatalism, and death, a repertoire of wartime terrors and sentiments. As the war began Matisse, like so many other French artists, had manifested an overt patriotism in his work, explicitly in the painting *La France*, made within months of Hitler's invasion of Poland in the fall of 1939. He soon followed this with a tricolour reworking of *The Romanian Blouse* (Musée National d'Art Moderne, Paris), as Sarah Wilson has observed.[10] These nationalist expressions were accompanied by doubts about his work. In a letter to Bonnard, Matisse despaired of finding the reconciliation he sought in his art, lamenting the difficulty of proceeding with his characteristic means, and saying, 'My drawing and my painting are separated from one another,' so that he was unable to make his work suggest 'light and spiritual space.'[11] When the German army pushed into France from the north, Matisse and many others headed south to the refuge of the Mediterranean, where they temporarily escaped wartime oppression. As the centre of the Free Zone, the Mediterranean region could seem a place of suspension from time as well as the last best hope of the French way of life. His near-death experience following major surgery in 1941 produced in Matisse the conviction that he had been blessed with a second life for realizing his goals; his subsequent physical limitations also introduced a practical advantage to his work in cut paper, less demanding than standing at an easel. When he had the opportunity to leave France, with invitations from the United States and a Brazilian visa in hand, he demurred, implying that his departure would impoverish French cultural life. During the war he was taken to be a living embodiment of Gallic values, not least by the communist Louis Aragon, and publications on his work ritually emphasized his essential Frenchness.[12] With Bonnard, he was made honorary co-president of the Union Méditerranéenne pour l'Art Moderne in 1946. Films were made of him at work, one of them sponsored by the Department of Cultural Relations of the Ministry of Foreign Affairs. The war years elevated Matisse to the status of a national treasure, sealed in an official sense by the award in 1947 of the rank of Commandant de la Légion d'Honneur.

The war over, however, nationalist imagery disappeared from his art. With his cut-paper technique, he embarked on a variety of decorative projects that drew heavily, in distinctly non-French motifs, on the classical and the Oriental, now supplemented with what we might call the oceanic, the outpouring of long-processed memories of his trip to Tahiti in 1930, as in his compositions for Ascher Ltd of London of white creatures of the sky and sea suspended on a beige ground, destined to be used in the creation of a sleek updating of France's tapestry tradition, more suitable for the modern middle-class apartment than for the château.

Images of plenitude, benevolence, salvation, and triumph come to fill enormous walls in his studios, transforming the terrestrial environment into evocations of ocean and sky and realms beyond. In the cut-out *Celestial Jerusalem* of 1948 (figure 6.4), an early project for stained-glass windows in the Vence Chapel, Matisse gives abstract coloured form to the promised heavenly kingdom in the East. Colour itself, whose splendour is concentrated by the absence of any explicit imagery despite the Oriental theme, expresses the hope of redemption in the life to come. The protagonist of the cut-out *Amphitrite* (1947; private collection), Greek queen of the sea, presides over the fantastic creations of her watery realm, a magical space of seemingly limitless depth and variety. Classical and Oriental motifs alike share in Matisse's project to create a transcendent decorative art in which the viewer could imagine a wholly separate and immeasurable space.

Still there are some differences in Matisse's treatment of his classical and Oriental themes. The cut-outs with Oriental subjects tend to be more intensely coloured and more densely arranged, with killer juxtapositions of saturated hues, as in *Zulma* (1950; Statens Museum for Kunst, Copenhagen), the image of a generalized Oriental, presumably North African, woman; and *The Sorrow of the King* (1952; Musée National d'Art Moderne, Paris), one of the very few elegiac images in the cut-outs. Derived in all likelihood from his thoughts about a never-realized project to illustrate the Song of Songs, the Old Testament theme of David playing for King Saul or, alternatively, Salome dancing before Herod conveys an image of loss and longing assuaged by art in the forms of music and dance, in accord with Matisse's belief in the benevolent effects of his own creations, especially when they were allowed to operate in a comprehensive environmental fashion, as at Vence in his chapel. These cut-outs with Oriental themes are also more pictorial and more narrative in quality than those with classical motifs, whose compositions tend to the iconic and tabular. *The Thousand and One Nights* (figure 6.2) unfolds across the surface like a story told on an unfurling scroll. The work is to be 'read' as a rebus of signs, a succession of specular, half-glimpsed images in the passage of a single night: a lighted oil lamp followed by dreamlike dancing forms, the starlit sky, the lamp at last extinguished, and the approaching dawn, all surrounded by an ambience of heart-inflamed love and accompanied by a parallel textual diminuendo whose ellipses leave much unsaid: '... she saw the light of day / She fell discreetly silent.' The so-called 'Arabian Nights,' the tales of Scheherazade, were a staple of Arabic literature and well known in France in translation as well as in adaptations for ballet. The stories themselves were not a pure Islamic expression, but a cultural mongrel, freely blending the traditions of Central Asia and the Maghreb, and projecting a generalized image that romanticized the Oriental Other in ways that resonated with eager consumers of this idea of the exotic Levant in France. Matisse's largest Oriental composition was one of his most derivative, but also one of his most sensual.

Some of the cut-outs combine characteristics of both classical antiquity and the east. Leaves of acanthus, native to the Mediterranean and an inexhaustible source of classical decorative motifs, spread gently in a cut-out design (1953; Beyeler Foundation, Riehen) for a ceramic tile mural, implying their capacity to cover the entire surface with the pattern of their regular and insistent radiance. In this way these leaves conform to Matisse's tendency to treat classical motifs as patterns. But when he saw acanthus plants forty years earlier, on his first trip to Morocco, they were exotic emblems of the Oriental; their sumptuousness made a deep impression on him. Previously, he had encountered acanthus only in casts of Corinthian capitals, after which he had made drawings as a student.[13] The intensely coloured paintings of his Moroccan sojourn, and the vivid chromatic symphony of the spreading arcs of leaves in the much later cut-out, express the deep impressions that the luxuriousness of North Africa's tropical foliage made on the French artist; his stylization of the leaves recalls the decorative abstractions of antiquity. The adaptable acanthus was thus a visual 'shifter,' a sign capable of expressing multiple realms, collapsing Mediterranean time and space.

*Apollo* (figure 6.1) is as multicoloured and as complex as *The Sorrow of the King* or *The Thousand and One Nights*, but this triumphant image of the most Greek of the ancient gods is shown in heraldic symmetry, source and master of all he surveys. He is god of the sun, which is radiating above his head like a crown. The sea below directly evokes the Mediterranean source of these ancient origin stories. In the pantheon of the gods Apollo also presides over the arts: architecture (columns at either side, echoing the framing device of the contemporaneous *Large Decoration with Masks*); sculpture in the three yellow relief elements at the bottom centre, sheets of fan-folded paper arrayed on a figure-like silhouette; and painting in the coloured plant forms that spread across nearly the entire surface of the composition. Finally, drawing, represented by the thin lines that emanate from the figurative form at the bottom, unites the three arts while also resolutely reinforcing the mural quality of the surface, its overall decorative cohesiveness.

So far it might seem, perhaps against expectations, that Matisse's decoration is more classical than Oriental, or rather that his use of classical motifs in the cut-outs is more decorative and less pictorial than his expression of Oriental themes. But both Oriental and classical seem to contribute something essential to Matisse's concept of decoration, the coloured density and sense of vividness of one in counterpoint to the aerated, but relatively static, qualities of the other. For the artist who kept plaster casts of a Greek Kouros and the Borghese Ares in his studio, as well as Moroccan and Ottoman fabrics and furnishings, not to mention many Asian artefacts, the mixture of antique and Oriental in his paper cut-outs was a natural extension of his own cultivated environment, in which Berber textiles could be juxtaposed with a composition for an Abduction of Europa, presided over by signs of the modern in the form of a Cézanne portrait or a Picasso still life in his collection.

Another difference between the classical and the Oriental in Matisse's cut-outs begins to emerge, a difference that swings the balance of the decorative scale back towards the Oriental. In the early 1950s he made many compositions large and small in nothing but blue paper cut into contours whose sole counterpoint is the white of the ground. These works in unalloyed blue and white are altogether more sculptural than the brightly coloured frieze-like structures of cut-outs like *The Thousand*

*and One Nights* or such figural compositions as *The Sorrow of the King*. In a silhouetted figure of Venus, volume swells irresistibly from within the simple structure of two irregular slices of blue that bracket what should be simply a white void or neutral ground. In the environmental composition *The Swimming Pool*, the viewer is surrounded by – more than that, figuratively immersed in – a complex transposition of blue and white, figure and ground, swimmer and water, submarine and surface point of view. In such works, Matisse's scissor-cuts in colour produce not only the illusion of volume but play havoc with the idea that volume can be fixed in any given shape, or that colour's assignments to form are stable. The blue and white collages remind us that Matisse characterized his technique in making the paper cut-outs as a sculptural process – '[C]utting directly into vivid color reminds me of the direct carving of sculptors' – an ancient metaphor for his new procedure that suggests its potential not only for large-scale decoration but for uncanny, if transient, illusions of depth and volume.[14]

In his several blue cut-paper compositions of a seated nude female figure (see figure 6.6), Matisse made some of his most sculptural, and therefore least decorative, paper cut-outs. In the ravishing series of *Blue Nudes*, not only did he use white to signify the space surrounding the figure, he treated the narrow white seams between blue forms as both shadow and reticulation, as if the white has been hewed out of the blue rather than the blue sheets affixed to the white ground. Moreover, the artist's extremely physical handling of the medium in these works – even in reproduction one can see how much reworking some of these pieces of paper have gone through, and how many discrete elements may form a broad sweep of thigh or arm – mimics sculptural procedures of both carving and construction. Across the range of his blue-and-white compositions, either colour or its absence can function as the figure, either as the ground, with no loss of the sense of sculptural volume.

It should come as no surprise that these apparently generic seated nude variants in their compact pose, though examples of a recurrent theme throughout Matisse's career, are more specifically tributes to his friend Aristide Maillol, whose sculpture *La Méditerranée* (figure 6.7) had helped write the recipe for a twentieth-century neoclassicism with a piquant aioli sauce. Maillol had created a figural sign for the Mediterranean, heavy-limbed, grounded, enduring, and virtually interchangeable with his other telluric nude figures – indeed, he originally entitled the sculpture (which Matisse had helped him to cast in bronze in 1905) simply *Woman*; soon it gained the more allusive designation *Latin Thought*, until finally acquiring the title by which it has long been known, and through which a fully allegorical, synecdochic figure incarnates the entire region.[15] Matisse, as keen as Maillol's early supporters had been to think of him as a creature of instinct completely formed by his heritage and surroundings, took the Provençal sculptor, who had died several years before, as a touchstone of Mediterraneanism; in so doing he would resort to cliché in his own work, creating Mediterranean images in the cut-outs that were not so much timeless as timeworn.

A venerable received idea also animates Matisse's several cut-outs depicting figures of women carrying amphorae on their heads, which doubly imply Mediterranean stability and fecundity in this supremely classicizing motif. Then, among the simplest of all – a single piece of paper, a few judicious scissor strokes, spacing carefully gauged to suggest the cant of sails (figure 6.8) or the gentle ripple of the sea. One of Matisse's major pursuits in the period of his work in cut paper was to theorize his artistic practice in terms of the generation of pictorial signs, stylized marks that would convey at once the essence of the thing represented and the artist's singular approach to it. Such signs, in Matisse's view, were vital additions to the vocabulary of art; he even asserted that 'the importance of an artist is to be measured by the number of new signs he has introduced into the plastic language.'[16] If a new sign was invention as well as individual expression, an old sign offered the comfort of familiarity and collective consciousness. These deceptively simple blue and white compositions do not further Matisse's pursuit of a decorative, environmentally based aesthetic, but their associative potency makes an important contribution to his iconography of the Mediterranean, as well as transcending any local context. In these late cut-outs, his most extreme distillations of form and his most reductive approach to colour, Matisse was after all reverting to familiar images of Mediterranean sun and sea, to the apolitical white and azure world that always, conveniently, offered a prospect of escape from uncomfortable contemporary realities.

## NOTES

1 The major exception is John Elderfield, *The Cut-Outs of Henri Matisse*, (New York: Braziller, 1978).

2 Kenneth E. Silver, *Making Paradise: Art, Modernity, and the Myth of the French Riviera* (Cambridge, MA: MIT Press, 2001), 119; see also 103–4.

3 On modern artists and the Mediterranean, see most recently the excellent catalogue of exhibitions held at thirteen museums in southern France, *La Côte d'Azur et la Modernité, 1918–1958* (Paris: Réunion des Musées Nationaux, 1997); and the insightful review of it by Kenneth Silver, 'An Invented Paradise,' *Art in America* 86 (March 1998): 78–87.

4 Peregrine Horden and Nicholas Purcell, *The Corrupting Sea: A Study of Mediterranean History* (Oxford: Blackwell, 2000), 25.

5 On Matisse's cut-outs generally, see Jack Cowart et al., *Henri Matisse: Paper Cut-Outs*, exh. cat., St Louis Art Museum and Detroit Institute of Arts, 1977; Elderfield, *Cut-Outs*; and Olivier Berggruen and Max Hollein, eds, *Henri Matisse: Drawing with Scissors, Masterpieces from the Late Years* (Munich: Prestel, 2002).

6 Matisse's decorative projects, most of them post-war commissions from patrons in France and the United States, are the subject of my book in preparation.

7 For oriental in this context I rely on the definition of 'the Orient' offered by Ary Renan, 'a vague word defined quite clearly by the frontiers of the ancient Muslim conquests,' or, broadly speaking, North Africa and the Middle East; cited in Roger Benjamin, *Orientalist Aesthetics: Art, Colonialism, and French North Africa, 1880–1930* (Berkeley and Los Angeles: University of California Press, 2003), 8.

8 On Matisse's persistent engagement with classicism, see Marie-Thérèse Pulvenis de Séligny, ed., *Matisse et l'Antiquité*, exh. cat., Musée Matisse (Nice, 1999).

9 On Matisse and 'oriental' (including Asian) art and culture, see *Matisse: 'La révélation m'est venue de l'Orient,'* exh. cat., Musei Capitolini (Rome, 1997).

10 Sarah Wilson, *Matisse* (New York: Rizzoli, 1992), 22.

11 Matisse to Bonnard, 13 January 1940, in Jean Clair and Antoine Terrasse, eds, *Bonnard/Matisse: Correspondance, 1925–1946* (Paris: Gallimard, 1991), 66.

12 This is a theme in several of Aragon's publications on Matisse during and just after the war; see, for instance, 'Matisse-en-France' (1942) in *Henri Matisse: A Novel*, trans. Jean Stewart (New York: Harcourt Brace Jovanovich, 1972), 1: 1–143. For a similar sentiment of Matisse as an embodiment of French culture in this period, see Pierre Courthion, *Le Visage de Matisse* (Lausanne: Marguerat, 1942), 107–8.

13 Jack Cowart et al., *Matisse in Morocco: The Paintings and Drawings, 1912–1913*, exh. cat., National Gallery of Art (Washington, 1990), 68.

14 Matisse said this in his 1947 text for *Jazz*; see Jack Flam, ed., *Matisse on Art*, rev. ed. (Berkeley and Los Angeles: University of California Press, 1995), 172.
15 Penelope Curtis, *Sculpture 1900–1945: After Rodin* (New York: Oxford University Press, 1999), 222.
16 'Conversations with Aragon: On Signs,' in Flam, ed., *Matisse on Art*, 150.

# 7 Classicism and Resistance in Late-Nineteenth-Century European Art: The Case of Greece

NINA ATHANASSOGLOU-KALLMYER

Some time around the middle of the nineteenth century, classicism in France, Germany, and England entered a new phase. Its most distinctive feature was a shift from the lofty Graeco-Roman classicism of the late eighteenth and early nineteenth centuries, best exemplified by the paintings of Jacques-Louis David, to a new form of classical imagery, quotidian, domestic, and sentimental in nature. Subjects were mundane and, as a rule, devoid of precise historical or literary references; the figures were most of the time anonymous (or, if historical or mythological, engaged in patently un-heroic actions); and settings, although crafted meticulously to appear archaeologically accurate, were intended less to situate the scene in a given context than to convey a convincingly antiquarian impression. One recurring feature is the preference for dazzlingly blue skies and sea, the markers of a Mediterranean location. A representative example of this late version of classicism is Lawrence Alma-Tadema's *A Reading from Homer* (1885; figure 7.1), in which a group of young men and women listen rapturously to a bard reciting the poems of Homer, whose name is inscribed in Greek letters on the marble wall behind the speaker.

A temporal and signifying disjunction lies at the core of such scenes: painted in a precise and illusionistic manner, the antiquarian costumes and accessories clash with the overt modernity of the figure types – some recognizable portraits of well-known models – and the naturalism of the depicted landscapes. The closest analogy is with the theatre: modern actors in ancient travesty enacting their given roles amidst convincingly realistic settings. As a result, the ancient past appears both remote and strangely actual. Commenting on this semantic bifurcation in 1869, a British critic referred to the 'idealism and the realism, the romance and the naturalism, which are so strangely blended in certain new phases of the English school.'[1] Such odd concoctions – it was felt – announced a new strand of classicism, modernized, brought up to date, one that contemporary audiences could live with, or, rather – as I shall argue here – live into.

This new classicism coincides with the period's larger concern with ancient Greece, an interest that superseded the mostly Roman-based earlier classicism. Over the years, modern scholarship has referred to this shift of taste variously as 'a turning away from Rome, the distinguishing and raising of Greece';[2] as 'the extensive nineteenth-century concern with ancient Greece ... essentially a modern factor in modern European intellectual life';[3] or even – with regard to Germany – as 'the tyranny of Greece over Germany.'[4] Roman subjects, of course, never disappeared from the artists' repertory, but Rome was increasingly viewed as a reflection of Greece, a screen through which the true, genuine antiquity of the Greeks could be experienced at one remove. Greece was the cultural fountainhead to which everything (and everyone) aspired, the Ur-Altertum and primeval core of Western culture. 'We are all Greeks,' exclaimed Shelley in a famous verse from his poem *Hellas* (1821). Reaching from elite to mass public, perceptions about a primal Hellas underlying its modern Roman reincarnation can be found in the popular literature and press of the time; witness, in that regard, the Dutch writer Carel Vosmaer's *The Amazon* (1884), a popular novel translated into several languages and illustrated by Alma-Tadema, with a preface by the German archaeologist Georg Ebers. In it one character, the sophisticated Dutch connoisseur Van Valborch, who lives permanently in Italy, declares that 'Rome had grown to be his favourite spot of the world ... in which the motherland, Hellas, has become practical and modern for all the world.'[5]

In recent years, this late form of classicism, dismissed in the past as merely an 'emasculated' survival of early-nineteenth-century classicism, has been attracting more scholarly attention.[6] But scholars tend to treat its individual national strands and their exponents separately, as unrelated to one another. There is no mention of it as a transnational phenomenon (which it was), nor of its ideological and political charge and its possible formal and representational consequences. My project – which this paper previews – proposes an approach that is at once multinational and ideologically informed. I consider the new classicism as an aesthetic language shared, in the late nineteenth century, among the most powerful European nations – primarily, England,

France, and Germany – in order to assert affiliation with ancient Greek culture at a time of aggressive imperialist expansion focused on the Mediterranean seaboard, the cradle of classical civilization and the coveted gateway to European colonial undertakings. Establishing direct affiliation with the classical tradition reconfigured in modern terms authorized Germany, England, and France – as I argue – to both pose as the heirs of Europe's most revered legacy and to lay claim to the land of its origin, Greece, a country made independent in 1828 after four centuries of Ottoman rule.

Although in principle free and independent, however, fledgling modern Greece was, in reality, little more than a powerless 'protectorate,' submitted to the immediate tutelage of the Great Allied Powers – Britain, France, Prussia, and Russia – the nations that had contributed to its liberation.[7] In 1833, the Allies appointed Greece's first king, a foreign prince, Otto von Wittelsbach, second son to King Ludwig I of Bavaria. Otto arrived in Greece accompanied by an extensive staff, including three Bavarian viceroys, a Bavarian court, a Bavarian army, and a crew of Bavarian bureaucrats. British and French diplomatic missions also formed part of his retinue. Peter von Hess, a Bavarian painter from King Ludwig's court, depicted Otto's arrival in the kingdom's new capital, Athens, after three years spent in the town of Nafplion, in the Peloponnese (figure 7.2). At the centre of the composition stands the prince in a smart blue uniform. He is flanked by his likewise uniformed Bavarian staff and cheering Greeks in colourful ethnic dress. More than the colourful gesticulating native Greeks, it is the western-clad Bavarians that appear as the direct heirs of the ancient heritage, a fact underscored by Otto's graceful contrapposto stance emulating classical sculptures. The Doric temple of the Theseion and the Acropolis, seen in the far distance, lend their sanctioning authority to the scene.

The consensual imagery of Hess's painting, with Greeks and Bavarians jointly welcoming the new ruler, conceals in fact a much more complex reality. For it soon became evident that the Greeks had exchanged one authoritarian master – the Ottoman Turks – for another, no less ferocious, in the guise of the Allied Powers.[8] With tacit French and British approval, the Bavarians exerted a repressive rule over the Greek population. Bavarian military forces (assisted by a Bavarian-trained Greek militia) roamed the countryside brutally suppressing peasant uprisings that demanded an equal distribution of land. In the cities, a Greek middle class, liberal, educated, and wealthy, called for increased participation in government affairs. Contemporary chroniclers described the prisons filled with insurgent Greeks (including revered chieftains of the revolutionary wars such as Colocotronis and Plapoutas, accused of conspiring against the regime). The guillotine, a punitive instrument unknown to Greece until then, was introduced in 1834 courtesy of France, and first used for the public execution of a Greek war veteran. Ludwig Köllnberger, a Bavarian lieutenant and amateur painter who served in Otto's guard from 1833 to 1838, left a precious record of these years of native resistance to foreign rule in a series of watercolours (figure 7.3).[9] Events climaxed in 1843, when a revolutionary uprising backed by the army demanded, with success, that the king accept a constitutional charter, while also calling for Bavarians to go home. Foreign civil servants were banned from top official positions, now reserved exclusively for native Greeks. But peace was never to be achieved. Opposition to the Bavarian regime kept swelling and eventually led to more insurrections, in the early 1860s, in Nafplion and Athens, including an attempt to assassinate Otto's spouse, Queen Amalia. In 1862 yet another uprising sent king, queen, and court packing (only, however, to have them replaced by another foreign ruler, a member of the Danish royal dynasty of Sonderburg-Glücksburg, who ascended the Greek throne in 1863 as King George I).

What follows is a case study of the relations between Victorian England and modern Greece and of its echoes in the realm of visual representation. For the British, Greece appeared as an attractive and strategic outpost that would extend their established foothold in the Ionian Islands, a British protectorate since 1815.[10] At Eton, Oxford, and Cambridge, the ruling elites were weaned in the Greek classics. A veneration for Greek social and political models pervaded educational and public spheres alike.[11] The Elgin marbles, displayed in 1816 in a magnificently refurbished room in the British Museum as a joint emblem of cultural affiliation and imperialist triumph, were an ever potent site of aesthetic and ideological pilgrimage.[12] As Richard Jenkyns writes, Ancient Greece – more than ancient Rome – was 'almost an obsession for many Victorians,'[13] and 'unless we realize how much the Victorians thought about Greece, we will not fully understand them.'[14] Indeed, according to Jenkyns, the Greek fad eventually superseded that other Victorian obsession, medievalism. In the words of one art critic of the 1860s, '[T]he medievalism which threatened to take possession of the English school is giving way to classicism, and accordingly we mark for better and for worse a tendency to exchange naturalism for idealism.'[15]

A self-portrait by Frederic Leighton, the knighted president of the

British Royal Academy and Britain's prime academic classicist, may be read as an emblematic summation of the significance of Hellenism for Victorian England (1881; figure 7.4). Leighton's lifelong fascination with Hellenism has been noted by all his biographers. A fellow of the Society of the Dilletanti – an association that since its inception in the eighteenth century sponsored archaeological projects – Leighton also became, in the 1870s, a founding member of the Hellenic Society. As a trustee of the British Museum, moreover, he was close to two of its curators, both well-known archaeologists, Charles Thomas Newton, who excavated in Asia Minor, and Alexander Stuart Murray, the Greek vase specialist. In the 1870s Leighton followed with keen interest Heinrich Schliemann's sensational discoveries of pre-classical Greek culture in Troy and Mycenae and participated in the ongoing debate about the identity of Homer and the origins and authenticity of the Homeric epics.[16] Although Leighton's self-portrait incorporates reminiscences of well-known old-master portraits (by Titian and Rembrandt, among others), it is Greece that really haunts the image. Against the ghost-like procession of the Parthenon's Panathenaic horsemen traversing its background, a slab from Elgin's booty at the British Museum, and assuming the imperious physiognomy of a new Jupiter, Leighton poses as a modern Phidias. In not so subtle terms the portrait represents Hellenic classicism as absolute power. For it joins the effigy of the mightiest figure in the British art establishment and the most celebrated tokens of British cultural imperialism.

His interest in the ancient civilizations compelled Leighton to travel twice in the Mediterranean. In 1867 he toured the Greek mainland, the Aegean islands, and the coast of Asia Minor. In 1868 he visited Egypt. Leighton's approach to the lands and cultures of his journeys conforms to the archetypal tourist's way of thinking: they reveal a dominant concern with natural sites, especially those that carried historical resonance, and a single-minded fascination with the monuments of the past. And it is no coincidence that his journey unfolded within the geographical sphere of British imperialist influence in the Mediterranean. In that way he once again followed a pattern set by many a European traveller in exotic lands in the nineteenth century. Travel was eased, and the pleasure and instruction afforded by tourism best savoured when conducted within the comforting safety net spun by prior European political and cultural presence. Travel then became a corollary of, and a metaphoric alternate for, imperialism. Some oil studies from Leighton's Greek trip show views from the islands of

Rhodes and Chios. They are panoramic vistas suffused with radiant light, a model connoting the controlling self-sufficiency favoured by the imperialist traveller, as Mary Louise Pratt has shown.[17] Above all they are empty vistas. Across from Chios, thought to be the birthplace of Homer, rise the violet-pink mountains of the coast of Asia Minor, the location of Homer's Ilion. The rugged shores devoid of human presence take on a primeval quality that transports us into the primitive Homeric age. Indeed, standing in splendid isolation in contemplation of the famous coastline, Leighton might have even fancied himself a latter-day Homer spurred to heights of creativity. Moving from the islands to Athens, Leighton was struck by 'the exquisite beauty' of the ruins of the Acropolis,[18] which he depicted in an oil study (figure 7.5). The historic hill, seen from the south and topped by its celebrated monuments, commands a virtual wilderness. Leighton significantly avoids the north-eastern slopes of the hill, which would have revealed the encroaching presence of dense modern construction, as witnessed by a photograph from the 1860s by the Greek photographer Dimitrios Constantinou (figure 7.6). In Leighton's rendering, instead, Greek urban modernity is elided, made invisible, reduced to a few dabs of white pigment on the far edge of the canvas. Land and ruins exist in mutual solitude, bonded in a timeless, elemental union by the translucent air and the ruddy-gold glow of the setting sun. As with the views of Rhodes and Chios, and putting his plein-air naturalism to deceptively convincing ends, Leighton portrays the Greek mainland as a primitive desert awaiting acculturation.

Leighton came back from Greece a true believer, his earlier infatuation with classical antiquity now transformed into an all-consuming passion. Scenes from Greek mythology and literature take on a concrete quality by their connection to the painter's first-hand experience of the real Greek landscape, the hues, light, and air of the Mediterranean south. His *Daedalus and Icarus* of 1869 (figure 7.7) – a sentimentalized and domesticized version of the story told by Ovid in *Metamorphoses* in which the main figures are modelled after ancient statues, including the Apollo Belvedere, much admired by Winckelmann[19] – combines ideal Hellenism in the foreground scene and the actual topography of a modern Greek island in the background, the bay and whitewashed village houses of Rhodes, based on the artist's travel sketches. Thus, straddling two temporal realities, one of the past as monument and museological display, the other of actual experience as panoramic landscape, the image symbolically encapsulates – much like a metaphor –

the two poles of European attraction to Mediterranean geographies, cultural heritage and physical territory, the joint targets as it were of the imperialist takeover on the march.

Leighton, along with many of his fellow new classicists, supplemented his travel sketches with photographs.[20] As a founding member of the Hellenic Society, he had access to its large collection of photographs of classical antiquities. His colleague at the Academy, Alma-Tadema, owned an extensive collection of photographs of ancient monuments and artefacts by well-known photographers, including Félix Bonfils, Pascal Sébah, and William James Stillman, and drew inspiration from them for settings and accessories.[21] The marble exedra of Alma-Tadema's *A Reading from Homer*, for example, is based on Bonfils's photograph of the marble seats of the theatre of Dionysus in Athens (figure 7.8). Photography, and pictorially emulated photographic accuracy, reinforce the air of veracity, the most distinctive component of Leighton's, and especially Alma-Tadema's antiquity. This purposefully convincing Grecian universe, in turn, lends an air of authenticity to its fictive inhabitants, Leighton's and Alma-Tadema's Victorian models in clinging veils striving at a Greek look despite their modern English features and rosy complexions.

The association – incongruous to a modern viewer – would have barely raised a British eyebrow at the time. As the sociologist Athena Leoussi has shown, such unlikely physical fusions between the southern Greeks and the northern Britons were common coin in contemporary discourse – backed by pseudo-scientific anthropological theories and historical studies. In his book *The Races of Men* (1850), for example, the Scottish anatomist Robert Knox (1791–1862) posited that the ancient Greeks were Aryans of Scandinavian-Saxon descent whose true heirs in the modern age were the Anglo-Germanic and Celtic populations of England, Germany, and France.[22] Knox admired the Elgin marbles, in which he found the reflection of the 'perfect type of man,' a type, he believed, that contemporary Englishmen, Germans, and Frenchmen perpetuated. The impact of these and similar theories is evident in two typical products of those years, Matthew Arnold's collected essays entitled *Culture and Anarchy* (1869) and Benjamin Disraeli's novel *Lothair* (1870). Arnold distinguishes two opposing impulses in contemporary British society, one Hebraic (or Semitic), the other Hellenic (Aryan). He associates the latter with humanism, spirituality, and an aspiration to perfection, harmony, and beauty, an ideal he urges his contemporary Englishmen to follow: 'Aristotle and Plato, and Thucydides and Cicero,' he told his students at Oxford, 'are most untruly called ancient writers; they are virtually our own countrymen and contemporaries.'[23] In turn, in *Lothair*, Benjamin Disraeli, Queen Victoria's Tory prime minister and a champion, jointly, of imperialism and superior British Aryanism (despite his own Semitic origins), features a fictional painter called Gaston Phoebus – a thinly veiled alternate for Frederic Leighton – who only speaks and dreams of ancient Greece. Phoebus entreats his fellow-artists to regenerate the Hellenic art of Phidias by striving to produce an 'Aryan form.'[24] In an uncanny fashion the imaginary Phoebus-Leighton's words anticipate those allegedly pronounced by the real-life Leighton in his 1883 address to the Royal Academy: 'In the art of the Periclean Age ... we find a new ideal of balanced form, wholly Aryan and of which the only parallel I know is sometimes found in the women of another Aryan race – your own.'[25]

But this sublime vision of Hellenism, minted abroad, conflicted with modern Greek reality and the modern Greeks as experienced in their native context. Dark, uncouth, and uncultured, the modern Greeks appeared 'barbaric' and a far cry from their ancient antecedents, as evoked in Winckelmann's writings and epitomized by the ideal beauty of the Apollo Belvedere. Indeed, centuries-old discourse portrayed the modern Greeks as a degenerate and mongrel breed, an alien race unrelated to their ancient forefathers and the founders of Western civilization.[26] In the 1830s the Austrian historian Jakob Philipp Fallmerayer (1790–1861), whose books King Otto of Greece read,[27] expounded the view that the original Greek race had degenerated, indeed ceased to exist, due to centuries of Slavic and Albanian infiltration and cross-breeding. His theories were embraced and amplified by the racial theorist Arthur de Gobineau (1816–82), a friend of Disraeli's and French ambassador to Greece from 1864 to 1868, who declared that the modern Greeks were entirely unjustified in laying even the slightest claim to the heritage of ancient Greece.[28] How such ideas came to colour the experience of reality, to provide ready-made explanations for it and assume the status of self-evident truths, is illustrated by this passage on Athens by the critic and archaeologist Edmond About, who spent two years in Greece in 1882 and 1883:

> The beauty of the Greek race has so been touted and travellers to Greece so firmly expect to find the family of the Venus of Melos there, that when they arrive in Athens they think someone has been pulling their leg. The Athenian women are neither beautiful, nor well-proportioned ... In town

> one only meets ugly women with flat noses, flat feet, and shapeless bodies. The reason for this [ugliness] is that some twenty-five years ago Athens was but an Albanian village. The Albanians constituted and still constitute nearly all of the population of Attica ... Athens has been settled by people of every possible ethnicity and kind. This explains the ugliness of the Athenian type.[29]

For About, as for his contemporaries, accusations of hybridity as physical ugliness implied a bastard racial status that automatically deprived the modern Greeks of cultural legitimacy. By contrast, About makes clear his allegiance to pure unalloyed types, which are, for him, synonymous with beauty: 'Beautiful Greek women, who are rare anyway, can only be found in some privileged islands or in some remote mountain valley, where invasions never reached.'[30] Edward Said and Johannes Fabian have shown how conceits of racial degeneracy and temporal regression are interrelated tropes of imperialist rhetoric intended to justify aggressive acts of territorial invasion, political oppression, and forced cultural rehabilitation.[31] Branding the modern Greeks savages and racially alien automatically discounted their claims to the land and culture of ancient Greece. Voided, transformed into an eerie 'no man's land,' Greece's geophysical and cultural territory was thus open to appropriation by those posing as the authentic racial heirs and cultural champions of the original Hellenes, the British, French, and Germans of the day. Politics and culture collaborated in the fabricating of a narrative whose ultimate purpose was to strip Greece of its legacy in order to reassign it to its 'protecting' nations. Along with it went classicism, turned into an exportable commodity eagerly incorporated by the host nations (on a par, one is compelled to note, with Chinese export porcelain, Indian tea, and black servants from Africa).

Three distinct but related practices were mobilized to that end: archaeology, tourism, and photography. Since the early nineteenth century, archaeology had developed from being largely an amateur pursuit in the previous century to an official, government-sponsored undertaking carried out within the precincts of 'institutes,' 'schools,' museums, and universities, as the historian Suzanne Marchand has observed.[32] These institutions became the outposts of what could be seen as an archaeological form of imperialism that often preceded, reinforced, or served as surrogate for actual foreign political involvement in the Mediterranean. Thus, in Greece, the implantation of a foreign-sponsored regime was accompanied by the foundation of foreign 'archaeological schools,' British, German, and French: the École française d'Athènes, created in 1846; the Athens branch of the *Deutsches Archäologisches Institut*, established in 1872; and the *British School*, inaugurated in 1879.[33] The 'schools' initiated excavations on a grand scale, staking their claim to Greece's most celebrated ancient sites, including the Athens Acropolis (German, French); Olympia (German); Delphi and Delos (French); and Crete (British). The sites were regarded as national turf by the schools and became the locus of nationalistic rivalries and, conversely, of nationalistic pride. Thus, the French archaeologist and director of the French school, Charles Diehl, who excavated at Delos, declared that 'the honour of this beautiful discovery belongs entirely to France and to the French School in Athens.'[34] In an exultant mood, the German archaeologist Ludwig Curtius, in charge of the excavation at Olympia, joined archaeology, technology, and military supremacy to the greater glory of Prussia:

> The time is ripe. In the whole Orient, as far as educated men live, Prussia will make good its new position of power in honorable and strong representation of the interests of art and science in the classical lands ... Can we imagine what could be achieved if our available energies could be harnessed together in the right way: the steam power of the navy; the technical know-how of the General Staff, the expertise of archaeologists and architects.[35]

Antiquities were also the prime lure for the many tourists who scoured Greece's landscape in single-minded search of the 'sacralized' sites of the past. By the 1880s Athens had become the necessary port of call for all tourists worth their salt, both low-budget clients of Thomas Cook's popular tours and upper-class grand tourists. The English traveller Richard Ridley-Farrer told how 'steamers of various lines touched at the Piraeus. Anglo-Indians contrive a short visit either going or coming home, and the ubiquitous Mr. Cook allows his little flock a day or two to get through the antiquities.'[36] Educated elites also formed the audience for the French 'voyages scientifiques,' the high-brow archaeological cruises in the eastern Mediterranean – Greece, Egypt, and Asia Minor – launched in the 1890s by the French magazine *Revue générale des sciences*.[37] Their itineraries were designed by famous archaeologists – French, British, and German – who also served as tour guides. An anonymous photograph of the early 1900s shows members of such a scientific voyage on a visit to Cnossos, in Crete. Leading the group, striding through the ruins with manifest proprietary pride, is Sir Arthur Evans, who discovered the palace (figure 7.9). In another photograph from the 1890s exuberant 'voyage scientifique' tourists at the ancient theatre of Delphi consume classical culture with the same relish – it appears – as the bottles of Greek wine at their feet (figure 7.10). As G.F. Bowen, author of the preface to John Murray's 1854 guidebook to Greece, put it: 'After a rapid walk of a few hours [amidst the classical ruins] every well-informed traveller may carry away in his mind a picture of the city of Pericles and Plato, which will never leave him until the day of his death.'[38]

Carrying away a picture of the coveted city of Pericles or Plato literally described end-of-the-century tourist practices, when most foreign visitors to Greece alighted from their boats armed with cameras. The critic Gaston Deschamps described a Cook's Tours shipload of British tourists on the quays of Piraeus, in 1892, with 'their good ruddy and admirative faces, [and their] photographic cameras mercilessly aimed at the Acropolis ... [their] white helmets enveloped in white muslin which ripples like flags in the air.'[39] Beside self-made photographs, visitors could also purchase the photographic souvenir albums and commercial photographs of classical antiquities produced by photographers of various nationalities who had set up shop around the Mediterranean, in Athens, Istanbul, Beirut, or Cairo. Photographs allowed a symbolic possession of the coveted past, including its physical birthplace. Evocative simulacra, they permitted even a modest tourist to share vicariously in the grand imperialist scheme. As was the case with Leighton's landscape paintings from Greece, in the tourist photographs ancient ruins are featured as if in complete isolation (a typical example is Bonfils's photograph, seen earlier, figure 7.8). No new structures or unseemly Greek natives profane the noble marbles (or if they do, their presence is intended to invite disparaging contrasts),[40] their absence thereby encouraging the fantasies of modern viewers who could imagine themselves clad in tunics perambulating among the monuments of the ancient land.

But so far I have been telling one side of the story only. After all, my title announces a 'resistance' to this classical scheme. To patterns of 'resistance' we must therefore now turn by evoking the unfamiliar and somewhat exotic counter-image to this Western European scenario. Doing so requires a reorientation of our cultural angle from the European 'centre,' as represented by the dominant nations of England, Germany, and France, to the European 'periphery,' to which Greece belonged, physically and politically. Greek resistance to imperialist representation took the form of a rejection of the classical mirage cultivated by the colonial imagination. Already in the early years of Greek independence, annoyed Greek voices had risen in protest against what was perceived as a foreign-minted vision of Greece. 'As to us, a historical race of people, what are we to do? What should provide us with spiritual nourishment? ... The past? Alas! We are allowing foreigners to represent it for us through the lens of their own prejudices, and according to the direction of their own systems and interests,' lamented Spyridon Zambelios, a scholar and pioneer folklorist from the Ionian islands.[41] Antiquarian constructions were denounced as part of a deliberately regressive scheme meant to position Greece within a fixed and inert past, with no access to the future and modernity. 'You are making a mistake in overestimating, like everyone else, the ancients. They were restless spirits, from which we, modern Greeks, can learn nothing useful,' wrote the Greek statesman John Capodistria.[42] Even the disgruntled About, who, as we saw, disparaged modern Greeks, had to admit that 'in Greece the past will always do injustice to the present.'[43]

Their vehement tone notwithstanding, we must not see these statements as wholesale rejections on the part of the modern Greeks of their classical heritage. Antiquity was Greece's most valuable asset in its foray into modern Europe, and Greeks knew that all too well.[44] Rather, the purpose was to mitigate antiquity's exclusive supremacy as single-mindedly cultivated by self-serving colonial constructions, and foster instead a more balanced, synthesizing approach to the nation's culture. Integrating the ancient past with later phases of Greek history and culture, such as the Byzantine Middle Ages and the modern period, marked by the recent experience of revolutionary insurrection against Turkey, became the goal of Greek nationalists eager to demonstrate the historical, racial, and cultural continuity of the Greek nation through time and history. Two scholarly disciplines were enlisted to that end: history and ethnography.[45] In the second half of the century, Greek historians wrote general histories of Greece in an effort to reconstruct the nation's identity as a flawless and unbroken narrative that smoothly led from, and linked, the remotest past to the present. A dominant strategy was the creation of historical analogies between events in the ancient past and modern occurrences: thus, the wars waged by fifth-century BCE Greeks against invading Persians from the East were shown as analogous to the liberation wars fought by the modern Greeks against the Turks in the 1820s. Similar analogic ancient-modern strategies were applied by ethnographers. Their foremost concern was to undermine the charges of racial extinction, along with those of cultural discontinuity. In 1882 the Historical and Ethnological Association of Greece was founded in Athens. Even before, however, amateur Greek ethnographers had set out with patriotic zeal to collect, study, and taxonomize local traditions, customs, folksongs, legends, and proverbs. One of them, Emmanuel Vivilakis, made his purpose clear: 'The goal of my study is to make a precise comparison between the traditions and habits of ancient and modern Greece so that I may provide, in that manner, evidence to the effect that ancient Greece is not yet defunct but rather that its first inhabitants of thousands of years ago are still surviving in their great-great-grandchildren.'[46] In the preface to his anthology of Greek folkloric verse, Michael Lelekos compared popular songs to the epics of Homer and declared that everywhere in them one encountered the same power of expression and beauty of descriptions as in the classical poems of Greek antiquity.[47] The final poem in this collection is not a traditional folksong, but rather one written by Lelekos himself. Titled 'To the German Fallmerayer,' it is an invective against the Bavarian historian (dubbed a 'black villain') who had denied Greece its identity. Its presence at the end of the little volume confirms the nationalist intent of Lelekos's ethnographic enterprise.

Greek painters and writers of the second half of the nineteenth century embraced historiographic and ethnographic nationalism as well. Significantly, and as opposed to their British, French, or German counterparts, not a single Greek work, literary or visual, deals with a classical subject. Rather, artists draw on the traditions and customs of their land and its recent history. The first generation of trained Greek artists was the product of the School of Fine Arts, founded by King Otto in Athens, in the 1840s.[48] After a first period of study, its most talented graduates were sent with a government stipend to pursue their work at the Academy of Fine Arts, in Munich. There, following the trend of younger Academy students, they were quick to reject the grand manner of their German teachers, such as Karl Theodor von Piloty (1826–86), known for his large and complex historical compositions. They opted instead for genre painting executed in a style of picturesque naturalism. Nicolaos Gyzis (1842–1901) and Nikiphoros Lytras (1832–1904), both born on the Aegean island of Tinos and trained at the Athens School of Fine Arts, were among the first such Greek painters to study in Munich in the 1860s and 1870s. Whereas Gyzis stayed in Munich and became himself a professor in the Academy, Lytras returned to Athens and taught at the School of Fine Arts. Both men worked in the naturalist idiom learned in Germany, which they applied to depictions of Greek subjects, producing contemporary genre scenes with a pronounced ethnographic quality. But concepts of cultural roots and continuity are present at every turn in the form of discreet iconographic allusions to the nation's ancient and medieval past. The paintings thus function on two levels simultaneously: they tell a lively everyday-life story, a sentimental anecdote replete with colourful detail; and by fusing allusions to diverse periods of Greek culture, from classical antiquity, to the Christian Middle Ages of Byzantium, and up to present-day folkloric culture, they construct a seamless narrative of the nation's unbroken cultural and national identity untouched by time and historical vicissitudes. In *Children's Betrothal* (1877; figure 7.11), Gyzis represents a children's engagement, a practice prevalent among wealthy Greek landowners during the uncertain times of Ottoman rule in view of securing, early on, the transmission of their estates among their heirs. The scene overflows with ethnographic detail, thus echoing the concurrent rise of ethnological study. Types, costumes, accessories, and settings are all reproduced with an eye for their exotic singularity, in what constitutes a glorious compilation of modern, vernacular Hellenism. Folklore is in turn linked with a long religious tradition and Byzantium, which the priest performing the sacred rite embodies.

Lytras's *New Year's Carols* (1870s; figure 7.12) brings together modern folklore, religious allusions, and the memory of antiquity. In the interior of a rustic courtyard of a well-to-do village home, children wearing ethnic costumes sing ritual New Year's songs accompanied by folkloric instruments, drums, metal triangles, and pipes. The mistress of the house, dressed in her best finery, listens on, her baby in her arms in the manner of a latter-day Byzantine Virgin and Child. Immediately below her, a broken marble statue of Venus, a pagan goddess of the hearth, paired with an ordinary broom as if another household item, links the modern Greek mother to her classical antecedent. A parallel case of ancient and modern celebrated concurrently as a statement of cultural continuity is found in the photograph of Athens by Constantinou we saw earlier (figure 7.6).

The theme of Greece as historically and culturally multiple, yet indivisible and one through time, also underlies Gyzis's *The Secret School* (1885; figure 7.13). During the centuries of Ottoman rule, when the Greek language was banned from schools, patriotic Greek children eager to be instructed in their native tongue secretly attended the makeshift night schools ('kryfo scholio') run by the Greek Orthodox clergy in churches and monasteries.[49] The dimly lit basement of such a church-school forms the setting of Gyzis's scene. Greek boys listen fervently to an old monk who reads aloud from a book, perhaps the Bible or an ancient Greek text. Ancient pagan or modern Christian, the book – a multivalent sign – symbolizes both the diversity and the seamless continuity of the Greek heritage. Antiquity is also present in the fragments of classical ruins – a marble capital and parts of a broken pediment – lying on the dirt floor. On the ruins sits a Greek chieftain holding his rifle. He is the appointed sentry who watches over the safety of the little group, but also a symbolic marker of the nation's recent struggle for independence. More than attentive pupils, the schoolboys themselves, dressed in a colourful array of ethnic costumes alluding to diverse regional origins – the mainland's white pleated skirts and red bonnets, the puffy pants and short dark vests over white shirts of the islanders – stand for the variety of the new nation's territory, at once multiple and harmoniously united.

Gyzis's reading scene is dated 1885, the very year of Alma-Tadema's *A Reading from Homer*, with which we began. Cast in vastly different styles and settings, the two scenes are nevertheless very much alike: for in both cases, the protagonists appear absorbed in a text alluding to Greece's venerable heritage. The two images – the antiquarian as much as the ethnographic, the British as much as the native Greek – constitute competing perceptions of Hellenism intended to serve competing political agendas, European imperialism versus Greek nationalism. In his book about the origins and function of modern Greek ethnography, the anthropologist Michael Herzfeld describes just such two different constructions of Greek history and culture confronting one another in the nineteenth-century imagination: 'The crux of the matter [is] that we are dealing less with questions of fact (since both images have some factual basis) than with ideological formulations ... This is not a distinction between 'ideal' and 'real' so much as a contrast between two 'realities,' two notions of what matters in the attempt to define Greek-ness.'[50] By enhancing this model with a political dimension in the guise of the larger framework of European imperialism in its opposition to nationalist affirmation, my project turns Herzfeld's equalizing view into an unequal one, affected by the power play between strong and weak. Such asymmetries, I argue, affected not only the historical fate but also the cultural and representational fortunes of the Mediterranean and its traditions. The artists on both sides of the divide, in this case British and

Greeks, forged a dialogic vision and an aesthetic whose contrasts (but also, to a degree, similarities, as we discussed) metaphorically articulated the tug of war underlying their respective cultures, although it ultimately seems that they fought over one single and perennial trophy, classical antiquity as origin, identity, and warranty for the future.

## NOTES

1 *The Saturday Review*, 5 June 1869, 743, cited in *Frederic, Lord Leighton: Eminent Victorian Artist*, exh. cat., Royal Academy (London and New York: Abrams, 1996), 162–3.

2 D. Constantine, *Early Greek Travelers and the Hellenic Ideal* (Cambridge: Cambridge University Press, 1984), 3.

3 F. Turner, *The Greek Heritage in Victorian Britain* (New Haven, CT: Yale University Press, 1981), 1.

4 E.M. Butler, *The Tyranny of Greece over Germany* (Cambridge: Cambridge University Press, 1935).

5 C. Vosmaer, *The Amazon* (London, 1884), 100. See also Rykle Borger, *Drei Klassizisten: Alma-Tadema, Ebers, Vosmaer* (Leiden: Ex Oriente Lux, 1978).

6 See, for example, the 1996 Royal Academy exhibition *Frederic, Lord Leighton* (note 1); also T. Barringer and E. Prettejohn, *Frederic Leighton: Antiquity, Renaissance, Modernity* (New Haven, CT: Yale University Press, 1999); and R. Barrow, *Lawrence Alma-Tadema* (London and New York: Phaidon, 2001).

7 For a brief history of Greece, see R. Clogg, *A Concise History of Greece* (Cambridge: Cambridge University Press, 1992).

8 J.A. Petropoulos, *Politics and Statecraft in the Kingdom of Greece 1833–1843* (Princeton: Princeton University Press, 1968). W. Seidl, *Bayern in Griechenland: Die Geburt des griechischen Nationalstaats und die Regierung König Ottos* (Munich: Prestel, 1981). Bavarian repression of Greece is described in G. Farmakithis, *O Zographos Athanassios Iatrithis (1799–1866)* (Athens, 1960), 240ff.; and the preface by Tassos Vournas to Edmond About, *I Ellatha tout Othonos* (*La Grèce contemporaine*, trans. from the French by A. Spiliou) (Athens, n.d. [first pub. Paris: Hachette, 1855]).

9 I. Meletopoulos, *Ta prota eti tis othonikis epochis is tas ithatografias tou Köllnberger* (The First Years of the Ottonian Period in the Watercolours of Köllnberger) (Athens, 1976). E. Papaspyrou-Karathimitriou, *Ikones apo tin Ellatha 1833–1838. Ithatografies tou Hans Hanke apo to ergo tou Ludwig Köllnberger* (Images from Greece 1833–1838. Watercolours by Hans Hanke

from the Works of Ludwig Köllnberger) (Athens, 2000). And *Athina-Monacho. Techni kai Politismos stin Nea Ellatha (Athens-Munich. Art and Culture in modern Greece)*, exh. cat. (Athens, 2000), 496–7. Köllnberger was one of several German artists, professional and amateur, who recorded events from Otto's early reign, including the history painter Peter von Hess and the landscape painter Carl Rottmann. There are 102 watercolours in two albums by Köllnberger conserved today in the Bayerisches Haupstaatstarchiv, in Munich. Several of these were copied by the artist Hans Hanke in 1909 and are part of the collections of the National Historical Museum, Athens.

10 The Ionian Islands came under British protection as part of the Treaty of Paris (1815), after having been part of Napoleon's empire. They were ruled by a British High Commissioner. A strong opposition movement within the islands demanded union with the new Greek kingdom, which was only accomplished upon the ascent of King George I to the Greek throne in 1863. See also E. Prevelakis, *British Policy towards the Change of Dynasty in Greece, 1862–63* (Athens, 1953).

11 R. Jenkyns, *The Victorians and Ancient Greece* (Cambridge, MA: Harvard University Press, 1980), 60ff. Also F. Turner, *Greek Heritage* and 'Why the Greeks and Not the Romans in Victorian Britain,' in G.W Clarke, ed., *Rediscovering Hellenism* (Cambridge: Cambridge University Press, 1989), 61–81.

12 On the Elgin marbles as British imperialist markers, see Gillen D'Arcy Wood, *The Shock of the Real: Romanticism and Visual Culture, 1760–1860* (New York: Palgrave, 2001), 130ff.

13 R. Jenkyns, *Dignity and Decadence: Victorian Art and the Classical Inheritance* (Cambridge, MA: Harvard University Press, 1992), 2.

14 R. Jenkyns, *The Victorians and Ancient Greece* (Oxford: Basil Blackwell, 1980), x.

15 Cited from the *Saturday Review*, 5 June 1869, 743–4, in *Frederic, Lord Leighton*, 162–3.

16 R. Asleson, 'On Translating Homer: Prehistory and the Limits of Classicism,' in *Frederic Leighton: Antiquity, Renaissance, Modernity*, 67–86.

17 M.L. Pratt, *Imperial Eyes: Travel Writing and Transculturation* (London and New York: Routledge, 1992). Pratt dubs this model 'the monarch of all I survey.'

18 *Frederic, Lord Leighton*, 151

19 R. Barrow, 'Drapery, Sculpture and the Praxitelean Ideal,' in *Frederic Leighton: Antiquity, Renaissance, Modernity*, 49ff. Another Greek sculpture proposed as a model for Icarus is Praxiteles' *Pouring Satyr* (Dresden, Albertinum).

20 In a letter Leighton described some of his sources as 'casts and photographs [of] ... the sculptures and some part of the architecture which I found there [in Greece].' *Frederic, Lord Leighton*, 151.

21 R. Tomlinson, *The Athens of Alma-Tadema* (Wolfeboro Falls, NH: A. Sutton, 1991); *Sir Lawrence Alma-Tadema*, exh. cat. (New York, 1997), 112ff.

22 A. Leoussi, *Nationalism and Classicism: The Classical Body as National Symbol in Nineteenth-Century England and France* (New York: St Martin's Press, 1998).

23 Jenkyns, *The Victorians and Ancient Greece*, 62. Arnold's tandem idea of Hebraism implied practical activity, social individualism, and political radicalism.

24 B. Disraeli, *Lothair* (London, 1870), 138.

25 Cited in Leoussi, *Nationalism and Classicism*, 112.

26 The discourse was widespread and encompassed accounts and information contained in official travel guides, such as the authoritative *Murray's Handbook for Travellers in Greece*. John Pemble, *The Mediterranean Passion: Victorians and Edwardians in the South* (Oxford: Clarendon, 1987), 231ff.

27 Elli Skopetea, *Fallmerayer. Technasmata tou antipalou theous* (Fallmerayer: Devices of an Opposing Ideology) (Athens: Themelio, 1997). Fallmerayer's racial views on modern Greece are to be found primarily in his *Geschichte des Halbinsel Morea während des Mittelalters*, published between 1830 and 1836.

28 Leoussi, *Nationalism and Classicism*, 21ff. Gobineau's experience of Greece and the Greeks is the subject of his *Deux études sur la Grèce moderne: Capodistrias. Le royaume des Hellènes* (Paris: Plon, 1905). The first essay was initially published in the *Revue des deux mondes*, in 1841, before Gobineau's stay in Greece; the second was published in *Le Correspondant*, of 1878, following Gobineau's tenure as ambassador.

29 Edmond About, *La Grèce contemporaine*, 2nd ed. (Paris: Hachette, 1855), 56.

30 Ibid.

31 E. Said, *Culture and Imperialism* (New York: Knopf, 1993); J. Fabian, *Time and the Other: How Anthropology Makes Its Object* (New York: Columbia University Press, 1983).

32 S. Marchand, *Down from Olympus: Archaeology and Philhellenism in Germany, 1750–1970* (Princeton: Princeton University Press, 1996), chapter 2, 'From Ideals to Institutions.'

33 On the 'schools,' see Georges Radet, *L'histoire et l'oeuvre de l'école française d'Athènes* (Paris: Albert Fontemoing, 1901); Ulf Jantzen, *Einhundert Jahre Athener Institut 1874–1974* (Mainz: P. von Zabern, 1986); and Helen Waterhouse, *The British School at Athens: The First Hundred Years* (London:

Thames and Hudson, 1986). Generally, see Andonis Zoes, *I Archaiologia stin Ellatha. Pragmatikotites kai prooptikes* (Archaeology in Greece: Realities and Perspectives) (Athens: Polytypo, 1990).

34 C. Diehl, *Excursions archéologiques en Grèce* (Paris: A. Colin, 1903); cited in H. Yiakoumis, and I. Roy, *La Grèce: la croisière des savants, 1896–1912* (Paris: Picard, 1998), 26.

35 Cited in Marchand, *Down from Olympus*, 92.

36 R. Ridley-Farrer, *A Tour in Greece* (Edinburgh and London: W. Blackwood and Sons, 1882), 58

37 Yiakoumis and Roy, *La Grèce*.

38 G.F. Bowen, *Murray's Handbook for Travellers in Greece* (London and Paris: John Murray, 1854).

39 G. Deschamps, *La Grèce d'aujourd'hui* (Paris: A. Colin, 1892); cited in Yiakoumis and Roy, *La Grèce*, 11.

40 Yannis Hamilakis, 'Monumental Visions: Bonfils, Classical Antiquity and Nineteenth Century Athenian Society,' *History of Photography* 25, 1 (Spring 2001): 5–12; Andrew Szegedy-Maszac, 'Félix Bonfils and the Traveller's Trail through Athens,' ibid., 13–21. See also *Athens, 1839–1900: A Photographic Record* (Athens: Benaki Museum, 1985); and H. Yiakoumis, *La Grèce: Voyage photographique et littéraire au XIXe siècle* (Athens: Plessas, 1997).

41 S. Zambelios, *Asmata thimotika tis Ellathos ekthothenta meta meletis istorikis peri messaionikou ellinismou* (Demotic Songs of Greece Published along with a Historical Study about Medieval Hellenism) (Corfou, 1852), 7.

42 L. Ross, *Errinerungen und Mittheilungen aus Griechenland* (Berlin, 1863), 32; cited in Klaus Fitsen, 'Archaiologikes erevnes stin Ellatha stin epochi tou vasilia Othona (1832–1862)' (Archaeological Excavations in Greece at the Time of King Otto 1832–1862), in *Athina-Monacho*, 213.

43 About, *I Ellatha tou Othonos*, 33.

44 'After all, powerless and almost politically extinct as a nation, modern Greece's dignity and influence depended almost entirely on its cultural legacy'; Marchand, *Down from Olympus*, 6. See also G. Jusdanis, *Belated Modernity and Aesthetic Culture: Inventing National Literatures* (Minneapolis: University of Minnesota Press, 1992), who suggests that the modern Greeks 'appropriated the ideology of Hellenism to gain favor from Europe and counteract the discourse of Orientalism, which portrayed them as barbarians' (145), and that '[t]he Greek case illustrates how a peripheral nation can gain recognition in the international arena by embedding itself in the identity formation of superpowers' (13).

45 M. Herzfeld, *Ours Once More: Folklore, Ideology and the Making of Modern*

*Greece* (Austin: University of Texas Press, TX, 1982).

46 E. Vivilakis, *Neugriechischen Leben, verglichen mit dem altgriechischen zur Erlauterung beider* (Berlin: Wilhelm-Besser Verlag, 1840). The text was published in Greek in the 1842 issue of the periodical *Rathamanthys*. Vivilakis was specifically writing to refute Fallmerayer.

47 M. Lelekos, *Thimotiki Anthologia* (Demotic Anthology) (Athens, 1868), Preface, iv–v.

48 For a history of modern Greek painting, see S. Lydakis, *Geschichte der Griechischen Malerei des 19. Jahrhunderts* (Munich: Prestel Verlag, 1972); C. Christou, *Greek Painting, 1832–1922* (Athens: National Bank of Greece, 1981); and National Gallery, Alexandros Soutzos Museum, *Four Centuries of Greek Painting* (Athens, 2000).

49 On this painting see the article by Antonis Danos, 'Nikolaos Gyzis's The Secret School and an Ongoing National Dicsourse,' *Nineteenth-Century Art Worldwide*, Autumn 2002, (www.19thc-artworldwide.org).

50 Herzfeld, *Ours Once More*, ix.

# 8 The Faces of Modigliani: Identity Politics under Fascism

EMILY BRAUN

Amedeo Modigliani presents an ideal case study for exploring the multiplicity of Mediterranean identities. His biography and art are rooted in the region's diverse and distant shores and in its fertile terrain of cultural species. The oppositional pairs that define Modigliani – Christian and Jewish, civilized and primitive, classical and Orientalist – attest to the competing ideological constructs of the Mediterranean as a sacred land, communal Arcadia, and geo-political entity. As a consequence, Modigliani's acanonical style, singular within modernism itself, generated paradoxical readings when French and Italian critics had their own nationalistic agendas to promote. Interpretations of Modigliani during the Fascist *ventennio,* in particular, show how his prestigious reputation was urgently accommodated under the regime's own propaganda of *mediterraneità* and *romanità,* despite the artist's obvious allusions to non-classical sources, let alone to non-Caucasian races. Beyond the Fascist period, however, Modigliani's art deserves continued scrutiny for its prescient depiction of a post-colonial Mediterranean visage, one of shared, rather than privileged, features, where loaded distinctions of ethnicity and gender are subtly transgressed.

At first glance, Modigliani's art gives the impression of monotony, of faces rendered according to a common template and uniformly resigned in mood. Yet it is a mistake to assume that his style is one of sameness, for the types he depicts are explicitly marked by difference. Modigliani was a painter of faces from various national, ethnic, religious, and class backgrounds. Read the titles of his portraits and the names inscribed therein: Poles (Leopold Zborowski, Lunia Czechowska), Russians (Léon Bakst, Oscar Miestchaninoff), Lithuanians (Jacques Lipchitz), Ukranians (Leon Indenbaum), Catalans (Pablo Picasso, Manuel

Humbert Estève; figure 8.1), Spaniards (Juan Gris), Mexicans (Diego Rivera), South Africans (Beatrice Hastings), Algerians (*L'algérienne*), Swedes (Thora Klinkowström), Roma (*The Gypsy Woman*), and Greeks (Mario Varvoglis). One also finds Americans (*Morgan Russell*) in search of their identity on the continent. Modigliani's bohemian friends defined the melting pot of modernism that was Montparnasse, a quarter in Paris where foreigners and émigrés felt at home, even if they did not belong to the French nation-state. Modigliani painted the French, too, but comparatively few, and more women than men – mostly the working class of domestics, and peasants at that. His portraiture can be read as an ethnographic project that pointedly asks: Who is defined as 'European' in the years around the First World War? And, how do his contemporary 'Europeans' disavow the traditional concept of the Mediterranean as synonymous with classical and Christian civilizations?

Modigliani represented his multicultural subjects with a hybrid of non-Western and Western styles that still defies categorization. Contemporary critics duly acknowledged his various sources in Paul Cézanne and the Pre-Raphaelites, early Renaissance and Cubist painting, Cambodian reliefs and Japanese prints. His mature style emerged from yet another layer of cultural epidermis: the African sculpture he saw in Parisian studios, which inspired the asymmetrically placed blank or black almond-shaped eyes, the ovoid mouths, and the rudimentary angled noses of his sitters. Modigliani shunned the masculine, aggressively sculptural approach to painting and the racial and misogynist content of scarification and bodily violence that marked Picasso's appropriation of African art. There is no grafting of mask-like colonialist stereotypes onto Modigliani's faces, but rather the miscegenation of the sub-Sahara with individual features of European origin.[1]

Furthermore, Modigliani graced his sitters, men or women, with stereotypically feminine qualities. He privileged languid, serpentine line over sculptural mass, and used poses passive and demure, including the submissive tilt or decanting of the head. The dominant arabesque of Modigliani's art embodied the exotic Oriental, as did the Slavic ethnicity Modigliani painted more than any other foreign identity – Poles (figure 8.2), Lithuanians, Russians – many of whose surnames were also 'recognizably' Jewish. In the names and non-Western stylistic mix of his images, the constellation of the feminine, the Slav, the Jew, and the bohemian emerges as a portrait of otherness within modern Europe. Here we have beatific effigies of the Jew, the Slav, the Gypsy, and the homosexual (Jean Cocteau, Max Jacob [figure 8.3] –

specifically those 'types' that would soon be the object of systematic extermination.

Born in Livorno to a once comfortable, but recently impoverished, family of Sephardic Jews, Modigliani was an Italian who made his international reputation in France. Moreover – and this is the interesting twist – his art was completely unknown in his native land during his abbreviated life. It was only after his death in 1920, at the age of thirty-five, that Modigliani was embraced as a native son, through two retrospectives at the Venice Biennale. The first of these, in 1922, occurred just months before Mussolini's rise to power; the second, in 1930, during the middle years of the dictatorship and the height of Il Duce's popularity. Modigliani's posthumous reception in Italy created a most awkward case of national self-representation for the Fascist regime and its interpretation of *mediterraneità*. Given his stylistic nomadism, his choice of otherness as subject, how could he possibly be turned into an essentially Italian artist after the fact? How could Modigliani, known for his cosmopolitan portraiture of internationals, let alone his mythic life of debauchery, take on the face of Fascist Italy?

In Paris, Modigliani was a Jew with a difference: he was Italian. His Mediterranean background and his language distinguished him from the Eastern Europeans, whether of shtetel or assimilated origins. Yet his status as an Italian created a different sort of tension, since France had repeatedly snubbed Italy in the diplomatic arena, considering it a subaltern nation. In geopolitical terms, Italy was a liminal land between north and south, its extreme Mediterranean boundaries dangerously close to 'backward' Byzantium and 'savage' Africa. Southern Italy in particular bore the image of a lascivious 'paradise inhabited by devils.'[2] Long before Paul Gauguin painted his ripe Tahitian women, French Salon painters captured the Neapolitan peasant as a backward, if picturesque, creature of fecundity. Of all the peoples Modigliani painted in Paris, only the unnamed sitter for *Italian Woman* can be securely identified as a compatriot. Those most characteristically Italian are his anonymous nudes, whose rose-flushed brown skin, dark hair, and full lips and bodies conform to the 'primitive' Mediterranean type, contrasting with the pale and urbane Parisian *grisette*. Modelling was the occupation of choice for Italian immigrants in Paris, and the indolence ascribed to the profession served to reinforce the southern stereotype. Nowhere does Modigliani draw the fault line between north and south more clearly and knowingly than in his depictions of the naked female body. That the *femme italienne* was merged in the French public eye with the image of the Oriental *belle juive* merely reinforced Modigliani's identification with his immigrant models as foreigners like himself.[3]

Modigliani, however, was no southerner. Livorno was a major port in Tuscany, the geographical and historical centre of the humanist tradition. He laid claim, by birthright, to the illustrious art of the Renaissance – a cultural patrimony that made even the French genuflect. His contemporaries in Montparnasse never failed to mention his Tuscan elegance and aristocratic bearing, descriptions whose subtext affirmed the artist's good breeding. Modigliani's harmonious, Latin good looks were at furthest remove from the anti-Semitic racial type – epitomized by the hooked Jewish nose.[4] With a visage often compared to that of a Roman emperor, and as a Jew versed in Dante, Modigliani could never be a parvenu: a rooted, 'authentic' culture coursed through his veins.

For Italians, in turn, Modigliani was a contemporary artist with a difference: He had made it big in France. As Giorgio de Chirico once quipped, 'There is no modern Italian painting. There is Modigliani and me, but we are really French.'[5] Italian intellectuals smarted at the idea of their cultural inferiority by comparison with the rest of Europe, and numerous artists and writers shed their parochialism by residing in Paris. In the years before the war, Modigliani, de Chirico, and Gino Severini were the most famous Italians abroad, but Severini alone was known in Italy at the time, because of his association with the widely publicized Futurist movement. Despite Severini's solicitations, Modigliani never joined the Futurists. His style had little to do with their Analytic Cubist language or with their aggressive brand of Italian nationalism. After the rise of Fascism (which the Futurists ardently supported), de Chirico and Severini exhibited their works regularly in Italy. Throughout the 1920s and 1930s they participated in shows organized by the regime for tour abroad, and they accepted state commissions. Of course, Modigliani did not live to see Mussolini's 'Fascist revolution' (though his brother, the Socialist deputy Giuseppe Emanuele Modigliani, became an anti-Fascist and fled to France in 1926).[6] Precisely because Modigliani was not alive, and his art newly arrived, the art establishment used his legacy to a variety of ends. Fascist critics of every ilk – progressive, conservative, even Jewish – fought over Modigliani's Italian identity. The French imprimatur made his repatriation imperative, most pointedly to make gains for Italy in the European modernist movement. As one enthusiast phrased it, Modigliani became 'an Italian whom Italy needs to glorify.'[7]

Italian exhibitions and criticism on Modigliani between the wars neither hid nor impugned his Jewishness, but set out to construct, instead, the indigenous qualities of his art. (Severini, for one, claimed he never knew Modigliani was Jewish until the artist was on his deathbed.)[8] How Modigliani's background was integrated with the Italian and Christian traditions tells much about Fascist cultural policy and the status of Jews under the regime. Assimilated nationals since the mid-nineteenth century, Jews in various regions of the peninsula had been at the forefront of the making of the new Italian state. Ethnically and linguistically, they blended in with their fellow citizens, and little besides religious observance set them apart. Moreover, Modigliani was from Livorno, a cosmopolitan city without a ghetto, where Jews had enjoyed the largesse of the Tuscan dukes since the end of the sixteenth century. In the posthumous literature on the artist, a curious pattern emerges: he is referred to as a Livornese, a Tuscan, or an Italian; or as a Livornese Jew, a Tuscan Jew, or a Jew; or as Jewish *and* Italian; but never as an *Italian Jew* (*ebreo italiano*). That term uses 'Italian' as a qualifier, emphasizing racial over national identity, whereas for critics of Modigliani – pro and con – his allegiance was unproblematically dual. If anything, the emphasis on Modigliani's Tuscan origins reveals the tension between regionalism and nationalism that erupted during the Risorgimento and heightened under Fascism. As Modigliani himself once remarked to an Italian colleague, 'There is no Jewish question in Italy,' as there was, by implication, in France.[9]

For the record, the Futurists were the first to claim Modigliani for the patriotic cause, when they hung his works in the Italian section of the Exposition Internationale d'Art Moderne, held in Geneva from 26 December 1920 to 25 January 1921.[10] Only with the XIII Biennale of Venice in 1922, however, did Modigliani appear before the Italian public, in a small exhibition of twelve canvases organized by the progressive and francophile critic Vittorio Pica. Among the exhibited works were *The Baroness d'Oettingen (Roch Grey), Portrait of Jeanne Hébuterne, Gypsy with Child*, and *The Little Servant Girl*.[11] That year the Biennale hosted ten posthumous retrospectives of Italian artists, including the sculptor Antonio Canova, the Ingres-like Francesco Hayez, Modigliani, and another Jewish artist, Mosè Bianchi. International in scope but hardly contemporary in its tastes, the Biennale exhibited Cézanne (with twenty-eight pictures) for the first time in 1920; two years later, French officials chose Maurice Denis and Pierre Bonnard, among other Post-Impressionists, for their national pavilion. In this context, the novelty – and aesthetic affront – of Modigliani's work was equalled only by the installation devoted to African sculpture – the first temporary exhibition of its kind at the Biennale, and anticipating that at any Italian fine-art museum. This fortuitous occasion allowed critics to make vivid the connection, mostly to Modigliani's detriment, between *l'arte negra* and the artist's modernist primitivism.

Modigliani's debut met with derision, but no greater than the standard hostility directed towards modernism by the general public in Italy, as in France, who dismissed the avant-garde as charlatans or marketing hucksters. Leading critics of a certain generation, for whom Post-Impressionism marked the threshold of acceptable taste, sensationalized the 'elongated necks,' attributing Modigliani's vision to an astigmatism, or deliberate farce. Good to give the public a shot of this kind of artistic bolshevism, wrote Enrico Thovez, in order to immunize it from further monstrosities.[12] Although the most negative attacks drew from the fin-de-siècle discourse of cultural degeneracy, of the modernist artist as madman, none of the reviews associated this pathology with race, nor did they mention that Modigliani was Jewish. The more up-to-date critics Ardengo Soffici and Ugo Ojetti gave qualified assessments, acknowledging his natural talents, but bemoaning his regression into African art. Of the rare laudatory reviewers, the Futurist Carlo Carrà defended the artist's 'blessed ingenuity,' and laid out the main arguments for Modigliani's critical apotheosis almost a decade later. Modigliani was 'one of the few young Italian artists who brought honor to Italy abroad,' wrote Carrà. A truly 'spiritual artist' of exquisite refinement, Modigliani painted images of women that invoked those of Sandro Botticelli. Carrà was the first to link Modigliani with the Italian tradition of the early Renaissance, where feminine grace and otherworldly vision were considered the norm, not an aberration.[13]

After the debacle of the 1922 Biennale, Modigliani continued to be ignored in the Italian press, save for the very rare notice in a book or a show abroad. One of the first to write on the artist's vagabond, if creative, existence in Paris was the critic Paolo D'Ancona, member of a venerable Jewish Florentine family. His comment that the artist was 'alone and abandoned' in the vice-ridden metropolis prompted an indignant response from the artist's sister, Margherita Olimpia. In order to dismiss this 'absurd legend generated from north of the Alps,' she detailed her mother's material sacrifices on Modigliani's behalf.[14] But there was never any mention of Modigliani's Jewish background. It subsequently came into play in 1927, when the Italian press excerpted a translation of Adolphe Basler's book *La peinture ... religion nouvelle.*

Basler highlighted the 'Jewishness' of contemporary French art and depicted Montparnasse as a modern 'Tower of Babel,' referring to Modigliani in this heady context as one of his own race, a 'Jew from Livorno.'[15] From then on, Modigliani's Mediterranean Jewish identity – when addressed – was considered favourably or, most important, distinguished from the foreign Jews of Montparnasse and from the 'corrupt' nature of Parisian life.

Modigliani's repatriation began in earnest in 1927, with the publication of the first Italian monograph, written by Giovanni Scheiwiller, a leading editor and one of the few to publish on contemporary art. Scheiwiller issued the volume as part of his series on modern Italian artists, thereby assuring Modigliani's position as part of the national patrimony (even though no Italian collectors or museums yet owned his work). Scheiwiller was responsible as well for the 1930 *Omaggio a Modigliani*, a limited-edition volume of thirty-five personal reminiscences by French, Italians, and other internationals.[16] In his 1927 monograph, Scheiwiller established the critical agenda of thrashing out the mutually exclusive influences of Paris and Tuscany, while avoiding chauvinistic or parochial denigrations of French culture. After all, for sophisticates like him the pre-eminent role of Paris in the development of modernism had to be affirmed in order to extol Modigliani's accomplishment.

In what became a standard interpretation of Modigliani's experience abroad, we read that the artist found his true self in an intoxicating atmosphere of misery, vice, and ecstasy; his 'purity came shining through.' After absorbing various contemporary trends, the artist's *italianità* revealed itself through his elegant line, in his masterly ability to penetrate to the essence of things, formally and spiritually. The 'aristocratic' Modigliani captured the grandiose sorrow and the tragic nobility of a common humanity. Scheiwiller went on to shape a dominant trope in the Modigliani literature: for their sheer emotional power of humility, Modigliani's magisterial portraits of women compared with old master paintings of the Madonna. Scheiwiller ended his monograph by reporting the artist's last words, *'Cara Italia!'* (Beloved Italy!), thus propagating for the Italian public an indelible image of the artist's deathbed allegiance to his homeland.[17]

Not once did Scheiwiller factor in the Jewish background of the now famous *peintre maudit*. He displaced his interpretation of an unwholesome yet inspirational decadence and Modigliani's restless personality onto the contemporary Parisian environment (with an accurate appraisal of Charles Baudelaire's aesthetics), avoiding the subtext of the stereotypical angst-ridden or unhealthy Jew. An accounting of Modigliani's racial 'qualities' was left to the critic Lamberto Vitali in his book on the artist's drawings, produced by Scheiwiller two years later. Vitali maintained that Modigliani owed little to his adopted country in forging his distinctive style. 'Indeed, in this Livornese,' Vitali wrote, 'the typical characteristics of two great races – the Italian and the Jewish – were combined and augmented. And so he carried inside him, as do all new artists, a blood that could not have been transfused from anyone else.' Vitali's prose revealed more about his own self-conscious identity as both an Italian and a Jew than about the actual development of Modigliani's style. Significantly, Vitali was also the first Italian critic to promote stereotypes (albeit positive) of Jewish religion and culture. About the frank eroticism of Modigliani's nudes, he claimed, as did others later, that the carnal 'weight of the flesh' was 'transfigured' into chaste emotion. Modigliani's refined sensuality drew from 'that great, though weary race that had always worshipped woman on an altar with the most ancient and beautiful of hymns.' With a sleight of art-historical hand, Vitali concluded by likening Modigliani's 'spiritual' use of arabesque line to that of the fourteenth-century Sienese painter Simone Martini, further linking his Jewish and Christian antecedents, the modernist and the Tuscan primitives.[18]

Modigliani's reputation reached its height at the Venice Biennale of 1930, which sponsored a retrospective exhibition of thirty-eight canvases, two sculptures, and forty drawings, his largest show to date (figures 8.4, 8.5).[19] Lionello Venturi (1885–1961), the pre-eminent art historian and professor at the University of Turin, curated the show. Among the major lenders were the French collectors Jones Netter and Roger Dutilleul and, most noteworthy, the Turinese industrialist Riccardo Gualino, who had made a fortune after the First World War in the production of artificial silk. With Venturi as his art adviser, Gualino had acquired seven Modiglianis by the end of the 1920s. He had already amassed an impressive collection of old masters, which he eventually donated to Turin's Galleria Sabauda. Only upon meeting Venturi, however, did he direct his businessman's taste for risk towards the patronage of modern art, particularly the nineteenth-century Tuscan Macchiaioli.[20] A prodigious scholar of aesthetics and Italian Renaissance art, Venturi was no chauvinist. French art, he acknowledged, led the way in the nineteenth and twentieth centuries and was the wellspring of modernism from which all artists – especially contemporary

Italians – needed to drink. As he seriously recommended: 'In 1666, France offered its artists an academy in Rome; I can only hope that in 1930, Italy will establish a similar institution in France.'[21]

For Venturi, modern art reached its finest expression in French Impressionism, especially in the work of Cézanne (for which he wrote the first catalogue raisonné, in 1936). Venturi held Modigliani as the best model for contemporary Italian artists, since he had distilled the lessons of Cézanne to form his own individual style. Radical art (including Cubism), the cult of novelty, and belligerent ideologies did not fall into Venturi's humanist and liberal model (although he was an ardent supporter of abstract art after the Second World War). Nor did he view revolutionary change as suitable in the Italian historical and political context. His refusal to pander to imperialist and nationalist movements, namely Fascism, inevitably led to polemics with Filippo Tommaso Marinetti, the Futurist leader and impresario. Marinetti took exception to Venturi's support of Modigliani, in large part because it threatened to eclipse the role of the Futurists as Italy's leading moderns. In Marinetti's opinion, Modigliani (whom the Futurists first recognized, Marinetti proudly recalled) was no innovator; his art brought to conclusion a now outmoded Impressionism, and hence was not avant-garde enough.[22]

Rather than the Futurists, whose antics 'could not even rouse the curiosity of deadbeats,'[23] Venturi and Gualino supported the local Turinese artists Felice Casorati and the Gruppo di Sei (Group of Six) – Carlo Levi, Francesco Menzio, Jessie Boswell, Gigi Chessa, Enrico Paulucci, and Nicola Galante. Influenced by Turin's liberal politics and by Venturi's Impressionist orientation, the Gruppo di Sei exhibited together between 1929 and 1931. They cultivated an anti-monumental, anticlassical style with delicately painted, hazily rendered glimpses of everyday life. Long before the rest of Italy, these artists had privileged access to the Modigliani works that Gualino 'hung serenely amidst his Titians and Botticellis.'[24] While Scheiwiller, in 1927, refrained from reproducing a single Modigliani nude for fear of violating obscenity laws, some two years later Chessa, Levi, Paulucci, and Menzio paid open homage to the sensuous line and languor of Gualino's brazenly erotic *Red Nude* (*Nu couché, les bras ouverts*; figure 8.6).[25] In an article published in Venturi's periodical *L'Arte*, Chessa rebutted the scurrilous view of Modigliani as a marketing invention of Parisian art dealers, and rehearsed Venturi's interpretation of the Livornese's inspirational style: Modigliani, the 'outsider of the art world,' exuded qualities of the Italian (as well as the French) tradition not by following a given program, but by remaining open to any and all influences.[26] A month later, in February 1930, Gualino exhibited his collection of Modigliani portraits in the foyer of the Teatro di Torino (which he had built); this generated a local succès de scandale, in anticipation of the Biennale that spring.[27]

The timing of the Modigliani retrospective in Venice proved critical, for in 1930 the Biennale implemented changes in administration that politicized its role as a vehicle of Fascist cultural policy. The new secretary general of the Biennale, Antonio Maraini, a conservative sculptor and bureaucrat, wrested the event from local Venetian control, and reorganized it as an autonomous state institution with the agenda of prescribing official tastes. In 1930 Maraini initiated prize competitions to encourage more didactic images of overt propagandistic content among younger Italian artists. (With submissions few and lacklustre, the competitions were deemed a failure that first year.) While Fascist cultural policy remained pluralistic throughout the 1930s (in distinct contrast to that of Nazi Germany), the regime increasingly resorted to 'benign' coercion, such as prizes, acquisitions, commissions, and official favours, as a means of encouraging a unified and more realistic 'Fascist' style. Willingly, or under pressure, modernist painters also couched their works in terms of classical or Latin traits. In the same Biennale of 1930, the French critic Waldemar George put his name to 'Appels d'Italie,' a show of Italian, French, and 'foreign' artists working in Paris – among them Severini, Massimo Campigli, Filippo de Pisis, and de Chirico's brother Alberto Savinio – whose work, George proclaimed, heralded a return to Rome and 'eternal' humanist values.[28] In this climate of intensified chauvinism, Modigliani's exhibition held the future of modern Italian art in the balance, as critics weighed his various identities: national and international, Italian and French, classical and expressionist, Latin and Jewish.

Curiously, it was Maraini who commissioned the exhibition from Venturi, early in 1930, just months before the opening: 'The reasons for this exhibition are so evident that I do not need to repeat them here. Thanks to you, above all, in Italy the public's interest in the artist has been highly stimulated. On the occasion of the tenth anniversary of his death, it would be singularly propitious for the Fatherland to do him justice.'[29] Venturi's father, Adolfo – the other famous art historian in the family – warned him against curating the exhibition, since the Italian public would never understand Modigliani's work and would see the long necks only as 'caricatures of swans': 'I think that Maraini wants to compromise you so that he doesn't compromise himself and can throw the wrath of the public on your shoulders ... Even I don't get the geniuses of today. I'm too antique!'[30]

The commission was politically loaded, and not just for reasons of artistic style.[31] Turin – the city of Venturi and Gualino – was a centre of liberal activism and militant anti-Fascism.[32] Venturi's rigorous defence of creative freedom predisposed him against the regime. And while Gualino did not work against Mussolini, he did not fall into line, as did another powerful Turinese industrialist, Giovanni Agnelli. According to Il Duce, Gualino was indifferent to Fascism, too independent in his tastes, and too heavily financed by foreign capital.[33] The affiliation of Gualino, Venturi, and the *déraciné* Modigliani posed an implicit challenge to official cultural politics. Venturi's essay on Modigliani in the Biennale catalogue notably refused to play the ethnic or nationalist parlour game, and presented the artist's work in strictly formalist terms. With his foundation in Cézanne and innate love of decorative line, Venturi said, Modigliani uniquely reconciled construction in depth and surface arabesque, the sensuality of nature immediately perceived and the higher reality of the imagination.[34] Although he did not fail to mention the Italian primitives among Modigliani's diverse interests, for Venturi (and by extension Modigliani) national identity had an ethical dimension: 'There are two ways of being a good Italian,' Venturi declared, 'One is to speak positively about everything to do with us, and speak badly of everything foreign; the other is to assimilate everything possible of things foreign in order to become better than before and better than all the others. I prefer the latter.'[35]

Modigliani's faces – the thirty-seven portraits (and one landscape) shown in this exhibition, identified here for the first time – were overwhelmingly well received. Critics lauded Venturi for his curatorial enterprise, but roundly ignored or debunked both his formalist interpretation and his European perspective. They stressed Modigliani's Italian heritage through biographical facts (his youthful apprenticeships in Livorno, Florence, and Venice), stylistic debts to indigenous old masters (above all the Trecento primitives Simone Martini, Pietro and Ambrogio Lorenzetti, and Botticelli), and, last, the emotive spirituality of his art. Critics frequently read 'Jewish' content in details of his close family ties, his melancholic disposition, the sensuality of his nudes, and his respectful adoration of women (stereotypical qualities that could also be applied to the Italian character). To be sure, Modigliani's portraits appeared as but infantile deformations to some, the product of a morbid sensuality, and his success was attributed to a conspiracy of venal (read: Jewish) dealers. But the anti-Semitic remarks remained tellingly couched in anti-Parisian terms: the unhealthy life of the cosmopolitan French capital – corrupted by Oriental Slavic culture and other nefarious influences – accounted for Modigliani's grotesque stylistic pastiche.[36]

Although negative reviews proved the minority, Modigliani's supporters had to counter one prejudicial discourse prevalent in European fin-de-siècle literature: the inability of the 'wandering Jew,' who lacked roots in a native soil, to generate an indigenous culture. Jews were 'assimilators' but not 'originators,' and their diaspora had spread modernism – for better or worse – throughout the European capitals.[37] For Italians, of course, the Jews had lived on the peninsula for two thousand years: hence, Modigliani was an 'Italian flower, cut before its time, and transplanted in Paris,' and not an opportunistic weed.[38] He was as much 'melancholic Jew' as 'nostalgic Italian in exile,' who found himself in the 'fetid ghetto of the French art world,' his work exuding longing for his beloved homeland.[39] His art balanced the classical tradition with assimilating tendencies, as befitted the dual heritage of his genius. 'In the same way that Simone Martini departed Siena for Avignon, bestowing traces of his art on the French primitives, so six centuries later, Modigliani left Tuscany to die on French soil, bequeathing a body of work equally influential.'[40] Yet Modigliani's style 'nurtured in blood and soil' had its price, one paid in racial currency, for Italian critics unanimously agreed that Modigliani could have no true followers, merely 'imitators of his exterior forms.'[41] Despite the glory he brought to Italy, no one, except Venturi, advocated his progeny.

Still others spun his story of exile and assimilation as a patriotic artistic quest rather than a racial malaise – for example, the journalist Margherita Sarfatti. One of the most powerful critics of the time, and Mussolini's cultural adviser, Sarfatti, a Venetian-born Jew, had her own agenda: she perceived Zionism (a competing allegiance) as a threat to the status of Jews in Italy and a catalyst for Mussolini's incipient political anti-Semitism. Sarfatti not only ignored Modigliani's Jewish identity but insisted that he realized his Italian self by exploring and rejecting diverse foreign influences, ultimately becoming the finest ambassador of the Tuscan spirit abroad.[42] Sarfatti left it to others to distance Modigliani from the international and Eastern European profile of the Jewish circle in Montparnasse. Though he was Jewish, 'it was not for nothing that Modigliani was Italian'; the Mediterranean calm of his art was clearly 'alien' to the abstractions of Marc Chagall and the tormented brushwork of Chaïm Soutine.[43]

For the majority of progressive Italian critics, Modigliani's portraits bore the venerable lines of old masters in the skin of an avant-garde style, conforming to the regime's own double-faced cultural policy. Above all, these critics found native affinities in the elongated features, tilted heads, submissive gestures, and 'sorrowful gazes.' The 'chaste eroticism' of his nudes compared favourably with the women of Botticelli, while the gendered quality of his serpentine line paid homage to the Trecento primitives, in whose works 'feminine meekness and mildness prevail over the masculine elements.'[44] Moreover, art history conveniently linked the Sienese school, like Modigliani (the Jew), to the Oriental Byzantine tradition. The bittersweet melancholy of his sitters resurrected the inner solitude displayed in the faces of beatific virgins and Madonnas. As the writer Giuseppe Marchiori elaborated, 'The saints of Simone [Martini] raise themselves up, like statues, immobile in the heaven of immortality; their gaze is at once severe and sad. Yet the face of Saint Clare of Assisi bears the same resigned sorrow as [Modigliani's] *Huguette*; the neck of the Madonna, who kneels on a marble choir stall, bends with the same rhythm as the *Haricot Rouge*; while the good *Madame Hébuterne*, the sweet companion of Modigliani, is overcome by the same stirrings of maternity.'[45] The centrality of the arabesque to Modigliani's style went beyond mere formal analysis; Venturi himself admitted, line embodied the anti-natural and thus the 'spiritual' value in art – 'synthesis, simplification, liberation from the contingent, and passion for the essential.'[46]

And so, Italian critics welcomed their prodigal son home from the vice-ridden studios of Paris by converting him: they merged stereotypes of Jewish suffering with Christian *misericordia*, the mystic Jew with the Christian mystery. 'Amedeo Modigliani, Israelite, was perhaps the most "Christian," that is, the most humanely spiritual painter of his time. By means of ascetic castigation, he achieved a style of expressive pathos, dominated by the qualities of candour, kindness, and sorrow,' Mario Tinti pronounced.[47] Modigliani's sanctification in the press occurred the year after the regime signed the Concordat with the Vatican, which signalled a new alliance between Fascism and the Catholic church.

New Testament allusions abound in the Italian criticism, as we read that Modigliani endured his Parisian experience like the 'road to Calvary.' He trod a *via dolorosa*, where despite the temptations of drugs and alcohol, he never veered from the spiritual path of his art. His work exuded a rare 'aesthetic and moral rectitude,' and 'innocence and purity,' evident in the sitters marked by the 'stigmata' of their suffering and humility. Modigliani cultivated neither public nor followers, because he was the 'hermit of beauty, not its apostle.' The diasporic Jew and the expatriate Italian came together in this 'martyr for art,' now reborn through the 'miraculous power' of his style, and 'baptized with success.'[48] As Alberto Savinio observed, 'To him, men and things appeared *sub specie doloris*. Jewish and Italian, not in the least pharisaic, he shared the destiny of all "good" Jews, that is, to relive the tragedy of Christ – to be Christianized. His paintings, and, even more so his drawings, are nothing but the expression of a limpid Christianity.'[49]

The 1930 retrospective enjoyed great success in the press, but Modigliani's proponents did not fare as well. The next year Venturi was one of thirteen university professors (out of 1200 throughout Italy) who refused to swear the oath of allegiance to Fascism; he fled to Paris, where he joined an anti-Fascist group in exile, Giustizia e Libertà, led by two Jewish brothers, Carlo and Nello Rosselli. That same year, Gualino was taken into custody, ostensibly for 'grave damage to the Italian economy,' his holdings seized and his collections dispersed. He was sentenced to five years of confinement on the island of Lipari. In 1934 Fascist authorities arrested Carlo Levi, of the Gruppo di Sei (whose 'ethical' approach to painting was most akin to Modigliani's 'for reasons of race,' one critic observed).[50] A clandestine member of Giustizia e Libertà, Levi was exiled to Lucania, where he wrote *Christ Stopped at Eboli*.[51] And what of the Modiglianis from Gualino's collection? Through forced sale, several went to private Italian collectors, but none entered a national museum – suggesting the still unorthodox dimension of Modigliani's art in the Italian and Fascist context. As fate would have it, the National Gallery in Berlin acquired *Head of a Woman*; an object of the Nazi degenerate-art campaign, it was sold at auction in Lucerne by Galerie Fischer in 1939.[52]

One work in the Biennale retrospective – *Ragazza* – had already been disparaged by the Nazi ideologue Paul Schultze-Naumburg in his 1928 book *Kunst and Rasse*, on the biological degeneracy of modern art (figure 8.7).[53] Modigliani's image was compared to photographs of the mentally and physically 'diseased' in an attempt to connect the 'sickness' of modernist artists with their subjects. In 1930 neither the rhetoric of nor a sincere belief in biological degeneracy made inroads into the Italian literature on Modigliani. From the closing of that year's Biennale well through the mid-thirties, Modigliani held his position as the most brilliant of modern Italian artists, the one who brought the most glory to his country abroad. As late as 1935, the regime chose eleven of his canvases for a feat of international cultural diplomacy – an exhibition of modern Italian art 'from Canova to de Chirico' organized for the Jeu de Paume in Paris.[54] All the Modigliani works came from French collections, and none depicted Italians or recognizably Mediterranean types, for that matter, thus revealing the special pleading in claiming the artist's essential *italianità*. On this occasion the French press acknowledged his dual artistic 'citizenship' (French and Italian), while explicitly attributing his brilliance to his Parisian experience. The party bureaucrats who organized the show – lead by Antonio Maraini – also hung works by the anti-Fascist Levi, already under arrest. The duplicity of the regime's promotion of Italian artists abroad mirrored the shifting faces of its opportunistic cultural policy.

Racial discourse in the culture wars between modernists and conservatives increased with the Fascist invasion of Ethiopia in 1935, and began in earnest with the racial laws three years later. The most ludicrous, yet virulent, rhetoric issued from a fanatical group bent on mimicking the Nazi degenerate-art campaign. The Italian version of this anti-Semitic, anti-modernist genre was largely unoriginal, and intent on slandering foreign influence, principally French, rather than 'Bolshevik,' art. Fascist fanatics writing for incendiary cultural presses set out to bait living Italian modernists, such as de Chirico, Lucio Fontana, the geometric abstractionists, and Rationalist architects. They especially vilified the Jewish artist Corrado Cagli, and the young Roman artists around the Galleria della Cometa. In avant-garde circles a more disturbing strategy emerged, of defending modernism against accusations of 'Jewishness' instead of denouncing the racial policies themselves. Ugo Bernasconi, who had contributed to Scheiwiller's *Omaggio a Modigliani*, defended the artist's 'deformations' as sincere and therefore artistically valid, but then equivocated, excusing the 'caricatural style' as a product of Modigliani's 'Israelite blood.'[55]

In 1937, Modigliani's infamous *Red Nude* (figure 8.6) was displayed in a state-sponsored exhibition of contemporary art in Rome; Giuseppe Pensabene, a prime instigator of racial hatred, disrupted the inauguration, heaping anti-Semitic slurs and other verbal abuse on Modigliani's painting.[56] *Red Nude* survived the indignities: it was later acquired by the collector Gianni Mattioli, but not before Mattioli had helped Lamberto Vitali escape to Switzerland during the Nazi hunt of Italian Jews in the fall of 1943. Vitali carried his own Modigliani, *L'enfant gras*, with him in flight.[57]

A survey of the anti-Semitic literature shows that Modigliani appeared rarely in the art press during these years, and not as a sitting target for anti-modern, anti-Semitic propaganda.[58] In one instance, Pensabene reproduced the detail from *Kunst und Rasse* that paired Modigliani's *Ragazza* and a 'pathological human subject,' but without any caption identifying the artist's work.[59] In another example, Italian Rationalist architects defended modernist deformation by claiming that 'Umberto Boccioni was no Jew,' and that 'portraits with long necks were not invented by the Jew Amedeo Modiglani, but by the Etruscans, the Byzantines, and the early Christians.'[60] Conversely, other publications gladly remarked on, without fear of repercussion, the presence of Modigliani's work in Italian private collections.[61] One finds also anti-Semitic writers who nonetheless vaunted Modigliani, 'the most faithful Gesù of painting.'[62] Dead, and having made his reputation as a great international abroad, Modigliani escaped the worst degradation by those attempting to cleanse current Italian art of modernist impurities.

The case of Modigliani and of modern Italian Jewry complicates more than confirms the thesis of recent cultural studies that see in Jewish stereotypes the construction of a threatening or diseased racial other.[63] Though a foreigner in France, Modigliani was no alien to classical culture or the Latin world. His 'otherness,' when perceived, depended on the context, and failed to materialize in his repatriation by Italian critics determined to make him belong. They deflected the negative connotations of the feminine and the Oriental by linking his style to a prestigious cultural patrimony. As to whether or not Modigliani himself felt estranged or 'different,' we can only conjecture. Did his affinity for African masks derive from the self-awareness that Jews, like blacks, were considered racially inferior by many Western Europeans? Or did Modigliani, as an Italian, feel part of the collective identity of what the writer Caryl Phillips has called the 'European tribe,' that exclusive club of white Christian nations who have written history as we know it and created monuments in the name of Western civilization?[64]

The answer lies perhaps in his art, in the depiction of the eyes. Modigliani evoked the common lack of belonging of his sitters through his signature blank or blacked-out gaze. Cézanne similarly obscured the eyes, impeding viewers' psychological connection with the sitter, while Matisse used mask-like faces to increase the perception of exoticism and eroticism. But Modigliani alone used the African-inspired dark and asymmetrical 'non-gaze' consistently, in a form of suppressed expressionism or as the locus of a prophetic multiculturalism. His ethnically diverse subjects lose their individual personalities in a collective portrait of the socially marginal. No merely stylized heads, Modigliani's faces represent the hybridization of the European tribe, a challenge to monolithic classical and Christian visages that perhaps only an artist both Italian and Jewish, an insider *and* an outsider, could conceive.

## NOTES

This essay was first given as a paper in the symposium 'Modern Art and the Mediterranean,' held at the Art Gallery of Ontario in November 2002. It was subsequently published in *Modigliani: Beyond the Myth* (New York and New Haven: The Jewish Museum and Yale University Press, 2004) and is reprinted here, with slight changes, with the permission of The Jewish Museum and Yale University Press. I am grateful to Vojtěch Jirat-Wasiutyński for inviting me to reprint the essay in this volume. When given, Ceroni catalogue numbers refer to Ambrogio Ceroni, *I dipinti di Modigliani* (Milan: Rizzoli, 1970).

1 Despite his use of African masks as a facial model, Modigliani did not depict any blacks, for which there is some historical explanation. There were no African, African-American, or Caribbean (West Indian) artists or writers in the circle of Montparnasse, although Jules Pascin employed such models as the Martinique-born Julie Luce and Simone, her daughter, in the 1920s. Josephine Baker and the Revue Nègre arrived in 1925. With very few exceptions, African American artists did not study in Paris until after the First World War. See Theresa Leininger-Miller, *New Negro Artists in Paris: African American Painters and Sculptors in the City of Light, 1922–1934* (New Brunswick, NJ: Rutgers University, 2001). Further, Italy had no empire until the conquest of Libya in 1912, and only with Ethiopia in 1935–6 did Italy colonize in black Africa. The lack of a colonial empire aggravated Benito Mussolini's rivalry with the European powers – France, England, Germany, and Belgium. There is no evidence that Modigliani saw African sculpture in Italian ethnographic collections before he went to Paris in 1906.

2 Nelson Moe, *The View from Vesuvius: Italian Culture and the Southern Question* (Berkeley: University of California Press, 2002).

3 Marie Lathers, *Bodies of Art: French Literary Realism and the Artist's Model* (Lincoln: University of Nebraska Press, 2001), esp. chap. 1, 'Paris Qui Pose.'

4 On modern stereotypes of the Jew see Sander Gilman, *Difference and*

*Pathology: Stereotypes of Sexuality, Race, and Madness* (Ithaca, NY: Cornell University Press, 1985); *The Jew's Body* (New York: Routledge, 1991); and *The Visibility of the Jew in the Diaspora: Body Image and Its Cultural Context. The B.G. Rudolph Lectures in Judaic Studies*, Syracuse University, May 1992. Modigliani's Italian contemporaries in Paris emphasize his physical beauty. See, for example, Osvaldo Licini, 'Ricordo di Modigliani,' *L'orto* 4 (January–February 1934): 9, 10; and Umberto Brunelleschi, 'Modigliani: Storia vera di Umberto Brunelleschi,' *Il giovedì*, 16 October 1930.

5 Giorgio de Chirico, *Il meccanismo del pensiero*, ed. Maurizio Fagiolo dell'Arco (Turin: Einaudi, 1985), 281.

6 Donatella Cherubini, *Giuseppe Emanuele Modigliani: Un riformista nell'Italia liberale* (Milan: Franco Angeli, 1990); Vera Modigliani, *Esilio* (Milan: Garzanti, 1946).

7 Raffaello Franchi, 'Alle Belle Arti: Amedeo Modigliani,' *La fiera letteraria*, 27 March 1928: 3.

8 Gino Severini, *The Life of a Painter: The Autobiography of Gino Severini*, trans. Jennifer Franchina (Princeton, NJ: Princeton University Press, 1995), 34. According to Severini – and in contrast to de Chirico's opinion noted earlier – in Paris, 'Modigliani and I were the only Italians considered avant-garde artists.' Ibid., 207.

9 Anselmo Bucci, 'Ricordi d'artisti: Modigliani,' *L'ambrosiano*, 27 May 1931. Bucci recalls what Modigliani told him in 1919 at the Café de la Rotonde in Paris: '"I'm Jewish you know," he declared. "I had never thought about it." "It's true. In Italy, there is no Jewish question. I'm Jewish, and you know the family bond we have among us. I can say that I have never been destitute, my family has always helped me. Even if the money order was for five francs, they have never abandoned me."'

10 The Italian section was curated by the artist Enrico Prampolini, who selected works by his fellow Futurists as well as by Modigliani and de Chirico. Marinetti later bragged about the Futurists' primacy in first recognizing Modigliani (see note 22 below).

11 *Catalogo della XIII Esposizione internazionale d'arte della Città di Venezia* (Milan: Bestetti e Tumminelli, 1922), 57. Although the official Biennale catalogue contained more than one hundred illustrations, not one Modigliani was reproduced.

12 Enrico Thovez, *Il filo d'Arianna* (Milan: Corbaccio, 1924), 318–19.

13 Arturo Lancellotti, *Le Biennali veneziane del dopoguerra* (Rome: E. Loescher, 1924), 87–8; Ardengo Soffici, 'Gli italiani all'Esposizione di Venezia,' *Il resto del carlino*, 16 June, 1922; Ugo Ojetti, 'La XIII Biennale veneziana,' *Corriere della sera*, 27 May 1922; Carlo Carrà, 'L'arte mondiale alla XIII

Biennale di Venezia,' *Il convegno*, June 1922: 289–92. See also Enrico Somaré, 'Note sulla XIII Esposizione Internazionale d'Arte della Città di Venezia,' *L'esame* 1 (May 1922): 145–6.

14 D. [Paolo D'Ancona], 'Peintres maudits (Modigliani–Utrillo),' *Le arti plastiche*, 1 May 1925, which is a review of Gustave Coquiot's then recent book *Des peintres mandits*, and P. [Paolo] D'Ancona, 'A proposito di Modigliani,' *Le arti plastiche*, 16 May 1925, with a letter from Margherita Modigliani. On D'Ancona, see Emily Braun, 'From the Risorgimento to the Resistance: One Hundred Years of Jewish Artists in Italy,' in Vivian Mann, ed., *Gardens and Ghettos: The Art of Jewish Life in Italy* (Berkeley and Los Angeles: University of California Press, 1989), 138.

The Archivio Centrale di Stato in Rome, Casellario Politico Centrale, busta 3328, holds the (1932–40) file on Margherita Modigliani 'antifascista,' which contains intercepted personal letters and documents pertaining to passport requests for her and the artist's orphaned daughter Giovanna (Jeanne), for whom Margherita was guardian.

15 'Arte Parigina,' *Le arti plastiche*, 1 June 1927; Adolphe Basler, *La peinture ... religion nouvelle* (Paris: Librairie de France, 1926). Basler was a Polish-born Jewish critic in Paris. As late as 1934, in the official Fascist *Enciclopedia italiana*, the entry on Modigliani does not mention that he was Jewish. Palma Bucarelli, 'Modigliani,' *Enciclopedia italiana* 23 (Rome: Istituto della Enciclopedia Italiana, 1934), 526–7.

16 Published in Milan early in 1930, on the occasion of the tenth anniversary of the death of the artist, and dedicated to his daughter, *Omaggio a Modigliani, 1884–1920* was issued in a limited edition of 200 copies at Scheiwiller's personal expense. The volume offered three poems by the artist, an introduction by Sergio Solmi, and brief testimonies by Ugo Bernasconi, Georges Braque, Carlo Carrà, Felice Casorati, Blaise Cendrars, Giorgio de Chirico, Jean Cocteau, Pierre Courthion, André Derain, Othon Friesz, Waldemar Georges, Paul Guillaume, Max Jacob, Moïse Kisling, Jacques Lipchitz, Eugenio Montale, Filippo de Pisis, Ezra Pound, Giuseppe Raimondi, André Salmon, Alberto Savinio, André Dunoyer de Segonzac, Gino Severini, Chaïm Soutine, Maurice de Vlaminck, and Leopold Zborowski. Reviews of the book were positive, adding to Modigliani's fame in Italy and to the eagerness for his retrospective at the Biennale that spring.

17 Giovanni Scheiwiller, *Amedeo Modigliani* (Milan: Hoepli, 1927), 5–13, with the text dated 1925. On the history of the Scheiwiller publications see Giovanni and Vanni Scheiwiller, *Seventy Years of Publishing, 1925–1995* (Milan: Libri Scheiwiller, 1996), the catalogue for an exhibition held

at the Italian Academy for Advanced Studies, Columbia University, New York.

18 Lamberto Vitali, *Disegni di Modigliani: Arte moderna italiana 15* (Milan: Ulrico Hoepli, 1929), 5–11. See also Vitali's 'Amedeo Modigliani,' *Domus*, March 1934: 40–2; and his 'Modigliani' (1946), in *Preferenze* (Milan: Domus, 1950), 95–102.

19 *La Biennale di Venezia: Storia e statistiche* (Venice: Ufficio Stampa dell'Esposizione, 1936), 124; Lionello Venturi, 'Mostra individuale di Amedeo Modi-gliani, Sala 31,' *Catalogo illustrato del XVII Esposizione Biennale di Venezia*, 2nd ed. (Venice: Carlo Ferrari, 1930), 116–21. In the catalogue (p. 121), twenty-eight of the forty drawings are listed as coming from the collection of 'Michaux' [*sic*; Michaud], Paris; two were lent by Giovanni Scheiwiller. Ettore Tito was the other Italian to receive a retrospective, and the stark contrast between Modigliani and this Belle Époque painter, beloved by the public, was commonly observed by the critics.

20 Gualino was the first Italian to own a work by Édouard Manet, *La Négresse* (a study for *Olympia*). For the history of the Venturi-Gualino collaboration, the latter's Modigliani collection, and the cultural milieu of Turin between the wars, I am indebted to the scholarship of Maria Mimita Lamberti; see her 'Un sodalizio artistico: Venturi, Gualino, Casorati,' in M.M. Lamberti, ed., *Lionello Venturi e la pittura a Torino, 1919–1931* (Turin: Fondazione Cassa di Risparmio di Torino, 2000), 16–47; and 'La raccolta Gualino d'arte moderna e contemporanea,' in AA.VV. [various authors], *Dagli ori antichi agli anni Venti: Le collezioni di Riccardo Gualino* (Milan: Electa, 1982), 25–34. See also Riccardo Gualino, *Frammenti di una vita* (Milan: Arnaldo Mondadori, 1931), and Lionello Venturi, 'The Collection of Modern Art of Signor Gualino and the Modigliani Room at the Venice Biennale Exhibition,' *Formes* 7 (July 1930): 9–10.

21 Lionello Venturi, 'Risposta a Ugo Ojetti,' *L'arte* 33 (January 1930): 97. On Venturi's antagonistic position with respect to other Italian critics (both conservative and progressive) of contemporary art, see Giulio Carlo Argan, 'Le polemiche di Lionello Venturi,' *Studi piemontesi* 1 (March 1972): 118–24. Ojetti, a staunch nationalist and chief art critic of *Corriere della sera*, supported Modigliani, but only by virtue of the artist's innate *italianità* (and because Ojetti could not ignore his reputation abroad). Ojetti refuted Venturi's Francophile perspective; see his 'Risposta a Lionello Venturi,' *Pegaso* 2 (February 1930): 225, and 'Seconda risposta a Lionello Venturi,' *Pegaso* 2 (May 1930): 610.

22 F.T. [Filippo Tommaso] Marinetti, 'Modigliani e Boccioni,' *La gazzetta del popolo*, 27 February 1930. For the larger debate between Marinetti, the

Futurists, and Venturi, see 'Il futurismo e la scuola in una conferenza polemica di F.T. Marinetti,' *La gazzetta del popolo,* 12 December 1929; Lionello Venturi, 'Il professore Lionello Venturi risponde a Marinetti,' *La stampa,* 18 December 1929; and F.T. Marinetti, 'Risposta a Lionello Venturi,' *La gazzetta del popolo,* 4 January 1930.

23 Venturi, 'Il professore Lionello Venturi risponde a Marinetti.'

24 Gigi Chessa, 'Per Amedeo Modigliani,' *L'arte* 33 (January 1930): 30.

25 Lamberti, 'Un sodalizio artistico,' 41.

26 Chessa, 'Per Amedeo Modigliani,' 30. The fact that Chessa's article reproduces only six of the Modiglianis in Gualino's collection suggests that the seventh, *Ritratto di ragazza* (Biennale cat. no. 7; Ceroni 138; figure 8.5, seventh from left), had not yet been acquired. One of the Gualino paintings, *Ritratto di donna* (Biennale cat. no. 6; figure 8.5, second from left), is not in Ceroni's catalogue raisonné.

27 This exhibition featured a canvas recently acquired by Piero Giuseppe Gurgo Salice, Gualino's brother-in-law, which would be exhibited at the Biennale as *Ritratto di donna* (Biennale cat. no. 8; figure 8.5, first from left). Clearly a portrait of Hanka Zborowska, this work was donated anonymously to the Musuem of Art, Rhode Island School of Design, in 1933. It does not appear
in Ceroni; a variant of the painting is reproduced as *La Zborowska* in J. [Joseph] Lanthemann, *Modigliani: Catalogue raisonné* (Barcelona: Condal, 1970), 265, no. 400.

28 Waldemar George, 'Appels d'Italie,' Sala 23, *Catalogo illustrato della XVII Esposizione Biennale Internazionale d'Arte,* 2nd ed. (Venice: Carlo Ferrari, 1930), 92–3. Mario Tozzi, another Italian artist in Paris, organized the show, which included Christian Berard, Eugène and Leonid Berman, Roger de la Fresnaye, Philippe Hosiasson, Onofrio Martinelli, Amedée Ozenfant, René Paresce, Pierre Roy, Léopold Survage, and Pavel Tchelitchew.

29 Unpublished letter from Antonio Maraini to Lionello Venturi dated 1 January 1930. Courtesy Archivio Lionello Venturi, Università di Roma 'La Sapienza,' file CXCII – Modigliani II.

30 Letter from Adolfo Venturi to Lionello Venturi, of 1930, reprinted in Lamberti, *Lionello Venturi e la pittura a Torino,* 40–1.

31 For his part, Maraini, an arch-nationalist, blindsided any view of foreign influence on Modigliani's art, using a metaphor of the poor emigrant that unwittingly implied Italy's inferiority with respect to the modernized West: 'Of all peoples, Italians are closest to and most like the French, but have absorbed the least from them. So it is with us Italians. Like the

emigrants who suffer far from home with nostalgia in their hearts, and who return with their hoard to construct the most expensive, beautiful houses and can only know happiness here, so our artists who have been forced into exile reap the full benefits of toil in foreign lands only upon their return. Carrà, Soffici, Bucci – it is all the same story. And Modigliani undoubtedly understood this as he died on the eve of his repatriation, invoking Italy with his last words.' Antonio Maraini, *Scultori d'oggi* (1930), reprinted in Paola Barocchi, *Storia moderna dell'arte in Italia III Dal Novecento ai dibattiti sulla figura e sul monumentale, 1925–1945* (Turin: Einaudi, 1990), 113.

32 In the early twenties in Turin, Felice Casorati had been championed in print by the liberal activist Piero Gobetti, who was close to the Communist Antonio Gramsci. In 1926 the exiled Gobetti died in Paris after an attack by Fascist *squadristi;* that same year the Fascists sentenced Gramsci to prison, where he died in 1937. The other critical spokesman for the Gruppo di Sei, Edoardo Persico, was also an anti-Fascist. See Anna Bovero, ed., *Archivio dei Sei Pittori di Torino* (Rome: De Luca, 1965).

33 Marco Fini, 'Per una biografia di Riccardo Gualino come capitano d'industria,' in AA.VV. [various authors], *Dagli ori antichi agli anni Venti,* 253–56.

34 Venturi, 'Mostra individuale di Amedeo Modigliani,' 116–18.

35 Venturi, 'Risposta a Ugo Ojetti,' 97. When pushed to defend himself against accusations of *esterofilia* (xenophilia), especially in a heated polemic with the formidable conservative Ojetti, Venturi opined: 'The art of Amedeo Modigliani is more Italian than that of Antonio Canova, because Canova did not have the strength to overcome his neoclassicism of a rather German taste, whereas ... Modigliani achieved a wholly Italian balance of antithetical cosmopolitanism.' Venturi, 'Divagazioni sulle mostre di Venezia e di Monza, con la risposta ad Ojetti,' *L'arte* 33 (July 1930): 405.

36 Among the negative reviews that characterized Modigliani's 'deformations' as unhealthy or infantile were Alfredo Borghesi, 'Amedeo Modigliani,' *Il giornale dell'arte,* 15 June 1930; Alberto Neppi, 'Alla XVII Biennale di Venezia: Il caso Modigliani,' *Il lavoro fascista,* 16 May 1930; Cipriano E. Oppo, 'Amedeo Modigliani,' *La tribuna,* 14 May 1930; Ettore Rigo, 'Amedeo Modigliani,' *Il giornale dell'arte,* 30 November 1930; Guglielmo Zatti, 'Amedeo Modigliani e l'arte,' *Regime fascista,* 4 November 1930; and Vincenzo Costantini, 'La XVII Biennale Veneziana,' *Le arti plastiche,* 16 May 1930; see also his *Pittura italiana contemporanea dalla fine dell'800 ad oggi* (Milan: Ulrico Hoepli, 1934), 157–64. Qualified, though in the end

positive, reviews included those by Filippo de Pisis, 'La pittura di Modigliani,' *Il corriere padano*, 16 January 1934; and Giorgio Castelfranco, *La pittura moderna 1860–1930* (Florence: Luigi Gonnelli, 1934), 82–4.

37 See, for example, Virgilio Guzzi, *Pittura italiana contemporanea* (Milan: Bestetti e Tumminelli, 1931), 26–8.

38 Emilio Zanzi, '"Modì," l'ebreo mistico e sregolato,' *La rassegna filodrammatica*, 1 July 1930.

39 Vincenzo Cardarelli, 'Un pittore maledetto,' *Il resto del carlino*, 30 March 1932.

40 Giuseppe Marchiori, 'Modigliani italiano,' *Il corriere padano*, 21 February 1931.

41 Aniceto Del Massa, 'Amedeo Modigliani e la critica moderna,' *La nazione*, 4 July 1930; Enrico Galassi, 'Dall'ex Caffè d'Europa: Modigliani,' *L'Italia letteraria*, 9 February 1936.

42 Margherita Sarfatti, *Storia della pittura moderna* (Rome: Paolo Cremonese, 1930), 79–80; and 'Spiriti e forme nuove a Venezia,' *Il popolo d'Italia*, 4 May 1930.

43 Raffaello Franchi, 'Modigliani alla Biennale,' *Il corriere padano*, 31 May 1930. Exceptionally, the critic Baccio Maria Bacci, in 'Uomini del Novecento: Amedeo Modigliani,' *Nuova Italia* 1 (May 1930): 183–6, gave an in-depth account of Modigliani's Livornese Jewish background; Bacci read his work in the context of the Jewish 'pathetic' art and defined him as an expressionist, but one with the gift of 'Italian clarity.'

44 Marziano Bernardi, 'Amedeo Modigliani,' *La stampa*, 24 January 1930; Mario Tinti, 'Omaggio a Modigliani,' *Il resto del carlino*, 7 February 1930. Duccio, Andrea Orcagna, Vittore Carpaccio, and Cosimo Tura are also frequently mentioned as influences on Modigliani.

45 Marchiori, 'Modigliani italiano.'

46 Venturi, 'Mostra individuale di Amedeo Modigliani,' 117.

47 Tinti, 'Omaggio a Modigliani.'

48 See, for instance, Giovanni Costetti, 'Amedeo Modigliani,' *Illustrazione toscana*, October 1930: 11–14; Diego Valeri, 'I veneti alla Biennale,' *Le Tre Venezie*, July 1930: 10–16; Italo Cinti, 'Amedeo Modigliani,' *Vita Nova*, August 1930: 662–6; Carlo Carrà, 'Amedeo Modigliani,' *L'ambrosiano*, 2 July 1930; Ettore Zanzi, 'Amedeo Modigliani e i facili seguaci,' *La gazzetta del popolo*, 8 May 1930; Michele Guerrisi, 'Modigliani,' in *La nuova pittura: Cézanne, Matisse, Picasso, Derain, de Chirico, Modigliani* (Turin: Erma, 1932), esp. 86–7; and Vincenzo Cardarelli, 'Un pittore maledetto,' *L'italiano* 8 (November 1933): 364.

49 Alberto Savinio, in 'Omaggio a Modigliani,' n.p.

50 Zanzi, 'Amedeo Modigliani e i facili seguaci.'

51 Fini, 'Per una biografia di Riccardo Gualino,' 253. Gualino was arrested on 20 January 1931 after the failure of his major financial lenders. He was fifty-two years old. He served two years of his sentence and, although under constant surveillance, rebuilt his fortune during the regime and into the post-war period. In Paris until 1939,Venturi wrote and lectured, while working actively with anti-Fascist organizations. Upon the Nazi invasion of France, he went to the United States and taught at several universities. He returned to Italy in 1945, going first to the University of Turin, and then to the University of Rome, where he was head of the department of history of art. Carlo Levi survived the period of the Holocaust in Italy and continued his career as a writer and a painter after the war.

52 See Stephanie Barron, ed., *'Degenerate Art': The Fate of the Avant-Garde in Nazi Germany* (Los Angeles: Los Angeles County Museum of Art, 1991), 12–13. *Testa di donna* (Biennale cat. no. 4, Ceroni 223), is currently in a private collection in Switzerland.

53 See Barron, *'Degenerate Art,'* 165. *Ragazza* (Biennale cat. no. 32) was lent to the 1930 Biennale by Georges Bernheim; it is now in the collection of the Dallas Museum of Fine Art.

54 *Catalogue illustré de l'Exposition de l'Art Italien des XIX et XX Siècles au Jeu de Paume* (Paris: Jeu de Paume, 1935), 103–4. The main lenders were Jones Netter and Roger Dutilleul.

55 Ugo Bernasconi, 'Equivoco interno alla pittura,' *Broletto* 2 (December 1937): 12–13.

56 See the exhibition catalogue *Omaggio a sedici artisti italiani* (Rome: Galleria di Roma della Confederazione Nazionale Fascista Professionisti e Artisti, 1937). On the fracas that ensued between Pensabene and Dario Saba-tello, the Jewish director of the Galleria di Roma, see Braun, 'From the Risorgimento to the Resistance,' 180.

57 See Laura Mattioli, 'The Collection of Gianni Mattioli from 1943 to 1953,' in Flavio Fergonzi, ed., *The Mattioli Collection: Masterpieces of the Italian Avant-Garde* (Milan: Skira, 2003), 18–19. Vitali later wrote the Giorgio Morandi catalogue raisonné, *Morandi dipinti: Catalogo generale* (1983; 2nd ed., Milan: Electa, 1994). *L'enfant gras* (Ceroni 74) is now in the Pinacoteca di Brera, Milan.

58 This survey considered the periodicals *Quadrivio, Il Tevere, Difesa della razza*, and *La vita italiana*, and books by Giuseppe Pensabene (*La razza e le arti figurative* [Rome: Cremonese, 1939]) and by Telesio Interlandi (*Contra judaeos* [Rome and Milan: Tumminelli, 1938]) and *La condizione dell'arte* [Rome: Quadrivio, 1940]. See Giuseppe Pensabene, 'L'influenza degli ebrei

sul mondo contemporaneo,' *Quadrivio*, 16 May 1937: 6, for a rare disparaging of Modigliani in light of international Expressionism and its 'reflection of the sadistic spirit of the Jewish race.' Here, too, Picasso, Vasily Kandinsky, and others are indiscriminately lumped together as Jews.

59 H.G. and G.P. [Giuseppe Pensabene], 'La "tradizione moderna" nella pittura e nella scultura,' *Quadrivio* 5, 34 (18 July 1937): 7.

60 Letter to the editor from Alberto Sartoris and Giuseppe Terragni, *Origini*, January 1939: 8. See also Richard Etlin, *Modernism in Italian Architecture, 1890–1940* (Cambridge, MA: MIT Press, 1991), esp. chap. 15, 'Italian Rationalism and Anti-Semitism.'

61 Raffaello Giolli, 'Come nasce una galleria d'arte moderna,' *Quadrivio* 10, 18 (1 March 1942): 3, lists three Modiglianis in the collection of Rino Valda-meri. See note 62 on another private collector, Feroldi.

62 Luigi Bartolini, 'Visita al collezionista Feroldi,' *Quadrivio* 5, 23 (4 April 1937): 5–6; and 'Diario variatissimo,' *Quadrivio* 5, 27 (2 May 1937): 7.

63 See note 4.

64 Caryl Phillips, *The European Tribe* (New York: Vintage, 2000), 53.

# 9 The Representation of Islamic Art in Israeli Museums: The Politics of Collecting

ALLA MYZELEV

The construction of history is a political act.

K. Whitelam

In this age of increasing globalization and rapid cultural and scientific exchange, museums are still seen as 'temples' that preserve national cultural heritage. They often display the traditions and customs a nation desires to emphasize. Those working in museums participate in the business of making history through careful selection, interpretation, and representation. The museums of Mediterranean countries demonstrate these processes with particular clarity since this region bears the marks of past and present political and cultural tensions. Power relations of the past two centuries have located the countries of southern Europe, such as Portugal, Spain, or Italy, somewhat on the periphery, aside the major colonial conquests of the nineteenth and early twentieth centuries. In the last few decades, the tensions in the Mediterranean region caused by the desire of the southern Mediterranean nations to overcome their colonial past and to be considered as major political and cultural players constitute a driving force behind the founding of many museums. Startling examples of how museums interpret and reconstruct national histories can be found in two National Struggle Museums situated on the Turkish and Cyprian sides of Nicosia. These countries created two conflicting narratives regarding the same historic event: the struggle for the independence of Cyprus.[1]

Jewish and Arab cultures have traditionally been part of the Western Orientalist discourse. Rooted in Middle Eastern culture, Jews and Arabs represent important material for the research of Western anthropologists and ethnologists; the lands of Palestine are full of archaeological treasures. While the early twentieth century saw the immigration of a significant number of European Jews to the Mediterranean region, the representation of Jews living there hardly changed. Photographs and paintings of the period still showed them wearing non-Western clothing and occupying themselves with activities foreign to Europe's educated classes.[2] Little changed in the perception of Jewish Palestine even after it received independence in 1948. The country was seen as one of the poor, war-torn countries of the Mediterranean region. Only the conscious efforts of national institutions could help to improve its image. Therefore, from the 1930s on, Jewish Palestine and then Israel associated themselves with innovative European cultural movements such as the Bauhaus and International Style architecture. In the field of museology, adopting Western approaches and representing Arab nations in the Orientalist mode helped Israel to construct itself as part of the West.

Establishing museums is often viewed as part of globalization, a process of diffusion of models of civilization and a subsequent particularization of national characteristics.[3] Accordingly, countering the tendencies of worldwide homogenization in terms of national distinctiveness, museums serve to register those elements that are peculiar and different from 'standard civilization.'[4] At the same time, many anthropological and art museums follow a common paradigm of cultural development dictated by increasing globalization and Western influences. The traditional history of Western civilization from Ancient Egypt to the First and Second World Wars serves as a backbone to their narrative even if the cultures that are represented had somewhat unrelated histories. It is important to look at the phenomenon of the creation of museums not only as the reflection of the globalization process, but also as an integral part of the processes of colonizing and, later in the twentieth century, de-colonizing the Mediterranean countries.[5]

Using such a framework, this paper will analyse the response of the Mayer Museum to the pressure of the political and cultural tensions of globalization and elevated national self-consciousness. Traditional strategies of museum-making – such as presentation of an object out of context as an aesthetic entity, an only partial interest in the real values and beliefs surrounding the object, a striving to put an object within existing categories without recognizing its uniqueness, and, finally, a desire to present an object as neutral, contained, and deprived of its original powers – should be assessed within the context of the partiality of those in charge of creating displays. Only after analysing the effects of such strategies on the dynamics, in this instance, of the relationship between Jews and Arabs is it possible to free the discourse of Islamic culture from the constraints of misrepresentations.[6] Said, in his pivotal work *Orientalism*, which became a milestone for the further analysis of Western responses to Islamic cultures, traces the production of Orientalist knowledge, demonstrating that this school of thought incorporated a set of fantasies and beliefs presented as pure and objective knowledge that were later used as the basis for Western colonial enterprise.[7] As Whitelam asserts, 'The realization that accounts of the past are invariably the products of a small elite and are in competition with other possible accounts, of which we have no evidence, ought to lead to greater caution in the use of such accounts to construct Israelite history.'[8] Thus, localized accounts of history, especially within the context of the Middle Eastern past and present political situation, are bound to be controversial. The existence of several competitive historical narratives challenges the position of any museum as a purveyor of the historical truth. Israeli museums have constructed a narrative that is best suited for the ideological and political aims of Israel and its cultural heritage.

The L.A. Mayer Museum for Islamic Art is presented to viewers because of the efforts of three people: Vera Salomons, Leo Mayer, and Richard Ettinghausen.[9] According to the museum brochure, Vera Salomons, philanthropist and scholar, dedicated the museum to her late lifelong friend, Leo Arie Mayer, professor of Middle Eastern archaeology. After Mayer passed away in 1959, Salomons decided to collect Islamic art in his memory, for which purpose she approached Richard Ettinghausen, a professor of Islamic Art at the Institute of Fine Arts in New York, to help her gather a 'representative' collection of Islamic art. The core of the collection consists of Mayer's privately owned artefacts and acquisitions secured by Salomons and Ettinghausen.[10]

The idea that the museum will help Jews and Arabs understand each other and live in peace has been interwoven into the construction of the museum narrative. The building of the museum was made possible by a change in political climate beginning in the early 1960s, and continuing into the late 1960s and early 1970s. The victory of the Labour party, first led by Golda Meir and then by Itzhak Rabin, signified a political turn to the left that led to the liberalization of Israeli society. After the Israeli victory in the Six Day War in 1967, Golda Meir succeeded in reaching a ceasefire agreement with Egypt in 1970. As a result, the period between 1970 and 1973 was relatively tranquil, and this helped to awaken interest in neighbouring Islamic countries. Furthermore, after the Yom Kippur War in 1973, followed by an interim agreement with Egypt in 1975 and Anwar Sadat's visit to Jerusalem in 1977, Israel attempted to demonstrate its peaceful intentions towards other nations, most importantly Arab ones. Part of this initiative involved displaying a respect and appreciation for Islamic culture; the Mayer museum opened its doors in 1974.

The museum collection consists of artefacts dating from the seventh to the early twentieth century. The earliest artefacts date to the Umayyad Period, seemingly a logical date to start since Muslim culture recognizes as its most important event the birth and subsequent preaching of Muhammad, which occurred in the sixth and seventh centuries. Muhammad died in 632 C.E. The museum brochure tells us: 'The Umayyads moved the Islamic capital from Medina to Damascus, where they were subsequently exposed to Late Classical culture.'[11] Hence, the starting point of the collection is tied in with Western civilization and classical culture. Peculiarly then, it is the Western tradition that legitimizes the importance of this period in Islamic art, not the development of the Islamic religion.

The first revelation of Muhammad has been traditionally used as a starting point in telling the history of the Arabs.[12] However, given the mandate of the Mayer museum, it would be especially important to look into the history of the Middle East, giving equal attention to the peoples living in the region long before the sixth century C.E. The life of Muhammad provides a comfortable and clear starting point similar to the birth of Christ and the agreement between God and Abraham in Christianity and Judaism respectively. Arab culture, though, existed long before Muhammad. Respected and feared by the Roman, Greek, and Byzantine empires, it flourished from the first to the fourth centuries C.E., declined in the fourth century, and then slowly gained back its power and prosperity with the advent of Islam. Incidentally, many of the small Arab states located on the Arabian Peninsula were able to survive the Roman onslaught and remain independent. Still, the history of these countries, their art, and documentary records are outside the art-historical canon.

Given the location of the museum in Jerusalem, one of the richest places for Arab archaeology, and the interests and preoccupations of the museum's namesake, Leo Arie Mayer, a professor of Middle Eastern archaeology, this absence of an account of Arab culture before Muhammad is telling. According to Whitelam, Israeli archaeology tends to privilege the archaeology of the Bible over Palestinian archaeology. Rarely do researchers set as their goal the excavation of artefacts that reveal the history of Arab predecessors. If these objects happen to be found while biblical scholars are looking for artefacts related to their projects, they are exhibited with other archaeological findings, mainly in the Rockefeller Museum of Archaeology. The main reason for this approach is, of course, Israel's attempt to show the territory as historically belonging to Jews.[13] To justify the present land dispute between Arabs and Jews, the political climate in ancient Palestine is usually presented as one of constant threat to the Jews living there. These threats, however, came from Egypt and Damascus and later from Greek and Roman governments, not from small Arab nations. As G.W. Bowersock, for instance, observes, during the Roman occupation of the Middle East region, 'the relation between Jews and Arabs in the territory south of the Dead Sea was a harmonious one.'[14] It would perhaps be even more just to say that the relationship between Jews and Arabs was similar to the relationships among other tribal nations. Once Jews became a settled nation, they attempted to protect their borders from any invaders, including Arab tribes.[15]

The art of the Ottoman Empire completes the museum's displays. Since the Ottoman rulers encouraged a preoccupation with art and allowed the representation of human figures, the Ottoman period is presented as a fruitful and interesting one. Ending with this period is also historically significant, since the Ottoman Empire was considered a major economic and military power by the Western world. Therefore, the last important period of the development of Islamic culture, as depicted in this museum, is once again the one closest to Western civilization.[16]

Those who are looking for an answer to how Islamic art developed after the demise of the Ottoman Empire are not going to find it in this museum. Actually, they are not going to find the answer in many museums of the Western world. As with the representation of Native and African cultures in anthropological and ethnographic collections in the West, Islamic art in Israel is represented as historic rather than contemporary and changing. Such displays refuse, in Fabian's terms, 'coevalness' to the art of the Islamic world.[17] Representations of their past and the omission of present situations constructs Arab peoples as set in the past and lacking any potential to create viable, contemporary cultures.

The arrangement of the collection display in chronological order, starting from the seventh century and divided into dynastic periods, reveals the typical Western desire to collect and organize. What is presented as a noble and wholehearted desire to create a venue for research into and study of Islamic art becomes a problematic undertaking. According to Handler and Clifford, any collection is rooted in a culture and, therefore, is either directly or indirectly related to collective identity.[18] By circumscribing earlier and recent histories such institutions as the Mayer Museum misinterpret and reinterpret both past and future. As Zerubavel reminds us, the actual process of remembering is often constructed by prevailing ideologies, and the commemoration of some events will necessarily leave out others.[19]

In comparing the L.A. Mayer Museum for Islamic Art with the Museum for Islamic Art on Temple Mount in Jerusalem, which was founded in 1923 by the Muslim High Authority during the British Mandate, one notices two different constructions of a narrative by two museums that deal with the same subject. Following canonical art-historical analysis, the Mayer Museum views its artefacts as part of the general history, culture, and craftsmanship of the Islamic world, while the Museum for Islamic Art on Temple Mount interprets Islamic art in connection to particular buildings (the neighbouring el-Aqsa Mosque and the Dome of the Rock). The mandate of the Museum for Islamic Art on Temple Mount 'to preserve Islamic Heritage and especially artistically significant parts of El-Aqsa Mosque and the Dome of the Rock'[20] gives justification to both the preservation of material culture and the connection to a particular place. The reason for this focus is easily identifiable if one looks at the ideological implications of Arabs constructing a narrative of ties with the Jerusalem they consider their own. By contrast, Zionist ideology cannot afford to associate Arab culture with a specific place, particularly within Israel, preferring the discussion of countries less related, or unrelated, to the Zionist project, such as Egypt, Syria, Iraq, Turkey, India, Afghanistan, Spain, and Iran.[21]

Moreover, any museum collection is manipulated by the ruling ideology to represent or stand for an abstract whole. For example, in the Mayer Museum prayer beads from nineteenth-century Uzbekistan stand for the abstract notions of prayer, Koran, and Allah in that country. In James Clifford's words, in the modern Western museum, '[an] allusion of a relation between things takes the place of a social relation.'[22] In the Mayer Museum for Islamic Art, this tendency can be seen in the clear division of the narrative into distinct periods. Not even one artefact is shown to belong to two periods; relationships occur only within the group, which creates an imagined overgeneralised representation of Islam. As Clifford puts it, '[T]he time and order of the collection erase the concrete social labour of its making.'[23]

In Foucauldian terms, what the museum produces is a general archive, 'which includes all literature, of all objects, of all places.'[24] The institution creates the epistemological system of knowledge from which one can draw information. This organized system of representation forms a substitute for whatever the reality might have been. According to Timothy Mitchell, this systematic approach characterizes modernist and colonial projects in general: 'What seems excluded from the exhibition as the real or the outside turns out to be only that which can be represented, that which occurs in exhibition-like form – in other words, a further extension of that labyrinth that we call an exhibition. What matters about this labyrinth is not that we never reach the real, never find the promised exit, but that such a notion of the real, such a system of truth, continues to convince us.'[25] Mitchell further mentions the modernist desire not only to categorize anything the eye can see, but also to turn it into a display separated from the world. As a result of this process, the representation of a culture becomes naturalized; in other words, the viewer does not see the process of categorization or representation. What one witnesses instead in an institution such as the L.A. Mayer Museum is the seamless result of categorization: the world represented according to colonial rule. Colonial power is so thoroughly naturalized that it becomes invisible. Since most Israeli museums and, indeed, most museums in the world are constructed in this way, the Western project of the naturalization of the hegemonic process of making Islamic culture marginal remains unnoticed by most visitors.

The L.A. Mayer Museum project fits well into the modernist and colonial discourse of preservation. Like a colonial power, Israel both 'suppresses indigenous cultural tradition and is fascinated by the custom of the "Other," which generates the desire to preserve.'[26] The process of transformation of material cultural history into loaded cultural imagery is part and parcel of the existence of many of the museums that preserve Israeli culture and commemorate Israel's fight for independence.[27] This nationalist cultural preservation can be seen as a process of detaching the preserved heritage objects (structures, places, etc.) from their original meaning and function. The original meaning is often displaced or lost, while the new one is usually constructed by those participating in the preservation efforts. Both Mitchell and Alsayyad argue that often the new meaning of the preserved object not only successfully substitutes for 'the thing itself,' but actually becomes the 'thing.' That is, since the original meaning or object is lost, the copy becomes the reality. The risk of creating such naturalized reality is especially acute in museums, since they take objects out of context and then attempt to reinterpret them. Such risk is even higher when a museum represents a culture that either has changed after the museum formed its collections or is little known to the majority of visitors. This disjuncture creates a responsibility that some museums have yet to acknowledge.

Another process that needs to be scrutinized is that of collecting. It is interesting to note that unlike many Western museums, whose collections have been the result of a gradual process of accumulation followed by the finding of an adequate place to house the gathered objects, the Mayer Museum acquired its collection for the purpose of creating the museum. Although the collection is built on the same principles as other Western collections, which again include the gathering of representative specimens, rigid classification, and an interest in the past rather than an interchange between past and present, this collection was brought together, not in the early part of the twentieth century, as most Western museums were, but much later, between 1965 and 1979.[28] The building was, in fact, inaugurated in 1974, and the core of the collecting project was finished by 1979. Accomplishing this undertaking was possible only on the basis of the belief that, as Mitchell argues, the world can be grasped as an exhibit. Part of modernist ideology is to see the world as something that can be represented, making it, therefore, possible to collect parts of it to stand for the whole.[29]

Richard Ettinghausen, who was entrusted by Vera Salomons with collecting for the museum, was faced with a difficult task because, as the museum brochure explains, he was in competition with museums from Arab countries that were trying to collect objects for their own purposes.[30] Ettinghausen's search for valuable artefacts and his attempts to outdo other collecting institutions can be seen in light of Susan Stewart's proposition that 'the boundary between collection and fetishism is mediated by classification and display in tension with accumulation and secrecy.'[31] Ettinghausen's description of the pursuit of an Egyptian carpet for the collection of Islamic art at the Metropolitan Museum in New York reveals the relation between collecting and desiring an object: 'Every art lover knows that many works of art contain a special inner force ... There is, however, a category of Near Eastern art that has been widely believed to be imbued with magical qualities.'[32] This passage begs a comparison to either an advertisement for a trendy, exotic perfume or the story of Aladdin and the Magic Carpet. Although masked by the explanations of a learned man, this collector's urge to acquire that carpet can be traced to the desire to possess a fetish.[33]

Another interesting aspect of Ettinghausen's account of carpet chasing is that nowhere is it mentioned how this object found its way to the Western world. In fact, as with many Native art objects and handicrafts, artefacts from the Middle East were often purchased for small amounts of money and at times were even stolen or confiscated by Europeans colonizers.[34] In the case of archaeological digs, excavated objects became the property of the nation that sponsored the archaeologist. Many thousands of such objects were taken to large national museums to showcase both exotic cultures and the achievements of the archaeological science of a given nation. Interestingly, this practice was never considered theft. For instance, while discussing the problematic relocation of the village of Gurna in Egypt to vacate the archaeological site for an open-air museum, Mitchell writes, 'It is curious that those Gurnawis are today considered "tomb robbers," while it is still difficult to describe the British Museum in London or the Metropolitan Museum in New York as collections of stolen goods.'[35] Another example is the Metropolitan Museum of Art's 2003 exhibition of materials from Ernst Emile Herzfeld's archaeological expeditions to Samarra, the temporary capital of Abbasid caliphs from 836 to 892 C.E. and one of the major archaeological sites in Iraq. As a result of excavations led by Herzfeld and other scholars, many artefacts from this site were moved to European museums. It is interesting, however, that the 2003 exhibition barely mentions the artefacts or collecting in general. Mostly, it is concerned with 'Herzfeld's notebooks, sketchbooks, travel journals, ... watercolours and ink drawings, site maps, architectural plans, photo albums, and photographs.'[36]

As Ariella Azoulay makes clear, the interest in preserving the past, and admiring and conserving artefacts, represses any concern for the ways that objects happened to come to a museum.[37] In addition, in Israeli museums in particular, the role of donor, founder, or collector occupies a special position. From the 1970s on, the merits of a single enthusiast were often inscribed into institutional histories; his or her role became not only part of the museum's narrative but, as perpetuated by tour guides, achieved the status of local mythology.[38] The private interests of the founder (such as obsessive collecting or personal choice of what is collected) are often erased; instead, this individual is constructed as a neutral, 'objective medium that transfers historic truths without embellishment.'[39] Interestingly enough, the narrative of the personal story of a museum founder often masks the involvement of governmental bodies, so that the interference of a dominant ideology is blurred. The founder then becomes the means through whom an inevitable event has come to take place. The official history of the Mayer museum transforms Salomons's interest in Islamic art and her desire to create a monument to her teacher in the form of a museum into an unmediated, disinterested cultural narrative.

Ironically, by preserving artefacts expropriated from the Arab world, this institution also preserves the memory of a Jewish scholar. A professor at the Institute of Middle Eastern Studies at the Hebrew University of Jerusalem, Mayer worked on inscriptions on Jewish gravestones and other epigraphic remains as well as archaeology. His research in this area resulted in his discovery of the ruins of the third wall of the Old City in Jerusalem. Mayer was also a world authority on Saracenic heraldry and Islamic artists.[40] The museum narrative constructs Mayer as a great advocate and connoisseur of Islamic art and archaeology, as one of the pioneer Jewish scholars who realized the importance of Islamic art. However, among sixteen works published by Mayer, only half deal with Islamic art and archaeology; the rest are on the subject of Jewish art, numismatics, or general archaeology.

Within the framework of this discussion, one particular book published by Mayer, *Some Principal Muslim Religious Buildings in Israel*, is worth a more detailed investigation. It discusses historically and artistically significant Muslim buildings for the purpose of their further preservation and, in some cases, urgent repair. The study, commissioned by the Ministry of Religious Affairs, notes that most of the buildings had suffered significantly from recent military activities and the departure of most of the Arab population. Mayer depicts Arab villages such as Lydda and Acre, and Muslim quarters in Jerusalem and Safed, as rundown and abandoned. Such representation contributes to the image of Islamic culture as one in need of salvage, protection, and help from Israeli authorities for its continued existence, a well established Orientalist trope.[41]

To some extent, the L.A. Mayer Museum for Islamic Art continues Mayer's approach by adhering to accepted Orientalist ideas.[42] A comparison of two texts discussing the Ottoman Empire, one a part of the museum catalogue and the other *Discovering Islam,* by Akbar S. Ahmed, illuminates such Orientalist strategies.[43] The museum publication concisely and 'objectively' describes the conditions of the flourishing of the arts under the Sultans of the Ottoman Empire and then proceeds to discuss and analyse different styles of art production. Ahmed, by contrast, discusses the Ottoman Empire in relation to other Muslim countries as well as other religions. His text closely relates the building of mosques to the development of other types of art, emphasizing the multicultural background of the ruling dynasties. Rather than avoid the controversial subject of the harem, the author explores it with empathy and openness. While the author of the museum classification and hierarchy, after two object-based, thematic collections, Rachel Hason, adapts an 'objective,' scholarly tone, Ahmed overtly recognizes that his position is subjective. Hason's discussion neatly falls into canonical art-historical analysis; she showcases the highlights of the collection, not shying away from generalizations. For example, she states emphatically that 'the *Tugra*, the most outstanding achievement of Ottoman calligraphy, became the main symbol of the Ottoman Empire.'[44] Ahmed, by contrast, discusses another charged notion in the representation of Islamic culture: the creation of the stereotype of Arabs as lazy, debauched, and ignorant. He documents the development and role of these stereotypes in the present. These two texts, aimed at general, non-academic audiences, demonstrate different approaches to describing the culture of the 'other.'

This difference reflects the privileging of a nationalist historical narrative that can, with great clarity, be seen at work in Israeli archaeology and museum display. The particular, marginal place of Islamic archaeology in Israeli scholarship is rooted in the same Zionist nationalist ideology. According to some scholars, the dominance of biblical studies is 'silencing the general history of the region' while, at the same time, what was once referred to as the archaeology of Palestine has now been changed to the 'archaeology of the Land of Israel.'[45] Consider, for example, the following paragraph from the catalogue of the Israel Museum, Jerusalem: 'The archaeology of the Land of Israel has its own peculiar array of motifs, ideas and practitioners. Two major themes stretch throughout the history of the Holy Land. The first concerns Israel's position as a bridge between the great civilizations of Egypt and Mesopotamia, while the second is the fragmentary, segmented character of society in a landscape that encouraged regionality and discouraged large-scale organization.'[46] Here, the term 'Land of Israel' not only reflects the governing ideology but also sets the tone for other Israeli museums. Also of interest is the positioning of the 'history of the Holy

Land' as the history that connects two major civilizations, Egypt and Mesopotamia, that have greatly influenced the West.

In accordance with this ideological framework, Islamic archaeology occupies the last place on the list of the eras and objects included in the archaeology department of the Israel Museum, following Prehistory, the Chalcolitic Age, the Bronze Age, the Iron Age, the Persian Period, the history of the Hebrew Script, the Second Temple Period, Hellenistic and early Roman archaeology, Roman archaeology, Byzantine archaeology, the oil lamp collection, and the glass collection. Placing Islamic archaeology in last place within the museum classification and hierarchy, after two object-based, thematic collections demonstrates that the institution's priorities reflect the ruling ideology as well as Islamic culture's placement outside canonical Western development from prehistory to Byzantium.

The same is true for the temporary exhibitions of the archaeological wing of the Israel Museum. Most of them have related to the archaeology of the Bible or to the classical tradition. Among the topics covered have been the prehistoric depiction of elephants, Canaanite representations of the storm god, sacred animals of ancient Egypt, and Greek coins. Only one exhibit, 'Coffee Culture,' was inspired by Arabic tradition, that of drinking coffee. An interesting comparison can be drawn between texts that appear in the exhibition catalogues of the L.A. Mayer Museum and the text describing objects from the Judaica and Jewish ethnography wing of the Israel Museum. Introducing such artefacts as spice boxes, costumes, Haggadah manuscripts, Torah cases, and mantles, the author pronounces, 'These objects, both ritual and secular, hold in themselves stories of survival to [*sic*] the Jews' continuity as a people despite all perils. They also convey a spirit of hope and a love of beauty in the face of hardship and persecution.'[47] Introducing similar artefacts used by Arabs, the Mayer museum catalogue explains, 'Islamic art typically consists of small objects intended for everyday use. These were made from simple materials, in observance of Islam's call for a modest way of life. Muslim artists and artisans, nevertheless, embellished their creations, inlaying brass vessels with silver threads, decorating pottery and glass with lustre paint, and gilding enamelware.'[48] Note the difference in tone of these two passages. While the first shows pride in and love for the objects, the other assumes an impersonal stance. The neutral, scientific style allows for the retention of the gap between the audience and the culture that the museum represents.

Finally, the museum emphasizes the stereotype of Islam as a cruel, military culture, perpetuating the belief that the Orient should be feared and controlled. Indeed, out of nineteen figurative images reproduced in the catalogue, five depict hunters or fighting, while only two depict religious or spiritual scenes, and six depict physical pleasure such as dance or lovemaking. The following three examples of explanatory text emphasize a militant Islam: 'The Mamluks were a military society ... They waged a relentless battle against the Mongols';[49] 'The Seljuqs were a Turkish people who had emigrated from Central Asia and Iran and seized power';[50] and 'Timur emerged from the steppes of Asia to invade the Islamic world ... He conquered Iran, overrunning Shiraz and Tabriz and subsequently vanquished Iraq.'[51]

The current trend is to shy away from this stereotype by emphasizing other aspects of Islamic history and art. For instance, the Metropolitan Museum of Art in New York recently (2003) presented 'The Legacy of Genghis Khan: Courtly Arts and Culture in Western Asia 1256–1353.' Although Genghis Khan is usually associated with military activities, enslavement, and cruelty, the rule of Mongols in western Asia also instigated the development of new forms of Islamic art.[52] The exhibit stressed intercultural exchange between western and eastern Asia: 'During this peaceful era, people, objects, and ideas moved with unprecedented freedom over a vast territory that reached from the Pacific Ocean to the Black Sea.'[53] Such a presentation avoids the compartmentalization process that museums often undertake, instead presenting the history of the Mongols and their art as multi-faceted and evolving.

'A Day at Qumran: The Dead Sea Sect and Its Scrolls,' on permanent display at the Israel Museum, provides an interesting comparison between the representation of Jewish and Islamic culture in Israel. The curator's goal was to use archaeological materials to reconstruct the daily life of a Jewish group of Essenes, whose religious scrolls became one of the most important symbols of the Jewish historic connection in this region. Methodologically, like the Mayer Museum and the Metropolitan Museum, it deals with cultural objects in order to reconstruct the past. However, 'A Day at Qumran' uses artefacts to represent Jews as spiritual, knowledgeable people who lived to pray and study in contrast to militant Arab tribes.

Even when the Mayer Museum's catalogue discusses the contribution of Islam to science, it emphasizes the role of Islam in the transmission of a classical and Hellenistic scientific heritage to the West rather than any original contribution. The West then adopted, cultivated, and furthered the classical legacy.[54] Many scholars do not share this opinion, however. For example, Bernard Lewis notes, 'For most of the Middle Ages, it was neither the older cultures of the Orient nor the newer cultures of the West that were the major centers of civilization and progress, but the world of Islam in the middle. It was there that old sciences were recovered and developed and new sciences created; there that new industries were born and manufactures and commerce expanded to a level previously without precedent.'[55] Further, the scholar C.A. Qadir writes: 'Islamic civilization ... inspired by Quranic teachings and influenced by the translation of Greek texts of science and philosophy, rose to the highest pinnacles of glory; and then, after losing their spirit of inquiry due to conformism ... sank to the lowest level.'[56]

Unfortunately, it is an ideological agenda that rules presentation in the Mayer Museum. For instance, along with praising Salomons for the 'cultivation of mutual understanding between Jews and Arabs,' Hason also recounts the following story about her loyalty to the Israeli/Zionist enterprise: 'We know that she once carried out negotiations with the Jewish Agency for the purchase of the Wailing Wall from the Arabs, and was ready to pay an enormous sum of money for the deal.'[57] Although Salomons's main achievement in the context of the Mayer Museum was creating an institution for the study of Islamic art, this quote serves to remind us of how priorities are set: the patron was first and foremost interested in Zionism. The mention of the Wailing Wall (Western Wall), one of the most sacred and contested sites in Israel, demonstrates that, although Arab culture and craftsmanship are given their fair due by the museum, the Palestinian Arabs are seen as representatives of an adversary ideology. As a result, like the majority of Western museums, the Mayer Museum for Islamic Art participates in the colonizing practices of exhibiting material culture for purely aesthetic pleasure, denying its original purpose, role, and context.

As a memorial to the scholar Mayer and a site for the preservation of Islamic culture, the collection acquires a double meaning, a double nostalgia. By commemorating the memory of this scholar the museum also creates a narrative of the development of Israeli academic life. By emphasizing an academic tradition of Islamic scholarship, the collection represents Israel as an enlightened Western nation. However, the feeling of nostalgia is exclusive. Bammer thinks of nostalgia as a sentiment that justifies one's right to space, which often means the exclusion of others from the same space.[58] Such cultural mis(re)presentations, as in the display of the Mayer Museum, create a mythic separation between cultures of the Middle East, such as those of the Arabs, Sephardi and Ashkenazi Jews. Although the mandate of the museum is (a) to exhibit the art and architecture of Muslim cultures and (b) to bridge the gap between Israeli and Arab cultures, it is doubtful that such representation of the historical culture of the Muslim world alone would help the Jewish people appreciate Arab culture.[59] To fulfil its mandate, the museum should situate the artefacts in the context of Arab life and present them as part of a living culture. Including the culture of Sephardi Jews, which often closely resembles Islamic cultures since it was formed in the same environment, in its displays would help Israelis to relate to materials presented in the museum.

The fact that not one artefact of the Sephardi Jews is included in the display only emphasizes the hierarchical structure of Israeli society in which the Arab population is located on the lowest level and the Ashkenazi group on the highest. Continuing the Orientalist tradition plays a major part in situating Israel on the cultural and economic maps of the Mediterranean and of Europe in general. Israel strives to have cultural and economic relations with the countries of the European Union rather than with its neighbours, both because of the political situation and because of its more advanced economic development. Of the Mediterranean countries, it aligns itself most with more developed countries such as Spain, Italy, and Portugal. For instance, in Israel, Sephardi Jews from these countries are associated by others or align themselves with the notion of the Golden Age of Jewish culture, while Oriental Jews of the Middle East are accorded a much lower status.[60]

One may ask where a different approach to the representation of Islamic culture can be experienced. Museums still do not view Islamic art and culture as an independent, historical narrative, separate from Western cultural discourse. The ideas of colonialism have taken root in the representation of Islamic culture; even the museums of the Islamic world, for instance the National Museum of Iran and the Egyptian Museum, tend to present their culture as an outgrowth of Western history and civilization.[61] Furthermore, the National Museum of Iran maintains Western museological standards of classification and chronological display and emphasizes the ties of Iranian culture to 'universal culture and civilization.'[62] Also, both Western and Eastern museums attempt to present Islamic culture in terms of 'development.' It is the departure from point A, the arrival at point B, and the changes that have occurred along the way that are important to the curators. For instance, the already discussed 'The Legacy of Genghis Khan' presents the process of cultural change and influence. Although such an approach is useful because it demonstrates cultural relations and the merger of traditions and styles, it is important to remember and represent the skills and creativity invested in the production of the objects on exhibit. The traditional techniques should be exhibited not because they may disappear or they represent a change, but rather because of the ingenuity and creativity of the producers regardless of their innovative value for that period of culture. Western museology tends to emphasize innovations in skills and/or content. This was not always the goal of cultures in the past; skilful interpetation should receive the respectful attention of the curators and historians.[63]

Finally, using Lavine's and Karp's terminology, what can be done to transform the museum as temple into the museum as forum, a 'contested terrain?'[64] In the case of the L.A. Mayer Museum, one would like to see the representation of both Arab and Jewish cultures, their present and past histories, and, most important, the way the dispute between the two cultures has found embodiment in cultural heritage. One attempt at representing the two cultures together took place recently. In the early 1990s, as a reaction to the start of the peace process, the Jerusalem Foundation, a semi-independent body whose goal was to fund and instigate cultural projects in the city, attempted to create a museum showcasing the lives of Arabs and Jews side by side in Jerusalem. Although the attempt failed, it is significant that the history of Jerusalemite Arabs could be documented alongside that of Jerusalemite Jews.[65] Another, more recent example is the exhibition 'Sudan: Past and Present,' which took place at the British Museum in 2004–5.[66] This exhibit included, along with historical and indigenous Sudanese art and craft, the modern work of Sudanese artists. The modernist works of the graduates from the College of Fine and Applied Arts in Khartoum reveal the connections between traditional and modern styles, and between Sudan and the West. It helped visitors to paint a multicoloured picture of Sudanese life, one that is not tainted by hunger and disease but is filled with ingenuity.

It is important to realize, as Homi Bhabha asserts, that every culture is constituted in relation to other cultures. Cultures are not autonomous entities, but rather are constantly evolving, living organisms that produce their own symbols to create difference.[67] Museums should recognize the uniqueness of each culture by representing them as flexible, hybrid entities. Turning the museum into a forum in this way would mean letting conflicting realities affect the museum's organizing principles. It would also, in a paradoxical manner, mean turning the art museum into an anthropological museum of sorts because, as Ruth

Phillips has demonstrated, anthropology along with the new art history is interested in microhistories rather than grand narratives.[68] In other words, one should create museums that through loosely structured classification allow smaller local histories to be told. Anthropology is helpful because it deals with culture by experiencing it directly, while art does so by creating distance between the viewer, or researcher, and the object. Ultimately, what is needed is to create a more democratic environment in which voices of difference can be heard and respected.

## NOTES

1 Yiannis Papadakis, 'The National Struggle Museums of a Divided City,' *Ethnic and Racial Studies* 17, 3 (July 1994): 400–19.

2 On the representation of the Jews in modern Europe see Richard I. Cohen, *Jewish Icons: Art and Society in Modern Europe* (Berkeley and Los Angeles: University of California Press, 1998); Ivan Davidson Kalmar and Derek Jonathan Penslar, eds, *Orientalism and the Jews* (Hanover, NH: University Press of New England, 2005); and Catherine M. Soussloff, *Jewish Identity in Modern Art History* (Berkeley and Los Angeles: University of California Press, 1999)

3 Papadakis, 'National Struggle Museums,' 27.

4 Martin Prösler, 'Museums and Globalization,' in Sharon MacDonald and Gordon Fyfe, eds, *Theorizing Museums* (Oxford: Blackwell, 1996): 27, 34.

5 Ibid., 22.

6 It should be noted that this paper does not discuss the audience of the Mayer Museum, but not because I view this as a matter not worth attention. On the contrary, the analysis of an audience's reaction to a museum display would be a most useful research tactic. Unfortunately, this piece of research was impossible to accomplish within the framework of this project.

7 Orientalism is understood here as 'a study of the genesis, evolution, and reproduction of a specific Western tradition of knowledge concerned with the Mashreq or the Eastern part of Arabo-Islamic world.' Amal Rassam, 'Comments on Orientalism: Two Reviews,' *Comparative Studies in Society and History* 22, 4 (1980): 505.

8 Keith W. Whitelam, *The Invention of Ancient Israel: The Silencing of Palestinian History* (New York: Routledge, 1997), 33.

9 Although Leo Mayer, the man to whom the museum is dedicated, did not actively participate in the founding of this institution, it is important to

mention him here since his work was inspirational for Salomons and Ettinghausen in their creative project.

10 Rachel Hason, *Masterworks from the Collections of the L.A. Mayer Museum for Islamic Art* (Jerusalem: Art Plus Ltd., 2000), 6.

11 Ibid., 16.

12 See, for example, Karen Amstrong, *Islam: A Short History* (New York: Modern Library, 2000); Michael Brett, *The Berbers* (Oxford: Blackwell, 1996); and Malise Ruthven, *Islam: A Very Short Introduction* (New York: Oxford University Press, 2000).

13 For more on this subject see Whitelam, *Invention of Ancient Israel.*

14 G.W. Bowersock, 'Palestine: Ancient History and Modern Politics,' in Edward W. Said and Christopher Hitchens, eds, *Blaming the Victims: Spurious Scholarship and the Palestinian Question* (London: Verso, 1988), 185.

15 For more on the history of the region see, for example, David Fromkin, *Cradle and Crucible: History and Faith in the Middle East* (Washington: National Geographic Society, 2002) and Bernard Lewis, *The Middle East: 2000 Years of History from the Rise of Christ to the Present Day* (London: Weidenfeld & Nicolson, 1995).

16 This point can be developed further: Palestine belonged to the Ottoman Empire then to the British Mandate and then to Israel. Thus, ending the timeline with the Ottoman Empire serves both the imperial and Zionist projects, since it demonstrates that Islamic culture has reached its peak under the rule of an enlightened regime, after which it either regressed or continued to flourish, depending on the viewpoint of those writing history.

17 Johannes Fabian, *Time and the Other: How Anthropology Makes Its Object* (New York: Columbia University Press, 1983).

18 Richard Handler, 'On Having Culture: Nationalism and the Preservation of Quebec's Patrimoine,' in *Nationalism and the Politics of Culture in Quebec* (Madison: University of Wisconsin Press, 1988), 192–215; James Clifford, *The Predicament of Culture: Twentieth-Century Ethnography, Literature, and Art* (Cambridge, MA: Harvard University Press, 1988).

19 Yael Zerubavel, *Recovered Roots: Collective Memory and the Making of Israeli National Tradition* (Chicago: University of Chicago Press, 1995).

20 Yehudit Inbar and Ely Schiller, eds, *Museums in Israel* (Jerusalem: Ariel Publishing House, 1995), 51.

21 Sadly, it appears that the museum for Islamic Art on Temple Mount has closed. All recent attempts to contact the museum administration have been fruitless.

22 Clifford, *Predicament of Culture*, 219.

23 Ibid.
24 Michel Foucault, 'Of Other Spaces,' *Diacritics* 16 (1986): 26.
25 Timothy Mitchell, 'Orientalism and the Exhibitionary Order,' in Nicholas B. Dirks, ed., *Colonialism and Culture* (Ann Arbor: University of Michigan Press, 1992), 313.
26 Nezar Alsayyad, 'Introduction,' in Alsayyad, ed., *Consuming Tradition, Manufacturing Heritage: Global Norms and Urban Forms in the Age of Tourism* (London, New York: Routledge, 2001), 6.
27 The process through which the gaze transforms the material reality of the built environment into a cultural imagery is sometimes called 'engazement.' For further discussion of preservation and nationalism in the Israeli context see Tamar Katriel, *Performing the Past: A Study of Israeli Settlement Museums* (Mahwah, NJ: Lawrence Erlbaum, 1997) and Ariella Azoulay, 'Museums and Historical Narratives in Israel's Public Space,' in Daniel Sherman and Irit Rogoff, eds, *Museum Culture: History, Discourses, Spectacles* (London: Routledge, 1994), 85–109.
28 Hason, *Masterworks*, 7.
29 Mitchell, 'Orientalism,' 312–14. For more on collecting a representative specimen in the natural history context see Donna Haraway, 'Teddy Bear Patriarchy: Taxidermy in the Garden of Eden, 1908–1936,' *Social Text* 11 (Winter 1984–5): 20–64.
30 The correspondence between Ettinghausen and Salomons related to the process of finding and acquiring artefacts was considered confidential by the museum staff and was not communicated.
31 Quoted in Clifford, *Predicament of Cultures*, 219.
32 Thomas Hoving, ed., *The Chase, the Capture: Collection at the Metropolitan* (New York: Metropolitan Museum of Art, 1975), 123–4.
33 Clifford, *Predicament of Culture*, 220.
34 Christopher Steiner and Ruth Phillips, 'Art, Authenticity, and the Baggage of Cultural Encounter,' in C. Steiner and R. Phillips, eds, *Unpacking Culture: Art and Commodity in Colonial and Postcolonial Worlds* (Berkeley and Los Angeles: University of California Press, 1993), 3–19.
35 Timothy Mitchell, 'Making the Nation: The Politics of Heritage in Egypt,' in Alsayyad, ed., *Consuming Tradition*, 224–5.
36 Accessed at http://www.metmuseum.org/special/se_event.asp?OccurrenceId=%7B9B2DD36-155A-11D6-9415-00902786BF44%7D.
37 Azoulay, 'Museums and Historical Narratives,' 102–4.
38 For more on the role of donor or founder see Katriel, *Performing the Past*.
39 Azoulay, 'Museums and Historical Narratives,' 102.
40 Hason, *Masterworks*, 7.

41 In the book's preface, which gives a political and scholarly framework to Mayer's research, the Minister of Religious Affairs quotes Psalms 105:35: 'May it be granted to us to witness the real truth of the words of the Sweet Singer of Israel: "Let sinners be consumed out of the earth, and let the wicked be no more."' This is a curious thing for someone in charge of the upkeep of Muslim and Druze religious sites, who was also responsible for the Ministry for War Sufferers of All Religions, to wish. Leo Arie Mayer, *Some Principal Mus-lim Religious Buildings in Israel* (Jerusalem: Government Printer, 1950), 2.

42 Edward W. Said, *Orientalism* (New York: Random House, 1979), 300.

43 Ibid., 301. Akbar S. Ahmed, *Discovering Islam: Making Sense of Muslim History and Society* (London and New York: Routledge, 1988): 65–9, and Hason, *Masterworks*, 52–8.

44 Hason, *Masterworks*, 57.

45 Whitelam, *Invention of Ancient Israel*, 34.

46 http://www.imj.org.il/eng/archaeology/index.html; accessed 14 Feb. 2004.

47 http://www2.imj.org.il/eng/judaica/index.html; accessed 14 Feb. 2004.

48 Hason, *Masterworks*, 8.

49 Ibid., 32.

50 Ibid., 36.

51 Ibid., 44.

52 Stefano Carboni, http://www.metmuseum.org/special/Genghis_Khan/legacy_more.htm; Accessed 29 Oct. 2004.

53 Ibid.

54 Hanson, *Masterworks*, 70.

55 Bernard Lewis, *What Went Wrong: Western Impact and Middle Eastern Response* (Oxford: Oxford University Press, 2002), 156.

56 C.A. Qadir, *Philosophy and Science in the Islamic World* (London and New York: Routledge, 1988): iv. Qadir also quotes the following from A.M. Iqbal:

> It was, I think, Nazzam who first formulated the principle of 'doubt' as the beginning of all knowledge. Ghazali further amplified it in his *Revivification of the Sciences of Religion* and prepared the way for Descartes' method. It was Ishraqi and Ibn-i-Taimiyya who undertook a systematic refutation of Greek Logic. Abu Bakr Razi was perhaps the first to criticize Aristotle's first figure, and in our time his objection, conceived in a thoroughly inductive spirit, has been reformulated by John Stuart Mill. Ibn-i-Hazm in his *Scope of Logic* emphasizes sense-perception as a source

> of knowledge, and Ibn-i-Taimiyya, in his *Refutation of Logic*, shows that induction is the only form of reliable argument. Thus arose the method of observation and experiment. It is not merely a theoretical affair. Al-Biruni's discovery of what we call reaction time and al-Kindi's discovery that sensation is proportionate to the stimulus are instances of its application to psychology. It is a mistake to suppose that the experimental method is a European discovery.

Allama Muhammad Iqbal, *The Reconstruction of Religious Thought in Islam* (Lahore, 1968), 129.

57 Hanson, *Masterworks*, 6.

58 Angelika Bammer, 'Editorial: The Question of "Home,"' *New Formations* 17 (1992): xi.

59 Hason, *Masterworks*, 6.

60 Daniel J. Schroeter, 'Orientalism and the Jews of the Mediterranean,' *Journal of Mediterranean Studies* 4, 2 (1994): 183–96.

61 Ibid. and see http://www.egyptianmuseum.gov.eg; accessed 1 Nov. 2004.

62 See http://www.nationalmuseumofiran.com/en/; accessed 1 Nov. 2004.

63 Cheryl Buckley, 'Made in Patriarchy: Toward a Feminist Analysis of Women and Design,' in Victor Margolin, ed., *Design Discourse: History, Theory, Critique* (Chicago: University of Chicago Press, 1989), 251–62.

64 Steven D. Lavine and Ivan Karp, eds, *Exhibiting Cultures: The Poetics and Politics of Museum Display* (Washington: Smithsonian Institution Press, 1991), 1.

65 Efran Ben-Ze'ev and Eyal Ben-Ari, 'Imposing Politics: Failed Attempts at Creating a Musuem of "Co-existence" in Jerusalem,' *Anthropology Today* 12, 6 (Dec. 1996): 7–13.

66 See http://wwww.thebritishmuseum.ac.uk; accessed 1 Nov. 2004.

67 Homi Bhabha, 'The Third Space: Interview with Homi Bhabha,' in Jonathan Rutherford, ed., *Identity, Community, Culture, Difference* (London: Lawrence and Wishart, 1990), 207–21.

68 Ruth Phillips, 'How Museums Marginalize: Naming Domains of Inclusion and Exclusion,' *Cambridge Review* (1993): 6–10.

# 10 Returning the Gaze: Orientalism, Gender, and Yasmina Bouziane's Photographic Self-Portraits

DAVID PROCHASKA

MOUKHTAR KOCACHE: Your work refers to historic ethnographic practices and the role that documentary and Orientalist photography plays in the construction of 'image' and its justification of certain ideological discourses. What brought you to this?

YASMINA BOUZIANE: Initially, when I first started out, I did documentary photography; more specifically, I studied Moroccan women in the work-force. My work shifted when I began to understand photography as a construction, with the power to alter truths and fabricate imagery ... At the same time, I had to take a closer look at myself as a woman photographer shuffling between at least three cultures ... The result is, in part, this series of self-portraits ...

Kocache, 'Conversation with Yasmina Bouziane,' 1997

Yasmina Bouziane is one of several contemporary visual artists based in the 'West,' especially New York, revisioning the 'East,' especially the Middle East and North Africa.[1] A striking number of these artists are women; gender figures prominently as well in the work of Ghada Amer, Jananne al-Ani, Mona Hatoum, Shirin Neshat, Mikal Rovner, and Shahzia Sikander, for example.[2] Usually the work of these and other artists is viewed in the context of contemporary art practices. To be sure, their geographical origins are noted, even emphasized, but this background is rarely examined in depth, rarely connected to the particular forms their art takes. Here I adopt Edward Said's contrapuntal approach and run the analysis in a different direction.[3] While I acknowledge, with Said, the critical insights stemming from a contemporary-art, ultimately Western, perspective, I focus on Bouziane's biographical and geographical background, and on the colonial and post-colonial contexts that her work addresses.

Bouziane is a filmmaker and photographer; her father is Moroccan, her mother French, and she lives in the United States. In her films and photographs she ranges from Morocco and Palestine to New York and Georgetown. She collaborates with her screenwriter sister Anissa on her films: *Imaginary Homelands* (1993), *Yellow Nylon Rope* (1994).[4] In her installation 'Inhabited by Imaginings We Did Not Choose'[5] Bouziane interrogates earlier Orientalist studio photography practices. In a post-colonial critique and reworking of colonial practices, Bouziane looks back and responds from her contemporary vantage point on the colonial past, although from her post-colonial location in New York, she addresses more a 'Western' audience than an 'Eastern' one. Fore-grounding her own body, her project has everything to do with gender: how the colonial photography studio was gendered, the gendered gaze of colonial postcards, and what it means to be a woman photographer and filmmaker of French and Moroccan background living in America and a post-colonial world today. Taken together, Bouziane's work simultaneously probes issues of identity and gender, hybridity and post-coloniality. Here I focus on the 'Untitled Self-Portraits' photographic series, from the 'Inhabited by Imaginings We Did Not Choose' installation, using them as a springboard for a series of reflections on Orientalist photography, especially postcards.

DAVID PROCHASKA: What is your personal experience of orientalist or colonial postcards and photographs? Did you know people who had postcard collections or family albums?

YASMINA BOUZIANE: My background as both French and Moroccan and as a photographer was very instrumental in my study of colonial postcards ... The interesting thing about how I started this series ['Untitled Self-Portraits'] was that I came across a photograph of my father's uncle and a friend of his, in a studio set-up (one with this strange flowered background and some kind of orientalist art) all the while they were dressed in traditional Moroccan garb. It so happens that apparently they had had their portrait taken at this photo studio and later on down the road had found it being sold on the streets as a postcard. This was done, of course, without their knowledge or consent. I own that postcard now and it is part of an installation ['Inhabited Imaginings We Did Not Choose']. As a personal experience it got me thinking some more about the nature of photography and the appropriation of someone else's image and the distortion of 'truth' with the use of photography.

David Prochaska / Yasmina Bouziane, email correspondence, 1999

'Untitled, Self Portrait' (figure 10.1) is Yasmina Bouziane's signature photo. It turns the tables. Instead of the Western male photographing Arab women in Orientalist studio settings, the Arab woman turns the camera on the implied Western male viewer. The voyeuristic male gaze of Orientalist painting and photography is reversed as the viewer becomes the viewed. The passive female object becomes here the active female subject, reinforced by Bouziane's serious mien, her direct gaze. The way the photograph is composed contributes to this effect. Everything here consists of lines and angles, nothing is softened by curves: the trapezoids are formed by the floodlights, and the triangles outlined by the tripod. Very much a constructed, posed photo, it is by no means naturalistic. Bouziane's right hand is on the (cocked) camera shutter (ready to shoot), but she is not looking at us through the viewfinder, she is looking at us slightly above and to the side of the camera. It is not 'natural' for her left arm to rest on her hip, thrust out, but it makes her pose more active, in your face. Key to the construction of this constructed photograph is the way it calls attention to its own making. The picture frame includes the top of the canvas backdrop and shows how it is attached to the wall behind it. The floodlights are starkly visible. 'Untitled, Self Portrait' presents both past and present, 'tradition' and 'modernity,' colour and black and white. The Turkish rugs, the spathiphyllum and red plastic flowers in a basketry container, and Bouziane's tooled leather cowboy boots (a nice touch) are rich in colour. In contrast, everything else is black or white.

A photograph such as this one risks being considered trite; once the viewer gets the point, repeated viewings are not necessary, its meaning is exhausted. But behind the end product is the process, the process of working through and beyond the accumulated weight of Orientalist photography and of colonial representation in general. Here Bouziane takes back the photograph of her great-uncle and his friend that was taken from them.

Bouziane evokes the space of the photographer's studio, but undermines the illusion of verisimilitude by calling our attention through her composition to how the space is used to create photographic effects. Generally, we may identify three kinds of postcard space. First is the space of the photographer's studio. Second is the space of the 'view' photograph, the physical world outside. A third or optical space refers to the ways in which the negative is manipulated after exposure and before printing by the publisher to achieve certain spatial effects.[6] Now, the archetypal space of the Orientalist postcard is a photographer's studio, a 'scenic space' arranged to create an 'Oriental' illusion. Besides indoor studios, Orientalist photographs were shot in interior courtyards and other spaces where natural light could be used in controlled environments. All these settings were outfitted in an Orientalist fashion with props and artefacts purchased for the purpose.

The organization of the Neurdein postcard catalogue for colonial Algeria for *scènes et types,* scenes and types, makes clear how Orientalist photographers fabricated the 'scenic space' for such photos. Produced by one of the largest French postcard publishers, the 1905 Neurdein catalogue lists 198 *scènes et types* cards.[7] The postcards themselves provide brief, generic titles; for example, the country, 'Algérie,' is the only place name usually given. But in the 1905 list for Algerian *scènes et types,* the cards are organized according to the town where they were photographed. Combined with the number of cards and card titles, this yields important information on the construction of this visual genre. Two examples are '104A Un Musicien,' taken in Blida outside Algiers, and '133A Femme Mauresque dansant au son de la derbouka,' taken in Tlemcen (figure 10.2). The 'Femme Mauresque' was photographed outside in full sun with a series of props arranged by the photographer – rugs, a sword, and the *derbouka* being played by one of the women.

Of 198 total *scènes et types* 81 were taken in the oasis of Biskra, the Biskra frequented by André Gide and Isabelle Eberhardt. The second highest number (44) were taken in the interior centre of Tlemcen, and the third highest (29) in the oasis of Laghouat. In contrast, the colonial port cities of Algiers (16), Oran (2), and Bône (0) are either little represented or not at all. The four largest Algerian cities in order of population are likewise little represented or not at all: Algiers (16), Oran (2), Constantine (6), and Bône (0). Thus, the two interior centers of Constantine and Tlemcen on the high plateau are represented nearly three times as often (50) as the three port cities on the Mediterranean (18). Towns in Constantine *département,* generally considered the most economically backward, account for many more cards (102) than towns in Algiers and Oran *départements* combined (72). Most striking of all is that the Saharan oases of Biskra and Laghouat together account for 110 of the total 198 *scènes et types* cards. All 16 cards picturing women (significantly, there are no men) of the Oulad Nail ethnic group, the basis for one of the most infamous Orientalist tropes connoting eroticism and exoticism, were photographed either in Biskra (5) or Laghouat (11). To a striking extent, therefore, more traditional, that is, more exoticist, urban agglomerations were chosen as locales for *scènes et types* cards.

Over and against such Orientalist imagery there exists a body of what may be called indigenous photography that is increasingly coming to light. Sarah Graham-Brown's images of Middle Eastern women were drawn largely from private family albums and featured institutional photos as well as personal portraits.[8] More recently, the Arab Image Foundation (AIF), based in Beirut and New York, has amassed more than 70,000 images taken by Middle Eastern professional and amateur photographers, especially in Lebanon, from the late 1890s to the present.[9] As such, the AIF holdings constitute a large-scale exercise in 'looking back' analogous to Malek Alloula's aim in his *The Colonial Harem* to 'return this immense postcard to its sender.'[10] Photography was introduced in the Mashreq and Maghrib and initially dominated by Western photographers, who, following earlier Western artists such as David Roberts, worked mostly in an Orientalist mode. For example, 'Jerusalem, the Golden Gate (1839)' (figure 10.3) is a contemporary postcard reproduction of a work by Roberts issued by Palphot, the leading Israeli postcard firm.[11] In ways that are still not well known, photographic techniques were disseminated to local, indigenous photographers. In the 1860s, for example, Yessai Garabedian, the Armenian Patriarch of Jerusalem, held perhaps the first photography workshop in the Middle East. Armenian exiles, including trained photographers, left what is modern-day Turkey and opened photography studios elsewhere in the Middle East.

The AIF documents certain of these activities in a travelling exhibition based on its collection entitled 'Mapping Sitting,' curated by Akram Zaatari and Walid Raad.[12] 'Mapping Sitting' consists of four components: studio passport photographs (several thousand passport photos by Armenian photographer Atranik Anouchian [1908–91], who was based in Tripoli, Lebanon, plus two passport albums from the Soussi Studio), institutional group portrait photographs (numerous group portraits, especially military portraits, taken by photographers active in Lebanon, Palestine, Syria, Egypt, and Iraq between 1880 and 1960, plus eight group portraits of nurses, all featuring Egyptian nurse Zainab Shalabi, which were recently purchased at the Cairo flea market), itinerant portrait photographs (numerous photographs taken by Hashem el-Madani [1930–] of Studio Shehrazade at the beach and elsewhere in and around Saida, Lebanon, beginning in the late 1940s), and street photographs known as *photo-surprise* (early 1950s photos taken by Setrak Albarian, Sarkis Restikian, and Joseph Koraunat of the Photo Jacques Studio in the main square of Tripoli). Hashem el-Madani's 'Beach series–reclining' (figure 10.4) in the exhibition consists of thirty large-format photos of people at the beach arranged in a large-scale montage that nearly fills a wall. These portraits exemplify el-Madani's photographic practice. Based in Saida, Lebanon, each day beginning in the late 1940s el-Madani went to the beach to drum up business. All of the individuals assume the same or a similar reclining posture, half reclining left and half reclining right; fifteen of them are posed on the same rock; and in three others the same buildings are visible in the background. What was sold as a unique personalized portrait was in fact structually similar to other photos of other people. Certainly these photographs present a Middle East different from that of Orientalist imagery. After all, they originate in a different visual economy, that is, a political economy of the visual patronized by local inhabitants for personal reasons (*photo-surprise* and itinerant photos), institutional imperatives (military, medical, and other group photos), and government purposes (passport photos). In the history of photography in the Middle East, therefore, they make present what previously has been absent.

In contrast, one of the key pictorial strategies of Orientalist (and other exoticist) studio photographs is the effect of the real they strive to achieve and which Bouziane's 'Untitled, Self Portrait' undermines.[13] These Orientalist photographs employ realist strategies of representation to convince the viewer of their 'other,' in this case, Oriental reality. Chief among these representational strategies is that they bear no mark of their making. Sometimes backdrops, often painted, are visible in Orientalist postcards, yet rarely, if ever, are the edges of the backdrops as visible as they consistently are in Bouziane's 'Untitled Self-Portraits' series. Photographs by Félix-Antoine Moulin (ca. 1800–after 1868) may be the exception that proves the rule. The first photographer to produce an important body of work on colonial Algeria, Moulin in *L'Algérie photographiée* gathered over four hundred photos taken during extensive travels in 1856–7. Moulin frequently rigged up canvas backdrops against which he posed his subjects, and in several photographs the backdrops are clearly visible.[14] Although Moulin left no record that tells us why he did this, it may well be simply haste, since he travelled more or less continuously.

Through the constant fabrication of Orientalist illusion based on realist pictorial strategies, the mimetic conceit that the photograph is a copy of the real is asserted. In the early decades of photography, people frequently took a photograph of an object for the object itself. In a humorous newspaper sketch in an 1890s colonial Algiers newspaper, author Auguste Robinet stages the first encounter of his lower class,

Spanish, *petit blanc* hero Cagayous with the then still relatively new photographic technology. 'I put on my Sunday trousers, a fancy shirt, the scarf that Remédio gave me for my birthday, and all the other stuff you need.' Cagayous goes at 5 a.m. because 'I was told that the earlier it is, the fresher your face looks.' Cagayous is told that the photographer M. Leroux sleeps until 7 a.m., so he has to wait. In fact, Alexandre Leroux (1836–1912) was one of the two or three leading photographers in colonial Algiers at the time.[15] He was loosely affiliated with the paper Robinet wrote for, and in this sketch Robinet mixes both his fictional Cagayous and the real-life Leroux. Once Leroux is ready to take Cagayous's picture, he tells Cagayous to lean on the stand (for the long exposure time required). Cagayous says there is no need; Leroux says no one will see it, since it is only 'a piece of iron.' Leroux now tries to get Cagayous into a pose and to hold it. 'My head is spinning, my chest is doing the same.' After all this, Cagayous moves, and they get into an argument. Half an hour later, 'the guy brings out a box, and has me look at my so-called portrait. "Come on, don't kid around. That's me?" ... Leroux: "That's the negative." Cagayous: "Negative ... Negative! ... Me, I came here for my portrait. Where is it?"'[16]

> An entire industry was there to serve him [the European]: coloured pictures showing some of the regional characteristics of the *mouquère* [Arab woman] – the young girl from the desert (Nailia) or the Aurès, the young Kabyle woman or the city woman from Algiers, Oran or Constantine, ludicrously attired, or in a state of 'Oriental' undress; postcards for tourists and soldiers; cheap novelties; bizarre or salacious tales peddled on street corners ...'
>
> Saadia and Lakhdar, 1961

This description in Graham-Brown's *Images of Women* (44) serves to set the historical scene for Bouziane's second signature photo, 'Untitled, Self Portrait 10' (figure 10.5). In it she reclaims for the Arab woman subject the studio space the Arab woman object occupies in Orientalist postcards. Here she turns the implied Western male gazing at the colonial woman back on itself. She uses light filters that suggest old, sepia-toned photographs. Partly clothed, wearing a see-through veil, her skirt dipping to reveal her navel, her arms raised and clasped behind her head, gazing directly at the camera – these are voyeuristic features of the Orientalist erotic postcard that draw us, the viewer in. In her pose Bouziane makes herself available to us, but our gaze is disrupted, turned back on us. It is precisely as though the peephole gaze has been caught and turned back at the voyeur. Certain of the props exacerbate our unease that something is not right – the modern electric fan, the incongruous pedestal, the floodlights clearly in view, the backdrop tacked on the wall – these mark the scene as 'almost the same, but not quite.'[17] What Bouziane is here restaging, mimicking, mocking is specifically the classic Orientalist trope of 'La danse du foulard' ('Dance of the Veil'), which in its postcard version as a staged studio photograph usually features a woman posing with a scarf or veil, a painted backdrop, and a prop such as a vase on the floor.[18] Similarly, a woman holds a scarf and strikes a dance pose in the postcard 'Mauresques, costume d'intérieur. Danse des Almées' (figure 10.6).

The antithesis of women unveiled, partially or entirely unclothed, inside the photography studio were postcards of veiled women out of doors. In colonial Algeria, for example, to go outside was to go veiled, which gave rise to a range of reactions. Women veiled head to foot with only a hole for an eyepiece drove some French crazy: 'They can see us but we can't see them.' A subgenre of postcards grew up, 'Mauresques en ville,' 'Femmes mauresques en promenade,' 'Mauresques, costume de ville.' In Algiers Jean Geiser (1848–1923), perhaps the leading photographer in Algeria in the last three decades of the nineteenth century, produced several such cards, including 'Mauresques se rendant au Marabout de l'Amirauté' (figure 10.7), in which four fully veiled women walk in one of Algiers's oldest districts.[19]

Much has been written in feminist film theory, art history, and related fields in the past twenty-five years on the gaze, mostly of men looking at women, mostly Western men looking at Western women. Although it is not possible to go into detail here, three observations are in order. The first concerns Malek Alloula's *The Colonial Harem*, certainly the single best-known republication of colonial postcards, and one that focuses specifically on colonial representations of Algerian women; the postcards in figures 10.6 and 10.7, for example, appear there (pp. 87, 12, respectively).[20] As opposed to the vast majority of other books that republish colonial postcards, Alloula's study is sharply critical, to which the reviewers' comments quoted on the cover attest. 'Imprisoned by the photographers' eye [these women] reclaim their historicity through the pages of this powerful book.'[21] 'By displaying and dissecting colonial pornography as an insider he [Alloula] brings into stark relief the violation of the patriarchal gaze at its harshest.'[22] Yet it has been correctly argued, especially by some feminists, that Alloula's book constitutes a nostalgic or sexist view of male–female relations in Algeria.[23] 'If Algerian women were vulnerable and disgraced by their original display on colonial postcards, they are once again exposed by their display in this book.'[24]

The problem is that Alloula ends up reproducing the gender system that prevailed during the colonial period, if not waxing nostalgic over it, in the way he orders his material. For the book is clearly a postcard compilation – many reproduced at larger-than-postcard size — with a message. Eschewing background and contextual information, forgoing a historical or geographical classification, Alloula arranges his cards in order of increasingly derogatory imagery. His chapter headings, culminating in an 'anthology of breasts,' make this clear.[25] In short, his narrative structure constitutes his argument for the postcards' meaning. Certainly Alloula's cards existed – they *were* produced – but the market, including Bouziane's native Morocco, consisted of more cards of more different types than Alloula's book conveys. And to situate colonial Algeria in context, it has been argued that while 'the most explicit versions of this sub-eroticism were produced mostly in the cities of North Africa and Egypt; they were more rarely seen in Turkey, Lebanon, Iran and Iraq, and seldom in Syria or Palestine.'[26]

Second, Alloula and other commentators generally assume that males, mostly metropolitan visitors, bought and sent such cards to primarily male correspondents. For Alloula, to 'return this immense postcard to its sender' is to mail it back to males in France.[27] However, two recent studies of postcard reception suggest that matters may not have been so straightforward.[28] A study of female collection practices based on admittedly fragmentary data suggests that one way such colonial Algerian cards were consumed was by bourgeois French women who mounted them in postcard albums that were prominently displayed in bourgeois drawing rooms to which both men and women had access.

> Collecting postcards of harem scenes was a rare socially sanctioned occasion for [French] women to view and to display images of other women in exhibitionist and sexually provocative poses ... Yet collection practices also suggest that French women identified with the erotic sexuality that Algerian women represented ... Through these possibilities for identification, women could use postcards within the bounds of social convention as a way to actively imagine and desire sexuality ... French women's exchange and collection of the postcards demonstrates that they accepted colonial depictions, including racial hierarchies, degraded labor, and eroti-

> cized feminine stereotypes. Yet by reordering, recategorizing, and displaying the cards in collections ... the colonial postcards did not merely reinscribe accepted hierarchies; they were also used [by French women] to displace and expand definitions of bourgeois femininity.[29]

It is relatively easy to critique along with Alloula the clearly sexist and culturally derogatory images in his sample of historical postcards. But, and this is the third point, what about the reproduction of these Orientalist tropes today, which Bouziane clearly targets in 'Untitled, Self Portrait 10'? It is more difficult to account for the continued pervasiveness of such imagery, its contemporary reproduction and circulation. For example, Lehnert & Landrock was one of the largest and best known photographic firms in the Middle East and Maghrib in the first three decades of the twentieth century. Rudolf Lehnert (1878–1948) and Ernst Landrock (1880–1957) met while travelling in Europe and decided to open a photography studio in Tunis around 1904. Lehnert spent extensive time taking photographs in Tunisia and Algeria. At the outbreak of the First World War their business was closed, and it was not until after the war that Lehnert recovered his photographic plates. Around 1923 he made a trip to the Middle East, where he took photographs, and with Landrock in 1924 opened 'Lehnert & Landrock' in Cairo selling postcards, photographs, and fine art pictures. In 1930 Lehnert quit the partnership and returned to Tunis. Decades later, in the 1980s, a book of reproductions featured numerous nude and semi-nude women plus some nude boys along with Lehnert's trademark landscape views.[30] This collection was entirely devoid of such information as title, date, size, or any other contextual data, which had the effect of reproducing all the colonialist and Orientalist trappings of the photographs for a contemporary audience. Much of Lehnert & Landrock's production could be termed soft-core pornography, but given the cachet of their firm, and the fact that their work catered especially to upper-middle-class Westerners, this is usually glossed over.[31]

> Bible metaphors and parables take on the vividness of their own sunny clime when viewed among the hills of Palestine; and Bible history appears as if acted anew when read upon its old stage.
>
> J.L. Porter, 1874

J.L. Porter wrote in the 1870s, but Bouziane's 'Untitled, Self Portrait 8' (figure 10.8) resembles a stock Orientalist 'biblical' scene.[32] Bouziane, dressed in 'biblical' clothes evocative of Palestine, looks down as if contemplating the infant Jesus in the manger. It recalls all those Bible scenes of the Holy Land from the nineteenth and early twentieth centuries, of shepherds herding their flocks, and women by the manger. 'Both the growth of tourism and pilgrimage to the Holy Places of Palestine ... produced a deluge of books, slides, postcards and other memorabilia of "biblical" Palestine and its inhabitants.'[33] These stock stereotypes coded Palestine as 'biblical.' To produce 'biblical' tableaux, photographers 'simply took pictures of daily life in Palestine and attached a caption with a biblical reference or quotation,' for example, 'The 23rd Psalm, portrayed in the land of its inception.'[34] Similar to Bouziane's image in expression is a photograph taken before 1914 titled 'A Judean home, suggestive of "The Wise Men Seeking the Christ Child."'[35]

What has been termed 'the biblical allegory,' or discourse, transformed contemporary Palestinians into past biblical figures.[36] Theological and literary works earlier employed the biblical allegory, but Frank Mason Good was the first photographer to adopt it in the 1860s and 1870s. 'Biblical' photos followed set lines. Named personalities were always Old Testament individuals. Unidentified background figures alluded to New Testament people. What makes the 'biblical' biblical in this photographic genre is the way contemporary Palestinians were transformed into past biblical figures, how nineteenth- and twentieth-century Arab Palestinians were made to stand in for Jews and Christians of 2,000 years ago. It also makes them Orientalist. Contemporary Palestinians became 'for the viewer Mary, David or a figure in one of Christ's parables.'[37] While Arab Palestinians were made to assume another ethnic identity, Jews are erased pure and simple. 'None of the models who portrayed biblical scenes was a Palestinian Jew; all figures named Abraham, Joseph, or David were represented by Arabs.'[38] Good's 'Jacob's Well' (figure 10.9) exemplifies all these conventions in which Arab Palestinians were pictured circa 1868 at the site of Jacob's well. This postcard was issued in conjunction with an exhibition, 'Photographic Heritage of the Holy Land, 1839–1914,' at the Tel Aviv Museum in 1980, and is, therefore, an instance of reproducing and recirculating earlier photographic imagery.

In another example of the biblical allegory, an American traveller in the 1890s describes how 'a shepherd lad in a scarf of many colors' became Joseph: '[I]n a momentary pause due to the sudden sight of an approaching cavalcade the kodak had eternalized him as "Joseph of

Today."' In Nazareth the same writer does not name names because she does not need to. 'A lad stands just within the threshold of a carpenter's shop. His tunic was blue serge with a red sash at the waist. At the sight of the levelled kodak, he laughs and his hands chafe one another nervously.'[39] This would have particular resonance for Bouziane, whose father is originally from Nazareth. As the narrator puts it in her film *Imaginary Homelands*, 'When I walk down the streets of the *medina*, rue des Consuls, the men speak to me in English. They think I'm a "Nasrania," the one from Nazareth. They think I'm from "El Kharij," from the outside ... But what am I supposed to do? I'm the daughter of a "Nasrania," who lives in "El Kharij" and speaks Arabic.'[40]

Bouziane's 'Untitled, Self Portrait 8' contests the persistence of these Orientalist 'biblical' tropes, not in so many words but through pictorial composition. 'The wide circulation of biblical stereotypes of Palestinians suggests a picturesque backwardness which has coloured Western views of them to this day.'[41] For what makes these 'biblical' images Orientalist is the way the Palestinians are made to inhabit a 'timeless Orient' as if unchanged for thousands of years. Photographers at the time wrote about their practices in terms that we would describe today as 'salvage ethnography,' or folkloric, that is, they were concerned to record traditions before they were overtaken by modernity. For example, Adrien Bonfils, the son of Félix Bonfils who founded the leading Western photography studio in Beirut in the 1870s, describes his approach as follows: 'Twenty centuries have passed without changing the décor or physiognomy of this land [Palestine] unique among all; but let us hasten if we wish to enjoy the sight ... [B]efore progress has completely done its destructive job, before this present which is still the past has forever disappeared we have tried to fix and immobilize it in a series of views.'[42]

Once the image was fixed it was available for circulation, and could be inserted in a visual economy of images largely bereft of their original referents. Thus, stereotypical 'biblical' photographs were made not only in Palestine. They could be set in Egypt, where Lucie Duff Gordon described a Bedouin woman who was 'walking away towards the desert in the setting sun like Hagar. All is so Scriptural in the country here.'[43] They could be set in Algeria, as Théophile Gautier noted in writing about the 1861 Paris Salon: 'The voyage to Algiers is becoming as indispensable for painters as the pilgrimage to Italy; they go there to learn of the sun, to study light, to seek out unseen types, and manners and postures that are primitive and biblical.'[44] Or they could be set among the Todas, an ethnic group in the Nilgiri mountains of southern India. The Todas inspired a voluminous written literature, from Richard Burton to Madame Blavatsky to W.H.R. Rivers.[45] Photographic representations of the Todas look 'biblical.' Romanticized visions of natives of such hill regions allowed the British to interpret the Todas's slide into decay as an inexorable evolutionary process. Richard Burton, for example, considered the Todas a demographically dying race. That images of such different ethnic groups from such different places could all nonetheless be glossed as 'biblical' constitutes a case of a discourse trumping difference. Bedouins in Egypt come from a different ethnic background and geographical locale than do Todas in India, but visual representations of both are constructed to exemplify the same 'biblical' discourse.

Bouziane's 'Untitled, Self Portrait 8' contests Orientalist 'biblical' tropes reproduced on postcards of Palestine. What her work does not do is engage other strains of postcard imagery in the region over time. There are at least four stages of postcard imagery of Israel/Palestine that require sorting out.[46] First of all there are the late-nineteenth and early-twentieth-century postcards that reproduce the visual strategies and Orientalist tropes of the biblical allegory already discussed. This body of work depicted Palestine as a 'living museum' in which postcard captions and texts that alluded to the biblical past were used in conjunction with contemporary photos. Individuals in a postcard labelled 'Carpenter's shop' were arranged to represent the Holy Family. A postcard of peasants harvesting grain that is captioned 'Field of Boaz' refers to the Old Testament parable from the Book of Ruth. Palestinian Arabs were used almost exclusively in these images, but in this first stage of postcards, Jews were also represented and in ways that were, significantly, similar to the Arabs. Side by side with 'Mohammedan women' are found, therefore, 'Jewish woman of Jerusalem' and 'Jews.' These Jews are not recently arrived immigrants but members of already existing communities. Such early twentieth-century postcards of Jews 'often invoked Christian anti-Semitic notions.'[47] Postcards of Jews sitting on their luggage, for example, recall representations of the 'Wandering Jew' found in Western art.

Jewish postcard representations changed as the Zionist presence in Palestine grew. Postcards of Zionist *sabras*, pioneers, reversed the negative valence of the earlier Orientalist representations of Jews.[48] One postcard series from the 1930s was entitled 'We Build up Palestine'; other cards were captioned 'Joy in Work,' 'The Gardener,' and 'Jewish Builders.' Such pioneer postcards became 'increasingly common' when Zionist firms began to produce and disseminate them from the 1920s. The 'We Build up Palestine' series was produced by the Palestine Photo Rotation Company, or Palphot, which was founded in 1934. Pioneer cards were 'often inspired' by Zionist settlers from Russia, who were influenced in turn by various strands of socialism.[49] Thus, early Zionist postcards drew on contemporaneous Socialist Realism as a visual mode of representation. An echo of such imagery is 'Hebrew Labourer' (figure 10.10), a postcard reproduction of an Israeli five-pound banknote in which a muscled worker with a pickaxe stands in front of a schematic rendering of a factory.[51] Moreover, Zionist women were pictured wearing modern dress and actively working alongside men. In contrast, early Zionist postcard representations of Arabs did not change, but instead reproduced earlier Orientalist-inflected imagery. Arab women are often depicted carrying large loads on their heads; the caption on one card, 'Fuel for thought – Arab women collecting wood,' underscores the point. Similarly, the Arab in 'Palestine. Native Shepherd carrying a lamb' in his tattered clothing contrasts with the newer 'Jewish Shepherd in Galilea,' the pioneer overseeing the land and his flock.[51] Such Jewish cards aided in constructing the Zionist myth of 'making the desert bloom.' Where earlier Christian Orientalist imagery erased Arabs to create biblical personages in their stead, now the Zionist myth of 'a land without people for a people without land' erased the Arabs from the land. Of course, the fact that Arabs were not entirely absent, even after 1948, creates an inevitable tension at the level of representation. The *sabr*, cactus fruit, was used by the Arabs to mark the boundaries of their land, so that even in Israeli postcards where the cactus is evoked as a metaphor for Zionist pioneers, it constitutes at the same time a visible trace of Palestine.

A third stage of postcard imagery began after 1948 with the creation of the Israeli state, which for the Palestinians was the *nadha*, catastrophe. In the new nation-state, Israeli postcards are produced overwhelmingly by Israeli firms; Palphot established a virtual monopoly on postcards sold in the country after 1948. Whereas earlier Zionist postcards were influenced by socialist ideals and Socialist Realist visuality, a major theme of Israeli postcards, especially after the 1967 war, was the so-called tough Jew, a reaction against alleged Jewish passivity during the Holocaust and now directed against the Palestinians. 'The Israeli Soldier' was, for example, a popular postcard series issued in the 1980s. In addition, a fusion of the military and religion also occurs in the 1980s, as in the postcard of a soldier praying at the Western Wall, 'Jerusalem.

Soldier by the Western Wall' (figure 10.11).[52] Israeli postcards depict Israeli women as soldiers and policewomen as well as *kibbutzniks*. Thus, 'Woman Soldier of the "Nahal"' (figure 10.12) reproduces in postcard format an Israeli half-pound banknote depicting a uniformed woman soldier holding a bushel basket of produce against a backdrop of patchwork farm plots.[53] In contrast, 'representations of the Palestinian-Arab population on Israeli postcards are in some ways quite similar to those found on postcards from the beginning of this century.'[54] An Israeli postcard issued by Palphot pictures an Arab woman carrying a large bundle of firewood on her head and captioned derisively 'Women's Lib.' Another Palphot card, 'Beduin Women [*sic*] with Her Water Jar on Her Head on the Way from the Water Well' (figure 10.13), both reproduces the Orientalist trope in a contemporary setting of a women carrying a water jug, and contrasts starkly with the Israeli woman in figure 10.12: 'traditional' versus 'modern' dress and economic activity. Yet another Palphot postcard makes the sterotypical 'traditional' versus 'modern' contrast implied in the biblical allegory explicit: 'Plowing the fields as in biblical times' (figure 10.14).

Where, in all of this, are the Palestinians? Individual Palestinians and Palestinian organizations have begun to produce postcards, especially after the first *intifada* that began in the late 1980s. On the one hand, images of 'resistance' (the Palestinian term) or 'terrorism' (the Israeli term) do not appear on postcards; on the other hand, with the end of the *intifada* political disillusionment was channelled in part into cultural resistance. One example is the postcards produced by Maha Seca, who comes from Beit Jala on the West Bank. In the 1980s she began to collect traditional Palestinian embroidered dresses in different styles from different regions. Since many of these areas were taken over by Israel after 1948, she reclaims in effect this former Palestinian territory simultaneously as she collects the dresses. From the 1990s Maha Seca started producing postcards in which young, urban, attractive Palestinian women modelled the dresses. 'I chose beautiful girls to present these beautiful dresses, to show our culture. We do not need to show backwardness, because the West has already done that.'[55] Her cards underline both Palestinian unity and diversity. One card labelled 'Jaffa' states on the reverse, 'Palestinian women near Jaffa in the traditional costumes of Majdel, Safiriyya, Neit-Dajan, Yabnah and Yazour.' All of these villages were destroyed or depopulated of Palestinians by the Israelis in 1948.

In Algeria in the late 1970s and early 80s you saw Algerian women who in their chic Parisian styles, expensive coiffures, and fluent French could well pass as French. My temporary Iraqi roommate, who brought his makings for tea from Baghdad, was typical of many from the Mashreq who looked down on Algerians for being 'uncultured' because they lacked Arab culture. Meanwhile, militant Algerians vehemently criticized the French for having *déraciné*, deculturated, them. For the French the Algerians were *complexé*, they had a psychological problem.

David Prochaska

In the affected, exaggerated pose of 'Untitled, Self Portrait 11' (figure 10.15), Bouziane looks like someone aping a *Vogue*-ish pose. Her head in profile, tilted up, she is posing, primping for the camera. Her outstretched fingers jabbing the air are a dead giveaway that she is poking fun at the attitudes of such wealthy women. The clothes she wears suit well her body language. Her red coat and heels, blue skirt, and black tights are all solid, primary colours. She drapes an animal fur piece around her neck, while an outlandishly large animal tail is attached to her expensive leather bag. Oriental carpets and a wood Mouton-Cadet box type this woman as French and Arab. This is not a new phenomenon. 'By the early twentieth century, the upper classes in these cities [of Turkey, Egypt, Syria, and Palestine] were looking to Paris for their fashions ... The wealthy paid visits to Europe where they bought clothes, and in large cities such as Cairo, Alexandria and Istanbul, department stores and dress shops opened.'[56] Bouziane's pose together with her sartorial get-up parodies the well-off, contemporary, Westernized Arab woman; it signs her as snobby and snooty, a person for whom Paris and things French are the epitome of sophistication, elegance, refinement, and culture.

Bouziane deals little in her self-portrait series with either politics or class. What about her own class position? We learn little from either her photographs or her films, except that there is considerable geographical mobility in this triangular Moroccan-French-American milieu. Her mother's family is French and her father's Arab, but otherwise we are left to guess. 'Untitled, Self Portrait 11' comes closest to an explicit comment on class in this satire of the wealthy Arab woman, by someone presumably coming from a slightly lower class position. The photography studio here might just as well be a changing room, from which this woman could emerge to continue shopping until she drops on Michigan Avenue or Fifth Avenue, Rodeo Drive or the Champs Elysées.

In 'Untitled, Self Portrait 6' (figure 10.16) we have the young professional with her signifiers, a laptop and red plastic whistle. As in 'Untitled, Self Portrait 11,' Bouziane's wardrobe runs to primary colours, but here there is more black: black tights; medium black heels instead of red ones, professionally, modestly short; black sequined vest over black blouse shirt; red above-the-knees puff skirt. Staring directly at the viewer, she again gives us that look with eyebrows lifted, forehead furrowed: 'Yes? You wanted something? You said something?' All of Bouziane's self-portraits play with juxtaposition, mixture, hybridity, East and West, new and old. Few of the studio props here, the Oriental carpets for one, sign this Western-looking woman as Arab. Past and present: the personal computer occupies exactly the same picture plane as the classical pedestal.

This photo is the young professional woman about town wearing the 'Don't fuck with me' look. Nothing here codes her as Arab. Once she emerges from this interior 'Oriental' space into the outside world she will pass as 'Western.' She has erased her Arab identity. She has become an other, another Western woman, but who exactly has she become? The juxtaposition – Western woman, Eastern setting – suggests the question, who is she? 'We never thought of entering ourselves in Moroccan society, I was a bystander to my own culture and people, allowed only to peek through the keyhole of the door we had locked outselves ... How may I choose one side over the other? How may I give up one part of my puzzle? Pull out any piece, and it all comes crashing down.'[57]

Perhaps in other, less expensive clothes an Arab woman cannot readily be seen in Paris or Washington as French or American. 'As an Arab woman you're suspect.' Outside the métro in Paris the subway police ask a friend for her papers. 'She didn't want to prove that she was what she was not. She was Arab but she was also French and her papers were French. What do they do, these keepers of law and order with those elements that straddle both?'[58] But dressed as Bouziane is in this interior studio space, is she not invisible as an Arab? Whereas '[T]wo suspicious-looking females were reported to the Washington, D.C. police ... [as] possibly of Hispanic origin ... Why is it that we have to go through so much to prove that we are legitimate? You see, I pay rent for the building on the edge of the sidewalk in Georgetown ... Does the colour of my skin determine where I can sit?'[59]

The woman in 'Untitled, Self Portrait 6' can perhaps be viewed as Western, but she still is a woman negotiating heavily male spaces. The red whistle she dangles has about it an aura of potential danger. She carries it just in case; she may need it. And it is because of her sex. In Paris and in Georgetown it is her race, her ethnicity that is reacted to. In the *medina* – which particular *medina* Bouziane does not specify – it is her gender that is responded to. Sexual comments, sexual taunting, sometimes sexual danger. In *Le Regard* (1993) a young Moroccan male street seller staring at her video camera holds up a pair of white panties, turns them inside out, stretches them, shows the crotch panel in a long sequence while Bouziane films him playing with them.[60]

> I thought I would write a story and a book called 'Where Are You From?' It would be about this kid who would go from one place to another asking people if they could help him find out where he was from not because he didn't know, but because there was too long an answer because there was a different answer depending sometimes on whom you were talking to.
>
> Yasmina and Anissa Bouziane, *Yellow Nylon Rope*

An exhibition of indigenous Middle Eastern photography such as 'Mapping Sitting,' discussed above, makes present the sort of photos that have been absent too long in the history of photography in the region. But beyond the function of 'looking back,' what exactly do the photographs mean, signify? To be sure, they offer glimpses, clues of what life was like in these places (Lebanon) at these times (especially the decades between the world wars) for these people (Zainab Shalabi). Yet in the overwhelming number of cases we have no information beyond the image itself; in all but a tiny number, we do not know the name of the individual snapped. In Hashem el-Madani's series of individuals reclining at the beach (figure 10.4), we do not know any of their names; the male gazing at the name 'Lillian' drawn in the sand (top row, second from right) remains enigmatic. Without additional contextual information, photos such as these constitute extensive rather than intensive data; they are information-poor versus information-rich, in contrast to a play, a poem, or a painting. In other words, they consist of interesting, even fascinating social data, but are ultimately inconclusive; we are provided sufficient information to pique our curiosity but not enough to draw a conclusion, or form an interpretation. The questions prompted by such historical clues quickly become epistemological ones: what does this image tell us, and how do we know it?

The curators of 'Mapping Sitting' do not engage such issues head-on;

no doubt they had no intention of doing so. Virtually no background or contextual information is provided in the exhibition beyond an introductory wall text plus individual labels that are art-museum brief, not natural-history-museum long.[61] Instead, the viewpoint of the curators is expressed in the way they mount the show, which is museologically striking and sophisticated. The several thousand passport photos are pinned side by side to the wall in clusters (women with different headdresses, men with light- or dark-coloured clothes), while the two old passport albums are placed in glass cases. Fifteen military group portraits have been put on one looped DVD and projected nearly lifesize on a wall, while Zainab Shalabi's eight nursing pictures are displayed behind glass. The itinerant photographs are mounted on three large panels, two 240 by 360 cm and one 300 by 360 cm. Each panel groups different individuals photographed at different times at the same spot in the same posture from the same camera angle (reclining on the beach, treading water, and sitting on what appears to be a ski lift). The *photo-surpise* photos have also been digitized on two looped DVDs and projected through TV monitors. One monitor consists of several hundred photos taken in the main Tripoli square facing north, and the second of an equal number taken in the same square facing south. The individuals are seen only fleetingly, but the background buildings in the square emerge distinctly. In the way the curators have displayed the photos, therefore, they underscore that what was a personal, individualized, unique portrait for the person who paid for it was, for the commercial photographer, a result of photographic practices repeated over and over to make a living. In short, these are instrumental photos in the sense that Allan Sekula has alerted us to.[62] The passport photos are identity photos, structurally similar to police photos, including Marc Garanger's photos of Muslim women taken during the war in Algeria.[63] The institutional group photos are broadly similar to the mining company photos that Sekula analysed; the ones in the show happen to be formal group portraits.[64] The *photo-surprise* and itinerant photos are structurally related to commercial studio photography. Taken out of doors, and more like candid snapshots, the routinized manner of their making betrays their aimed-for spontaneity and reveals their basis in a capitalist transaction. One of the questions that Raad and Zaatari pose in materials that accompany the exhibition is 'What can we learn about notions of identity from these [photographic] portraits?' I think I have answered that question: nothing more specific than the sort of general statements made above, certainly nothing concerning the identity of a particular individual. In making present indigenous commercial photography that heretofore has been generally absent, 'Mapping Sitting' raises questions about identity that, however, it cannot answer in detail or in depth.

Bouziane takes a very different approach to identity. She, too, 'looks back.' She has a connection not to commercial but to documentary photography. 'I came from a documentary photography background, so the issue of truthfulness in representation was quite important to me. Turning the tables around and placing myself in the photograph was pivotal here.'[65] This issue connects in turn to the production and reproduction of stereotypes, especially Orientalist ones. 'We are not what you think' is a theme Bouziane stages in her juxtaposition of past and present, using the present to interrogate the past, drawing on the present to critique old stereotypes. Hers is a series of staged studio portraits that, through the poses she adopts as so many changes of clothes, leads us to raise questions about identity that push us to rethink especially Orientalist studio photography. Just as Said in *Orientalism* resisted conjuring an alternate, let alone 'real' Orient, so, too, is Bouziane's enterprise primarily a deconstructive one. As such, her project runs the risk of narcissistic self-regard. For as Moukhtar Kocache points out, 'Yasmina Bouziane's project faces two dangers ... Her practice of self-examination might run the risk of "othering the self" rather than "selving the other" ... [Hal Foster] notes the danger that "self-othering can flip into self-absorption, in which the project of an ethnographic self-fashioning" becomes the practice of a philosophical narcissism.'[66]

Identity drives Bouziane's photographic project, her aesthetic. Stealing identity: her great-uncle's photo for sale on the streets. It happens to French *petit blanc* colonizers, too. Some time after Cagayous finally got his portrait from M. Leroux, he noticed one day walking past the studio that it was on display in Leroux's store window. Fashioning an identity: no single photograph sums up, completely constitutes Bouziane. Her 'Self-Portraits' do not reveal her self as those, for example, by Rembrandt or Matisse do. Bouziane's 'Self-Portraits' are more accurately staged personas; the different people, the poses she adopts do not collectively add up to an understanding of who Bouziane is. Instead, in every one of her photos she dresses up, plays a role. Yet as facets, faces of identity, her approach to identity emerges. Postmodernism as pastiche, indeterminacy, and body parts intersects in Bouziane's work with post-coloniality as diasporic, multicultural identity. But Bouziane's post-colonialism is not so much beyond colonialism as it is what comes after colonialism.[67] Bouziane's oeuvre presents us with neither history, in the form of documentary, nor class, nor politics, let alone 'straight' autobiography. Rather, Bouziane self-consciously uses autobiographical materials to essay an identity, one based on body parts and multiple personae that is liminal and contingent. As the narrator in *Yellow Nylon Rope* expresses it, '[W]ho I am has been defined by my struggle to fill that chasm between East and West. That struggle to complete a circle around two points that shall never meet.'[68]

Yet however shattered, fragmented into shards – however much metaphors of chasms or of circles that do not meet are employed – Bouziane's identity lies behind the different identities she stages. Her identity fragments are not given raw; they are mediated, processed, constructed, performed. All of which assumes an identity, an authorial presence, an author in charge; in short, a Bouziane identity who stages these facets of her identity. 'I am the product of those cultures that according to you can never meet. Don't say nobody, because I'm somebody, and that chasm is me.'[69] This identity is sufficiently strong and ego-centred to perform its own identity as autobiography. 'Caught between two worlds of not belonging to one or the other side neither Muslim nor Christian. It is a hurt ... not many would willingly impose on anyone else. Yet it is an identity, my identity.'[70]

NOTES

The opening epigraph is from Moukhtar Kocache, 'Conversation with Yasmina Bouziane,' *aljadid* 21 (Fall 1997): 11.

1 See, among others, David O'Brien and David Prochaska, *Beyond East and West: Seven Transnational Artists* (Urbana, IL: Krannert Art Museum; Seattle: University of Washington Press, 2004). The seven artists were Jananne al-Ani, Ghada Amer, Mona Hatoum, Y.Z. Kami, Walid Raad, Michal Rovner, and Shahzia Sikander. After opening at the University of Illinois, the exhibition travelled to Dartmouth College, Williams College, and Louisiana State University.
2 For orientation, see the references in O'Brien and Prochaska, *Beyond East and West*, and in particular Michael Archer, Guy Brett, and Catherine de Zegher, *Mona Hatoum* (New York: Phaidon, 1997); Georgio Verzotti, ed., *Shirin Neshat*, exh. cat. (Milan: Charta, 2002); Sylvia Wolf, *Michal Rovner: The Space Between* (New York: Whitney Museum of Art, 2002); and *Shahzia Sikander*, exh. cat. (Chicago: The Renaissance Society and University of Chicago Press, 1999).
3 Said describes how his contrapuntal approach originates in his experience

as an exile. 'Most people are principally aware of one culture, one setting, one home; exiles are aware of at least two, and this plurality of vision gives rise to an awareness of simultaneous dimensions, an awareness that – to borrow a phrase from music – is contrapuntal' (Said, 'Reflections on Exile,' in Russell Ferguson et al., eds, *Out There: Marginalization and Contemporary Culture* [Cambridge: MIT Press, 1990], 366). Said applies his approach to Jane Austen's *Mansfield Park* in his *Culture and Imperialism* (New York: Random House, 1993), 80–97. See also David Prochaska, 'Edward Said: The Contrapuntal Self,' unpub. ms. Another approach rooted in Western contemporary art practices would situate Bouziane's project in relation to the work of artists such as Cindy Sherman. See, among others, Cindy Sherman, *Cindy Sherman: Retrospective* (New York: Thames & Hudson, 2000).

4 Yasmina Bouziane, *Imaginary Homelands*, ¾" video, 20 minutes, tri-lingual (English/French/Arabic) (1993); script by Anissa Bouziane. Yasmina Bouziane, *Yellow Nylon Rope*, ¾" video, 18 minutes, tri-lingual (English/French/Arabic), English subtitles (1994); script by Anissa Bouziane.

5 La Maison Française, Columbia University, New York, 1997.

6 Aline Ripert and Claude Frère, *La carte postale: Son histoire, sa fonction sociale* (Paris: Éditions du CNRS; Lyon: Presses Universitaires de Lyon, 1983).

7 Neurdein postcards of colonial Algeria in 1905 are divided in turn into nearly 1300 view, or landscape, cards (pp. 258–73), and *scènes et types algériens* (273–7). An annex (522–8) lists additional view cards. Algerian view cards are further broken down geographically, first by *département* (Algiers, Constantine, and Oran), and within each *département* by town.

8 Sarah Graham-Brown, *Images of Women: The Portrayal of Women in Photography of the Middle East, 1860–1950* (London: Quartet Books, 1988).

9 The AIF archive is the single largest collection of indigenous photography that I know of anywhere. The Foundation's website is located at http://arabimagefoundation.org and includes background information as well as numerous photos.

10 Malek Alloula, *The Colonial Harem* (Minneapolis: University of Minnesota Press, 1986), 5. On Alloula, see below.

11 See David Roberts, *The Holy Land, Syria, Idumea, Arabis, Egypt and Nubia* (London: F.G. Moon, 1842–9). For more on the so called 'biblical allegory' and Palphot, see below.

12 After travelling in Europe for two years, the show opened in North America at the Grey Gallery, New York University. Its second North American venue was the Krannert Art Museum, University of Illinois.

A book has been published in conjunction with the exhibition: Karl Bassil, Zeina Maasri, and Akram Zaatari, eds, *Mapping Sitting* (Beirut: Mind the Gap, 2002).

13 Roland Barthes, *The Rustle of Language*, trans. Richard Howard (New York: Farrar, Straus and Giroux, 1986), 141–8.

14 André Rouillé and Bernard Marbot, *Le corps et son image* (Paris: Contrejour, 1986), 66; and David Prochaska, 'All in the Family,' unpub. ms.

15 His business card is reproduced in *Photographes en Algérie au XIXe siècle* (Paris: Musée-Galerie de la Seita, 1999), 132. On Leroux, see *Photographes en Algérie* and Malek Alloula, *Alger photographiée au XIXe siècle* (Paris: Marval, 2001).

16 Auguste Robinet, *Les amours de Cagayous: Pochades algériennes* (Algiers: Imprimerie de la Revue Algérienne, 1896), 'Chez le Photographe,' 69–75 (trans. Jane Kuntz). On Cagayous, see David Prochaska, 'History as Literature, Literature as History: Cagayous of Algiers,' *American Historical Review* 101 (1996): 670–711.

17 Homi Bhabha, *The Location of Culture* (New York: Routledge, 1994), 86.

18 David Prochaska, 'The Archive of *Algérie imaginaire*,' *History and Anthropology* 4 (1990): 394.

19 Serge Dubuisson and Jean-Charles Humbert, 'Jean Geiser, photographe-éditeur d'Alger, 1848–1923: Chronique d'une famille,' in G. Beaugé and J.-F. Clément, eds, *L'image dans le monde arabe* (Paris: CNRS Éditions, 1995), 275–90.

20 Alloula, *The Colonial Harem*. Representative critical studies include Annie Coombes and Steve Edwards, 'Site Unseen: Photography in the Colonial Empire, Images of Subconscious Eroticism,' *Art History* 12 (1989): 510–16; Irvin Cemil Schick, 'Representing Middle Eastern Women: Representation and Colonial Discourse,' *Feminist Studies* 16 (1990): 345–80; Winifred Woodhull, *Transfigurations of the Maghreb* (Minneapolis: University of Minnesota Press, 1993), 37–45; Carol Shloss, 'Algeria, Conquered by Postcard,' *New York Times Book Review*, 11 January 1987: 24; and Jean-Noël Ferrié and Gilles Boëtsch, 'Contre Alloula: Le "*Harem colonial*" revisité,' in Beaugé and Clément, eds, *L'image dans le monde arabe*, 299–304.

21 *Village Voice.*

22 *Women's Review of Books.*

23 Coombes and Edwards, 'Site Unseen,' 511–12; Woodhull, *Transfigurations of the Maghreb*, 37–45.

24 Shloss, *'Algeria, Conquered by Postcard.'*

25 Alloula, *Colonial Harem*, 105.

26 Graham-Brown, *Images of Women*, 44.

27 Alloula, *Colonial Harem*, 5.

28 Rebecca J. DeRoo, 'Colonial Collecting: Women and Algerian *Cartes Postales*,' *parallax* 4 (1998): 145–57; and Saloni Mathur, 'Wanted Native Views: Collecting Colonial Postcards of India,' in Antoinette Burton, ed., *Gender, Sexuality and Colonial Modernities* (New York: Routledge, 1999), 95–115.

29 DeRoo, 'Colonial Collecting,' 154–5.

30 Philippe Cardinal, *L'Orient d'un photographe: Lehnert & Landrock* (Lausanne: Favre, 1987). Another volume that republishes work by the firm is Charles Favrod and André Rouvinet, *Lehnert & Landrock. Orient 1904–1930* (Paris: Marval, 1999).

31 In a further twist, Landrock sold the store to his son-in-law, Kurt Lambelet, on the eve of the Second World War. The store evolved into a bookstore specializing in fine arts, technical, and foreign language books; in 1972 a branch opened in the Cairo Museum. As of the mid-1990s the business was still run by Lambelet with his son, Édouard, and daughter-in-law, Roswitha Lambelet. What exactly does it mean, therefore, for contemporary post-colonials in Egypt to reproduce and sell Orientalist photographs taken nearly 100 years ago in Tunisia and Algeria?

32 J.L. Porter, *The Giant Cities of Bashan and Syria's Holy Places* (London: T. Nelson & Sons, 1874), iii, quoted in Nissan N. Perez, *Focus East: Early Photography in the Near East, 1839–1885* (New York: Abrams and Jerusalem: Domino Press and Israeli Museum, 1988), 95. Porter lived in Damascus from 1849 and wrote a standard guidebook to Syria and Palestine published by John Murray in 1858. In 1887, two years before his death in 1889, his *Jerusalem, Bethany and Bethlehem* appeared.

33 Graham-Brown, *Images of Women*, 45. One of the most important early productions was Roberts, *The Holy Land*, see figure 10.3.

34 Graham-Brown, *Images of Women*, 46.

35 Ibid., 105.

36 Yeshayahu Nir, *The Bible and the Image: The History of Photography in the Holy Land, 1839–1899* (Philadelphia: University of Pennsylvania Press, 1985), 144–7.

37 Graham-Brown, *Images of Women*, 46.

38 Nir, *The Bible and the Image*, 147.

39 Quoted, ibid.

40 Yasmina Bouziane, *Imaginary Homelands*, script by Anissa Bouziane.

41 Graham-Brown, *Images of Women*, 46.

42 Quoted ibid., 45.

43 Lucie Duff Gordon, *Letters from Egypt* (London: Virago, 1983), 21.

44 Théophile Gautier, *Abédécaire du Salon de 1861* (Paris: Dentu, 1861), 253.
45 Dane Kennedy, 'Guardians of Edenic Sanctuaries: Paharis, Lepchas, and Todas in the British Mind,' *South Asia: Joural of South Asian Studies* 14 (1991): 57–77.
46 See, among others, Erik Cohen, 'The Representation of Arabs and Jews on Postcards in Israel,' *History of Photography* 19 (1995): 210–20; Annelies Moors, 'Embodying the Nation: Maha Seca's Post-Intifada Postcards,' *Ethnic and Racial Studies* 23 (2000): 871–87; Moors, 'From "Women's Lib" to "Palestinian Women": The Politics of Picture Postcards in Palestine/Israel,' in David Crouch and Nina Lübbren, eds, *Visual Culture and Tourism* (New York: Berg, 2003), 23–39; Moors and Steven Wachlin, 'Dealing with the Past, Creating a Presence: Picture Postcards of Palestine,' in Moors, Toine van Teeffelen, Sharif Kanaana, and Ilham Abu Ghazaleh, eds, *Discourse and Palestine: Power, Text and Context* (Amsterdam: Het Spinhuis, 1995), 11–26; and R. Oren, 'Zionist Photography, 1910–1941: Constructing a Landscape,' *History of Photography* 19 (1995): 201–10.
47 Moors, 'Dealing with the Past,' 17.
48 'Sabra' refers to Jews born in Israel/Palestine; literally, it is the cactus fruit found in the region (Arabic: *sabr*) which has been appropriated as a metaphor for the Israeli character, 'prickly on the outside, sweet on the inside.' Moors, 'Dealing with the Past,' 19.
49 Moors, 'From "Women's Lib" to "Palestinian Women,"' 31.
50 This series of banknotes dates from 1958 to 1971.
51 Moors, 'Dealing with the Past,' 18.
52 In addition to the quadrilingual caption on the reverse in Hebrew, English, French, and German, a passage from Isaiah 61 drove the point home: 'For Zion's sake I will not hold my peace and for Jerusalem's sake I will not rest.'
53 This series of banknotes dates from 1958–1971.
54 Moors, 'Dealing with the Past,' 21.
55 Quoted in Moors, 'From "Women's Lib" to "Palestinian Women,"' 34.
56 Graham-Brown, *Images of Women*, 125.
57 Yasmina Bouziane, *Yellow Nylon Rope*, script by Anissa Bouziane.
58 Bouziane, *Imaginary Homelands*.
59 Ibid.
60 Yasmina Bouziane, *Le Regard*, ¾" video, 12 minutes, tri-lingual (English/French/Arabic) (1993).
61 Wall labels for the itinerant photo panels by Hashem el-Madani do list individuals by name for those whose names he remembered when interviewed. What is impressive is how many names he remembered years

after taking the photographs; what is striking is the high number of unnamed individuals simply labelled 'Palestinian.' Zainab Shalabi is not named anywhere in the exhibition, nor are the two views of Tripoli's main square identified. Instead, much of this background information was provided by Walid Raad during a gallery talk on the occasion of the opening of the exhibition in Urbana. I thank Walid for his generosity, his unfailing willingness to respond to my numerous queries, and, most important, his support of my work on and participation in both 'Mapping Sitting' and 'Beyond East and West.'

62 Allan Sekula, 'The Body and the Archive,' *October* 39 (1986): 3–64.

63 Marc Garanger, *Femmes algériennes 1960* (Paris: Contrejour, 1982).

64 Allan Sekula, 'Photography between Labour and Capital,' in Benjamin Buchloh and Robert Wilkie, eds, *Mining Photographs and Other Pictures* (Halifax: Nova Scotia College of Art and Design, 1983), 183–267.

65 Email communication to David Prochaska, 8 February 1999.

66 Kocache, 'Yasmina Bouziane's "Inhabited By Imaginings We Did Not Choose": Photography, Identity and Choice,' *aljadid* 21 (Fall 1997): 11.

67 Kwame Anthony Appiah, 'The Postcolonial and the Postmodern,' in his *In My Father's House: Africa in the Philosophy of Culture* (New York: Oxford University Press, 1992), 137–57.

68 Bouziane, *Yellow Nylon Rope*.

69 Bouziane, *Imaginary Homelands*.

70 Bouziane, *Yellow Nylon Rope*.

# Contributors

**Nina Athanassoglou-Kallmyer** is Professor of Art History at the University of Delaware. Her interests in art and cultural politics inform her articles and books on a variety of topics ranging from Romanticism, Delacroix, Géricault, and Cézanne, as well as her forthcoming work on classicism and imperialist expansion in the Mediterranean.

**Emily Braun**, Professor of the History of Art at Hunter College and the Graduate Center, CUNY, has written extensively on modern Italian art and on culture of the Fascist period. She is the author of *Mario Sironi and Italian Modernism: Art and Politics under Fascism* (2000) and co-author of *The Power of Conversation: Jewish Women and Their Salons* (2004), which won a National Jewish Book Award.

**André Dombrowski** is Assistant Professor at Smith College, where he teaches the history of nineteenth- and early-twentieth-century European art and architecture. He is the author of essays on Adolph Menzel and Paul Cézanne, and a book on Cézanne's early scenes of murder and sexually laden domesticity is forthcoming.

**Anne Dymond** is Assistant Professor of Art History and Museum Studies at the University of Lethbridge, Alberta. She has published on Signac's articulations of the Mediterranean as anarchist utopia and on representations of the Arlésienne, and she is working on a book that considers the cultural construction of Provence in art, museums, exhibitions, and tourist paraphernalia.

**Vojtěch Jirat-Wasiutyński** was Professor of Art History at Queen's

University, Kingston, Ontario. The author of several books, including *Technique and Meaning in the Paintings of Paul Gauguin* (with H. Travers Newton, 2000), Vojtěch's many publications on late-nineteenth-century topics as diverse as Paul Gauguin, Vincent Van Gogh, Odilon Redon, and painting technique inspired a generation of scholars. His sudden death shortly before the completion of this volume shocked us all, and he is sorely missed.

**John Klein** is Associate Professor of Modern and Contemporary Art at University of Missouri-Columbia and author of *Matisse Portraits* (2001). He is writing a book on Matisse's late decorative projects in a variety of media.

**Francesco Loriggio** is Professor of Italian and Comparative Literature at Carleton University, Ottawa. Most recently his research has centred on questions of time and space in Italian and European culture.

**Alla Myzelev** is a lecturer at the University of Guelph and the Ontario College of Art and Design. Her main research interest is the role of women in the history of design and applied arts. Her co-edited volume *Collecting Subjects: Meaning and Pleasures of Material Culture* will be published in 2008.

**David Prochaska** teaches history and postcolonial studies, with an emphasis on colonial visual culture, at the University of Illinois. He is the author or co-author of two books, co-editor of two forthcoming collections, and curator or co-curator of two museum exhibitions.

**John Zarobell** is Associate Curator of European Painting at the Philadelphia Museum of Art. He is currently preparing his manuscript *Empire of Landscape* for publication in 2008.

www.ingramcontent.com/pod-product-compliance
Lightning Source LLC
LaVergne TN
LVHW020431080826
844660LV00034B/1386

* 9 7 8 1 4 8 7 5 6 4 8 0 3 *